The Riddle
of
Emily Dickinson

HOUGHTON MIFFLIN
LITERARY FELLOWSHIP AWARDS

To E. P. O'Donnell for *Green Margins*
To Jenny Ballou for *Spanish Prelude*
To Robert Penn Warren for *Night Rider*
To Clelie Benton Huggins for *Point Noir*
To Dorothy Baker for *Young Man With A Horn*
To David Cornel DeJong for *Old Haven*
To Maurine Whipple for *The Giant Joshua*
To Mary King O'Donnell for *Quincie Bolliver*
To Helen Todd for *A Man Named Grant*
To A. Fleming MacLeish for *Cone Of Silence*
To Mary Benton for *Old Bullion* *
To Donald MacRae for *Dwight Craig*
To Joseph Wechsberg for *Looking For A Bluebird*
To Ann Petry for *The Street*
To Beatrice Griffith for *American Me*
To Elizabeth Bishop for *North & South*
To Helen Mears for *Mirror For Americans, Japan*
To Arthur Mizener for *The Far Side Of Paradise:* A Biography of
F. Scott Fitzgerald
To Eugene L. Burdick for an untitled novel *
To Anthony West for *The Vintage*
To Fred Ross for *Jackson Mahaffey*
To Katharine DuPre Lumpkin for a novel based on the life
of Eli Wright *
To Rebecca Patterson for *The Riddle of Emily Dickinson*
To Siegle Fleisher for an untitled novel *
* *In preparation*

The Riddle
of
Emily Dickinson

by

REBECCA PATTERSON

HOUGHTON MIFFLIN COMPANY BOSTON
The Riverside Press Cambridge
1951

THIS BOOK WAS WRITTEN UNDER THE HOUGHTON MIFFLIN
LITERARY FELLOWSHIP AND THE MARGARET LEE WILEY
FELLOWSHIP, AMERICAN ASSOCIATION OF UNIVERSITY WOMEN.

For permission to use excerpts from the works of Emily Dickinson or
from the prefaces of her editors, the author gratefully acknowledges
her indebtedness to the following sources:

Poems of Emily Dickinson (1937), edited by Martha Dickinson Bianchi
and Alfred Leete Hampson, copyright, 1914, by Martha Dickinson
Bianchi, by permission of Little, Brown & Co.; Prefaces to *The Single
Hound* (1914) and *Further Poems of Emily Dickinson* (1929), edited
by Martha Dickinson Bianchi, by permission of Little, Brown & Co.

Bolts of Melody (1945), edited by Mabel Loomis Todd and Millicent
Todd Bingham, copyright, 1945, by Millicent Todd Bingham, and
Ancestors' Brocades (1945), by Millicent Todd Bingham, copyright,
1945, by Millicent Todd Bingham, by permission of the Harvard
College Library, and Harper & Brothers.

"Poems of Emily Dickinson: Hitherto Published Only in Part," by
Millicent Todd Bingham, *New England Quarterly* (Vol. XX, No. 1,
March, 1947, pp. 3–50), by permission of *New England Quarterly*
and the Harvard College Library.

Emily Dickinson's Letters to Dr. and Mrs. Josiah Gilbert Holland
(1951), edited by Theodora Ward, by permission of Harvard University
Press.

Letters of Emily Dickinson (1931), edited by Mabel Loomis Todd, by
permission of Millicent Todd Bingham.

Life and Letters of Emily Dickinson, and *Emily Dickinson Face to
Face*, edited by Martha Dickinson Bianchi, by permission of Houghton
Mifflin Company.

The Riverside Press
CAMBRIDGE . MASSACHUSETTS
PRINTED IN THE U.S.A.

CONTENTS

PREFACE

IN A FEW PAGES it would be impossible to explain or defend
the thesis of a long, complex book. It must be read for itself —
and with an understanding that every part of it is dependent
upon every other part. To isolate any single piece of evidence
would be as meaningless as to isolate a single bit of stone from
a mosaic. Here I can only thank the many friends who have
helped me and illustrate the manner in which they have helped.

First of all, and very gratefully, I acknowledge my indebtedness to Millicent Todd Bingham, author of *Ancestors' Brocades*
and co-editor with her mother, Mabel Loomis Todd, of Emily
Dickinson's *Bolts of Melody*. Without these two books I could
not have written, or even begun, my own book.

In January, 1947, I read *Bolts of Melody* for the first time,
and I was much interested. Here was not only sound scholarship, here was a new Emily Dickinson, altogether different
from the creation of her biographers, yet oddly familiar and
all of a piece — if I could only find the clue. I read the book
many times and was struck by Mrs. Bingham's reference to
the "too-much-loved woman friend" and by her arrangement
of the volume. Then I began to notice the highly personal

character of many poems. I received a distinct impression that they had been held back from earlier publication, not because they were inferior (although some of them are youthful and imperfect), but precisely because they were too revealing. I now began to reflect upon the peculiar reticences of the Dickinson family, the long, strange history of publication, and the personality of Emily Dickinson herself. I noticed certain striking coincidences, particularly during the period of 1859 to 1861. One fact led to another, and all of them held together and explained each other. I now became convinced that the "too-much-loved woman friend" had been Kate Scott Anthon, the intimate friend of Emily's sister-in-law, Susan Dickinson.

At this time I knew very little about Kate Anthon. All my information I owed to three letters from Emily Dickinson to Kate Anthon (published by Mrs. Todd in the 1894 collection of Emily's letters) and to references in various biographical sketches by Emily's niece, Martha Dickinson Bianchi. I did not yet know that Mrs. Anthon had been twice married, although I was beginning to suspect it. In fact, an attentive reading of Emily's poems and letters was giving me an extraordinarily detailed picture of a woman whose importance has escaped every biographer except Mrs. Bianchi. I can explain only by means of analogy.

For many years the eccentric behavior of the planet Uranus was as inexplicable as that of Emily Dickinson. Astronomers refined their calculations; they increased the mass of Saturn to an improbable amount (apparently they did nothing so bizarre as to suggest the influence of an asteroid or two — that is, a Hunt or a Gould). But all their efforts failed to account for the strange perturbation which retarded the progress of Uranus and drew it out of its path, "comme si une cause attractive eût séduit le voyageur dans sa marche, et l'eût fait devier de son chemin tracé. On calcula que, pour produire en cet endroit une attraction de telle intensité, il fallait qu'il y eût de ce côté du système, plus loin qu'Uranus, une planète de telle masse pour telle distance." Kate Anthon (who marked the passage in Flammarion's *Merveilles célestes* which I have just quoted) could not guess that she would be the planet Neptune to me.

Before I saw a photograph or read a line of Mrs. Anthon's diaries and letters, I knew that she was tall, dark-eyed, dark-haired, handsome, and remarkably emotional. I knew that she had a commanding personality, and I could surmise that she was passionately fond of music and of books, especially poetry. Mrs. Bianchi, who gave no other description, referred to her as a woman of vitality, charm, and humor, saddened by great tragedy. Afterwards I was to learn that she was almost an exaggeration of the qualities I had found in the poems.

On a snowy day of March, 1948, I went for the first time to Mrs. Anthon's birthplace in Cooperstown, New York. Here I was shown an old photograph in a family album, and for a moment it was a dismaying shock. I stared at blue eyes, fair hair, and a sweet, insipid face under a frothy lace cap, and then I knew that this was not the woman. But I hesitated to tell my hostess that she was mistaken. I waited until she left the room. Then I moistened a thumb, whipped the photograph out of the album, and turned it over. On the back was a name I had never heard of. Satisfied, I leafed rapidly through the album, looking for a face I would recognize. I stopped with conviction at the portrait of a young girl with dark hair, beautiful dark eyes, full mouth, and strong chin. On the back of this photograph was Mrs. Anthon's name.

My hostess, who was immediately taken into this little joke, will forgive me, I hope, for recalling it. To her I am grateful for many pleasant visits and for a generosity that permitted me to borrow, copy, and photograph many documents. I remember appreciatively her kindness in listening to my thesis and making suggestions of her own. But debts of friendship like these cannot be repaid. I am still a debtor.

As my research broadened, I saw clearly that I must go to

Europe. Mrs. Anthon spent several early years in southern France, Italy, and Switzerland, and, except for brief periods, she lived in England from 1881 until her death in 1917. Many events of her life are comparatively recent; many people are still living who would be injured by an invasion of their privacy. I had to know how they wished certain material handled, and I had to speak to them face to face. A generous fellowship from the American Association of University Women made my trip possible. On July 10, 1949, I flew to England.

I expected to encounter surprise and even dismay, and I found them. The complete truth about any human life — even if it is a tragic, generous life — commonly waits for the death of generation upon generation of interested persons. By that remote period, alas, the truth has usually disappeared. To tell even part of the truth I was prepared to disguise the rest. Accordingly I suppressed or altered several names, and I became purposely vague about dates and place names and occupations. In this book there are persons without surnames, also a Lady Bertram and a Lady Russell who owe their new titles (but not their personalities) to the works of Jane Austen, and finally a Florence Eliot, a Henry Layton, and a Charles family who would not recognize themselves by those names.

When I returned to New York on August 25, 1949, it was to learn that the Hampson collection of Dickinson manuscripts would be sold. This collection, bequeathed to Alfred Leete Hampson, her co-editor, by the last surviving Dickinson, Martha Dickinson Bianchi, represents a sizable part of all existing Dickinson material. For two years I had been hearing rumors of a probable sale, but this was certainty. And in May, 1950, the collection was indeed sold to a generous purchaser, Gilbert H. Montague, who in turn presented it to the Houghton Library of Harvard University. Long before that time — in fact, as early as August 25, 1949 — I had received a good general notion of the contents and was satisfied that they would not materially affect my thesis.

Although the collection now at Harvard is very substantial, it is far from complete. Letters and poems are scattered about among other libraries, and a considerable part of the Dickinson material is still in the hands of private owners. It is problematical how soon all these scattered hoards of manuscripts will be available to interested scholars — but, in all likelihood, not for many years. Nevertheless, I considered the wisdom of deferring my own study for this problematical number of years.

An examination of *all* surviving manuscripts would undoubtedly result in some textual changes of poems and letters and would allow of a broader, more accurate picture of Emily Dickinson's parents and remoter ancestors. However, the existing published texts of the poems are accurate enough for my purpose. I have also had the advantage of examining the manuscripts with which I am principally concerned. And my book would be seriously unbalanced by a detailed study of Emily Dickinson's ancestry. It is outside my purpose. My conclusion was that I could better serve the interests of scholarship by publishing my own material, which will never be available to any library, than by permitting new errors to accumulate in the interpretation of Emily Dickinson.

I must add that I did not enter lightly upon a delicate subject. I spent almost three years gathering evidence and testing my conclusions before I began seriously to write. Meanwhile I collected hostile opinions from several Dickinson scholars. These troubled me less than my own ignorance of the subject with which I was dealing. I read the psychologists and found them confusing — and confused. Gingerly I came to the conclusion that there is much bias even among supposedly detached scientists, and I resolved to leave theoretical matters alone.

Nowhere have I tried to "explain" Emily Dickinson. I have limited myself to establishing the identity of the person about whom she wrote her poems. And I do not pretend that Kate was responsible for Emily's disastrous life. Emily would have broken down in any event — and I say so plainly — but it would have been a different kind of breakdown, and if she had written any poems at all, which I doubt, they would have been very different poems. I believe that Kate converted a sterile breakdown into a fruitful one. Beyond that I cannot speculate. Any single, simple explanation is bound to be false.

It is easy to show that all three Dickinson children were unhappy, and the temptation to blame their parents is very strong. Certainly the fussy, silly mother and the possessive, domineering father did not provide a healthy environment. But children of unusual intelligence and vitality are uncomfortable in any setting. If they too blame their parents, it must be remembered that parents are not only the most convenient scapegoats, they always make enough mistakes to render the charge plausible. The commonplace child slides easily and smoothly through life; the child handicapped by too much intelligence clings to his parents and loathes his captivity.

In the course of this book I remark that Emily emphasized "power." She preferred it to the "kingdom" and the "glory," she said, for it included the other two. She knew that her position was weak almost to impotence — not merely against her parents but, far more importantly, against the entire world, of which her parents were simply the nearest representatives and agents. Someone has suggested that many a woman anciently burned as a witch was in truth a vigorous, gifted woman with no outlet for her abilities. Again and again Emily wrote uncomfortably that she was too "large" for her environment; her own explanation of herself is worth noting. She faced a world that was hostile to everything she wanted to do, inimical to the realization of herself, and she fought it with the only weapon in her possession — withdrawal. In seclusion she drew up her "letter to the world." It is the age-old recall of man to himself, to his own proper ends — to have life and to have it more abundantly. That Emily herself, for her complete and healthy functioning, needed this woman Kate, or one very like her, puts the problem of life in its most difficult and delicate terms.

On several occasions my work took me to Amherst. There I paced Emily's bedroom and noted that it was a "chamber facing West." What impressed me most, however, was the lightness and airiness of the old brick house. I had thought that it would be dark and dismal, but I found no shadows there.

It remains only to thank various persons for the assistance they have given me. For more than four years my husband, Thomas McEvoy Patterson, has patiently listened to my ideas, read manuscript, encouraged me, and given our children the attention that I was sometimes too preoccupied to give. To my friends in England I am grateful for more benefits than they permit me to acknowledge. To the two grandnieces of Kate Anthon, who lent me manuscripts, books, photographs, and other material not available to any previous biographer of Emily Dickinson, I express my deep gratitude. To Richard Sewall of Yale University, I am indebted for encouragement and very material assistance in my research; to Theresa N. Swezey, for research in New York archives; to Alice C. Dodge, Utica Public Library, for information regarding the Dering family and the Utica Female Academy; to Alfred Leete Hampson, for copies of letters from Kate Anthon to Susan Dickinson; to the late Mary Margaret Kirkby, for a photograph of Mrs. Anthon and many personal recollections; to Charles R. Green, Jones Library, Amherst, for weather information regarding Amherst in March, 1859; to Mr. and Mrs. Douglas T. Johnston, for a description of Campbell Turner and other kindnesses; to Theodora Ward, for copies of unpublished letters from Emily Dickinson to Dr. and Mrs. J. G. Holland; to John McClelland of Stanford, California, for painstaking correction of my manuscript; and to the many friends, doctors, psychologists, and others, who gave me technical advice or simply encouragement but asked to remain unnamed.

Part One

I

I shall not murmur if at last
The ones I loved below
Permission have to understand
For what I shunned them so —

Divulging it would rest my heart
But it would ravage theirs —
Why, Katie, treason has a voice,
But mine dispels in tears.

EMILY DICKINSON

ALTHOUGH this poem has been in print for several years, it has not attracted any particular notice. Yet it offers a clue for interpreting the life and work of Emily Dickinson. Alone among her poems, it names the real name of a person known to her, and it connects this name with the most puzzling circumstance in her life and suggests an explanation.

The plain meaning of the poem is that Emily Dickinson has been desperately hurt. In some manner the woman named Katie has injured her. The wound is deep and lasting. In her pain Emily avoids even the persons she loves. She would like to confide in her family or friends and be comforted by them, but she is afraid to tell the truth. Perhaps after her death the truth will not harm them; meanwhile she can only shut herself up and weep.

This poem cannot be dismissed as the expression of a passing mood. It records feeling too deep and painful for a trivial event. Also it is connected with other poems accusing a woman of treason or of cruel behavior. And these poems are related to still others which disguise the friend's sex. Finally, and most

3

significantly, it appears to say that Emily secluded herself because of her friend's cruelty.

Now whatever else her readers conjecture or misinterpret about Emily Dickinson, they have correctly observed that in her early thirties she withdrew from society. The explanations are numerous and contradictory, but the seclusion is a fact. In 1861, during her thirty-first year, she began to hide even from her old friends, and in her writing she called herself a prisoner and lamented the hard necessity that shut her away from life. She was not a contented recluse.

When her friend Samuel Bowles, editor of the *Springfield Republican,* called at the Dickinson house in the fall of 1861, and again in March, 1862, Emily refused to see him. She was not indifferent or hostile toward Bowles; nor was she trying to pique his interest. She was simply afraid of bursting into tears. In former times she had welcomed him, and she was to welcome him again, but during these hours she could not trust herself. "Something troubled me," she wrote to him apologetically, and Bowles had reason to know what she meant. In her mind he was closely associated with the lost "Katie."

It would be misleading, of course, to suggest that Emily Dickinson was an ordinary young woman who changed over-night into an anguished hermit. Behavior is never so simple — or so inexplicable. There is plenty of evidence in her early letters that she felt uncomfortable, ill at ease, vaguely conscious of a difference from others. "Old-fashioned" was a word she often applied to herself to describe this feeling of difference. Her eventual seclusion, even without any special crisis in her life, might almost have been foretold.

But the result of her seclusion could not have been predicted. It might have been an uncreative withering. Instead, like a barren tree that has been severely pruned, Emily flowered surprisingly. She was, in her own words, the "wounded deer" that "leaps highest," the "smitten rock that gushes." In pain she found herself, and she sang "unto the stone of which [she] died" until the symbolic death merged with the real, and the prison on the second floor of the old house in Amherst was exchanged for the lasting prison of the grave.

The manner of her withdrawal was just as surprising and unpredictable. For it is clear that a gradual retreat quickened suddenly amid almost intolerable pain. And the beginning of her real seclusion followed hard upon a last conspicuous approach toward other people. In 1859 and 1860 she had been happy, she had made new friends, her letters had sparkled with excitement. In 1861 she was frenzied. Her letters spoke of constant weeping, of the fear of madness and death, of a terrible blow that had struck her down during May or April. There was a marked change in her handwriting. By 1862, according to her niece, Mrs. Bianchi, she had entered upon her long retirement.

For some time she may have continued to visit her brother's house next door. In 1864 and 1865, during her thirty-fourth and thirty-fifth years, she made two long stays in Boston for medical treatment. There is no record, however, of any other trips outside her father's grounds following the crucial year 1861. By the late sixties she was beginning to remain invisible even when she entertained old friends: they sat in the parlor and Emily talked with them from an adjoining room. About the same time, or perhaps earlier, she began to dramatize herself by wearing white dresses. As an example of her morbid shyness, it is said that she had these dresses fitted on her sister rather than on herself. Sometimes she persuaded friends to address her envelopes, and sometimes she cut letters out of newspapers and pasted them together to form addresses. It was as if she could not bear even the most distant and indirect contact with strangers.

Her last public appearances were at the teas given by her father during Commencement week of Amherst College. Upon a lull in the conversation she was accustomed to sweep into the room, apparitional in her white dress, bow left and right, and then disappear without saying a word. After her father's death, in 1874, the teas were given up, and Emily became only a shadow on the curtained window or a distant figure in the garden. If a grocer's clerk appeared at the back door, Emily vanished, heedless of the fate of her cooking. Or a knock sounded at the front door, and she was gone up the stairs. From her bedroom window she looked down with interest and occasional mockery at passing townspeople, but few of them ever saw her face. In her own lifetime she became a legend.

Every detail of this picture is drawn from the letters of Emily Dickinson or from the accounts of trustworthy witnesses. Unverified tales have been discarded without any loss, for the truth was strange enough. It has troubled her biographers, who have been tempted, as Emily wrote, "to dilute to plausibility." In the face of manifest abnormality they have stressed her normalcy, and in trimming her to satisfy conventional prejudices, they have impaired the unique quality of a life and work. It would have been wiser to admit frankly that Emily Dickinson was abnormal — that is, she departed from the conventions of her society — and to challenge the common notion that abnormality means disease.

In the opinion of her neighbors Emily Dickinson had suffered a "disappointment." She was either an Elizabeth Barrett who lacked spirit to defy a tyrannical father and elope with her Robert Browning, or she was a George Eliot without courage to live openly with a married man. The disappointed bachelor was a George Gould or a George Howland or an unnamed Boston lawyer. The married lover was the Reverend Charles Wadsworth or Major Hunt. Theories multiplied to the point of absurdity and produced several biographies and stillborn plays. Finally this very absurdity drove some persons to an interesting conclusion: If, in one poor fashion or another, any man could be made "to do," then probably no man had ever existed. According to Emily herself, the gap in her life could be filled only by the "thing" that had caused it. If anything else were inserted, it would simply "yawn the more." There is a great yawning in the biographies of Emily Dickinson.

The confusion was natural, however, for Emily herself took pains to disguise the evidence. She had good reason for her distrust. Although she suggested, in the poem to "Katie," that she would be willing to have the truth revealed after her death, she became increasingly anxious to hide it. As a poet she had need of an audience, but she feared that it would accept her only upon its own terms. Her efforts to adapt herself to those terms are recorded in the poems.

Of the many interpretations of Emily Dickinson, the most common is the most improbable. She did have intellectual attachments to men and was profuse in gratitude to those she called her "tutors," but she was extravagant in all things. Thomas Wentworth Higginson called her his "partially cracked poetess." She described him, no doubt sincerely, as her "safest friend." There is a believable tradition that Major Hunt, the first husband of Helen Hunt Jackson, disliked Emily and thought her "uncanny." Other men seemed to share this vague feeling of discomfort. With some few, like Samuel Bowles, Emily had comradely relations, and towards still others, if they were old enough, she was filial. But from the days of her childhood women attracted her emotionally, and women alone had power to wound her. In one of her perverse self-analyses she remarked to Higginson: "Women talk; men are silent. That is why I dread women." Undoubtedly she had come to dread women.

There is no man — no real man — anywhere in the poems. With an audience in mind, Emily tried to create a male lover; that is, she tried to redirect genuine emotion into an unfamiliar channel, and the effect is sometimes odd. Wherever the poems become real, however, the personality that emerges is not that of a man. Masculine readers have spoken of the "intellectual" quality of her love poems. They have shown awareness that the poems were not addressed to them.

"Unworthy of her breast," wrote Emily Dickinson. "To see her is a picture," she wrote elsewhere, in a poem describing the futility of her life now that a woman friend has turned away from her. The poem beginning "Frigid and sweet her parting face" accuses some woman of cruelly abandoning her. The same meaning attaches to poems beginning "I showed her heights she never saw" and "The Stars are old, that stood for me." A short but significant poem ("Not probable — the merest chance") begs another person to explain what Emily has said or done to give offense. It ends with a desperate appeal to the woman who has forsaken her — "oh phantom Queen!" Still other poems express poignant feeling about some unnamed woman. For one reason or another these poems escaped revision, but Emily appears to have altered a good many others to make them more acceptable.

The disguise employed is very thin. It consists of a number of masculine pronouns, or "bearded" pronouns, as Emily called them, and an occasional "sir," "signor," or "master." These expressions are oddly formal. They may replace an earlier, more natural "sweet" or "beloved," and in one poem they will be shown to do so.

Pronouns do not make a man in the poetry of any woman. There must also be what might be called a woman's image of a man. It may be quite subtle, without physical details, and not dependent on any single real person. Essentially it is a projection of her ability to love a man, and as such it is unmistakable. There is no such image in the poetry of Emily Dickinson. In a poem beginning "Although I put away his life," she drew a vivid picture of herself sowing flowers for her lover, soothing his pains, playing his favorite music, and bringing an apronful of sticks to their cottage fire. The man himself is invisible; he has no trait, physical or psychical, identifying him with some man whom Emily knew or indeed with any man who ever existed. Once Emily referred to her lover's "shaggier vest," and she gave a consistent impression that the other person was taller than herself. In two large volumes of poetry there is no other detail which suggests a man.

On the other hand, many poems show a conscious avoidance of description. Some are so deeply involved in symbolism as to be unreadable. Still others witness a bitter struggle with pronouns — for instance, the use of neuter pronouns or plurals to refer to the beloved (in certain poems, clearly a woman, as betrayed by other evidence), or the existence of two versions of the same poem, one employing feminine and the other masculine pronouns. Finally, despite Emily's alterations, there survive many poems of intense emotion addressed to a woman.

2

In the little poem already quoted, Emily Dickinson accused a woman named Katie of treason. Katie was a very common name in the mid-nineteenth century. There were doubtless many Katies in the life of Emily Dickinson. Her favorite aunt was named Katie Sweetser, and her friend Mrs. Holland had a young daughter Kate. Emily may well have known many others of that name who have not been recorded. One Katie, however, occurs again and again in her history, and at times and in connections that are unquestionably significant. This woman was Kate Scott, a schoolmate and lifelong friend of Emily's sister-in-law, Susan Gilbert Dickinson. Apparently she was also the woman whom Emily Dickinson called the "phantom Queen."

In March, 1859, about the time of her twenty-eighth birthday, Kate Scott paid the first of many visits to Amherst. She came at the entreaty of her old school friend, Susan Gilbert, to spend several weeks in the Italianate villa of Sue and her husband, Austin Dickinson. Next door, in the old red-brick house among the pines, lived Austin's sister Emily. In this simple, unforced manner the crisis of Emily Dickinson's life began.

The imagination is not taxed to contrive meetings or to explain why Emily, in her verse, placed the person she loved in the "chamber facing West" on the second floor of the Dickinson house. Kate Scott was in and out of the house, upstairs and downstairs, many times during those wintry weeks and in the several visits that followed. As a woman she was admitted to Emily's bedroom and to a friendly intimacy that no man, except a husband, would have known. There was nothing miraculous in their attachment, for they were together daily, almost hourly. Even in the short space of two or three weeks they had plenty of time to fall in love.

On pleasant days the two young women strolled with the venerable dog Carlo, Emily's playmate and guardian for the past nine or ten years. During snowy weather they had delightful rides in Austin's sleigh, as Kate was to recall sorrowfully long after Emily was dead. More often the visitor sat in the parlor of the Austin Dickinson house, one arm around her slighter, red-haired friend, and talked in her lively, excited manner. Or she stood beside the piano, a tall, handsome woman, dark-haired and dark-eyed, and listened raptly while Emily played. A half century later this sensitive, emotional lover of music recalled with awe and sadness the rhapsodic melodies that Emily had invented for her. Or they amused each other like girls released from school. In a letter of this same March, 1859, to Mrs. Holland, Emily sketched a vivid picture of their clinging together, more in affection than in alarm, after fleeing from unwelcome callers. There is no reason to doubt the evidence of the poems, or of Emily's letters to Kate, that the attraction between them was swift and strong, but it was also founded upon abundant opportunity.

The story told in the poems was surprisingly literal, but the poetic mind of Emily Dickinson *was* literal. Her symbolism was only a word-play used to present familiar things in a new and startling light. She was a wit, not a mystic, and she invented nothing. In her poetry the hummingbird was real, the pine at her bedroom window was real, and real also was this story of love and betrayal by her intimate friend. With perhaps some heightening and rearrangement, the incidents of this friendship — the breathless declaration of love, the demonstrative tenderness, and the bitter and eternal parting — were to form the material with which Emily worked. Invention was unnecessary, for Kate was fully able to supply a story — and not for Emily alone.

Long years afterwards, and in reference to another woman, Kate was to mark these lines of her favorite poet Shelley:

> Something within that interval which bore
> The stamp of *why* they parted, *how* they met.

The story of that other woman, the young English girl Florie, will be told in its place. So also will the story of how Kate Scott and Emily Dickinson met and of how they parted "as the central flint were cloven with an adze." At present it is enough to say that about April, 1861, with pain and reluctance, Kate wrote a letter terminating a hopeless attachment, and for the rest of her life Emily was never sure whether she herself was mad or sane.

In her poems Emily Dickinson described a tall woman who loved music and poetry. Readers looking still higher in search of a man, Charles Wadsworth, who wrote stilted, religious verse and described all music other than church hymns as "fashionable agonies," need not be surprised that their eyes have met only vacancy. "Alas! alas!" as Kate was to write so often in her diaries and letters.

It is true that the importance, almost the existence, of Kate Scott has escaped the attention of every biographer except Martha Dickinson Bianchi. But Mrs. Bianchi was the daughter of Susan Dickinson, who was Kate's intimate friend and Emily's sister-in-law. The daughter of Sue Dickinson had unusual opportunities for learning the truth. That Mrs. Bianchi was acquainted with the history of Emily Dickinson and Kate Scott, however partial and inaccurate her report, seems obvious upon an examination of her two biographies of Emily Dickinson.

Perhaps no other members of the family were so well informed. Emily's brother Austin might not notice — it would be too trifling and insignificant a relationship to catch the attention of a man — although there is evidence that he was uneasy about publishing his sister's poetry. Emily never fully confided in her sister Lavinia, who was absent, moreover, during a good part of Kate's two most important visits. Of course, Lavinia must have guessed, for one fact would be painfully obvious. The girl who had been Emily's inseparable companion during the Amherst visits, and who had written weekly, perhaps oftener, now ceased to write, and Emily suffered. "When the head aches next to you," as Emily had said of her sister, "it becomes important." Lavinia would be indignant with Kate and protective toward Emily.

During Emily's lifetime, however, Lavinia saw only a few poems. She could not guess just how calamitous this friendship had been until Emily died and the hoard of manuscripts came to light. Then, as Lavinia's editor, Mabel Loomis Todd, read the poems aloud and asked for explanations, Lavinia undoubtedly suffered. There could be only one explanation. Still Lavinia was an isolated, unsophisticated woman; she did not immediately see beyond the poems to their curious, gossipy readers. After November, 1890, however, an excited village and a larger public clamored for the name of Emily's lover, and even Lavinia must have realized that poems which readers persistently read as love poems to an actual person could not be suitably explained as the result of Emily's friendship with Kate. In the fall of 1891 Lavinia tried to see Kate Scott — in order, as she afterwards wrote, to discuss "mutual interests." This effort failed, thanks to the interference of Sue Dickinson, and under increasing pressure Lavinia was driven to invent her own explanation of the poems. An incident of February, 1894, reminded her of her brother's classmate, George Gould.

At this time Lavinia and Mrs. Todd were collecting Emily's correspondence. Mrs. Todd wrote to George Gould, among others, to inquire about Emily's friend Ben Newton. Neither Lavinia nor her brother Austin had thought of asking Gould for letters. They were surprised to learn that he too had once treasured some letters from Emily. He had looked diligently for them, Gould added, and would look again. From his casual reference it is clear that they were not love letters. But this new piece of information gave Lavinia's mind something to work with. Emily had liked Gould well enough to write to him, as she had written occasionally to Vaughan Emmons and other young men. Inquisitive neighbors would be satisfied with Gould's name and would be less likely to stumble upon the real story. Apparently Lavinia did not begin spreading this tale until after her brother died, in August, 1895. Even then she was obliged to be very careful, for Gould was still alive and could deny it.

In the last year of her own life Lavinia employed a young woman named Mary Lee Hall to copy Emily's poems for publication. Miss Hall was curious about the identity of the "man" in the love poems she was copying. Lavinia thought best to satisfy this curiosity. She gave a rambling account of Emily's love for a poor minister, whose suit had been rejected by a cruel, possessive father. Miss Hall asked why Emily did not marry her lover after her father's death. The obvious reply was that he had married someone else, but Lavinia, flustered and unprepared, gave the wrong answer. After the death of Edward Dickinson — so Lavinia explained — they were just as much afraid of his wrath as during his lifetime. The man Emily loved, she added, was George Gould. Miss Hall remarked that she had heard him preach and admired him very much. This was more than Lavinia had bargained for. She appeared much surprised, Miss Hall remembered innocently. (Suppose the story got back to Gould himself?) As young Miss Hall was about to leave, the older woman rose, put a hand on her arm, and warned her that she had been entrusted with a great secret. Much embellished, this "secret" was later imparted to Genevieve Taggard and served up as a biography of Emily Dickinson.

The Gould story, of course, explains nothing about Emily Dickinson, but it does throw a revealing light upon Lavinia's accounts of her father. A stern, jealous parent was a necessary element of the plot, and Lavinia sacrificed her father without a qualm when it became a matter of saving Emily and Emily's poetry. Who would be the wiser? Who would recall that two girls had once strolled arm in arm and had written scores of letters to each other? Outside the uncomfortably knit Dickinson households, nobody would notice or remember anything.

Without question Susan Dickinson knew, for whatever knowledge she failed to gain from observation, Kate was to supply. In her youth Sue had been loved by both women, emotionally and naïvely; she was acquainted with their temperaments as even a sister could never be; and she was Kate's hostess and a constant spectator of the intimacy between her own best friend and her sister-in-law. She brought them together, and she may have been partly instrumental in separating them. The "treason" of which Emily complained on four different occasions may have been Sue's rather than Kate's. Sue kept the friend whom Emily lost — by what means, Emily could only speculate.

During her long seclusion, as the world knows, Emily Dickinson composed hundreds of poems. Many are of great beauty, but their meaning is often obscured by the mystery of her experience. Only four poems and a valentine jingle were published during her lifetime. When she died, in 1886, in her lonely Amherst prison-house, she left all her possessions to her sister Lavinia. Totally unprepared for the responsibility, Lavinia was obliged to seek help in editing the poems. Although she had long been on uneven terms with Susan Dickinson, she turned to her almost of necessity. Sue was intelligent, well read, even somewhat scholarly in her tastes, and she admired Emily's poetry. Lavinia could expect Sue to edit the manuscripts competently. As a result, the poetry came for some time into Sue's hands.

At first Sue was enthusiastic. On December 31, 1886, a few months after Emily's death, she submitted a poem to the editor of *The Century*, and she may have offered poems to other magazines. Then she became hostile to the idea of publishing Emily's poetry and even tried to dissuade Lavinia. Lavinia's explanation was that Sue was clever but lacked "mental energy to complete." Indeed, there was a weakness in Sue's character which brought all her ambitious plans to nothing. But as she delved deeper into the poetry, much of which was undoubtedly new to her, it is possible that she began to be afraid of it. For she not only tried to keep Lavinia from publishing; she also worked diligently to keep the poetry in her own hands.

When Sue became troublesome, Lavinia grew indignant. She wrested the poetry from Sue's reluctant hands and entrusted it to a friend and neighbor, Mabel Loomis Todd. Under the editorship of this capable, intelligent young woman, the first volume came out in November, 1890, and was an astonishing success.

It was now Sue's turn to be outraged. In a letter of about mid-December, 1890, to Thomas Wentworth Higginson, she denied Lavinia's statement that she had refused to edit the poems. She had intended, she said, to spend the coming winter arranging a volume of poetry and prose, to be privately published and privately circulated in order to avoid criticism. The prose would have consisted largely of passages from Emily's youthful, adoring letters to her. These surpassed, Sue added sentimentally, even the correspondence of the unhappy Karoline von Günderode with Bettina von Arnim. But other portions of Sue's letter to Higginson suggest a vague uneasiness. She was distressed by the "personal detail" in newspaper reviews of Emily's poems. She shuddered at the thought of the world reading Emily's "heartbroken convictions," and she found herself constantly saying "poor Emily."

Now some of this may be sentimental posturing, but there is evidence of real anxiety. An intelligent, cultivated woman like Sue, who had admired Elizabeth Browning from her girlhood, and who was now warmly encouraging her own daughter to publish, would not be influenced by supposed Victorian reticences about women appearing in print. She must have had other reasons for wishing to limit or prevent the appearance of Emily's work. To W. H. Ward, editor of *The Independent*, Sue wrote that she "had moved slowly, dreading publicity for us all."

Her behavior, however, would suggest that Sue was of two minds. And that was not at all surprising. Every member of the Dickinson family, like other people, was moved by several different and often conflicting motives, and the strongest was not always the most obvious. Sue could be afraid of Emily's poetry and yet feel robbed of her share of the excitement and of her position as Emily's sponsor. After Lavinia had taken the dare of publishing Emily's poems, Sue would be tempted to try her hand with a few little things — if for no other purpose, then to annoy Lavinia. In the early spring of 1891 Sue again submitted a few poems to various magazines. She also tried to sell her daughter's satirical sketch of Lavinia — a curious piece of behavior for a woman who "dreaded" publicity for the family.

Lavinia now intervened to stop Sue's unauthorized sale of poems to Ward's paper and others. Sue was defiant. On March 23, 1891, she wrote again to Ward to say that she would do as she pleased with her copies of the poems, and that she intended to write an article about Emily. Perhaps she would have carried out her threat except for one thing. In the summer of 1891, while Mrs. Todd was bringing out a second volume of poems and preparing to collect Emily's letters, Kate Scott returned unexpectedly from England and made a short and per-

haps significant visit to Amherst. Sue Dickinson was silenced —
not merely for the rest of Lavinia's life-time but also for the
fourteen years between Lavinia's death and her own.

3

At this point it is necessary to cast back into the history of Kate
Scott, who had been for many years the widowed Mrs. John
Anthon. After several long stays in Europe, she had sailed for
the fourth time, in early 1878, to make her permanent home
abroad. Family troubles had recalled her, much against her
will, for a period of two years; but by April, 1886, she was once
more abroad, and had now been living in England for almost
five years without discovering either the desire or the necessity
to return home. There was indeed little to attach her to her
own land. All members of her immediate family — parents,
brother, sister, and husband — were dead; the only living person with whom she had close ties was her sister-in-law. Early in
1891, however, she began for the first time to write of a desire
to visit her homeland. Was it coincidence that this was at the
very time when English reviewers were discovering the poetry
of Emily Dickinson?

The English edition of the poems did not appear until the
summer of 1891, when Kate Anthon was already on her way to
America. As early as January, 1891, however, English reviewers
of the American edition had begun a series of the most slashing
attacks to be visited upon any poet since the days of Shelley and
Keats. The reviews were enough to make a shrewd person
realize that something momentous had occurred, and they appeared in newspapers that Mrs. Anthon read with an attentive-
ness that overlooked nothing. Her feelings must have been
curiously mixed. In her youth she had acclaimed a new poet,
predicted a brilliant future for her, and fallen in love with the
poet herself. Afterwards she had broken off their friendship

with a cruel abruptness that might have destroyed a smaller talent. For all she knew, the *poet* died young, and only a ghost (aloof, increasingly eccentric, and dressed in appropriate white) slipped through the hedge to the Austin Dickinson house when Kate Anthon made her later visits to Amherst. For Emily continued to see Kate.

On this point Mrs. Bianchi was strangely insistent. Indeed she went out of her way to assert that Emily Dickinson interrupted her seclusion to visit her brother's house whenever Kate was there. And the poems bear out this statement. Plainly Mrs. Bianchi's mother told her a great deal about the friendship between Emily and Kate, for the visits to which Mrs. Bianchi alluded took place before her own birth, or in her very early childhood.

Emily Dickinson came — to observe, talk, laugh, be silent. How was Kate Anthon to guess what poems Emily would write when she returned to the little upstairs chamber that she called her prison? Or did Mrs. Anthon guess? She had received enough of the early poems to be curious and perhaps a little disturbed. She had thought that Emily was dead — dead many long years before the visible death of May 15, 1886 — and now, in this year 1891, the ghost came again in power.

By late April, 1891, Kate Anthon was in a fever to be at home, but her voyage was delayed. Unexpectedly her sister-in-law came to England with an invalid son, and Mrs. Anthon canceled her reservation and postponed her trip in order to care for them. So great was her impatience to be gone, however, that she engaged passage on an earlier steamer than theirs, and was in New York about a week before her sister-in-law and her nephew returned. She could not, or at least did not, immediately go to Amherst. Originally she had planned to be in America by spring, but the delay had thrown her arrival into the hottest part of the summer, a period when Sue Dickinson was commonly away from home. This may explain why Kate

Anthon's visit to Amherst was the last she performed before she returned to England.

After a few days in New York, Mrs. Anthon called upon former schoolmates in Utica and spent some time with her sister-in-law in Cooperstown. And everywhere she went — in New York, in Utica, or in Cooperstown — she talked eagerly of her old friendship with Emily Dickinson. All at once she became silent. In the late fall her friend Mrs. Alfred Corning Clark took pains to send her a newspaper clipping about the poet. But when Kate referred to this kindness, she was brief and cool — a curious circumstance, for she habitually spoke of even slight acquaintances with a wealth of kindly detail. Meanwhile, however, she had had her interview with Sue Dickinson, and she may have grown anxious to dispatch the subject of Emily Dickinson as swiftly as possible.

Kate Anthon reached Amherst on the evening of September 20, 1891. Austin Dickinson had met her at the railroad junction of Palmer and had escorted her the rest of the short distance. The hour of her arrival, as Kate noted with her usual methodicalness, was eight o'clock. The following afternoon the Dickinsons and their guest set out for a drive in the delightful early fall weather.

The tall, slender, exquisitely neat woman who entered the carriage with Austin and Sue had been absent for many years. On the last of her earlier visits, about 1876 or 1877, she had been forty-five or forty-six. Now she was sixty, and her hair was completely white. The beautiful dark eyes, however, shone as brightly as of old, and the ivory skin was clear and not so deeply lined as might have been expected. Although life had dealt cruelly with Kate Anthon, she was still a very attractive woman. As always, she was dressed in deep black, perhaps in the handsome black dress, with the fine lace at throat and shoulders, in which she was photographed a few weeks later. And as always, the pleasant voice rippled on from the solemn to the gay to the nonsensical. No one could tell a story better, not even Sue Dickinson, who had much the same talent. In the memory of Mrs. Anthon's friends, her irrepressible Irish wit ranked just below her unfailing generosity and warmth of heart. Kate Anthon brought to Amherst the very breath of life, Mrs. Bianchi was to recall gratefully. The words echo the language of Emily Dickinson's poetry.

The other members of the carriage party were, in their way, as remarkable and individual as their guest. Sue Dickinson, strikingly handsome as a young girl, was now both stout and grey, but the remnants of former beauty were still evident in the mold of her face and in the fine dark eyes. Between the two friends there were indeed some likenesses, along with still more important differences. Both women were amusing and often brilliant in conversation, and both were excited by ideas and books, but with these traits any resemblance in personality ended. Sue Dickinson excited admiration and gave an impression of competence. Kate Anthon, intense, emotional, aroused protective feelings even in strangers, though she managed her difficult life with a courage that belied appearances. Sue Dickinson was calm, unemotional, undemonstrative; she would rarely be wounded but would have skill to wound. Kate Anthon was all generosity and fire and eagerness. She loved recklessly, and in the process injured herself no less painfully than she injured others. Like Emily Dickinson but unlike Sue, she had a capacity for tragic feeling, which her life had already tested to the full.

The third occupant of the carriage was a man of sixty-two. Austin Dickinson, in a photograph of this period, had a tired, lined face, clean-shaven except for sideburns, with deepset eyes under heavy, overhanging brows, and, framing his face, a large, bushy wig. His wig was a coppery red, perhaps in memory of his red-haired father, and his eyes were a piercing blue. When he spoke, it was in a booming bass that could astonish even those who knew him. He was at this time wholly estranged from his wife, but appearances were kept up before their old and honored friend.

Martha Dickinson may have made a fourth in the carriage (Mrs. Anthon was not explicit in reporting the drive). Less need be said of her, for she was no more than an absorbed spectator at the last act of the drama. A young woman in her middle twenties, with a good deal of her mother's dark beauty, she was already anxious to win fame as a writer and to see the great world of which her mother's friend had long been a denizen. Years later she was to make a belated, foolish, and unhappy marriage with a foreigner named Alexander Bianchi, travel widely in Europe, and write inferior poetry and novels. In this fall of 1891 she would have found Mrs. Anthon an intensely interesting figure, and like virtually everyone else she succumbed to the charm of that extraordinary vitality and warmth. As the friendship grew steadily with the years, the inscriptions in Mrs. Bianchi's books progressed from a respectful "Mrs. Anthon" to an affectionate "beloved" or "dearest Aunt Kate." In *Emily Dickinson Face to Face,* written long after Mrs. Anthon's death, Martha Dickinson Bianchi spoke with warm admiration of a woman whom she had seen only a few times in her life.

The visit to Amherst, which lasted about a week, "was short and very pleasant in many respects," wrote Mrs. Anthon to her sister-in-law. Although she hinted at some of the respects in which it had *not* been pleasant, she was, on the whole, very reticent for so communicative a woman.

If young Martha Dickinson was present, and she probably was for much of the time, the conversation would have been somewhat general, but there were moments of uninterrupted intimacy. As the two older women sat on the east porch, so dear to Kate's memory, and looked across at the opposite house, they would inevitably be drawn to the subject that engrossed both their minds. Yet it was not an easy one to approach. "The past is such a curious creature," Emily had once written. And for the unguarded, who might venture too near, she had added a warning, "Her rusty ammunition might yet reply!" The past, the long-ago past of the Civil War, rained grapeshot and Minié balls upon Kate Anthon during those pleasant September days.

"I was sorry," she wrote afterwards, "to find that Sue and her sister-in-law were not on friendly terms. I mean Mr. D.'s sister Vinnie, who lives next door, now alone since the death of her parents and Emily. Sue was very fond of Emily, the poetess, but never greatly attached to Vinnie. Now she has no intercourse with her, and says she has treated her (Sue) very badly."

Even to her own trusted sister-in-law Kate Anthon dared say little more than this. She could only add a caution: "Don't let anyone know I have said anything in regard to this estrangement between Sue and Vinnie. It was so sad when I remembered how happy we were all together in years gone by." It was much sadder, in fact, than she cared to tell.

In the old Dickinson house lived a woman in late middle age, alone with her cats and her elderly housekeeper. Once a lively, handsome young girl, she was now wrinkled and gnarled, bitter of tongue, slovenly in dress. One great interest sustained her — the publication of her sister's poems, for which she felt, as she once wrote, the crusading zeal of a Joan of Arc. Across the hedge, in a newer, more ornate Dickinson house, lived another woman, now fat and grey, but still handsome, still careful in dress and manner. And between the two houses, separating them as nothing else could have done, were the explosive poems of Emily Dickinson.

As Kate Anthon observed, there had never been any real warmth between Sue and Lavinia. But they had borne with each other and had turned to each other at need. It was Sue who dressed Emily for burial, and it was Sue to whom Lavinia looked as her best hope of getting Emily's poems into print. Then Sue began to behave very oddly about the poems. And when she learned that Lavinia had entrusted them to Mrs.

Todd — young Mrs. Todd, their neighbor, in whom Austin
Dickinson was showing a great interest — open warfare began.
Lavinia talked much of Sue's petty cruelties (her favorite name
for Sue was "Old Scratch") and told stories of dogs turned
loose in her shrubbery and of compost heaps stolen from her.
They sound like the delusions of an isolated old woman. Even
if true, they do not explain Lavinia's very obvious fear of Sue.
Lavinia had been afraid of what Sue would do when the poetry
came out. Afterwards she veered between desperate appease-
ment and desperate boldness, and for the remaining years of
her life went in dread of Sue's mysterious power. Now the only
real weapon that could have been in Sue's hands was an understanding of the poetry.

Kate and Sue spoke of Emily's poems — so much is certain —
although they did not use the language of modern psychology.
As the two older women sat on the east porch and looked at
the silent house opposite, Sue would speak of Lavinia's trea-
sonable behavior in taking the poetry away from her and entrusting it to Mrs. Todd. But she would touch Kate most
sharply with the charge that Lavinia was recklessly publishing
poems which she herself would have suppressed. Of course Sue
loved Emily and had understood her (though she had never
been "greatly attached to Vinnie"), and she knew how Emily
would exaggerate and imagine situations. Still there were
things in the poetry which could be misinterpreted. Sue herself had been the recipient of one of Emily's uncomfortable
adorations, and she understood Kate's position. In such words,
or phrases still more guarded, the conversation must have been
carried on. But in the end Kate knew what Emily had written,
and Sue witnessed the concern on her expressive face. All the
later conduct of the two friends suggests strongly that there had
been a mutual enlightenment. Kate Anthon was to act like a
woman who had experienced a dreadful shock.

Lavinia sent flowers and a note begging Kate to call. Kate
would have gone if Sue had not made clear that it was a choice

between her own friendship and the visit to Lavinia. The
aging woman remained with Sue but looked mournfully across
the narrow hedge which separated her from the house and the
sister of the friend she had once known and loved so well. She
would never again cross that hedge, never roam in the house
whose every nook and cranny had once been so familiar, never
again climb the stairs with Emily to the little chamber facing
west. She was now an old woman and Emily had been dead
these five years. In a letter to her sister-in-law Kate openly
deplored the slight to her dead friend's sister. "Vinnie was
always very fond of me," she wrote sadly.

Now Lavinia's real feelings toward Kate must remain a
riddle. If she ever guessed, as she must have guessed, that Kate
had injured her sister, she would have been slow to forgive her.
But as between the enemy at a distance and the ever-present
enemy next door, she would doubtless prefer Kate. Then there
was a sweetness about Kate — a reluctance to wound — that
made her more attractive than the slightly feline Sue. Finally,
Kate was not simply a pawn, she was the all-important "phantom Queen," in the game being waged between Lavinia and
Sue. Afterwards Lavinia would show plainly that her object
had been to separate the other two women and attach Kate to
herself. Failing that, she was still determined to get the letters
and poems that Emily had written to Kate. For the news of
their survival (an admission from Kate to Sue) had gone from
Sue to Austin to Lavinia.

Undismayed even by Kate's refusal to cross the few feet of
lawn to the old Dickinson house, Lavinia obtained her address
— undoubtedly by way of Austin — and wrote to England. The
letter was a plea for copies of Emily's correspondence and
poems. In referring to it, Kate said merely that Lavinia had
written to her and that she was unwilling to answer because of
her friendship with Sue. But it is obvious that Lavinia persisted, for eventually, and with much reluctance, Kate Anthon
sent copies of several letters and poems which she had carried

with her during the many years of her nomadic life.

Meanwhile she had been reading Emily's poetry. During her stay in New York she had asked a friend to buy her a copy of the first volume. She marked it with thoroughness, probably during her return voyage to England, and suffered bitterly for many months afterwards. Although she was to be reserved about her Amherst experiences, the evidence of a violent emotional upheaval can be traced with certainty through her correspondence for the next two years. A letter from Sue or a bare reference to Amherst was enough to bring on a storm of passionate regret — for what, she dared not say, but she talked much of her youth. Did she communicate her pain to her old friend Sue, with whom she was once more in frequent correspondence?

The poetry, of course, was no longer at Sue's disposal. Quite apart from this difficulty, Kate Anthon was not a person who made demands. Despite the pain, there was probably a melancholy pride in having inspired so deep and lasting an attachment. There must even have been moments when she longed to be associated with the memory of Emily Dickinson. After much hesitation and several denials, she permitted the publication of some of Emily's letters to her, and she spoke of buying the second volume of the poetry. There is no evidence, however, that she did buy the book or any later works of Emily Dickinson. Perhaps she found Emily too painful to read. Now if Sue Dickinson understood that her friend suffered, she had an added reason for dissociating herself from poems which she already considered of doubtful propriety.

At all events, from the moment of Kate's visit in late 1891, Sue Dickinson, who had been busy with the poetry as recently as the preceding March, made no further attempts to publish any of it. Even when Lavinia died intestate, and the poetry came wholly and finally into her own hands, Sue Dickinson suppressed it and imposed the same prohibition on her daughter. Many years later, to be sure, Mrs. Bianchi was to assert that her Aunt Lavinia was responsible for the suppression. The story was good publicity for the poetry that Mrs. Bianchi was now issuing in driblets calculated to excite public interest. It created melodramatic visions of a mad Lavinia secreting poems in the wainscoting or in other unlikely places, and it had the further merit of exonerating Mrs. Bianchi's mother. But it was wholly untrue to the personality of Lavinia Dickinson. Lavinia would have published the text of the Black Mass, and would have convinced herself that it was Holy Writ, if it had been composed by her idolized sister. She was indignant with those delicate persons who withheld or burned any of the letters they had received from Emily.

With Lavinia's approval, Mrs. Todd continued to publish the work of Emily Dickinson. The second series of poems appeared in November, 1891, the letters in November, 1894, and the third series of poems in September, 1896. It would not appear that Lavinia was anxious to suppress any poetry. All her desires ran the other way. Nevertheless, signs of strain were developing between Lavinia and her hard-working editor.

For the rest of her life Mrs. Todd would appear to wonder why Lavinia turned against her. She would refer to Sue's mysterious power over Lavinia but would give no hint as to its nature. Yet it is hard to believe that she was entirely ignorant. As the intimate friend of Austin and Lavinia Dickinson she learned many family secrets. She was to insist upon the necessity of seclusion for a woman of Emily's temperament, and was to deny authoritatively, even contemptuously, the many stories connecting Emily with one man or another. These stories, she said, merely amused Austin Dickinson, adding that he told her many things about Emily "unsuspected by others." Over the poems themselves she exercised a curious censorship. For she omitted every poem showing strong feeling for a woman, accusing another person of cruelty or treason, or describing the love affair in too intimate or realistic detail. The poem beginning "Is bliss, then, such abyss," is not an exception. Mrs. Todd struck out the telltale last three lines, which alone show that the "bliss" depended upon another woman.

A possible explanation is that Mrs. Todd associated the poems with Sue, whom she heartily disliked. But the most revealing poems were written in 1859 and in the eighteen-sixties, long after Sue's marriage to Austin Dickinson, and the love described in them was strong, dangerous, and mutual. Austin would not have laughed at the memory of a love affair between his sister and his wife, nor would Mrs. Todd have misread the poems so grossly. Indeed she may have known that the woman was Kate. For when Kate yielded to Lavinia's pleading, she apparently sent copies of more letters and poems than were ever published. Either Mrs. Todd knew the reasons for minimizing Kate's influence, or Lavinia selected the letters before entrusting them to her editor. Certainly Mrs. Todd would have had no reason to like a woman whom she knew only as the source of Emily's heartbreak and the intimate friend of Sue Dickinson.

There is no need to discuss — or, rather, to guess — the circumstances which alienated Austin Dickinson from his wife and sent him for companionship to young Professor Todd and Mrs. Todd. The alienation was profound and unbridgeable long before 1881, the year in which the Todds came to Amherst. Some Amherst people would sympathize with Austin, others with Sue. But Mrs. Todd would eventually be the chief sufferer. For the rest of her life she would replace Sue's name with asterisks or with blanks in the letters of Emily Dickinson. These are facts, and they must be reckoned with in understanding why Lavinia and Mrs. Todd came to their fateful parting. Sue Dickinson would wish to injure Mrs. Todd with any means in her power, and she would find Lavinia her most convenient tool.

Lavinia was afraid of Sue. As early as 1890 she tried to keep Mrs. Todd's name off the title page of the poems. Later on she was anxious to minimize her editor's work with Emily's letters. There is a suggestion of jealousy, even of a penurious desire to

keep all the royalties to herself, but again and again, in her letters, Lavinia can be seen throwing a fearful look over her
shoulder toward the house in which Sue glowered and bided her
time. Then Austin Dickinson died on August 16, 1895, and
with him went Lavinia's last bulwark. In the fall of 1896 she
brought suit against Mrs. Todd to recover a small tract of land.

Now this lawsuit of Lavinia's was as curious as anything else
in the history of the Dickinsons. The land itself, a part of the
Dickinson estate bordering on the Todd property, was of little
value to anyone except Mrs. Todd and her husband. Austin
had wanted them to have the land as a partial return for Mrs.
Todd's years of work with the poetry. After his death Lavinia
took counsel with all her friends and worried and pondered,
but at last decided to carry out her brother's wishes. But she
insisted upon secrecy; the deed was not to be recorded. Mrs.
Todd explained to her own lawyer that Sue would make trouble. Unfortunately she did not — or could not — tell him that
Sue's power to make trouble was something far more substantial
and dangerous than petty cruelties. He must have felt that he
was dealing with some very foolish, unbusinesslike women, and
in Mrs. Todd's absence he had the deed recorded. This long
absence would appear to have been crucial. For several months
Sue had a clear field with Lavinia. When Mrs. Todd returned,
she was met by Lavinia's lawsuit.

It can be shown that Lavinia must have had a powerful
motive. By her conduct she was to alienate the only person who
could help her with the poetry; she was to lose her good friend
and business adviser, Mr. Hills, to whom she was emotionally
attached; and she was to throw herself completely into the
power of Sue Dickinson. To achieve these dubious gains, she
was obliged to go to court, perjure herself, and give the lie to
her own friends who testified for Mrs. Todd. Afterwards some
persons would think that Lavinia was painfully disturbed by
her treachery to Mrs. Todd. Is the lawsuit sufficiently explained

by saying that Lavinia resented Mrs. Todd's success with the poetry — or feared that Sue would turn a dog into her shrubbery?

Probably Sue Dickinson would never have used knowledge which would injure Kate or Emily, not to mention her own family pride. But with so jealous and unpredictable a woman, could Lavinia ever be entirely sure? About this time Lavinia apparently began confiding her tale of Emily's love for George Gould. At need, it would have been a useful backfire.

Sue's children, Ned and Martha, accompanied their Aunt Lavinia to the courtroom and lent support through a difficult time. Sue herself remained in the background, but she was evidently very much in the minds of persons attending the trial. The proceedings could only have been inspired by a desire to injure Mrs. Todd. For her courtroom appearance Lavinia wore yellow shoes, a blue flannel dress, and a long black mourning veil. With an adroitness and a wit that belied her, she testified that she was a simple, ignorant woman and had not understood the nature of a deed. In April, 1898, the deed was declared void.

Lavinia Dickinson survived her disastrous lawsuit little more than a year. But neither failing health nor the lack of Mrs. Todd's assistance deterred her from trying to continue the work of publication. Whatever fears inspired the Gould story, Lavinia had a flaming faith in the poems. And she loved and understood her dead sister — and Kate also — rather better than she expected others to love and understand. If she could have edited the poems herself, she would have done so. It was bad eyesight, an impossible handwriting, and editorial incompetence which led her to seek the help of Sue Dickinson, Mrs. Todd, and Mary Lee Hall.

A few little poems strayed into print during the winter of 1897–98 and the following spring. Undoubtedly they were furnished by Lavinia, who was paving the way for a new collection of poetry. In the winter of 1898–99 she employed Mary Lee Hall to copy enough poems for the new volume of poetry, but it was not to appear. Lavinia died the following August, and significantly all publication came to an end for many years. The obvious conclusion must be that it was Sue Dickinson, not Lavinia, who suppressed the poetry of Emily Dickinson.

If it is asked why Sue suppressed all of the poetry rather than the fraction which dealt with Katie, the answer can only be another question: What fraction? Sue was aware, as the casual reader is not, that poems about Katie masqueraded as nature poems, poems on ethical questions, poems on death and immortality. She could never be sure where Katie stopped and something else began. Better to have nothing at all to do with the poetry.

During the last year of her life (or so Mrs. Bianchi was to write in the preface to *The Single Hound*), Sue Dickinson read and reread the poetry and the emotional letters which she had received from the young Emily. According to her daughter, she was trying to decide whether she ought to destroy both poems and letters. The story has the aspect of truth, and it is now possible to understand Sue's concern. If Emily Dickinson had had an orthodox and hopeless love for a married man, as the common story goes, Sue Dickinson would not have faced any great dilemma. She died with her dilemma unresolved. During her lifetime, however, she made sure that nothing was published which would injure the memory of her sister-in-law or the feelings of her friend Katie.

Thus for fourteen years, from the death of Lavinia, in August, 1899, until Sue's own death on May 12, 1913, the poetry was as good as buried. Sue Dickinson was hardly in her own grave, however, before Martha Dickinson Bianchi was engaged in preparing a volume published about the first of October, 1914, under the title *The Single Hound*. The dates of Sue's death and the publication of *The Single Hound* follow each other too closely to be explained as coincidence.

Mrs. Bianchi prefaced the book with absurd stories about her aunt's numerous male admirers and with a vague reference to a love affair. Although these fictions would not deceive her mother's friend, they at least distracted attention from Kate Anthon. And Mrs. Bianchi sent a copy of the book to her "beloved Aunt Kate from Emily's niece and Susan's daughter." Mrs. Anthon thanked her with a wistful letter in which she recalled the evenings when Emily had come with her dog and lantern and had played enchanting melodies of her own composition. Those evenings were gone forever, she added with a sigh; she could only live on the memory of them.

The Single Hound, incidentally, was a somewhat more cautious selection than the three volumes published by Lavinia Dickinson and Mabel Loomis Todd. Although it was impossible to find any large number of poems unconnected with Emily's attachment to Kate, Mrs. Bianchi did her best to avoid giving pain to her mother's old friend. Kate Anthon could have read few poems that referred clearly to herself. In fact, the most revealing poetry published by Sue's daughter was to wait upon the death of Kate Scott Anthon.

In the long preface to *The Single Hound,* which mentioned scarcely any other names, Mrs. Bianchi was careful to refer to her Aunt Emily's friendship with Kate Anthon, linking Kate's name with that of Samuel Bowles. A decade later, and again, almost a decade later, she was to refer to the time when Emily and Kate and Bowles had spent joyful evenings together in her mother's house. These evenings occurred well before Mrs. Bianchi was born, and she would have heard of them through her mother. It has already been pointed out that she was well instructed in the history of her Aunt Emily and Kate Anthon, for she was correct in saying that Bowles was closely associated with those wintry evenings. Little wonder that Emily refused to see him in the fall of 1861, and again in March, 1862. He admired Katie and was all too likely to speak of her. And Emily was not yet able to hear that name without a "stop-sensation in [her] soul and thunder in the room."

4

This is the story of three women: Emily Dickinson, her sister-in-law Susan Gilbert Dickinson, and most especially, Kate Scott, about whom least is known. It is also the story of a fourth woman, shadowy as yet, who replaced, or merged with, the image of Emily Dickinson in the mind of Kate Scott Anthon. Still other names come into the story, but they were of little importance to the poet who wrote with truth that she could select one individual from a populous nation and "then close the valves of her attention like stone."

It is often necessary to refer to the three women by their given names. Usage has not yet sanctioned the terseness of "Dickinson." Susan Gilbert married Emily's brother and became a Dickinson herself. Kate Scott bore, in all, three surnames. During the period of her intimacy with Emily Dickinson she was the young widow Turner, but, to the further confounding of the biographer, she preferred that her Amherst friends use her maiden name. Afterwards she became Mrs. John Anthon.

To Sue she was "Katie Jane." To her sister-in-law she was "Katie Ann." To her stepmother she was "my Katrina." To Emily Dickinson she was many names, ranging from a playful "Goliath" (because of her height) to a significant "Ishmael." Emily called herself "Ishmael" as well, for she felt that both were outcasts and that every man's hand was against them. She may even have had in mind the translation of the name, which is a hopeful "God will hear." It is probable that she also referred to Kate under the names "Saxon" and "Gabriel."

To her own niece, Kate Anthon was "Aunt Tommy" or

"Aunt Thomas." To her young English friend Florie, she was "Mud" (mother?) or "Mr. Pump." In her last years she wrote wistfully to Sue Dickinson: "*Do* throw your arms around my neck and kiss me and call me Katie — 'Katie Jane.' I am so tired of the everlasting 'Mrs. Anthon.'"

II

CATHERINE MARY SCOTT was born March 12, 1831, in Cooperstown, New York. She was three months younger than Emily
Dickinson.

The village of Cooperstown lies at the southern end of Lake
Otsego, where the Susquehanna River takes its rise, in the
southeastern part of New York State. In its broader geograph-
ical relations, it is due north of New Jersey and — of greater
significance to Emily Dickinson — due west of Amherst, Massachusetts.

Students of the poetry have long been aware that Emily
Dickinson's symbolism looked westward, but they have mistakenly spanned the continent. West is west, whether it be next
door in the house of Austin Dickinson, where Kate invariably
stayed during her visits to Amherst, or many miles farther westward in the village of Cooperstown. Emily's bedroom faced
west. If she looked toward the setting sun, she saw her
brother's house, and beyond that, in imagination, the dim western region to which Kate returned. When she wrote that her
"Sun" had removed "to other Wests," she meant that Kate had

withdrawn from the literal wests of Austin's house and of Cooperstown to the symbolic wests of psychical distance, estrangement, love's death.

Emily Dickinson never saw Cooperstown, but for several
years it was a joyous and then a painful stimulus to her imagination. She never forgot that her friend, like the sun, disappeared below the western horizon. The letter ending their
friendship came to her from Cooperstown.

During the War of the Revolution the country around Lake
Otsego was not always secure, and the smoking, bloodstained
ruins of nearby Cherry Valley long remained in memory as a
witness to the terror. After the war, however, the Indians
melted away like the ice on Lake Otsego in a spring thaw. In
1794 a last wandering band appeared on the outskirts of Cooperstown. They never revisited their forests of pine, or the
maples they had tapped for sugar, or the lake they had fished
for bass or crossed in their darting canoes. In the late seven-
teen-eighties William Cooper made his surveys and early set-
tlements in perfect safety; and his son James, who was to give
the redskins an enduring and international fame, got his Indian
lore from books or the recollections of older persons.

From the height of Mount Vision, on the southeast, where
James Fenimore Cooper often took his stand, much of the
region lies open to view. Immediately below is Lake Otsego,
Cooper's "Glimmerglass," which, for size and beauty and for
its relation to the surrounding mountains, has been compared
to the lakes of northern England. It is about nine miles long
and from a half-mile to a mile wide, being in some places ex-
panded into graceful little bays and in others pinched by mountains or penetrated by jutting spurs. At its foot, perhaps a mile
from Mount Vision, lies the village of Cooperstown, clustered
around the point where the youthful Susquehanna, accompanied by the highway, takes off southward through its own
valley. At the opposite end of the lake is another opening,

through which the highway enters from the north, but east and west the main valley is enfolded by lofty, wooded hills. The site of the town is rugged and picturesque enough to suggest that it was chosen for its scenery. With some such picture in mind, Emily Dickinson wrote to her absent friend: "Oh, our condor Kate! Come from your crags again!"

During the winter and even later than the early March day on which Kate was born, the nine-mile lake was usually frozen over to a considerable depth. Sportsmen built huts on the lake, chopped holes in the ice floor of the hut, and fished in the comfort of their restricted quarters and of their good stove, often warmer than many a family in town. The snow lay heavy and long on the mountains that rim the lake, on the lake itself, and on the little cluster of houses at its outlet. Sleighing was good, particularly on the lake, though caution was necessary when a spring thaw was imminent. Ice skating was another favorite sport. In the early spring, before the snow was gone, the sap rose in the maple trees, and the village young people often went out in parties to tap the trees, boil the syrup and cool it in the snow.

In late March or early April, the snow vanished. The hills, which had glittered under the winter sun, became a somber brown, then flushed with new green life. The ice melted with astonishing suddenness, and the lake rippled under a spring wind. The trees at the water's edge, bare poles all winter, now leafed out and obscured the lake and the opposing mountains. By June it was safe to begin gardening. In the summer young people rowed on the lake or went fishing.

Rowing and walking were young Kate's chief diversions, but she took part in all village activities. With other young people she went picnicking and fishing, she skated and took sleigh rides, and she learned to dance and to flirt with the village boys.

Although Cooperstown grew rapidly at first, it never answered the hopes of its founder, Judge Cooper, but remained small and isolated. During Kate's girlhood the population was not much over fifteen hundred, and it scarcely exceeds twenty-five hundred today. The hop vineyards, once the chief resource, declined in value, and the town came to depend more nearly upon its scenery, in which it abounds, and upon the increasing wealth of native or adopted sons, who made their fortunes elsewhere and settled in Cooperstown to enjoy them. The new proprietors dispensed patronage and discouraged the commercialism that threatened their summer retreat. Even before Kate left it permanently, Cooperstown was fast becoming a feudal preserve.

With wealth came a new atmosphere, or rather a widening of the atmosphere that had always surrounded the Cooper family. The harsh Puritanism of the early settlers, so distressing to the aristocratic feelings of Cooper, gave place to an aura of cosmopolitanism, of leisurely European travel, of winters in New York City or Florida. Great houses were built: among them, Hyde Hall, which was said to be haunted by a rather mild, domestic ghost in a bathrobe; Woodside, to which President Van Buren paid a visit; Edgewater, with its handsome twin stairways and fine view of the lake; and last of the big houses, Fernleigh, the vast stone mansion of Kate's friend Alfred Corning Clark. In the early days, however, all Cooperstown was under the shadow of baronial Otsego Hall.

Kate Scott did not live in the "old Fenimore Cooper mansion" — a picturesque detail contributed by Mrs. Bianchi. She lived in her own house, only a decade or so less old than Otsego Hall, though much smaller and less pretentious; but she must often have visited the house of her family's close friends. Perhaps she described it to Sue Gilbert; or Sue may have seen it herself, for she visited Cooperstown before Otsego Hall was destroyed. It was scarcely a hundred yards from the Scott house, and must have been a notable landmark. Here Cooper liked to surround himself with parties of young people, and

Kate was among their number. On the night of February 12, 1848, she came with her foster cousin, a daughter of Cooper's friend Nicoll Dering of Utica, as Cooper noted with pleasure in his diary.

It is true that Cooper was not on good terms with all his neighbors. Shortly after his return from Europe in 1837, he plunged into a quarrel, originally over public access to a favorite picnic spot, which ramified until it engaged national attention. Locally it was confined to Cooper's Whig opponents and a few hotheads. Kate's father was not involved. Henry Scott was a man of peaceful disposition, a banker (who had learned to walk softly in neighborhood feuds) — and a Democrat and an Episcopalian. He had no reason to quarrel with his fellow Democrat and Episcopalian. The two men were closely associated in the affairs of town and church. The names of James Fenimore Cooper and Henry Scott stood high on every public subscription list, and for like amounts, and they served as the two wardens of Christ Church. When Cooper died in late 1851, Henry Scott was deeply affected. "Going into the room once," wrote Cooper's daughter Susan on the morning after his death, "I found Mr. Scott and Mr. Battin there, both in tears." Years later, in a letter to Henry Scott's daughter Margaret, Susan Cooper recalled the warm friendship between the two men.

Mrs. Scott worked companionably with the younger Cooper women in the many duties connected with Christ Church. Scott's daughter Margaret named a street in Flatbush, Long Island, "Fenimore," in honor of her father's old friend; and Kate's references or messages to the Coopers, during her European sojourns of 1864 and afterwards, were many and cordial. Miss Susan and Miss Charlotte, Cooper's daughters, took a warm interest in Kate's journeys, which paralleled their own earlier travels; and Kate sent them pictures of European scenes and asked that they be shown her letters. She was amused by Miss Susan's proposal to scatter lemon peel and almond shells in her path to persuade her that she was still in Italy.

2

Kate's birthplace, the old Scott house at the corner of Elk and River Streets, unlike Otsego Hall, is still standing after almost a century and a half, and looking probably much as it looked in her girlhood. It is a pleasant, rambling, two-story clapboard house, painted brown, with a wing at right angles and other additions, for in the casual manner of old houses it has grown by accretion as family needs required. Kate lived to congratulate the family from overseas on the installing of the first bathroom.

In the front part of the house, separated by the entrance hall, are the customary two parlors, each with its fireplace against the outside wall. These fireplaces, more cheerful than warming, were probably supplemented in Kate's youth by large, clumsy iron stoves. The floors are covered with oriental rugs, and the walls with engravings and family portraits. In the north parlor the bookcases on each side of the old sofa are filled, in good part, with Kate's own books; and in the south parlor and the bedrooms upstairs, on tables or on shelves, are still more of her books. From the entrance hall a stairway rises to the large, old-fashioned bedrooms above. Beyond the hall are the dining room and the various service and storage rooms. Everywhere there is a pleasant informality.

Despite the early inconveniences, this was a comfortable house, remembered with affection by everyone who ever lived in it. Even for a guest, the old house has a great deal of charm, perhaps not so much in the details of architecture, however, as in a recollection of the warmth of life and the tragic fates of the persons it sheltered. Long after she had left it forever, Kate wrote mournfully: "My happiest and saddest days were passed under that roof, and the last memories will ever remain — my dear husband's long, weary illness, confined to his bed for five months in my old room. I cannot think of it without the bitterest tears."

On the north side of the house, so close as to be almost under the windows, is the graveyard of Christ Church, the church itself, a plain and dignified building of red brick, being set back a little distance behind it. This church, in which she was brought up, was always dear to Kate, and its many associations — the sewing circle, a new screen, the Christmas decorations, or a photograph of the chancel — continued to excite her warm interest long after she had seen it for the last time. The bell rings pleasantly on Sunday mornings, and the churchyard is not so lugubrious a neighborhood as the visitor would at first suppose. But of course the graves are old and have lost the bleak sharpness of recent death. In Kate's youth they were fresh enough. Here the Coopers were interred beneath massive slabs of marble, and here also, for a short time, Kate's young first husband was buried.

Crowded as the house is, on the north by the churchyard and on the east by River Street, the most attractive part of the grounds has always been the expanse of lawn and garden, with its margin of stately trees, at the corner of Elk and River Streets. During the summers of Kate's girlhood it was almost a mass of flowers. "My *own* mother in my childhood's days," she once wrote to her sister-in-law, "had the most beautiful garden in Cooperstown. She almost lived in it. It was only of late years that the numerous flower beds were destroyed and replaced by grass. I remember when each bed was laid out and exactly where the flowers bloomed. Maggie and I used to help Mother weeding and transplanting by the hour." And she ended sadly, "Happy, careless days, now gone forever!"

There are only three or four casual references to her own mother in all her correspondence, but as the first Mrs. Scott died when Katie was twelve, there would have been fewer associations. The most lasting effect of the mother's death was to give the little girl a premature sense of responsibility and a brooding tenderness for the younger children, especially the six-year-old brother. Two years later Kate's father married his dead wife's younger sister, Margaret Elizabeth Strong, who was the "dear mother" of Kate's letters and of her very warm devotion.

The two successive Mrs. Scotts were members of the ramifying Strong clan, inhabitants of New England from the very early days of settlement. Selah Strong, Kate's great-grandfather, was a delegate to the first Continental Congress and afterwards a captain in the Revolutionary army. Some members of the family, however, were too comfortably established to take a warm interest in revolution. Kate's attitude toward the Strongs was one of innocent and forgivable pride. It was nothing more than that she took for granted the position into which she was born, and that she moved freely in a New York society where her Dickinson friends would not have felt at home. What this society was like can be briefly illustrated. Kate's niece, Mrs. Stuyvesant Fish, introduced writers at her dinner parties. It was an innovation almost as surprising as the elaborate parties for dolls and dogs with which "Mamie" Fish carried on her warfare against stodgy Mrs. Astor. Of course Kate herself was brought up among writers and had a hearty respect for them. She liked to remember that her cousin Sally Baxter had captivated Thackeray during his American visits, and she was convinced that Sally had furnished a model for "the saucy, beautiful Ethel Newcome."

Kate's own branch of the Strong family migrated to Cooperstown, and then to Flatbush, where they intermarried with the old Dutch families, themselves so much intermarried over the centuries that virtually everyone was related to everyone else. Joseph Strong, Kate's grandfather, sent his son, afterwards pastor of the Dutch Reformed Church in Flatbush, to Princeton, and gave his two daughters as good an education as was customary for women of the period. Kate seemed to have no doubt that her stepmother would recognize and enjoy an obscure allusion to Tasso, and she never complained, as her friend Emily complained of the elder Mrs. Dickinson, that her mother did not "care for thought."

The second Mrs. Scott was equal to the responsibility of the three charming, lively, book-loving children whom she inherited. She was a woman of salt and common sense, who often had reason to deplore the extravagant emotionalism of her stepdaughter Kate but loved her in spite of it — perhaps largely because of it. During their long separations the two women wrote to each other weekly, and even a few days' delay in receiving a letter from Mrs. Scott was enough to give Kate sharp anxiety. But though she loved her stepmother, it is clear that she was even more devoted to her father.

On her father's side Kate was Irish, as Mrs. Bianchi observed, or more probably Scotch-Irish. Her paternal grandparents migrated from Ulster toward the close of the Revolutionary War and settled in Otsego County. The first Henry Scott served two terms in the New York legislature and eventually became a judge. His son Henry, the "dearest Papa" or "blessed man" of Kate's letters, looks out smilingly from his portrait in the hall of his old house — a genial, elderly man with scant white hair, blue eyes, and rosy cheeks and chin above the tall, white stock and dark broadcloth of a banker and a substantial citizen.

"He possessed great liveliness and vivacity and wit," wrote his daughter long after his death. "One would perceive at once that he was either of Irish or French extraction. Dear, dear man! so delicate and sensitive and sympathetic." And she remembered that he had often asked her to read aloud from the Waverley Novels during long winter evenings.

Shortly before Kate was born, Henry Scott was appointed cashier of the first bank organized in Cooperstown, a position he held for more than forty years. Apparently he was contented with modest success and a very pleasant domestic life, for after a year as president of the bank he returned voluntarily to his old position. As a father he was kindly and generous, and his children not only loved him but also were at ease with him — a circumstance the more noteworthy as he was almost forty when the eldest, Kate, was born. His daughter had always a wholehearted, uncritical respect for him, and long after his death wrote with passionate regret of the days when he had been alive: "Oh! for one (only *one*) of those blessed evenings. How happy we were! Father and Mother sitting there so lovingly in the old parlour — I could weep to think those days are gone. Father was perfectly charming, was he not?"

At the time of this letter she was reading the published poetry of her friend Emily Dickinson and undergoing one of the blackest periods of depression she had ever known, a period in which she seemed almost to long for death and reunion with the father who had always comforted her; but many passages at other times reveal the same devotion. Relations among all members of the family, as reflected in Kate's letters, were unusually close. They were a warm, demonstrative family.

The Maggie who helped Katie with the gardening was a younger sister, Margaret, of comparatively short and pathetic history. As a little girl of thirteen she wrote an engaging letter to "dear Kate," then sixteen, in order to give her sister "a brief account of our delightful visit, & which would have been rendered still more if we had had your company." The other Scotts, including Margaret, had apparently been making a round of family visits, while Kate remained with their cousin Sarah Dering in Utica. The most memorable event of Margaret's trip was a performance by the midget Tom Thumb, but there were also many vivid, amusing sidelights on a typical family journey of the period — the slow progress by boat or "cars" or stage ("an old distressed stage," the little girl wrote), the leisurely visits with numerous cousins and uncles and aunts, the interweaving of a hundred strands of domestic feeling and interest which have frayed out with the decline in large family groups.

On June 1, 1859, Margaret Scott married Dr. Homer L. Bartlett of Flatbush and went to live in a large brick house on the street she herself named "Fenimore." Kate was a frequent visitor in the Bartlett house, and from this place she set out on some of her early journeys to Amherst.

Margaret resembled her older sister in extravagant wit and enjoyment of life. Even when she lay dying in Mentone, far from home and separated by an ocean's width from her husband and children, she rallied to entertain her new friends, and all the efforts of her sister Kate, who was her companion and nurse, were unavailing to quiet her. Long afterwards, in a letter to Sue Dickinson, Kate spoke of the dullness of her present existence after "living my life with a sparkling creature like my brilliant sister Maggie. Oh! did you ever know any one to exceed her? I have never met any one over here who remotely approached her in genius, wit, vivacity — Life!"

The youngest member of the family was the third Henry Scott, born March 5, 1836. There is a pleasantly misspelled letter of his, written at seven to his Aunt Margaret, afterwards his stepmother, repeatedly urging her to visit him. Of course the little boy also wanted things, "a good stout knife and a fidle and a saving bank," also "a Walet or a purse," and most of all, some new rabbits. When he had gone to feed his "pair of Rabits," he wrote sadly, "I open the dor and found my Rabits stole." Two years later his sister Margaret reported fresh calamities: "Henry's hen was killed by a dog & 5 of his last brood of little chickens were smothered by a cat."

There is not much more to tell about the little boy who tried to raise chickens and rabbits in the garden of the Scott house. Several letters survive in his clear, angular handwriting, gently scolding Kate for her mistakes, describing the measures he had taken to improve her income, and tacitly revealing his love for his impulsive older sister. A lover of books, like all his family, Henry Scott sent Kate his own parodies of Wordsworth and was as devoted as she to the works of Dickens. In 1868 he married Kate's friend Eliza Synnott, the "Lila" of Kate's many letters, and settled in New York as cashier of the publishing firm founded by Cooper's son-in-law Henry Phinney. His last illness, which brought Kate home from Europe in 1884, recalled some poignant memories: "Henry has always been especially dear to me. He was only six years old when our Mother died and he seemed left as my particular charge. You know how I loved him and understood him."

Concerning Kate's childhood there is no record except her own recollection that she was happy. Indirectly, however, it is possible to learn what she was like. She had a habit of marking passages in her books that described her own emotions, tastes, or experiences. She was interested in her own reactions and kept an emotional diary by penciling lines that seemed peculiarly appropriate to herself. When she marked a line in Lamb's essay "Witches and Other Night Fears" ("Parents do not know what they do when they leave tender babes alone to go to sleep in the dark"), it is certain that the irrational fears of her childhood were strong enough to leave a painful memory. That she was an oversensitive child is clear from other evidence. Thunderstorms and loud noises were sources of unreasonable terror. She could not bear to be alone during severe storms, and the infrequency of thunderstorms in Europe was to be one of the satisfactions of her life abroad. Another was her absence from America on "the noisy Fourth of July." "I am constitutionally susceptible of noises," wrote Lamb in "A Chapter on Ears," and Kate bracketed the passage and then vigorously underlined each separate word. In this she resembled Emily Dickinson, who was also a sensitive, nervous child. They were alike too in their hatred of cats, which with Kate amounted sometimes to a phobia, and both were extravagantly fond of birds.

There were compensations in this overstrong susceptibility. "I am not without suspicion," wrote Lamb (and again Kate marked the lines), "that I have an undeveloped faculty of music within me." She played nothing, sang with only an amateur's enthusiasm, but listened rapturously to those who could play or sing; the musical ability of a new friend was always the first thing mentioned in her letters. She responded sensitively, though uncritically, to color and form in art, and with still greater enthusiasm, to color and form in nature. She wrote with equal enthusiasm of the food she found abroad, and many a marked passage in her copy of Lamb's essays dealt with the pleasure of eating.

The night-terrors and the fear of noises were of no great importance in a life that was lived with gusto. She had every reason to be happy. Brought up in a comfortable, middle-class home, indulged by affectionate parents, she did, within reasonable limits, pretty much as she pleased. There were no restrictions on reading except her father's kindly insistence that she read in a good light, and she ranged at will through all the books available to her. But she liked social activities equally well, and to everything and everyone she brought her own overflowing zest for life.

When Kate was about seventeen, she was sent away to school. The impulsive, affectionate girl entered the Utica Female Academy, where Susan Gilbert was also a student. This school, founded in 1837, was well regarded and well patronized. During its first year it had an enrollment of 168, and the number of students may have been larger when Kate entered in 1848. At that time it was under the direction of Miss Jane E. Kelly. Upon Miss Kelly's "lasting and meritorious work" (wrote the historian of the town of Utica) it was unnecessary to enlarge, so well known were "her capacity as a moral as well as intellectual Mentor, her skill and tact in the management of this numerously attended institution, the able corps of teachers she from time to time collected to her assistance." It is possible that Miss Kelly sometimes needed all of her skill and tact to handle her lively new student.

Traditions (but no anecdotes) of Kate's madcap behavior

at school were reported by Mrs. Bianchi, and they appear to fit
the person. It is not hard to believe that, excepting her strong
appetite for books, young Kate was more noted at Utica for
prankish humor than for studiousness. There still survives a
French textbook, the *Fables* of La Fontaine, on the flyleaf of
which appears the name "Kate Scott" in a schoolgirl hand. The
first several pages show a conscientious attention to her studies,
but the remaining pages are immaculate. Years later, in her
European days, Kate lamented this earlier idleness, as she
struggled anew with the French language. To her sister-in-law
she wrote to urge setting her young niece "at the French —
while she is young." And she added, "I could cry that I was
neglected so in my youth in this respect." In time she learned
to speak and to read French fairly well.

"Oh! those happy school days!" she wrote to Sue Dickinson
long afterwards. "Will I ever forget the public examination
and the class in 'Wayland's Moral Philosophy'! You were monitress that day, and knew the agony I was suffering, as you sat in
the hall near the door of No. 37. I just escaped reciting by one;
the girl next to me had begun, when I whispered to her, 'Ask a
question.' The hour expired, and you rang the bell, loudly and
vigorously! The excruciating part of the affair was the fact that
two very clever Boston (Harvard) students were present. I
knew them and had danced and flirted with them a few
evenings before, but to discuss 'Moral Philosophy' with them
(I was 17 years old) was utterly out of the question!!"

Even the narrow world of the Utica Female Academy contained more interesting things than moral philosophy. There
were her Cousin Sarah Dering's stepdaughters, Annie, Sarah
(Kate's "first friend away from home," who unhappily lost her
mind in her early twenties), and the two younger girls, Kitty
and Fanny. The latter were to be Kate's closest friends in the
Dering family, although she was always fond of Annie and retained a tender memory of poor Sarah. In her correspondence
she recalled still other friends of her school days, with whom

she renewed acquaintance on every visit to Utica. The warmth and spontaneity of her temperament were very attractive to others, and with few exceptions she kept the friendships she swiftly made. At Utica the most loved of her new friends was apparently Sue Gilbert.

"Dear Sue," wrote Kate in their last years, "I remember how I dreaded being sent to the Utica boarding school. I cried and protested against it. Now what an awful thing if I had not gone — I should never have known *you!* Never have known you! It is too appalling to contemplate for a moment! I cannot conceive of my life without a Sue Gilbert Dickinson!" But she ended in the comfortable faith that predestined friends would have met somehow.

Kate Scott lost no time in declaring her attachment to a new friend. On the night when Sue, the new monitress, stopped at Kate's door during the course of her duties, the two girls were still virtual strangers. Impulsively Kate embraced her and kissed her cheek, and Sue looked at her with wondering eyes. "Non-demonstrative Sue!" This was what her classmates called her, wrote Mrs. Bianchi, and perhaps it was Kate who described her.

It was easy and natural for young Kate to love. She had grown up in warmth and security. But Sue Gilbert was of a different temperament, and her early life must have suppressed any tendency toward easygoing demonstrativeness. She was born December 19, 1830 (Emily, Sue, and Kate were, in that order, almost of an age), the youngest of a large and unprosperous family. Her father, Thomas Gilbert, managed successive taverns in various Massachusetts towns, drank heavily, and led his family through a haphazard, unsettled life. Both parents died while Sue was still a little girl, and the children were parceled out among their relatives. Sue fell to the lot of an aunt, Mrs. Van Vranken, of Geneva, New York. Here she probably learned to be self-reliant and prudent and to cultivate no feelings that could be easily hurt.

As to Sue's very real charm, the best evidence is that both Kate Scott and Emily Dickinson loved her. She was a witty, intelligent girl, interested in books and showing some ability for mathematics. At the academy she probably studied in a manner that Kate would never have imitated, for she knew that she might have to earn her living. In fact, she taught school during her twenty-first year. And she was admirably self-reliant, capable, and good-humored during a year's exile from home. Brilliant and beautiful, she was a natural magnet for emotional young girls. There is no evidence, however, that her own feelings ever became sufficiently engaged to give her pain. It is a curious fact that the letters Kate wrote to Sue in old age, like the letters Emily had written to her in youth, seem to plead always for more affection than the writer expects to receive.

Yet Sue was apparently the more faithful with respect to Kate. She tried to maintain the correspondence when Kate seemed willing to let it drop, and the hiatus of their middle years would seem to be of Kate's making. After the death of Emily Dickinson, however, the two women drew together again. Letters became frequent, visits were exchanged, and the whole tone of their intercourse grew warmer as life declined. In extreme old age Kate Anthon described Sue as "my dearest friend in America," and about the same time, grieving over Sue's failing health, she wrote simply: "I have loved her ever since I was seventeen years old."

To Sue Dickinson herself Kate wrote: "Dear, dear Sue, I have loved you always, since the first night you were 'monitress,' and I hardly knew you, but kissed your dear face simply because I could not help it! Your sweet eyes looked into mine, and I could never forget them! Now we are doomed to live widely separated, with a terrible ocean between us!"

From Utica it was no more than a brisk carriage drive or sleigh ride to Cooperstown, where the Scott home was always open to Susan Gilbert. Henry Scott treated her with his usual gentle kindliness, and Mrs. Scott became very fond of her. But if these visits were a pleasant experience to the orphaned girl, who had no real home and only occasional contact with her own brothers and sisters, they were still more warming to Katie. "This is too blissful!" she exclaimed over and over in an adolescent fever of admiration for her new friend. The words characterized her for Emily Dickinson long before Emily met her.

Many years afterwards, in a letter to Mrs. Scott, Sue Dickinson wrote gratefully of her youthful visits to Cooperstown:

My dear Mrs. Scott.

I cannot let my letter to my long beloved Kate go without a word of special love and tenderness to you for so kindly writing me of her. Your individual and remarkable hand-writing has reopened a most tender past with its memories and associations — most lively among them my school-girl visits to you, when you and your gentle husband received me with almost parental warmth. Kate will read you the tidings with which I am constrained to greet her, and I realize how fervently you will give your loving sympathy to us all. Dear Mrs. Scott, I cannot believe you have infirmities. Your writing belies that. I wish you may be always young in the only sense worth anything and that when you lift the veil it may be in a pleasant dream.

Yours with the fondest recollections,
SUE DICKINSON.

School days came to an end, and the two girls rarely met. Susan Gilbert went to live with her sister, Harriet Cutler, in Amherst, where she became acquainted with Emily Dickinson. Kate remained at home, finding what diversion she could and learning to cook and sew in preparation for almost the only life then open to women. Indeed she seemed never to have a desire for any other, unless it was the life of the unattached traveler.

About this time she received a long visit from her cousin Sally Baxter and her foster cousins Kitty and Fanny Dering. "They made our dear old home ring with laughter and merriment!" Kate recalled. "We used to sit up late in the spare bedroom listening to Sally, and I can hear Mother coming to the foot of the stairs and calling out, 'Go to bed, children, it is *very* late.'"

In June, 1856, Susan Gilbert made what was probably the last of her several visits to Cooperstown. "I was thinking the other day," wrote Kate Anthon, "of the short visit you made me on your way to Geneva to be married. I see my dear Father meeting you, and putting his hand on·your head, 'And is this Sue Gilbert?' and then we all went out to tea and were so happy, so joyous — so joyous, and trouble and sorrow seemed far away. 'Oh! Death in life — the Days that are no more!'"

It is difficult to understand this passage, unless she meant that Sue's visit had given her a temporary respite from sorrow. The days to which she alluded could have been anything but joyous to her.

The preceding autumn, on October 29, 1855, Kate Scott had married Campbell Ladd Turner of Cooperstown. Campbell Turner, born March 13, 1831, was a day younger than Kate. He was a grandson of Cooper's good friend Robert Campbell and a son of Levi C. Turner, then county judge, afterwards Judge Advocate in the War Department of President Lincoln. In his portrait Campbell Turner appears tall, thin, and erect, with reddish-blond hair, dark eyes, and a long, straight nose above a full beard. The beard is worn short, with sideburns and a small mustache. Apparently he was an intelligent, serious young man, but he died too early to leave much record of accomplishment. As he spent most of his short life in Cooperstown, the two young people grew up together and may have had a long engagement.

Campbell Turner was a doctor, a graduate of the medical school of the University of Pennsylvania. At the time of his graduation, and before his marriage to Kate, he knew that he had tuberculosis. He had made an accurate diagnosis of his own case and knew that his chance of recovery was not good. By June, 1856, the date of Sue's visit, his illness had become alarming.

During the following August, or perhaps earlier, he was confined to bed in his father's house. Here his young wife nursed him devotedly, seldom stirring from his room. If she had a turn for any profession, it was that of nursing. Deft, gentle, patient with the most querulous, she attended her two husbands and her sister through long, mortal illnesses, helped with the care of her brother, and nursed her dying stepmother. As if this were not enough, she acquired an interest in still other invalids whom she met abroad. Of course there were moments of weariness and even of rebellion. In 1876 she wrote mournfully that her nursing days were almost over; her strength was failing, she said, and she begged for help with her dying sister. Ten years later she asked her sister-in-law to keep secret the date of her voyage to England; otherwise she was sure to have some invalid put upon her. But three years later she spent weary months in the house of a dying friend. Perhaps invalidism had a certain attraction for her.

Referring long afterwards to this August of 1856, she recalled that she had once left Campbell's room for a few minutes to attend a wedding but had not been able to stay for the wedding breakfast. "Campbell was *very* ill at the time, and I returned to the house and back to his sick room. How well I remember it all." Elsewhere she spoke of her "youth and marriage to Campbell and those sweet sad days."

When she learned, in 1892, that her mother-in-law was dying, Kate Anthon wrote sadly: "I have thought so much, so much of Mrs. Turner for weeks past as if I had a presentiment of coming sorrow. I always live over every spring each day and hour of that trip to Boston and that dying scene at the Tremont House. Mrs. Turner was always with me day and night."

Three weeks before his death the young man, with his wife and parents, made a desperate pilgrimage to Boston. There was no reason to think that even so distinguished a physician as Dr. Salter could help him now, but the dying man may have hoped for another kind of miracle. During his illness Campbell Turner had become interested in theology and had promised himself that if he lived he would give up medicine and become a minister. He was determined to see Bishop Southgate. The trip from Cooperstown to Boston must have been dreadful. In the primitive trains of that period even a healthy man would have been uncomfortable, and Campbell Turner was dying. His parents and his young wife must have suffered as they attended to him. And after all there was no miracle. Campbell Turner died in the Tremont House on May 26, 1857, and his body was brought back to Cooperstown and buried in the churchyard under the windows of the Scott house.

Not long after the young widow returned to her old home, and while she was upstairs one morning brushing her hair, she heard sounds of activity in the churchyard below. From her window she looked out to see workmen digging up the coffin that contained the body of her young husband. Her permission had not been asked, nor had she even been notified of the intended removal. The shock was profound and lasting. But if the incident produced any coolness between her and the Turners, it had been forgiven by 1864, for her messages to them of that period and afterwards were invariably warm and affectionate. But the story may partly explain why, during the several intervening years, she preferred that her Amherst friends call her Kate Scott.

Emily Dickinson spoke of her as "K.S." in a letter to Mrs. Holland on Kate's first visit in 1859. Kate herself, beginning a manuscript cook book in Amherst, deliberately erased the word "Turner" (still faintly legible), which she had written

first out of habit, and immediately wrote over it the word
"Scott." Long after her marriage to John Anthon, she apparently rediscovered the book during a visit to Cooperstown
and began using it again, copying new recipes under the date
of August, 1872. Apparently at this time she added "Turner"
to the words "Kate Scott" on the flyleaf. The difference in ink
and in the period of handwriting is unmistakable, but the
meaning of the change cannot be fathomed.

According to Mrs. Bianchi, Kate was still Kate Scott when
she became acquainted with Emily Dickinson. Probably Mrs.
Bianchi was ignorant of the first marriage and remembered
only that Kate married John Anthon some years afterwards.
In one sense, however, the two young women did know each
other long before they met, for each had heard a great deal
about the other. The intermediary, of course, was Susan
Gilbert. The friendships between Sue and Kate, and between
Sue and Emily, began at about the same time; that is, when all
three girls were in their late adolescence. For more than a
decade the two intimacies roughly paralleled each other, not
yet merging but insensibly affecting each other by way of the
one person who was a party to both.

After her boarding-school days Susan Gilbert came to live in
Amherst, and here she talked to Emily of the Cooperstown girl
and doubtless read aloud many of Kate's letters. In writing to
Sue in the spring of 1854 Emily adopted one of Katie's exuberant expressions, "It is too blissful" (a formula so persistent that
it recurred as late as 1906 in a letter from Kate to Sue), adding
with a precision unusual for Emily that she had never seen the
girl herself.

There were good reasons why Kate and Emily did not meet
before early 1859. Sue Gilbert had no home of her own to
which she could invite friends until her marriage to Austin
Dickinson on July 1, 1856. Mrs. Bianchi was undoubtedly correct in saying that Kate paid her first visit to Amherst after
Sue married and moved into her own house. By July, 1856,

however, Kate herself was already married, and shortly afterwards she was fully occupied with the care of a dying man. After Campbell Turner's death in May, 1857, she would hardly have paid such a visit, even if she had wished to leave home, until a period of deep mourning had ended. Finally, Emily's references to her in a letter of March, 1859, to Mrs. Holland, as well as a letter of the same date to Kate herself, show plainly that the acquaintance was new.

No friend of those early days has left any record of Kate's appearance, except Emily Dickinson, whose descriptions have hitherto gone unrecognized. A daguerreotype, probably made about the time of Kate's boarding-school period, is the only surviving portrait of her youth. The abundant dark hair, gathered into a schoolgirl knot at the back and tied with a big bow, the striking dark eyes, the full mouth, and the strong nose and chin give some notion of the girl Emily Dickinson knew. According to persons who knew her in her last years, she was quite tall, not less than five feet eight inches. The daguerreotype suggests that in her youth she had the weight to match her height and might be described as Junoesque. Later on she became very thin.

A much better photograph, taken at the age of sixty, shortly after Kate's visit to Amherst in the fall of 1891, shows a sensitive, distinguished face, with the same beautiful eyes and strong chin and nose; but the mouth is somewhat thinner and fined down, and the hair is snow-white. Kate seemed to feel that no one would care for the portrait, and perhaps it too is an imperfect likeness. A young friend who knew her in 1880, when she was forty-nine, described her with enthusiasm as "the most beautiful thing I have ever seen," and her niece gave an admiring description of her at the age of fifty-six. In extreme old age she was still a very handsome woman.

To a good face and figure Kate added good clothes. On a small income she managed to dress with distinction. Although she was not ridden by fashion, she devoted a good deal of thought to her dresses, coats, gloves, and veils, and she knew how becoming were the little caps that crowned her white hair. "I always liked and remembered her clothes," said a woman who had been taken in childhood to visit Kate Anthon at Harrow. Mrs. Anthon, she remembered, was quite "neat-looking, with lovely snow-white hair, very *very* dark expressive eyes, and a smooth, clear, deep ivory complexion, very attractive with her white hair. I always saw her dressed in deep black, with just a white collar which seemed exactly to match her hair." As a widow, of course, Kate was expected to wear a good deal of black, but of her own choice she wore it exclusively. In fact, her mourning black, like Emily Dickinson's mourning white, was something of a fetish.

Her extraordinary emotionalism, reflected in the poems of Emily Dickinson, is corroborated by everything that Kate Scott wrote or did. It was distressing to her stepmother; it was well nigh fatal to Emily Dickinson. She wept, she laughed, she was swept away by her own enthusiasms, and she carried the susceptible with her. "Oh! the joy of being with you," she wrote to Sue Dickinson, "to plunge into the very abyss of things, to be natural, unconventional, earnest, impassioned, to say anything — everything, sure of divine sympathy." And elsewhere: "Shall we ever again have one long tremendous laugh before we die?"

"To hear her is a tune," wrote Emily Dickinson. Friends of Kate Anthon recalled a musical voice of unusual quality. When she was excited — and she frequently was — the tone altered surprisingly. She was a good reader, somewhat dramatic in style, and was often called upon to read aloud. Like her friend Sue she was also an excellent mimic. She enjoyed "taking off" people and was interested in peculiarities of dialect. More than once she copied down whole conversations on scraps of paper, carefully revising them from memory in order to reproduce the oddities of each speaker. Apparently she intended to use them for the entertainment of her friends. Examples are

flat on paper, and only the ear of imagination can still hear
the flexible voice rendering skilfully (and no doubt with many
absurd improvisations) the contrasting tones of the inquiring
lodger and the simple landlady:

> "*Yes! there* is *a back parlour as I clings to* & *wh. nothing
> will ever make me part from.*"
> "*Is there any objection?*"
> "*Yes, there is an objection, as I will not deceive you, wh.
> is the* Stairs."
> "*Is the room dry?*"
> "*You might sleep there for seven yrs.* & *be dry,* & *there
> might come a night when a* wet sop *as would be nothing
> to you.*"

Upon the dead, and somewhat desolate, calm of Emily's
twenty-ninth year, this lonely, emotional young widow broke
with the destructiveness and terrible beauty of a spring storm.
For years afterwards Emily Dickinson was occupied in gathering up the wreckage of her life; at desperate times she felt that
it was hardly worth the effort. But the effect of this experience
cannot be understood or credited without an understanding of
the personality of Emily Dickinson. She was peculiarly vulnerable.

III

Amherst, the birthplace of Emily Dickinson, is a pleasant little town in rural Massachusetts. It is fixed upon a shelf of the Connecticut valley and bounded far and near by the wooded ridges of hills. Closest are the Pelham hills on the east. Southward they diminish to a gap, of which roads and railroads take advantage, before the land swells again in the Holyoke range from Norwottock to Mount Tom. Westward beyond the valley of the Connecticut river is the distant curve of the Berkshires; and to the north is the rugged Toby range. Although it lacks the dramatic beauty of Cooperstown, Amherst is attractive enough to be the birthplace of a poet. Emily's poetic horizon, however, extended far beyond her lovely but unromantically named hills. There are no Mount Toms or Toby ranges or even Pelhams in her verse but instead exotic Himalayas, Alps, and Apennines, and many volcanoes, from Etna and Vesuvius to Popocatapetl and Chimborazo.

In her youth forests covered much of the lower ground as well as the hills around Amherst, and from a height the village itself would have seemed a wilderness. Amherst was then a town of some twenty-six hundred to three thousand inhabitants (it is not much larger today), and it lacked many conveniences now taken for granted. There were no street lights, no public water system, no sidewalks, no paved streets. Belated travelers carried lanterns, and on rainy days the streets became morasses. Helen Hunt Jackson, another daughter of Amherst, found it "untidy and huddled" during a visit of the seventies. As for private houses, Amherst had nothing to compare with the large, stately buildings of Cooperstown. The square, red-brick house of the Dickinsons was referred to as a mansion.

While Cooperstown was building its fine homes, Amherst was building a college. And this college, spare in architecture, beset with poverty, and dedicated to the spreading of Calvinism, expressed much that was characteristic of the town. From surrounding villages and farms came ambitious, often poor, youths, to sit upon comfortless benches and drill for the pulpit and the mission field. One Amherst graduate suffered martyrdom. Others returned with stories of hardships and with bags of pebbles collected in holy lands. The people of Cooperstown were wide travelers too, but they did not go to the same places; and they gathered no pebbles and suffered no hardships on their leisurely tours of European capitals and watering places. Pious enough, they lacked the moral fervor that occasions martyrs.

In Cooperstown people danced and played cards. They saw nothing wrong with the reading of novels, since they were in the business of producing them. There was much visiting in New York, with a resulting increase in the worldliness and cosmopolitanism of the little town. Materialistic it undoubtedly was (so was Amherst), but it wore its wealth debonairly and not as the outward sign of spiritual prosperity. At Christmas time people decorated the church with evergreens (it was young Kate's usual task), sounded the organ, and met each other with a "Merry Christmas."

To Amherst, in the early decades of the nineteenth century, Christmas was a pagan festival, reading for entertainment was suspect, and cards and dancing were tools of the devil. In

Emily's childhood the precentor's pipe was music enough for the congregation; the introduction of an organ was bitterly resisted. Plainness, even ugliness, in the church was a symbol of spiritual purity, and the gospel preached was a Calvinism that had not lost all of its harsh strength. The earnestness and idealism of the community, admirable in themselves, were painfully inelastic. There was little margin for sheer living and no margin at all for doubt.

In later years Austin Dickinson was to shudder at the memory of doleful hymns. His wife, Sue, who spent part of her girlhood in Amherst, would deplore their restricted youth. And in letters and poems Emily would remember the crime of being young "in a godly village." Amherst sometimes weighed upon its young people. But however the village may have oppressed Emily Dickinson or strengthened her sense of isolation, her discomfort had more complex sources than the limitation on life "in a godly village."

2

There are families which are uncomfortable for no clear reason. Their joys are intenser, their disappointments keener, as if they were sensitive to extremes of the emotional spectrum not felt by an ordinary person. Like grown children, the members of such families are demanding, intolerant of compromise, and prone to expect more of the world than they ever realize. Even in kindness, they wear upon each other's nerves and upon the nerves of any moderately susceptible person within range. They make their own sufferings, and in a sense they enjoy them. But if they succeed in harnessing their uncomfortable energies, they may do notable work and minimize their discomfort in the pride of achievement.

Emily Dickinson, who was the quintessence of the Dickinsons, once met a family of cousins and wrote to her brother with wonder and perhaps some complacency: "The Newmans seem very pleasant, but they are not like us. What makes a few of us so different from others?"

The building of Amherst College brought forward the first of the uncomfortable Dickinsons whose driving power left a mark on the town. Emily's grandfather, Samuel Fowler Dickinson, emerged from an ancestry of undistinguished town officials, tradesmen, and farmers. After graduating from Dartmouth, he became a lawyer and prospered enough to build, or perhaps only to buy and remodel, the large brick house where Emily was born and where she died. At the height of his prosperity he suggested changing the local academy to a college for religious training, and he subscribed to the necessary funds and signed the guarantee bond. When funds for the first college building were exhausted, he repeatedly pledged his own property. And he sent his own teams and laborers, boarded still other laborers, and paid their wages himself. In the service of a religious ideal, he exhausted himself and his modest fortune. Having lost his independent livelihood, he ended his days as a fiscal agent of Western Reserve College. Emily Dickinson did not know him but received his influence through her heritage.

Perhaps Samuel Dickinson's misfortunes were a lesson to his son, for Edward Dickinson was not receptive to enthusiasms. Even when he yielded, belatedly, to the call for religious conversion, his pastor had to remind him that he could not enter heaven as a lawyer but must come on his knees as a sinner. A sincerely religious man, he was distrustful of emotionalism. His daughter Emily said that he "never learned to play." Like his community, he was inelastic, and he carried himself stiffly, as if he feared that to bend would be to break. To his young bride he proposed a life of rational happiness, and after his graduation from Yale he devoted himself single-mindedly to retrieving the family's position.

There were hard years. When Emily was ten, the Dickin-

sons gave up the large brick house and settled themselves in
one half of a two-family house. Gradually their circumstances
improved, and in Emily's twenty-fifth year they returned to
their old home. In 1839 and 1840 Mr. Dickinson served in the
Massachusetts legislature; in 1842 and 1843 he was a member of
the state senate; at one time he held an honorary appointment
on the staff of Governor George N. Briggs. In 1852 he was a
delegate to the Whig Convention in Baltimore, and from 1853
to 1855 he was a member of Congress, where he helped found
the Republican party. In the fall of 1860 he declined nomination for the post of lieutenant governor in the "Bell and
Everett party."

During these years he did not neglect his legal practice or
the welfare of the community. He took an interest in his own
church and others, acted as trustee of Amherst Academy for
nearly forty years, and from 1835 to 1873 was treasurer of
Amherst College. In the early eighteen-fifties he was the prime
mover in bringing a railroad to Amherst to replace the old
stagecoach. His daughter Emily wrote delightfully that he had
been field marshal on the day of celebration and had paced
solemnly at the head of a procession, "like some old Roman
general upon a triumph day." This railroad, incidentally, was
not a very rapid means of travel. According to the Amherst
paper of July 3, 1857, a passenger who had missed the train by
two minutes was able to overtake it by sprinting through "the
deep cut in Judge Dickinson's pasture." But the race might
have ended differently, the newspaper added, if the engine had
been the "Vermont" instead of the "Bates."

In 1873–74 Mr. Dickinson entered the General Court in
order to help promote the Massachusetts Central Railroad. He
all but died on his feet during the course of a speech at Boston.
He was carried to the Tremont House, where Kate Scott's
young first husband had died more than a decade before, and
here his own life ended. Emily wrote that his heart had been
"pure and terrible" — a hyperbolic description of an able, up-

right country lawyer. She could not have written, with the tender simplicity of her friend Kate, "Father was perfectly charming, was he not?" Mr. Dickinson was an excellent man, but he was not charming.

It would be wrong, however, to describe Mr. Dickinson like the villain in a nineteenth-century melodrama. His older children, Austin and Emily, suffered in good part because they were so much like him. If he had been as alien to them as their mother, they would have ignored or evaded him. They could not escape their resemblance to him. As a youth at Amherst Academy he once helped some friends drink gin and cherry-rum and keep up an annoying disturbance until one o'clock in the morning. It was probably not an isolated prank. Perhaps for this, as well as for other reasons, his father was anxious to see him join the church, but Edward, like his daughter Emily afterwards, would not pretend to a conversion that he did not feel. He joined the church at the age of forty-seven. Years later he was to worry about Emily and to have her religious beliefs solemnly investigated by the family minister. He saw her difficulties in the light of his own. Emily thought he could not play, but there was at least a solemn playfulness in his strutting at the head of village processions. He liked to drive the fastest horses in town, and he could ring the church bell to call attention to a brilliant sunset. In old age he went out in his slippers on a snowy day to feed the birds. There was a vein of poetry in him; otherwise Emily and her brother Austin would not have loved him. Unfortunately he suppressed it and tried to suppress it in his children.

Without question he was an autocrat. A dominant man in a paternalistic society would inevitably rule his family — in the name of duty. And Mrs. Dickinson abetted her husband. On his return from work there was never any noise or confusion, every trace of domestic upheaval was concealed, and the women of the family stood at attention to receive his hat or hand him the evening paper or minister to his comfort in some other way. "Girls, your father!" was the watchword of the household. As the two daughters had a healthy sense of humor, they may have found some amusement in this irksome restraint, and the ceremonies gave a finish and an importance to their days. To make the puddings and the bread that her father liked was one of Emily's pleasantest duties.

They were a devoted family, who suffered under their inability to express their devotion. When her father once showed pleasure in her company Emily was embarrassed. He would have died for them, Lavinia thought, but could not express his love even with a good-night kiss. Austin kissed his dead cheek with a murmured regret that he could not have done so in Mr. Dickinson's lifetime. Years earlier the son had written to his fiancée that he had been brought up not to show tenderness. It was part of the rigid New England code of manners. There must have been other fathers in Amherst like Mr. Dickinson, but none other had a daughter like Emily whose words would be remembered against him.

"I never knew how to tell time by the clock till I was fifteen," Emily remarked to her friend Higginson. "My father thought he had taught me, but I did not understand and I was afraid to say I did not know and afraid to ask anyone else lest he should know." It was a curious story. Higginson looked with particular care at Edward Dickinson, who, he decided, was "not severe . . . but remote." If he had looked closer, he would have seen a man of strong passions under rigid control. Mr. Dickinson was an impatient man. He expected his children to behave like little adults. When they failed to do so, he stalked out of the house to avoid giving way to his temper. Surviving legends suggest that the children were not particularly afraid of him. If Emily could smash a cracked plate because her father complained about it or hide in the cellar rather than go to church, she was not living in terror. Nevertheless, there is evidence of unpleasant tension. In a family with nerves so close to the surface, it must often have seemed best to walk around provocation.

Emily also told Higginson that her father did not wish them to read anything but the Bible and was much displeased to learn that her brother had hidden Longfellow's *Kavanagh* under the piano cover. Another tale was that a student in her father's law office hid books for them in a bush by the door. These stories certainly involved some coloring of the truth. Upon reading Emily's youthful letters and noting her frequent references to books, Higginson dismissed her confidences as "yarns." Her brother insisted that Emily "posed" for Higginson's benefit, and in a sense he was right. But there are truths and poetic truths. Her grievances were real, and at the same time they were so vague and nebulous that she could not relate them in prose. A woman of forty, seldom outside her own door, she was chafing under prolonged dependence in a household of prickly nerves. How could she express her discomfort to this none-too-subtle stranger by any other means than exaggeration? If Higginson had looked deeper, he would have discovered that even the accounts of her reading had a basis in fact.

In the spring of 1854 Emily wrote to her brother that their father had given her "quite a trimming about 'Uncle Tom' and 'Charles Dickens' and these 'modern literati.' . . . Then he said there were 'somebody's rev-e-ries,' he didn't know whose they were, but he thought them very ridiculous." With respect to Ik Marvel's *Reveries,* Mr. Dickinson showed himself a discriminating judge, though he might have been more gentle with a young reader. But he himself read little outside his profession, and he was disturbed by the romantic absurdities with which his children were filling their heads. Emily spent a great deal of time reading and left too much of the housework to her mother and her more obedient sister. It was poor preparation for a life of rational happiness, and her father laid down the law.

"We don't have many jokes, though, now," Emily wrote to her brother, "it is pretty much all sobriety; and we do not have much poetry, father having made up his mind that it's pretty much all real life. Father's real life and mine sometimes come into collision, but as yet escape unhurt."

Almost nightly the Dickinson parlor was filled with company, quite often the young tutors or students from the college. Lavinia's diary of 1851 refers to many young visitors and completely disproves the legend that the Dickinson children were brought up in isolation. But Emily had formed the habit of remaining upstairs with a book or with her incessant letter-writing. Her father called her down, and she came unwillingly. Her remoteness from practical life must have disturbed him tremendously. Few fathers would have been more understanding in his place. As Emily grew older and might be presumed to be incurable of the bad habit of reading, Mr. Dickinson grew more generous. With a half-humorous understanding of her father's point of view, Emily wrote to Higginson: "He buys me many books, but begs me not to read them, because he fears they joggle the mind."

Nowhere in the history of Emily Dickinson and her father is there any picture like that of Kate Scott sitting down on winter evenings to read the Waverly Novels aloud to gentle Mr. Scott. Nor is there any record of Emily, like young Kate, going into a Boston shop to buy the works of De Quincy in one large, expensive purchase. Emily had no pocket money, no independence. How could her father suppose that she needed them? The power of the purse is never more vigorous than when it is wielded unconsciously.

Austin, too, was a problem. Although he showed more readiness than Emily to settle down, he had an uneasy youth. He ranged through books like his sister, and together they criticized the church and the established order in a way to disturb, even outrage, their father when he happened to overhear. Without at all understanding, Mr. Dickinson must have felt that they were too nervously overstrung, too poetic, too demanding for a prosy world. But they could not learn his severe lessons, and they preferred to stay out of earshot.

Emily wrote to Austin: "I don't love to read your letters all out loud to father — it would be like opening the kitchen door when we get home from meeting Sunday, and are sitting down by the stove saying just what we're a mind to, and having father hear. I don't know why it is but it gives me a dreadful feeling, and I skipped about the wild flowers, and one or two little things I loved the best." At another time she apparently sent her brother a discreet warning that Mr. Dickinson had begun to open all family mail at the post office.

In her late thirties she wrote to Higginson regarding an invitation to Boston: "I had promised to visit my physician for a few days in May, but father objects because he is in the habit of me." Later she wrote to him: "I must omit Boston. Father prefers so. He likes me to travel with him, but objects that I visit." This was certainly an excuse to avoid a meeting which her shyness would have made an ordeal. It is apparent, however, that Mr. Dickinson had fallen into a comfortably selfish dependence on his daughter. It suited her own inclination to remain at home, and she had no real complaint. There is no record that she traveled, even with her father, after her middle thirties.

On the other hand, Mr. Dickinson showed a watchful tenderness for his children. When Emily was a little girl and was thought to need fresh air for her health, he took her with him on his trips to the mill. And he dosed her with medicine and decided when she was strong enough to attend school and when she ought to be withdrawn. He arranged visits for her if she seemed to need a change of air, and certainly made no objection to her youthful visits to friends out of town. He took his children to hear Jenny Lind, and though he disliked the performance, the wish to give them a treat is obvious. Emily, too, cared little for the singing; she loved the singer: "*Herself* and not her music was what we seemed to love."

In the spring of 1854 Mr. Dickinson wrote from Washington to invite his wife and the two other children — "and Emily, too, if she will, but I will not insist upon her coming." Emily had shown a tendency to remain at home and brood over the death of her friend Ben Newton; also she was expecting Susan Gilbert that spring. A few weeks later, however, she did go to Washington with her sister Lavinia, and Mr. Dickinson showed them all the sights of the capital.

There is little evidence that Mr. Dickinson interfered with his children's social activities. The two daughters had as much freedom as any other girls in Amherst, and that was a great deal. They went about unchaperoned in mixed groups of young people — to reading clubs and "sugaring-off" parties and chowder parties, even to a highly secret and forbidden dancing club. Mr. Dickinson, of course, was not the only Amherst father who had to be deceived by the mysterious initials P. O. M., the Poetry of Motion society.

The two young girls walked or rode horseback or took buggy rides with young men, and young men called freely at the house to flirt with Lavinia or to read serious books with Emily. If either of the two girls had wished to marry, Mr. Dickinson could have done nothing to prevent them. A woman of any determination, like Elizabeth Barrett or James Fenimore Cooper's daughter Caroline, would have eloped in defiance of her father, or would have argued him down, as Dora Wordsworth did her own father. Only a girl who had no real wish to marry could have been discouraged by coldness or opposition on the part of her father. There is no evidence that Mr. Dickinson even wanted to prevent the marriage of his daughters. Emily was either disinclined or too unconventional to marry, and her younger sister came early under her powerful influence. There does not seem to be any other explanation.

Emily Norcross, the rather pretty girl whom Edward Dickinson had married, was a woman of little force and narrow interests. "My mother does not care for thought," her daughter wrote to Higginson. Elsewhere she spoke with contempt of her mother's appetite for stale gossip. On another occasion she did an elaborate burlesque of her mother's fussy solicitude, which the older woman was not clever enough to understand. Mrs. Dickinson was remembered as a charitable woman and a fanatical housekeeper. Lacking other interests, she concentrated on her house and kept the two girls dusting and polishing. When Emily was away at school she seemed almost more surprised than pleased to receive a letter from her mother, and wrote that she would not expect to hear often from her.

"I never had a mother," Emily remarked to Higginson in 1870. "I suppose a mother is one to whom you hurry when you are troubled." Even after her mother was paralyzed, Emily wrote to Higginson: "I always ran home to awe when a child, if anything befell me. He was an awful mother, but I liked him better than none." She meant, of course, that she had found solace in the grandeur and mystery of the world, but to describe this solace as her only mother was to aim a sharp blow at Mrs. Dickinson. She was not joking or trying to scandalize the tender-minded Higginson. In the depths of her consciousness she believed, whether justly or not, that her mother had ill prepared her to live and had failed her in a desperate crisis. The absence of her mother, not the presence of her father, was the cardinal fact in Emily Dickinson's life. Much of her behavior reads like a vain search for a mother.

Years of tender care of the bedridden woman altered the daughter more than they changed the mother. After her mother's death Emily could still say that they had never been congenial, but Mrs. Dickinson's long illness, transposing the relations between them, had drawn them closer together. The daughter was able to forgive an injury never specified but undoubtedly related to the central crisis of her life. A letter to the Norcross cousins is reminiscent of the ancient and long-cherished bitterness: "She was scarcely the aunt you knew. The great mission of pain had been ratified — cultivated to tenderness by persistent sorrow, so that a larger mother died than had she died before."

In temperament and in passionate, unhappy fate Austin Dickinson resembled his sister Emily. Outwardly his life ran a smooth and successful course. After his graduation from Amherst College in 1850, he taught school for a while, then entered Harvard Law School, and was admitted to the bar in 1854. Shortly afterwards he was tempted to try his luck in Detroit, but his father, by the gift of a house and a partnership, persuaded him to remain in Amherst. Here he led a prosperous but quiet and restricted life. Succeeding his father as Amherst's leading attorney and treasurer of Amherst College, he preferred to remain in his own small community and lived and died without other achievement than the respect of his fellow townsmen. Perhaps the times were against him. The New England life that was strong in his father's day was ebbing in his own, and the family that had begun vigorously with Samuel Fowler and Edward dwindled with Austin and died out with the latter's son Edward.

Inwardly the course of Austin's life was far from smooth. Like his sister Emily, he was poetic, passionate, neurotically intense; like her, he was affected by a family life unbalanced between a meek, commonplace mother and a strong-willed father. In his youth Austin struggled to assert himself and was often at "fisticuffs" with his father. But already he was dyeing his blond hair red like his father's, and in later years he wore a coppery red wig. He wrote verse and shared young Emily's fondness for sentimental novels. In maturity he bought paintings, landscaped Amherst College, and beautified the village, but he could not lose himself in the aggressive political and business life that had absorbed his father. Unlike his father,

Austin married a clever, ambitious woman and learned that he could not satisfy her.

Sue Dickinson never chose to present her own side, and her daughter Martha glossed over every sign of domestic unhappiness. In such matters one party is never wholly to blame. Sue might have made an excellent wife for an ambitious man who could have used her brilliant abilities and given her a life of color and excitement. Long afterwards she was to cherish the memory of Samuel Bowles more tenderly than that of her husband. She was totally unsuited to the quiet, puritanical little town or to the tense, uncomfortable Dickinsons, and instinctively she appeared to realize it.

Although the full evidence is not yet available, Sue was apparently in no hurry to accept Squire Dickinson's son. She drew back from Austin's first advances, but his persistence wore her down. After they were engaged she still had fears that she could not please him; the lover was certain that she answered perfectly. Her coolness, however, may have been one of the irritants of their long engagement. It was a period of stress, particularly for Austin. Every postponement, every trifling or imagined difficulty, upset him beyond reason. Even the few published excerpts from the letters of his courtship reveal a personality in striking contrast to his father's.

As a young girl Sue had had a taste of independence. She was not easily reconciled to a life of stagnation. Apparently she had vague hopes of distinguishing herself and sometimes went so far as to draw up ambitious plans, but laziness or irresolution brought them to nothing. It was easier to give parties and to dominate the social life of the little town.

Mrs. Austin Dickinson was no puritan, according to Professor John W. Burgess, who visited Sue's house during his student days in the middle sixties, and again during his teaching days in the middle seventies. In context, however, the statement was not unfriendly. As a Southerner in a New England town, Professor Burgess had been made to feel the coolness of his puritan neighbors. He remembered gratefully the warm understanding that Sue and her sister-in-law Emily had shown to him and other southern boys in the difficult period after the Civil War. Nevertheless, he noticed that Sue's wit was a little too sharp, her ambition for social prestige a little too aggressive, and her imagination so vivid as to be untrustworthy.

Outside the Dickinson atmosphere Sue continued to be charming, and she had many friends and admirers, among them such discriminating men as Samuel Bowles and Frederick Huntington. But her husband often failed to appear at her brilliant parties, and the gulf between them, visible even from the beginning, widened with middle age. Their quarrels split the two households asunder. Sue's surviving children, Ned and Martha, supported their mother; the two Dickinson sisters took their brother's part. Obviously Sue was not the kind of woman to tolerate any behavior on the part of a husband, however unloved, which caused gossip or lessened her own self-importance. The position of Austin Dickinson was still more painful. A passionate man who was most certainly a puritan, he had no chance of escaping great unhappiness. Shortly before his death he was said to be seeking a divorce.

Lavinia, the youngest of the three Dickinson children, appeared to lead a more contented life than her brother and sister. She was less demanding. Her attention was absorbed by her cats and friends and household cares, still more by the protection of her older sister, for whom she had a fierce, blind devotion. She was a pretty girl, with lively, dark eyes and dark-brown hair and handsome shoulders that she would have liked to show off more than her father permitted. In her youth she wrote innocuous poems, kept a diary, and flirted. Except for Emily, her affections did not appear to have deep or painful roots, and if she suffered when the young men took their attentions elsewhere, she left no record. In middle life, however,

Emily referred mysteriously to some bitter disappointment which Lavinia was then suffering. In old age Lavinia was inclined to brood over her loneliness, still more poignantly over her sister's, as it was revealed to her in the poems. The quarrels with Sue must have been lacerating, and doubtless she suffered because of her treachery to Mrs. Todd. She would have been still more lonely and bitter if she had not had the gratification of spreading Emily's fame.

Among the three Dickinsons, a visitor might have felt least uncomfortable with Lavinia. Even Austin, though accustomed to dealing with many people, had reserves that would be felt to be impenetrable, and Emily could be terrifying. Lavinia was not commonplace — no child of Edward Dickinson was that — but she was clever without being complex. With her mischievous, at times malicious, tongue, she provided a brilliant show that did not make excessive demands on the intellect or the sympathies. The visitor could admire the fireworks and dodge the occasional spark. Despite her coruscating tongue and her many eccentricities, Lavinia was a simple woman. The most important service of her life, as she herself recognized, was the jealous protection that she gave to her sister and, after Emily's death, to that sister's poetry. Without Lavinia there would have been no Emily Dickinson.

3

The little girl born on a wintry December 10, 1830, was the most uncomfortable Dickinson of them all. To paraphrase Emily's own words, she never felt at home on earth and doubted that she would feel at home in heaven. Still more revealing is the poem "A loss of something ever felt I." Her earliest recollection was a feeling that she was bereft of some unknown thing, that she was a mourner among the other children,

> . . . bemoaning a dominion,
> Itself the only prince cast out.

Although she was now older and wiser, she still searched for her lost palaces but with a suspicion that she was looking on earth for what was properly of heaven. "Misères d'un roi dépossédé," Pascal had written. Shelley, too, wrote sadly of "seeking in a mortal image the likeness of what is perhaps eternal."

In another poem, "It would have starved a gnat," Emily Dickinson recalled her fruitless search for affection. Elsewhere she wrote that she had once heard a woman call her "poor child," and that she had wept:

> . . . something in her voice
> Convicted me of me.

Although self-pity is a symptom that calls for attention, it is not attractive. It grows intolerable to the ordinary person when he realizes that he could bankrupt himself without satisfying the insistent demands upon his affection and sympathy. Fortunately the reader who finds a good deal of self-pity in Emily Dickinson is repaid by other qualities — irony, brilliant wit, and a searching intellectual honesty.

There was no obvious reason for the discomfort of her childhood. She had a good home, to which she was much attached — a loyal brother and sister, good parents. The mother, though she had little to offer, was a gentle, inoffensive woman who probably suffered more from her imperious daughter than she ever put upon Emily. The father was shy and reserved, perhaps a little harsh or unreasonable on occasion (the position of a father is not an easy one, and few men, even with the best intentions, fill it gracefully at all times); but his daughter knew the measure of his devotion, and despite her occasional slaps at him, left convincing testimony of her love. By turns Emily dealt harshly with every member of her family; yet their only drawback as a family would seem to be that they were not easy with each other. Instead of deciding that one and all were abominably cruel to her, it might be wiser to look for the discomfort in Emily herself.

Austin Dickinson thought his sister suffered morbidly on account of her plainness, that she secluded herself because she knew "how plain she was." The ugly duckling in a handsome family is always at a disadvantage. Emily was undeniably plain, although a loyal friend remembered that she had many beauties. Her eyes were large and fine, of a color, as their owner wrote to Higginson, "like the sherry in the glass that the guest leaves." Her hair, she wrote, was "bold, like the chestnut burr." The sherry-colored eyes and the two smooth bands of auburn hair were her best features, but the small teeth were pretty and the pale skin was clear. Nose and mouth were too large, it is true, and the long upper lip was markedly bad. Not a pretty girl certainly, but not a hopelessly repulsive one either. The only authentic likeness of Emily Dickinson, a daguerreotype made in her late teens, reveals a great deal of charm as well as strength. It is possible to imagine that when her face brightened in fun she would have been attractive. She was attractive to some women.

Her height is variously remembered as small or medium. She felt tiny beside her friend Kate Scott but tall in relation to Mrs. Holland, who was just under five feet. Perhaps the best average of these guesses is about five feet two inches. Her comparatively small size and her high, breathless voice gave visitors an impression of childlikeness, which was probably increased by her long years of isolation.

"I am growing handsome very fast indeed!" Emily wrote at the age of fourteen to her friend Abiah Root. "I expect I shall be the belle of Amherst when I reach my 17th year." It was meant as a joke. Some fifteen months later she wrote in the same vein: "I have grown tall a good deal, and wear my golden tresses done up in a net-cap. Modesty, you know, forbids me to mention whether my personal appearance has altered." The "golden tresses," of course, made part of the joke. Her hair was red. At seventeen, the period when she was to be the "belle of Amherst," she wrote wistfully to her brother that she supposed Lavinia and other girls had received scores of valentines, "while your *highly accomplished and gifted elder sister* is entirely overlooked." The ironic italics are her own, and the passage is another joke at her own expense.

In a poem, "He touched me, so I live to know," she described the transfiguring effect of love upon her "gypsy face." The self-portrait in her letter to Higginson was a discreet touching up of her best features. She refused to send him a photograph. When they met some eight years later, he may have felt that she had heightened the picture, or perhaps he went prepared to find no attractions in an eccentric spinster of forty, who annoyed him, moreover, by her excessive cleverness.

"A step like a pattering child's in entry," he wrote on August 16, 1870, "and in glided a little plain woman with two smooth bands of reddish hair." She was dressed "in a very plain and exquisitely clean white piqué and a blue net worsted shawl," and carried two day lilies. These she handed him "in a sort of childlike way," referring to them as her introduction "in a soft, frightened, breathless, childlike voice." He wrote flatly that she had not a single good feature. She talked continuously, as if for relief, and Higginson added, with something like a shudder, that he had never before met anyone who so thoroughly drained his nerve power. He was glad that he need not live near her.

When he returned to Amherst in late 1873, she astounded him with the complacent remark, "There is always one thing to be grateful for, — that one is one's self and not somebody else." Higginson's wife, to whom this was reported, thought it sadly inappropriate in Emily's position; yet it was typical. Emily knew she was not handsome, but she liked herself very well. There was no awkward self-consciousness in her regret that a gifted writer like George Eliot should be housed in so homely a case, and she was never preoccupied, as was Charlotte Brontë, with the idea of physical beauty.

Emily's playmates, ordinary, well-adjusted girls, did not know that a mourner lurked among the children. They remembered her as a humorist, a teller of such funny stories that they collected around her at recess. In the light of these kindly memories the poetry makes curious reading. Emily described her early friends as "paste," "shells from the coast," which she mistook for pearl, and the cause of "many a bitterness." Those friends who came forward after her death to speak of their old intimacy showed clearly that they had long been out of touch with her. Perhaps she made too heavy demands on their sympathy and intelligence, or perhaps, as is very common, the young women busy with household affairs dropped their unmarried friend.

The early letters of Emily Dickinson reveal a sensitive, egocentric child, troubled by her plainness, rebuffed by her preoccupied, reserved parents, too old for her playmates, and too young to be taken seriously by adults. And she remained much the same throughout her life. Children were never old enough for her and adults were never young enough.

The lonely girl was a warmth-needing person. The earnest, long-continued search for affection suggests that she was born with a need for more tenderness than the average child, and that the need was poorly supplied by her busy family. She fell in love with all her teachers — among them, good Mr. Taylor and Miss Adams (a favorite, whose absence left Emily disconsolate), and young Rebecca Woodbridge, of whom she wrote ardently:

She is tall and rather slender, but finely proportioned, has a most witching pair of blue eyes, rich brown hair, delicate complexion, cheeks which vie with the opening rosebud, teeth like pearls, dimples which come and go like the ripples in yonder little merry brook, and then she is so affectionate and lovely. Forgive my glowing description, for you know I am always in love with my teachers.

In childhood and youth the loneliness was of the spirit and not of the flesh, for she had many young friends. They played together, competed with each other in the making of herbariums, and wrote voluminous letters in absence; or rather — and this is characteristic — Emily wrote: the other girls, for the most part, were too busy with new scenes and activities to answer.

During her middle teens Emily's closest friends were Abiah Root and Abby Wood. Neither of these friendships was to continue smoothly into later life. In the summer of 1853 Emily sent Abiah Root a subtly sarcastic letter with the apparent intention of breaking off an unsatisfactory relationship. There is no record that they ever wrote to each other or saw each other again. Still earlier Emily had had difficulties with Abby Wood and had reacted with characteristic intensity.

Abby Wood was an independent, strong-willed young woman. Perhaps she grew restive in the rarefied atmosphere that Emily inhabited. Certainly a poet who described her early friends as "paste" and "shells" could not have been an easy person to live with. Early in 1851 Abby experienced a religious conversion, and Emily remained "one of the lingering *bad* ones." It was the beginning of a difference.

In August, 1851, Emily wrote to Abiah with pain:

I see but little of Abby; she cannot come to see me, and I walk so far not often, and perhaps it's all right and best. . . . She is more of a woman than I am, for I love so to be a child.

The estrangement continued to trouble Emily through the autumn and into the winter. A few weeks after this letter to

Abiah, she was writing to her brother of the blessedness of home, where doubts and distrust never entered: "I feel it more and more as the great world goes on, and one and another forsake in whom you place your trust." In December, about the time of her twenty-first birthday, she heard a sermon, preached by Professor Park of Amherst College, which affected her powerfully. Edwards Amasa Park was famous for his "Judas sermon." That this was what Emily heard, and that she identified Abby Wood with Judas, seems indicated by a letter from Emily to her Norcross cousins some twenty-three years later:

> *The loveliest sermon I ever heard was the disappointment of Jesus in Judas. It was told like a mortal story of intimate young men. I suppose no surprise we can ever have will be so sick as that. The last "I never knew you" may resemble it.*

The following year, in June, 1852, Emily wrote more happily to Abiah:

> *I often see Abby — oftener than at sometimes when friendship drooped a little. Did you ever know that a flower, once withered and freshened again, became an immortal flower — that is, that it rises again?*

The resurrected flower was soon to fade. The attention of Abby Wood was absorbed by the courtship of a young man named Daniel Bliss. In the fall of 1855 they were married and left Amherst for the Near East, where they remained for many years. In 1873 Abby returned to Amherst and sought out her childhood friend. And Emily made some astonishing conditions as to the terms on which they were to meet again. Abby Wood Bliss sensibly refused to sit in the parlor and exchange messages with an invisible Emily through an open door. They met finally on more reasonable terms. There is evidence, of course, that Mrs. Bliss was not the only friend treated in this manner. Yet Emily never made these absurd requirements of Helen Hunt Jackson, Maria Whitney, Emily Fowler Ford, or such friends as Bowles and Higginson.

The religious crisis which disturbed relations with Abby Wood and spoiled a school year at Mt. Holyoke had been long building in Emily's mind. As a child she was struck with a doubt of immortality, and the doubt and the need to resolve it troubled her the rest of her life. In her sixteenth year she wrote to Abiah Root that she had "perfect confidence in God and His promises, and yet I know not why I feel that the world holds a predominant place in my affections." In a postscript she acknowledged her friend's persistent concern for her soul. When she entered the Mt. Holyoke Female Seminary at South Hadley in the autumn of 1847, she plunged immediately into a situation characteristic of New England at that time.

Mary Lyon, the founder and principal of the school, was a good and noble woman, but in her zeal to rescue souls she did not scruple to work upon the feelings of emotional, adolescent girls with the strong poison of Jonathan Edwards. It was not enough to be good and to believe; the convert must first be reduced to an hysterical conviction of sinfulness. Lessons and the usual routine went on, of course, and the average schoolgirl may have welcomed a touch of hysteria. But to the sensitive unbeliever the proceedings must have been flavored with a hint of sadism. To Susan Gilbert, Emily wrote that "sermons on unbelief" were very attractive to her. Her poetry was to be colored with a lasting resentment toward the harsh Calvinistic God of her fathers.

In a sentence commonly overlooked by her sentimental admirers, Emily wrote proudly that she preferred the "power" to the "kingdom" and the "glory." The obstinacy with which she defended her position against the combined pressure of teachers, schoolmates, and friends is a witness to strength. A conversion would have demanded no material sacrifices of a life already so austere. She had literally nothing to give up except —

and this would seem to be the whole point of her refusal — the right of inquiry. She would wrestle with God for an answer (the story of Jacob and the angel attracted her), but she would not stifle her inquiring mind. And she thought rather better of God than to suppose He would demand such a sacrifice. The year at Mt. Holyoke, to which she had looked forward eagerly, ended in disappointment and a desire for home.

The next several years, as reflected in her letters, were somewhat painful. During her last term at Mt. Holyoke she had written distressfully to Abiah of the pressure she was under and of her regret that she could not "give up the world." On January 2, 1851, she wrote, with an undercurrent of defiance, that she would not subdue her mind. Although the shores of religious and social orthodoxy were unquestionably safer, the girl of twenty-one proposed to dare the open sea. "Oh, I love the danger!" she cried emphatically. In those days she was in love with Susan Gilbert, and she feared neither earth nor heaven as long as Sue remained firm. Later on, when she encountered the serenely aesthetic religion of Kate Scott, she was surprised and attracted. Catholicism was to interest her, and she was to find solace in the platonism of the Gospel of St. John. She never joined the church.

When Emily returned to Amherst in the late spring of 1848, she was seventeen and a half. Her formal education, always somewhat desultory and broken by illness, may now have come to an end. She had studied mathematics through the elementary branches, but without enthusiasm, if there is truth in a surviving legend that she traded English compositions for help in arithmetic. She had received a beginner's introduction to chemistry and to a moral philosophy on the order of that which had so little interested Kate Scott at Utica. There were smatterings of Latin and of French, and at the insistence of her father, a semester of German, but her later writing showed scarcely a trace of these languages. Throughout her life she read widely, and even indiscriminately, in English literature, and of course the best education of poets is self-education.

What she lacked — and her poetry was to show the ill effects — was the discipline of an audience and of intercourse with like minds. Probably she could have broken out of her prison, but she chose to strengthen the bars. Without doubt she could have found her way to publication if she had shown half the determination of her sister Lavinia. Although she read Emerson and was influenced by his work, it is evident that she never saw his forthright declaration that he distrusted the genius of a man too proud to publish. In the spring of 1848, however, Emily did not yet know that she was to be a poet. She was still struggling to find her place in society.

Any seventeen-year-old girl would know — she could not help knowing — that her society expected her to find a husband, but Emily was not comfortable in the rôle assigned to her. Admittedly she was plain and bookish; yet plain, bookish girls married every day, and often married well. Nor was there any lack of men. Amherst and the Dickinson house overflowed with young men — her brother's classmates, Lavinia's friends, the tutors and students who came to pay their respects to the college treasurer, even serious youths who wanted to discuss books with Emily. All too often, she was reserved or bored and they were disturbed. In time they appeared to sense that she was a barren flower, and they left her alone.

Marriage involved growing up, and Emily did not wish to grow up — at least, not along the narrow lines marked out for her by society. She was almost twenty-one when she wrote to Abiah, in a passage already quoted, "I love so to be a child," and she was disturbed by Abby Wood's new womanliness. A year later she was writing to Susan Gilbert of a wish that they "might ramble away as children . . . and each become a child again." In the spring of 1853, when she was twenty-two and a half, she wrote to her brother: "I wish we were always children, how to grow up I don't know." In her poetry she was to write that the "larger" lives are slow in reaching maturity.

Her childhood ended, by her own reckoning, when she was nearly thirty, but Higginson used the word "child" three times in a brief passage describing the forty-year-old woman. By conventional standards she remained somewhat childlike all her life.

On her return to Amherst, in 1848, Emily Dickinson struck up a warm friendship with Emily Fowler. Their correspondence began in this year with an exchange of locks of hair. Emily Fowler, daughter of an Amherst professor and granddaughter of Noah Webster, was a handsome, popular girl about three years older than Emily Dickinson. She was apparently the belle of Amherst that the younger girl had jokingly aspired to be. During the next several years they were much together, sometimes strolling by themselves through the neighboring meadows or making longer trips to Mount Norwottock for flowers. In December, 1853, Emily Fowler married Gordon Ford and left Amherst. Her friendship with Emily Dickinson gradually attenuated. After Emily's death Mrs. Ford, in an affectionate but confused memoir, tried to recall the personality of the young Emily.

Although Emily was shy and reserved among strangers (Mrs. Ford remembered), she was lively and talkative with intimates and entered freely into all the parties and frolics of the village young people. Among these were an essay club, a Shakespeare reading club, secret dancing parties, and excursions to Sunderland for the "sugaring-off" of the maple sap. Spiritedly Emily refused to read from an expurgated edition of Shakespeare, and she wrote her essays and valentines in a robust, frontier style of humor.

"She loved with all her might," wrote Mrs. Ford, "there was never a touch of the worldling about her, and we all knew her truth and trusted her love." Elsewhere she remarked that the girls of their group had been "in the adoring mood" and inclined to idolize each other. Looking back over the long gulf of years, she wondered whether Emily Dickinson, even in her later seclusion, had not been longing for "poetic sympathy."

Probably Emily Dickinson wrote fewer letters to young men than to young women. Of these letters, still fewer would be saved. They were apparently much in the style of her vanished prose essays. The strained jocularity of surviving prose valentines and jingles, and of letters to her young uncle and to George Gould, would suggest that little has been lost. Later on she wrote a few pleasant notes to Vaughan Emmons, thanking him for books or urging him to bring his fiancée to call. But she never seemed wholly at her ease in this correspondence, or with the young men themselves. The only serious loss, from the biographical viewpoint, would seem to be her letters to the man whom she afterwards described as her "tutor" and her "earliest friend."

Emily's "earliest friend" has been plausibly identified with a certain Ben Newton, a law student in her father's office between 1847 and late 1849. There is no evidence that they were acquainted before Emily returned from Mt. Holyoke in the late spring of 1848. Newton became her "earliest" friend, of course, only after she wiped out of memory the ungrateful girls who had preceded him. They lived and grew apart from her; Newton died in 1853, while the friendship was still warm, and Emily enshrined his memory.

In the year and a half before Newton left Amherst the two became pleasantly acquainted. He had a milder religion than that to which Emily had lately been exposed; she turned to him for help in her religious problems. After his death, however, she was to be painfully uncertain that he was among the saved. He was a lover of books, and Emily cherished the friends who discussed books with her. But there is no evidence that she was ever romantically in love with him or that she mourned him as a possible suitor. If the idea had occurred to her, it would have destroyed the ease of her relationship with him. Newton was an unlikely suitor at best. He was sickly, very poor, and ten years older than his young friend. She would

have thought him safely "old." Newton himself did not appear
to be romantically interested in a young girl; shortly after leaving Amherst he married a much older woman. This marriage,
incidentally, made not the slightest difference in Emily's correspondence with him. He was her tutor and elder brother; she
was his pupil. It was a relationship that committed her to
nothing.

Newton left Amherst about December, 1849, or in early
January, 1850. On January 23 Emily wrote to Jane Humphrey
that she had received a letter and a copy of Emerson's *Poems*
from "Newton." As her "tutor" he was replaced by another
young man, to whom Emily referred, somewhat distantly, as
"Mr. Humphrey" and, after his death, as "the departed
Humphrey." Leonard Humphrey was engaged to be married,
and his interest in Emily was doubtless casual. Another pleasant acquaintance of this period was Mr. Bowdoin, a young lawyer in Mr. Dickinson's office, who lent books to Emily. In
December, 1849, she returned *Jane Eyre* with a note and some
box leaves. In February, 1850, she wrote him a nonsensical
valentine jingle, and in 1851, a prose valentine. Mrs. Bianchi
made him the hero of a "spicy affair" with Emily, and he is as
good — or as poor — a candidate as any other man she knew.
In May, 1850, some young man called at the Dickinson house
and asked Emily to ride with him in the woods. Because of her
mother's illness, she was obliged to refuse. As Emily wrote to
her young uncle Joel Norcross, in a jocular letter of January
11, 1850, it was apparently a season when beaus were to be
"had for the taking."

If Newton's absence created any disturbance, it took the form
of an unusual hilarity. Emily seemed not so much distressed
by the absence of her friend as excited by the making of new
friends. About this time she became acquainted with Susan
Gilbert. And Sue was to influence her more profoundly than
Newton or any other friend of her youth.

IV

THERE WAS nothing mysterious about Emily Dickinson. The mystery is the work of her niece, Martha Dickinson Bianchi. For Mrs. Bianchi was deliberately misleading about the two most important events of her aunt's life. She suppressed parts of letters and even whole letters from Emily Dickinson to Susan Gilbert, and misdated most of those she published. Then she invented a romance, false on its face, between the young Emily and a middle-aged, married clergyman. Finally, disturbed by the enormity of what she had done, she apologized to the spirit of her dead aunt. After speaking of her duty to present Emily's life, "as far as it concerns others," Mrs. Bianchi continued:

> For which may her shy soul pardon the revelation; may it never be a betrayal of her spirit, still so vivid and real that to grieve her would be the supreme act of blasphemy against the Holy Ghost, which truly was her guest on this earth. Wherever she is, whatever she knows, may she know this!

This apology is ambiguous, like many other things she wrote about Emily, but the tone is earnest. Mrs. Bianchi could easily have felt a superstitious twinge about her distortion of Emily's history. She would have had to be morbidly prudish to blush for so unexceptionable and pure a Victorian idyl as the supposed love story between Emily and Charles Wadsworth. By her own account, Mrs. Bianchi was no prude.

It is true that Mrs. Bianchi was a poor scholar. She could not be accurate even in such simple matters as Emily's birth and death dates and middle name. Her talent was creative rather than scholarly. Also she inherited her mother's imagination, which Professor Burgess described gently as exceedingly vivid — so vivid, in fact, that it "confounded its pictures with objective things." But the distortion of Emily's friendship with Susan Gilbert and the substitution of Charles Wadsworth for Kate Scott went far beyond mere carelessness or a taste for romance. Mrs. Bianchi was concerned to present an acceptable picture.

This falsifying was a gradual and haphazard development. Originally Sue herself had no awkward doubts about Emily's letters to her and only a vague apprehension about the poems. She was flattered by Emily's tributes to her. After 1891 she apparently changed her mind. Instead of publishing the letters, as she had once proposed to do, she wanted to destroy both them and the poems. According to her daughter, she did, in fact, destroy some of Emily's letters to her, and the remaining letters and the poems almost suffered the like fate.

Of course, the destroyed letters might have spoken too revealing of Emily's love for a married man. Doubtless Mrs. Bianchi wished to leave this impression, although she avoided any definite statement. But the legend of a married lover does not explain why Sue wanted to destroy *all* the letters and *all* the poems. Nor does it explain why Mrs. Bianchi suppressed those letters and those passages which contained the warmest expression of Emily's love for Sue. Nor does it explain why Mrs. Bianchi rearranged the dates of her mother's friendship with Emily in order to minimize the appearance of a brief, schoolgirl infatuation.

There is only one explanation which takes account of all the shuffling and evasions and plain lies. As the situation became clearer to Sue, both from Kate's revelations and from a reading of the poetry, her real fear of conventional prejudice began to operate. Kate's experience, deeper and more understanding, illuminated her own earlier experience with Emily. She feared that both letters and poems would make the pattern of Emily's life as clear to others as it was to her.

It is true that none of these women fully understood the emotions involved. But two of them must have felt their painful difference from society, and they were bound to study it. The need to belong, to be accepted, is the most powerful human emotion. It can lead to suicide, to self-mutilation, to hypocrisy so deep as to be unconscious, even to abominable cruelty — where cruelty is fashionable. It would drive these two women on an agonizing voyage of self-discovery.

In her set of De Quincey's writings, which she bought some three or four days before her meeting with Emily Dickinson, Kate Scott discovered something of great interest to her. A certain Lady Carberry (wrote De Quincey) had been much attached to a friend of her youth. After their marriages separated them, Lady Carberry became reserved and melancholy and turned to religion for consolation. Even the esteem that she felt for her husband did not lessen her suffering. "There are women," De Quincey added (and Kate emphatically marked these lines), "to whom a female friendship is indispensable, and cannot be supplied by any companion of the other sex." What De Quincey had the acuteness to observe, Kate found in her own experience. All her life she was to be unusually responsive to poetic descriptions of women or to accounts of strong, emotional friendships between women. She was attracted by the history of the famous "Llangollen ladies," Lady Eleanor Butler and Sarah Ponsonby, who spent some forty years together in a little Welsh town. In middle life Kate made a pilgrimage to Llangollen, underlined the name of the town on her map of Wales, wrote a note about the two women in the margin of her

map, and in her copy of Wordsworth marked a long explana-
tory note on his sonnet to the Llangollen ladies. In her books
she checked line after line passionately invoking the image of
a woman. The history of her life leaves no reason to doubt that
she finally understood her own personality.

Emily studied herself with an equally painful interest. A
significant percentage of her poems is devoted to this crucial
problem in human behavior. She read attentively Shakespeare's
sonnets and Sir Thomas Browne's passionate eulogies of his
friend, and probably became acquainted with Thoreau's writings about friendship. Certainly Thoreau was one of the writers
she admired. The Gospel of St. John gave her some support for
a diffuse and sublimated love which took no account of sex,
and in the manners of her own period she found a good deal of
allowance for emotional attachments. Her friend Higginson
asserted that Sappho was only a Greek Margaret Fuller surrounded by adoring schoolgirls. With a candor impossible
today, he described his own passionate attachment to a college
friend.

If Emily had ended her self-discovery at the point reached
by Higginson, she might have been happier, but she would
not have written with the searing honesty that distinguishes her
poetry. In a moment of unguarded passion she discovered that
the line between emotional and physical behavior was a social
convention. It was a discovery that exploded the ignorance in
which she had been reared. As she looked about with unsealed
eyes, she wondered if her sufferings were unique. In a poem
beginning "I measure every grief I meet," she observed the
"fashions of the cross" —

> Still fascinated to presume
> That some are like my own.

There is no reason to suppose that Sue Dickinson resembled
her friend or her sister-in-law. Apparently she was incapable
of a passionate attachment to man or woman. By receiving and

not giving love, she satisfied the minor canons of respectability. As long as the attachment between the two other women seemed no more than her own shallow sentimentality, she was undisturbed. When she learned that it had been deep and anguished, she became anxious to conceal it. But she was now old and uncertain. After destroying letters which may have expressed too ardent feeling for Kate or for herself, she bequeathed to her daughter the task of confusing Emily's history.

2

As a matter of pride, Mrs. Bianchi would wish to establish her mother's very real influence on Emily Dickinson. But here the truth would not do. For the truth is that Emily's attachment to Mrs. Bianchi's mother, beginning about their twentieth year, was a youthful infatuation which reached its climax before Sue became engaged to Austin Dickinson, then declined to a calmer good will. After the unhappy friendship with Kate Scott, Emily's feelings toward Sue appeared to oscillate between pitiable dependence and hatred. Some years later she came to rest in the bitterness of disillusionment. Perhaps in her last months she experienced an autumnal glow of her old affection for Sue; her last notes to Sue appear to express genuine feeling.

In the *Life and Letters* Mrs. Bianchi wrote that Susan Gilbert and Emily Dickinson became friends in 1847, at the age of sixteen. For evidence Mrs. Bianchi misdated some letters. In *Emily Dickinson Face to Face* she stated, more accurately, that the friendship began after Sue completed her studies in Utica and came to live with her sister, Mrs. Cutler, in Amherst. The few scattered paragraphs which Mrs. Bianchi assigned to 1847 are too short for accurate dating, but two fragments ascribed to 1848 were written not earlier than August 21, 1853, and probably months later. On that date the Reverend Edward S. Dwight, mentioned in these scraps, became acting pastor of the

Dickinsons' church. Of the sixteen early letters published in *Emily Dickinson Face to Face,* the majority can be shown to be misdated by as much as one to four years. With the evidence of such inaccuracy, it becomes impossible to rely safely upon any date or fact given by Mrs. Bianchi.

If Emily Dickinson knew Susan Gilbert at all before the spring of 1850, the acquaintance was very slight. As a young girl Sue lived with an aunt in Geneva, New York, making perhaps only brief visits to Amherst. In handwriting of her seventeenth year Emily listed all the girls attending Amherst Academy with her, among them Sue's older sisters, Mary and Martha Gilbert, but Sue herself was not named. During the next year, 1847–48, Emily was a student at Mt. Holyoke Seminary, and in the following year, 1848–49, Susan Gilbert was a fellow pupil of Kate Scott's at the Utica Female Academy. It is not yet known where she spent the winter of 1849–50. By the spring of 1850 she was certainly in Amherst. In the fall of 1850 Emily mentioned Sue for the first time in a letter to another person, and about the same time she wrote Sue herself a letter which shows clearly that the acquaintance was new.

On May Day, 1850, Austin Dickinson, who was then a youth of twenty-one in his final year at Amherst College, left a basket of arbutus at Sue's door. Her note of thanks and his reply began their correspondence. On July 14, 1850, Sue's older sister Mary died at their brother's home in Michigan, and Sue's acquaintance with Austin was interrupted by the proprieties of mourning. When he suggested a drive on a secluded road, Susan Gilbert declined. A few weeks later they met at a tea, and he renewed the invitation. Sue was evasive. Although her reluctance continued for some time, as shown by a plaintive note from the young man, he was persistent. By early 1851 they were exchanging prim letters on religion.

In the fall of 1850 Austin went to Sunderland to teach, and from early 1851 to August, 1852, he taught school in Boston. As a result of his long absence, Emily had little opportunity to see her brother and Sue together and to judge the strength of their mutual interest. In these early months it would appear to have been very slight, and clearly Susan Gilbert was the less interested of the two. Meanwhile she was beginning to be on terms of intimate friendship with Austin's sister Emily.

The death of Mary Gilbert, which had been an obstacle to Austin's courtship, was no bar to Emily but rather an incitement. Painfully sensitive to the idea of death, she was stirred to a warmer interest in an orphaned girl for whom she already felt sympathy, and she wrote a letter of condolence. Judged by the one published excerpt, in which she longed to have "as many dear friends as you in heaven," it was not an easy letter. About this time she must also have written the first of the many poems that she gave to Sue.

Mrs. Bianchi assigned "I have a bird in Spring" to the year 1848, a date with no better authority than others which are demonstrably false. It looks very much like a poem written to console someone on the death of a friend or relative. The poet, speaking for the bereaved, says that she has a bird which disappears each summer with the coming of the rose. She does not mourn, however, for she knows that the bird is learning a new melody beyond the seas and will return to her. Although the dead do not return, the bereaved has the consolation of thinking that her own lost "bird" will send a melody to her from its "distant tree." Susan Gilbert, a girl of nineteen, would have been both touched and impressed.

Although any statement by Mrs. Bianchi is open to question, she may have been correct in her guess that this was the first of Emily's poems written for Sue. If so, it is also the first poem Emily is known to have written, except for an absurd valentine jingle of February, 1850, given to Mr. Bowdoin. The poem looks youthful and has a plausible connection with Mary Gilbert's death in July, 1850, when Emily's friendship with Sue was both new and tentative. Emily was proud of these early verses. Writing to Abiah Root on January 2, 1851, she apparently alluded to them with the words "if my 'bird has flown' in which world her wing is folded." In August, 1851, she wrote to Abiah in similar fashion: "too quickly flown, my bird, for me to satisfy me that you *did* sit and sing beneath my chamber window!" In a letter of early 1854 to her friend Mrs. Holland she quoted a stanza of the poem.

Most poets, it is true, write some verse before the age of nineteen. Emily's poetic development was slow, however, and for years her verse did not live up to the promise of her letters. Friends remembered early prose essays, but no one saved or even recalled any youthful poetry. It appears likely that Emily began to write poetry under the stimulus of Mary Gilbert's death and a growing attachment to Sue. During the next two or three years she was eagerly writing verse and seeking criticism and approval — with Susan Gilbert as her first and most important audience. Afterwards, for reasons of her own, she chose to forget Sue's influence.

During the summer of 1850 Sue and Emily spent a great deal of time together. Perhaps it was a day of this summer that Emily recalled, in the spring of 1854, with the words "when love first began — on the steps at the front door under the evergreens." In the spring of 1852, during Sue's absence, Emily looked forward hopefully to the time when they two would again be "sitting out on the broad stone step mingling our lives together!" Emily's family was then occupying one half of the Deacon Mack house, and the broad stone step and the evergreens belonged to a house that has long since been razed. There was also a "golden gateway beneath the Western trees," toward which Emily was accustomed to look for the approach of her friend.

It is curious — and it may have been significant to Emily — that her two best-loved friends came from the west. Kate lived due west of Amherst in Cooperstown and visited in the Austin Dickinson house, which was west of Emily's house. Sue had lived still farther west, in Geneva, to which she often returned during her acquaintance with Emily, and in Amherst she came from the west to visit Emily in the old Deacon Mack house. Both women also became involved in Emily's "southern" symbolism. To Emily the South represented love and escape from irrational puritan restraint. She associated both friends with the South even before Susan Gilbert went to Baltimore and Kate Scott to Italy. The "blue peninsula" of Emily's poetry is a complex symbol deriving from her dreams of Italy.

There was enough likeness of circumstances between Kate and Sue to make the ascription of many poems seem doubtful. But it must be remembered that at the time of their attachment Sue and Emily were young, naïve, and inexperienced. Sue was scarcely able to sustain the weight of Emily's adoration, let alone respond to it. She was not passionately attached and she made no commitments. Emily had no hope of permanence in their relations. She expected her friend to marry, and though the idea made her unhappy, the only question was the identity of the man. The few surviving notes from Sue to Emily are entirely unemotional, and the plaintiveness of Emily's letters suggests that her friend was far from satisfying an insistent demand for affection. Sue did not like Emily's love poems. She preferred what she called the "metaphysical" poems and insisted that they were Emily's surest title to fame.

Almost all of Emily Dickinson's poetry was written after her meeting with Kate Scott, an older, more experienced, and more passionate woman than young Sue had been. In these poems Emily described an intimacy so deep and fervent that it could be symbolized as a marriage. She called the other woman her "bride," remembered the summer in which they were "wed" to each other, described very clearly a proposal of intimacies, and looked forward, half hopefully, half despairingly, to a consummation in heaven that must be denied in this world. In fact, the real significance of her girlhood attachment to Sue would seem to be that it prepared her for a later, crucial experience with another woman — and introduced her to that woman.

In the fall of 1850 Sue and Emily were just beginning to be acquainted. At this time Sue's sister Martha, who was only a year or two older than Sue and was the latter's usual companion, returned to Amherst from a long visit to their brother in Michigan. Emily feared that her new friend would forget her. In a letter to Sue she begged her to remember "the little friends who have tried so hard to *be* sisters, when indeed you were alone!" And she invited a pleasant disclaimer by a reference to her "little unwelcome face." The intimacy has made strides, for she addressed Sue as "my dear one," but the whole tone of the letter and the "Very aff. yours" of the signature are a far cry from the rhapsodic letters of the 1851–53 period and the emphatic "Your Emily" which often concludes them.

On January 2, 1851, Emily wrote a melancholy letter to Abiah Root. She mourned in set terms for "the departed Humphrey," her kind ex-principal who had died the preceding November. But the letter as a whole suggests that Humphrey was a pretext for more personal griefs. For one thing, Abiah was growing away from her, and Emily was no longer satisfied to hear at rare intervals that her friend was alive and flourishing: "I do not care for the body. I love the timid soul, the blushing, shrinking soul; it hides, for it is afraid, and the bold, obtrusive body — "

Now among the odd and sometimes irrelevant memories of Emily Fowler Ford regarding her friend Emily Dickinson, the following item was preserved. The younger Emily once asked her if it did not make her "shiver to hear a great many people talk — they took 'all the clothes off their souls.' " Kaleidoscopic Emily! The soul was what she cared about. Apparently she feared that she had ventured too far in divesting young Abiah's soul, for in the next breath she interrupted with a distracting "Pray, marm, did you call *me?*"

After two more sentences of digression the letter resumed

the plaintive appeal for warmer relations between them. She
was lonely, she wrote, for some of her friends were gone, and
some were "sleeping." Humphrey was the friend who was
"sleeping," but Susan Gilbert was probably the friend who
was gone. Without occupation or other interest than that of
eventually securing a husband, Susan Gilbert made many visits
away from Amherst. Now if, in January, 1851, Sue was gone or
was showing coolness toward Emily, the latter would turn to
her childhood friend Abiah for consolation and would bring
up every reason for grief except the real one. It was a stratagem
that she was to employ with Abiah in the spring of 1852.

If Sue left Amherst during the winter of 1850–51, she returned in time to make one of the party that journeyed to
Sunderland for the spring "sugaring-off." At about the same
time, in late March of 1851, Emily and Sue read *Ellen Middleton,* a once popular novel, which Austin had given to his
sister. It made a deep impression on Emily, who was almost
tremulous in her letter of thanks to Austin. Perhaps she was
most impressed by some verses in which the childhood of the
heroine is compared to "the haze that veils the glorious skies
at morning prime," and her maturity to an elemental storm.
But who, declaimed the author, would not find in this storm

> A deeper and more glorious sense of life
> Than in the calm of silent apathy?
> Who would not stand within the Sun's full blaze,
> Though scorched and dazzled by his burning rays?

The imagery, commonplace though it was, must have set
Emily thinking. In a fragmentary letter to Sue, she recalled
that they had been strangely reserved about one subject. At
times they had begun to talk of love and marriage, and then
had shunned the idea, like children shutting their eyes against
the bright sun. She had often wondered if there was "no dear

fancy illumining" Sue's life. Her friend had seen flowers in the morning with the dew upon them and at noon "bowed in anguish before the mighty sun." Did Sue believe that they would be satisfied with dew? "No, they will cry for light and pine for the burning noon, though it scorches them, scathes them." But she reminded Sue ominously that many neglected wives would envy the unplighted maiden. Apparently she had no idea that her friend might be interested in her own brother Austin. "Dew," "sun," and "noon" were to be symbols for love in the later poetry of Emily Dickinson.

During the spring and summer of 1851 Emily was closely associated with Susan Gilbert. This was the period of their warmest intimacy. The friendship, which had been somewhat tentative in the late fall of 1850, and perhaps interrupted soon afterwards by one of Sue's long visits away from Amherst, now became close and affectionate. Their favorite recreation was an evening walk with reveries after the fashion of Ik Marvel, a writer whom they both admired. They might do even better than Marvel, who "*only* marvelled," whereas they two "would *try* to make a little destiny" of their own. Perhaps they spent some nights together, for, as Harriet Beecher Stowe observed tartly, New England girls of that period had no other dissipation. The confidences and tenderness usual on such occasions might account for the charged tone and the mystifying references in some of Emily's later correspondence with Sue.

The summer of 1851 may also have witnessed the beginning of the "southern" symbolism. Although Emily's interest in the South was to be magnified by Sue's year in Baltimore (and by later associations with Elizabeth Browning and Kate Scott), it began before Sue left Amherst.

Musing over some unpublished material (doubtless letters to Sue), Mrs. Bianchi was tempted by the idea of Emily's reincarnation. "How else," she wondered, "did these hanging gardens of Babylon in her nature get themselves implanted?"

How explain this "craving for the sultry Orient," this attachment to "the Egypt of Cleopatra?" There are no hanging
gardens of Babylon in Emily's published letters and poems,
but there are several allusions to *Antony and Cleopatra* and
perhaps to *Romeo and Juliet*. Years later Emily compared her
sister-in-law's calls to Antony's supper: "and pays his heart for
what his eyes eat only." On another occasion she sent the three
words: "Egypt — thou knewest." In the spring of 1852 she
wrote to Sue in Baltimore: "Loved One, 'thou knowest.'" Here
the quotation marks suggest an allusion to Juliet's speech beginning "Thou knowest the mask of night is on my face." To
a New Englander, the Italy of *Romeo and Juliet* was still more
sultry than Egypt. Emily was to refer to the play, and apparently her poetry was influenced by it.

It is probable, and indeed provable, that Emily became attached to the "peninsula" of her symbolism as early as her
schoolgirl enthusiasm for Susan Gilbert and Ik Marvel. Admiration for *Reveries of a Bachelor,* which devotes chapters to
a romantic interlude in the Apennines, would carry over to
other books dealing with Italy, for example, Longfellow's
Golden Legend, which Emily read at about the same time. It
was a rare poet in the nineteenth century who did not feel that
Italy was his spiritual home, and Emily Dickinson was never
more than uncomfortably at home in New England. In an
early letter to Sue she mentioned the Apennines, and they reappear in her poetry.

During their evening walks or on nights spent together, the
two girls may have quoted or read aloud from their favorite
books or the Shakespeare play to be discussed at the next club
meeting. In this manner a body of allusion would be built up
which would remain forever obscure to the outsider. At all
events, in the winter of 1852–53, Emily concluded a letter to
Sue with a passionate and tearful invocation of some memory:
"and the South, the love South, Susie, — you know the rest!"

3

In the fall of 1851 Susan Gilbert went south to teach in a private school in Baltimore. There she remained until July of the following year. She may have gone, or made plans to go, as early as August, 1851, for in that month Emily wrote to her brother: "It is very still and lonely — I do wish you were here." At this point the letter was abridged by Mrs. Todd, the original editor, who consistently eliminated all references to Sue. Very likely the omitted passage spoke of Sue, and the melancholy of the preceding sentence suggests that Sue had already left Amherst or was soon expected to go.

Emily's letters to Baltimore can be identified by several characteristics, regardless of the dates assigned by Mrs. Bianchi. Sue was to return to Amherst on the first Saturday in July, 1852. Several times Emily referred to the hot July day on which she expected to clasp her friend once more in her arms. The months in Baltimore were a long, exhausting "pilgrimage," and Emily, who never worked at a job in her life, was divided between grief for her friend's exile and awe for the work that Sue had undertaken. Sue lived in a little "chamber" high up in the sky, as would be natural for a teacher in a boarding-school dormitory of several stories. Books were mentioned as new and interesting which were certainly coming out in this period. Finally, the Baltimore letters contain no identifiable references to Austin, an extraordinary omission if they are supposed to have been written after Austin's engagement to Sue in 1852–53. Yet Sue's daughter, Mrs. Bianchi, assigned the majority of the Baltimore letters to the winter of 1854–55, long after Austin became engaged to Sue.

Mrs. Bianchi could not have made an innocent mistake. Sue's teaching engagement was of great interest to the Gilberts, and

Mrs. Bianchi had family correspondence dealing with it. She had also Lavinia's diary for 1851, which would have mentioned Sue's going to Baltimore. When one of Emily's letters to Baltimore mentioned the appearance of Longfellow's *Golden Legend* (1851) at the local bookseller's, Mrs. Bianchi was careful to explain that this was evidence of a lack of local enterprise. She added that Emily and Sue had already spoken of the *Golden Legend* as early as 1851 (in unpublished letters); plainly she herself was aware of the discrepancy in dates and was afraid that it would be noticed. Unfortunately for her story, Mrs. Bianchi forgot that presidential conventions are more easily dated than books. In a postscript to a letter dated by Mrs. Bianchi as of June, 1855, but written in June, 1852, Emily regretted that she could not be a delegate to the Whig Convention in Baltimore. Immediately the whole mystification of the Baltimore letters collapsed.

Mrs. Bianchi's motives are very important in unraveling the mystery which she made of Emily Dickinson. Apparently she had several reasons for misdating Emily's Baltimore correspondence. For one thing, the real dates would make altogether too obvious the fact that Emily's attachment to Sue was a short-lived infatuation. Mrs. Bianchi accordingly lengthened and attenuated the friendship by dating some letters as early as 1847, three years before Emily's real acquaintance with Susan Gilbert, and by dating highly emotional letters as late as 1854–55, when Emily's attachment to Sue had already cooled. Another reason for assigning the bulk of the letters to 1854–55 was that Austin's engagement to Sue would disguise their real nature. Puzzling as the letters were, they would still have to be dismissed as the overflow of sisterly affection. Another important consideration was that Mrs. Bianchi had invented a passionate attachment, in the spring of 1854, between Emily and a Philadelphia clergyman, Charles Wadsworth. Although the letters were manifestly youthful and immature, any sadness and

over-emotionalism in them could be attributed to Emily's supposed infatuation with Wadsworth.

The Baltimore letters themselves may be briefly summarized.
The majority of them, as well as the most emotional passages
of those already in print, have not yet been published. It is
evident that they must originally have been numerous. Sue
was gone from Amherst about ten months. She was expected to
write a weekly letter that would reach Emily on Saturday.
Though she was often remiss (to Emily's pain) and Emily was
sometimes compelled by pride to omit her own weekly letter,
it is highly probable that there were at least forty letters to
Baltimore. Scarcely a fourth of them have been published, and
these have not been published in their entirety.

Emily sent poetry to Sue. Once she apologized for having no
poem to send. She begged for letters, made excuses for Sue's
carelessness, wrote too fervently, was abject in apology. "Oh,
my darling one, how you wander from me, how weary I grow
of waiting and looking and calling for you." Sometimes she
anticipated Sue's marriage, "and I could have wept bitterly
over the fancy of ever being so alone." On a Sunday early in
1852 she begged Sue "to come with me this morning to the
church within our hearts, where the bells are always ringing
and the preacher whose name is Love shall intercede for us."
Once she asked desperately, "Is it all murmuring — or am I
sad and lone and cannot help it?" But she was afraid that such
thoughts were wrong and that God would punish her by taking
Sue away. And God had been good to her by giving her Sue's
letters, "but my heart wants more." Sue's indifference was a
perpetual grief to Emily. She reminded Sue that one or the
other of them might die; they must make haste to love each
other while they could. In June, 1852, she wrote painfully of
a wish that they "might ramble away as children among the
woods and fields and forget these many years and these sorrowing cares, and each become a child again." Indeed it is not

surprising that Mrs. Bianchi should have tried to diminish the force of these letters.

In early 1852 Emily apparently became concerned about Sue's interest in some man. Closing a letter of this period, she sent her love and referred to "some others who don't dare to send love." Then, in a postscript, she asked who loved Sue best and most and thought of her when others forgot, adding, "'Tis Emilie." A few weeks later she wrote that her sister Lavinia wanted *that little note.*" In her next letter she acknowledged the note to Vinnie and spoke of a journal which Sue was keeping: "I want you to get it bound at my expense, Susie, so when he takes you to live in his new home I may have some of you." It sounds almost as if Austin had formed a secret engagement with Sue and had confided in Emily, who in turn had confided in her sister Lavinia. In June, 1852, Austin asked for leave of absence from his school to accompany his father to Baltimore, but he was refused. However, there is no evidence of an understanding between Sue and Austin before the winter of 1852–53.

Undoubtedly something was amiss between Emily and Sue in the spring of 1852. Emily's letters were unusually mournful. Apologetically she wrote, "And you will be happy now — for all my sadness — won't you?" She could not forgive herself, she added, if she had made Sue unhappy; but the letter ended with a melancholy vision of their both resting in their grave "neath one willow tree." In April Emily wrote to Jane Humphrey, dwelling upon their childhood memories and hoping that they were equally dear to Jane. At almost the same time she overflowed very markedly in a letter to Abiah Root. With some bewilderment Abiah pointed out that Emily had written "more affectionately than wont." Whatever the reason, there is no doubt that Emily was unhappy about Sue in the spring of 1852 and was turning to other friends for comfort.

Sue returned to Amherst in July, 1852, but Emily's hopes for a renewal of their warm friendship were disappointed. For some reason Sue apparently decided to put a space between herself and Emily. She called often at the Dickinson house but avoided the intimate walks and conversations of the past. By the winter of 1852–53 she was certainly engaged to Austin Dickinson. Not long afterwards she left Amherst to visit friends in Manchester, and Emily wrote her some extraordinary letters.

At the time of the first letter Sue had been gone only a day or two. Yet Emily felt that she had not seen her friend for a long time. More emphatically, she added, "It is a long time, Susie, since we have been together, so long since we have spent a twilight and spoken of what we loved." She addressed Sue as "my Absent One," and declared that she was "hoping the days away" and "training the stems" of her flowers. A few months earlier she had addressed Abiah Root as "my absentee." It is not improbable that about this time she wrote an early version of the poem beginning "I tend my flowers for thee, Bright Absentee!" In spite of the masculine pronouns, the poem need not have been inspired by a man. It could have been written to Sue.

This first letter to Manchester (which, oddly enough, contained no reference to Sue's fiancé, Austin Dickinson) continued in a suppressed, deliberately childlike manner until near the close. Then, as if she had ripped off a mask, Emily exclaimed that she must cry out to Susie "in the old, old way," and she wrote two paragraphs of mature passion, claiming her friend as "my gift — my own — my own!" and tearfully invoking "the South, the love South."

Sue did not answer, and Emily was alarmed. After a period of anxious suspense she inquired whether her "quick letter" had contained anything which Sue found difficult to answer. Consciously she returned to the childish tone which characterizes most of her letters to Sue, and for the first time she spoke in detail of Austin and appeared to recognize his superior claims on Sue. In a subsequent letter she was still more careful to reinstate herself with Sue as Austin's sister. Her unhappiness escaped, however, in an attack upon her "silent home" and the bleakness of her surroundings. Much distressed, Sue apparently wrote to Austin, suggesting that Emily needed more tenderness and attention. The brother replied with amused scorn. He needed no bidding, he observed, to love his sisters, but he had been brought up not to show affection.

Gradually Emily reconciled herself to the situation. The letters became calmer, and the signature a cool "Aff. Emilie." Her poetry was claiming more and more of her thoughts. In a fragment to Sue, perhaps written in the early spring of 1853, she thanked Sue for her praise and wrote hopefully of making her and Austin proud some day. As she was to do in a like situation years later, she turned to one of her masculine friends and began sending poetry to Ben Newton for praise and criticism. She did not know that he was dying of tuberculosis. In his last week he wrote that he wished he might live to see her become a poet. The emphatic quality of his praise and the intoxicating effect it had upon Emily suggest that he was seeing her poetry for the first time. When he died a few days later, on March 24, 1853, Emily lost both a good friend and a valued critic. Nine years later she wrote to Higginson that the early phase of her poetry ended with the death of her "tutor." It is questionable, however, whether Newton's death affected her quite so dramatically as she wished afterwards to believe.

On May 17, 1853, Emily wrote with some melancholy to her brother Austin. She had been feeling lonely, she told him, and had not been able to write so often as in the past. In late June she watched a parade celebrating the completion of the railroad, but hid in the woods "and then ran home again for fear somebody would see me, or ask me how I did." The remaining letters of that year, however, seem cheerful enough, and in the fall she made a happy visit to a new friend in Springfield, Mrs. J. G. Holland, whose husband was then assistant editor of the *Springfield Republican*. With the Hollands Emily was to be on intimate terms for the rest of her life.

In midsummer, 1853, Abiah Root invited Emily to pay her

a visit in Philadelphia. After a rather lengthy silence Emily answered negligently, "I don't go from home, unless emergency leads me by the hand, and then I do it obstinately, and draw back if I can." But it is difficult to take Emily with entire seriousness. No emergency led her by the hand on her pleasant visit to Springfield in the fall of 1853, and she was under no compulsion to make an equally pleasant trip to Washington and Philadelphia the following spring. Apparently this letter ended her friendship with Abiah, who married a few months later and disappeared from Emily's history.

The engagement between Austin and Sue was announced at the Dickinsons' Thanksgiving dinner in 1853. For some months it had scarcely been a secret, but now it could be mentioned openly. The Gilbert family overflowed with rejoicing, and Emily listened, with mixed feelings, to their praise of Austin.

In mid-December, 1853, Emily attended the wedding of her old friend Emily Fowler and was morbidly affected by it. Five days later she could not write of it without tears. Her friends were marrying and growing away from her, Ben Newton was dead, and she was left shivering in her loneliness.

On January 13, 1854, Emily wrote to Newton's pastor to ask if her friend had died peacefully and with hope of a future life. She had waited a long time, almost ten months, to ask a question of such moment, but had written within a few weeks after the emotional upheaval produced by Sue's engagement and Emily Fowler's marriage. It seems likely that Newton's death loomed larger as other friends dropped away. It did not put an immediate and dramatic end to her early writing, for in the spring of 1854 she sent a poem to Mrs. Holland and quoted a stanza from "I have a bird in Spring."

In late March, 1854, Emily, now twenty-three years old, was planning, halfheartedly, to accept her father's invitation to Washington. Her friend Sue was expected to return soon from a long visit to Geneva, and in earlier times Emily would not have left Amherst. Now it was easier to go. She went to Washington and wrote animatedly to Mrs. Holland and rather wistfully to Sue, who was once more proving a bad correspondent. After some three weeks in Washington she accompanied Mr. Dickinson and Lavinia to Philadelphia on a visit to her old friend Eliza Coleman. There she met a middle-aged, married clergyman, Charles Wadsworth, with whom she was to have a puzzling, lifelong friendship. On this slender fact her niece, Mrs. Bianchi, was to rear a towering structure of fantasy.

4

The legend of Wadsworth sprang from the necessity of providing an explanation for Emily's love poems. No doubt Emily had been a center of gossip during her lifetime. After her death and the appearance of poems that described a tragic love, the gossip became insistent. The *Springfield Republican* of November 16, 1890, asserted the public's right to inquire into the experience which had produced "so exceptionally personal utterances." Sue Dickinson was alarmed and angry. For years the Dickinson family took turns concocting stories to fit the poems. If they had ever agreed upon a plausible story, they might even have made it stick. Only by degrees, however, and amid much contradiction, did the poems finally attach themselves to the name of Wadsworth.

It has already been pointed out that Austin Dickinson laughed at the stories about various men. He wished Mrs. Todd to believe that Emily's seclusion and eccentricities were the result of self-consciousness about her plain face. What Mrs. Todd suspected, however, seems indicated by her care in suppressing poems dealing with a woman and by her impatient statement that Emily was more interested in her poetry than "in any man." With some disapproval, she noted that Emily had had "fervent attachments to several persons . . . [and had] invested commonplace persons with her own magic," but in time had become "more discriminating." Obviously Austin and Lavinia — and Mrs. Todd as well — would wish to minimize, even in their own minds, the strong, enduring influence of Sue Dickinson and Kate Anthon.

How Lavinia accounted for Emily's love poems has also been related in an earlier chapter. Probably her fear of Sue's unpredictable malice had much to do with her invention of a love story between Emily and George Gould. But Lavinia may also have wished to persuade herself that Emily would have led a conventional life if their father had been less aloof. The facts in Lavinia's hands undoubtedly puzzled her a great deal, and she must have groped for an explanation. The cruelty which she attributed to Mr. Dickinson appears to have almost as little foundation as her romantic tale about George Gould.

Sue Dickinson had still another story. In their youth (Sue recalled) Emily had been loved by a poor but promising law student. Although Mr. Dickinson was a kindly, indulgent father, he considered the match unsuitable and persuaded Emily to give it up. Afterwards the disappointed suitor became a prominent Boston lawyer. This is a pleasanter story than Lavinia's but equally irrevelant to the poetry.

The wife of Emily's cousin Willie had her own theory (unreported — except that it enraged Lavinia), and Mrs. Samuel Fowler Dickinson thought vaguely that Emily had "met her fate" in Washington or Philadelphia. But these stories were unauthorized and represented merely an attempt to share the family limelight. Emily herself wrote that her secret was known only to God. She did not confide wholly in anyone (not even her Norcross cousins, who were obviously best informed), and most certainly not in the wives of her distant relatives.

When Martha Dickinson Bianchi published *The Single Hound,* in 1914, it is doubtful that she had even thought of Wadsworth. She wished merely to give a brief and plausible explanation of the love poems. According to the preface to *The Single Hound,* her aunt Emily had been very attractive to men, and had fascinated the brothers and even the fiancés of her friends. There had been many warm friendships, "Platonic, Plutonic . . . and at least one passionate attachment whose tragedy was due to the integrity of the Lovers, who scrupled to take their bliss at another's cost." This passage is ambiguous. The reader may be supposed to think that Emily Dickinson renounced a married man, but Mrs. Bianchi was careful not to say so. In 1914 Kate Anthon was still alive, and Mrs. Bianchi sent a copy of *The Single Hound* to her "beloved Aunt Kate from Emily's niece and Susan's daughter."

With the publication of *The Life and Letters of Emily Dickinson,* in 1924, seven years after Kate Anthon's death, Mrs. Bianchi enlarged the story. For material she had her own luxuriant fancy plus a family tradition that Emily had met a man in Philadelphia who became a lifelong friend. Mrs. Bianchi knew nothing about Wadsworth, not even his name. The lover she created for her aunt's biography was a figure out of her own romantic novels and had no connection with the real Wadsworth.

During a visit to Philadelphia in the spring of 1854, according to Mrs. Bianchi, Emily Dickinson met an unnamed married man, and they were instantly attracted to each other. The man is not characterized in any way. He is nameless, ageless, without known profession, appearance, or personality. His behavior might suggest that he was impetuous, however, for when Emily returned in panic to her own home, he followed and urged an elopement. A pale, breathless Lavinia hurried for help to "Sister Sue," who was quietly sewing, presumably in the house next door. The elder Dickinsons were away, "that man" had come, and Lavinia was afraid that Emily would elope with him. But Emily made her refusal even without Sue's help. The disappointed lover moved to a city on the other side of the continent and died prematurely. Emily secluded herself. Sue was her only confidante, but, surprisingly, Emily once begged friends to name their baby "Robert" in honor of the man she loved. Except for these lapses she preserved an unbroken silence to the grave. Thus Mrs. Bianchi.

Readers who assumed that Mrs. Bianchi had Wadsworth in mind were quick to find errors. Of course Emily's correspondence had been deliberately misdated, and they did not see clearly that nothing unusual had happened in 1854. But obviously Sue was not then married to Austin Dickinson, the house next door had not yet been built, and Lavinia would have had to cross a good deal of Amherst to find Sue. The "Robert" for whom Emily asked the Bowleses to name their son was simply Robert Browning, the newly bereaved husband of a woman whom Emily idolized. Charles Wadsworth did not move to California until the summer of 1862, and he died in 1882 — somewhat delayed reactions to an allegedly fatal love affair.

But Mrs. Bianchi was not interested in Wadsworth. The phantom of her imagination was far more adaptable. In the preface to *Further Poems of Emily Dickinson* (1929), this phantom became a clergyman, young and handsome, whose preaching had held Emily spellbound even before they met. But Mrs. Bianchi no longer attempts to picture their meeting. The earlier, detailed account of a crucial interview in the Dickinson house gives way to an uncertain "it was held by her Sister Lavinia as well as her Sister Sue" that Emily had taken the initiative in breaking off the attachment. Mrs. Bianchi, of course, did not attempt to deal with the problem that Emily Dickinson did not "break off" anything with Wadsworth. They continued to write and — on rare occasions — to see each other until he died.

In *Emily Dickinson Face to Face* (1932), Mrs. Bianchi refused to indulge in any further, dangerous flights of fancy. She contented herself with affirming the truth of her earlier stories, insisted that her father and her Aunt Lavinia, though manifestly estranged from her, had given her their full confidence, and brought forward vague affidavits from other persons that

Emily had "met her fate" either in Washington or in Philadelphia.

It is interesting to remember that in the *Life and Letters* Mrs. Bianchi prayed that her dead aunt would forgive her for the stories that she had told, and that she seemed reluctant to translate the handsome, vivacious young Katie into a homely, middle-aged, basically unattractive man. In the preface to *The Single Hound* and in *The Life and Letters* and *Emily Dickinson Face to Face*, Mrs. Bianchi gave a surprising amount of space to the unknown Kate Anthon. With each book she increased the number of lines devoted to a woman who attracted no attention from other biographers. In her last years she apparently wished to do still more. She hunted out the letters of Kate Anthon and put them conveniently to hand. But if she intended at last to tell the truth, she died before she could do so.

In a biography of Emily Dickinson, *This Was a Poet* (1937), George Whicher demolished the legend of the impetuous lover. Charles Wadsworth had not been the young, handsome, headstrong lover of Mrs. Bianchi's creation. He had been a plain, middle-aged man, a narrow, orthodox, almost bigoted clergyman, whose profession was his life. It was inconceivable that such a man should propose abandoning his life work and his devoted, beautiful wife in a sudden gust of passion for an odd, homely young woman without attraction for men. Or if it was not absolutely inconceivable, it was so implausible as to demand a great deal more evidence than the perjured testimony of Martha Bianchi. Professor Whicher concluded that the love story was a product of Emily's imagination.

The truth of Emily's friendship with Wadsworth may be briefly summarized. She did meet Wadsworth in the spring of 1854. But as her sister Lavinia did not meet him — on this or any later occasion — it is unlikely that Emily saw him more than once during this brief visit. About 1860 Wadsworth came to Amherst. He had been visiting his friend James D. Clark in the neighboring town of Northampton, and the drive to Amherst would have been a short and easy one. Again Lavinia failed to meet him; she was away during the spring of 1860, and this may have been the period of Wadsworth's visit. There is no evidence that he called specifically on Emily, but she did see him and was surprised to note the mourning band on his arm. If they had corresponded at all prior to this time, it must have been infrequently and without intimacy, for she did not know that his mother had died in the fall of 1859. There may have been another call either shortly before or shortly after 1860. Emily's undoubted friendship with Wadsworth seems to require the support of this additional meeting, and the ease of coming from Clark's residence in Northampton would sufficiently explain another meeting. With far greater inconvenience, Thomas Wentworth Higginson paid two calls on a writer of interesting letters, and yet no one has suggested that he was in love with Emily Dickinson.

In 1862 Wadsworth exchanged his Philadelphia pastorate for one in California. Apparently he wished to escape from the divided sympathies of the Civil War. In 1869 he returned to Philadelphia. During the middle seventies, under cover of her friends Dr. and Mrs. J. G. Holland, Emily began to correspond with him, but it may have been quite by accident that she discovered his return to Philadelphia and turned to him as her spiritual adviser.

The fact that her correspondence was clandestine requires an explanation altogether different from the usual. Neither Dr. Holland nor his wife would have given cover to an intrigue. It is plain that they knew her reason for seeking Wadsworth and that it was a reason they could approve. Nor would a man like Wadsworth have consented to a secret correspondence if he had not been well assured (and he was an intelligent, sensible man, capable of judging in such matters) that her need of him was wholly unerotic. To his family he spoke of Emily's extraordinary interest in immortality; they saw nothing unusual in his occasional correspondence with her.

At that time an unhappy person like Emily Dickinson could turn for help to no other person than a minister. She loved Wadsworth, she was dependent on him, precisely as any suffering creature would love or depend on the physician who gave ease and hopeful assurance. Her tributes to his memory (whether he or any man could have deserved them) were of a nobleness that would be stained by an erotic interpretation. After his death she wrote that he had been shy. His tastes were unknown to her; "he never spoke of himself." But she remembered that he had once said to her, "My life is full of dark secrets." And he had shuddered as he spoke. This was so remarkable a confidence from a reserved man that it must have had a deeper history than she cared to tell. Certainly there were passages in her own life that troubled her, and she was afraid that she would not merit Paradise. If she ever hinted these fears to him, he would have answered, like an honest man and a true Christian, that no human being was without a secret shame. There were dark secrets in his own experience; he had received confidences that acquainted him with the underside of life.

In letters to his friends, the Clarks, she made still clearer the nature of her dependence on Wadsworth. He gave her reassurance when she was overcome by the fear of death. And she entreated the like solace from them. To C. H. Clark she wrote: "Are you certain there is another life? When overcome to know, I fear that few are sure." Later she sent Mr. Clark one of her many poems inquiring into the nature and reality of immortality, with this anxious comment: "These thoughts disquiet me, and the great friend is gone who could solace them. Do they disturb you?"

The position that Wadsworth assumed in Emily Dickinson's life was undoubtedly that of her spiritual father. It was not about him that she wrote poems describing a passionate love, endearments, a night spent together, a cruel jilting. After Wadsworth died she continued to write poems about Katie.

5

In 1854, the young Emily returned from Philadelphia, as she had gone, with a dreary feeling that life was empty of promise. On July 1, 1856, Austin and Sue were married — after delays that drove the young man almost distracted — and Emily had the mixed pleasure of welcoming as her neighbor the woman whom she had once loved with a jealous, exclusive passion. The process of withdrawal continued, but at too quiet a rate to excite notice. She paid calls and received visitors. In the Cattle Show of 1857 she won a prize for bread she had baked, and in the following year she was named one of the judges of the bread division. These were meager enjoyments for a passionate, turbulent nature.

It is curious that she should write to Sue, just before the grossly magnified visit to Philadelphia, that she must "take the words of that sweet Kate Scott I have never seen, and say, 'It is too blissful!'" It is strange that Kate and Emily should meet — so fatally alike, so fatally unlike. Emily was to write, "Who's doom — to whom?"

A<small>FTER</small> a hundred years," wrote Emily Dickinson, "nobody knows the place." By this she meant the slow wastings and concealments of time, which bit by bit erodes the truth of history and buries it in its own debris. In her own history, however, truth, like a victim of enchantment, fell asleep for almost a hundred years, while the briars grew denser and thornier, and memory faded to rumor and rumor to forgetfulness.

She has been dead more than sixty years; "agony, that enacted there," began some ninety years ago; and the briars, meanwhile, have grown all but impenetrable. In another decade essential papers might well have been destroyed, and with them all remembrance of the personality that decisively affected hers. Even though the clue has been found, it is still no easy matter to thread so intricate a maze — to penetrate a mystery strengthened by every attempt to enter it.

On March 7, 1859, Kate Scott was in Boston with Nora Salter, a daughter of the physician who had failed to save Campbell Turner's life almost two years earlier. During this visit she bought a set of De Quincey in twenty volumes and wrote the date on the flyleaf. Long afterwards she was much concerned with the safety of her De Quincey, which had been stored with a friend in New York. She wrote many anxious letters about the books, describing the flowers collected from De Quincey's grave in Edinburgh and the De Quincey manuscript pasted to the flyleaf of *The Confessions of an English Opium-Eater*. Other references in her letters and many marked passages in her books show that De Quincey was a favorite author. In old age at Grasmere she was flattered by a visit from one of his descendants. Her admiration of De Quincey is worth noting, for she introduced Emily to his works during this first visit to Amherst in March, 1859. Probably she brought one or two volumes to read on the train from Boston to Amherst.

A few weeks after Kate's visit Emily sent a note to a friend, Mrs. Haven, begging for the loan of De Quincey's *Klosterheim* and *Confessions of an Opium Eater*. She had already tried another Amherst friend without success. A year later she wrote to Kate: "You do not yet 'dislimn,' Kate." The reference, including the quotation marks, is to a passage that Kate knew well and had marked in *Suspiria de Profundis*: "Faces begin soon (in Shakespeare's fine expression) to 'dislimn'; features fluctuate; combinations of features unsettle."

Kate reached Amherst shortly after March 7. About this time Emily wrote with an undercurrent of excitement to her young cousin Lou Norcross of Boston: "I've had a curious winter, very swift, sometimes sober, for I haven't felt well, much, and March amazes me!" Two Sundays ago the weather had been springlike, "but it snowed since, and we have fine sleighing, now, on *one* side of the road, and wheeling on the other, a kind of variegated turnpike quite picturesque to see!"

The only snowstorm in March, 1859, began on the evening of March 3 and ceased about seven o'clock the following morning. Apparently Emily's letter was written some days later, perhaps about March 9 or 10, for on March 12 a heavy rain spoiled the sleighing for the rest of the season. Forty-eight years later Kate was to recall sorrowfully their sleigh rides with

Austin. If this was the visit to which she alluded, then she was
in Amherst before March 12. Furthermore the tone of Emily's
letter suggests an unusual and pleasant excitement, not at all
checked by the fact that her sister Lavinia was to leave in a
day or two for a long visit with the Norcross cousins in Boston.
Emily had reason to be excited.

On a day of early March, 1859, a tall young woman, swathed
in long furs, her dark hair crowned by a fashionable black hat,
her dark eyes brilliant behind a widow's black veil, stepped
down from Austin's sleigh to the snowy driveway of the Austin
Dickinson house. Many bags and parcels were to be carried in,
for this was to be a long visit of some three weeks. But Kate
would not stop to oversee the moving of her luggage; she would
hurry up the walk toward Sue. There would be exclamations
and laughter and warm embraces for Sue; but at some point
Kate would turn toward the small, auburn-haired young
woman waiting eagerly to meet her. Emily had been hearing
about Kate Scott for almost nine years. She was ready to like
her, and if she was not already prepared to love her, then the
love followed swiftly upon a sunny laugh, a musical voice, and
the most excitable, moving personality that Emily was ever to
know. There is the best of evidence — Emily's own first letter
to Kate — that the attachment between them was swift and
deep. They seemed almost to recognize each other.

Emily began to spend all her evenings at Sue's house, and of
course she met Kate on other occasions. Sometimes Kate would
cross the snowy lawn and ask the servant where Emily was.
Then Emily would draw her upstairs out of reach of Mrs.
Dickinson's solicitous interruptions. The southwest bedroom
had long been a favorite place for entertaining guests. Apparently it was also the scene of an important event commemorated in the first two stanzas of a poem beginning "When I
hoped, I recollect."

The day on which Emily "hoped" (so runs the poem) was
one of sleet and frost. The air was rough, and Emily wore a

merino shawl to protect herself from the cold. As it happens, any one of three days in mid-March, 1859, would satisfy the conditions of this poem. The morning of March 16 was stormy, the whole of March 19 was blustery, with snow squalls in the evening, and March 20 was another blustery day. Clearly the day of the poem was actually stormy, for Emily drew a striking contrast between her inner, emotional warmth and the bitter weather outside.

On this blustery day Emily was in her bedroom, a "chamber facing West." Now the Dickinson parlor directly below has a west wall, with a fireplace, but the room is properly described as facing south toward the street. Besides, Emily would not have called the family parlor, a "chamber." She had in mind the intimacy — and the coldness — of her upstairs bedroom. In her letters she often spoke of it as her "chamber," and she valued the privacy and freedom to be found there. Unquestionably she was standing in her bedroom, when something occurred, so unexpected, so exciting, that it engraved on her memory every detail of the weather and even of the spot where she had stood. Apparently someone was with her, and in Emily's bedroom it could only have been another woman.

Kate Scott was an impulsive person, very ready to be attracted and equally ready to show that she was attracted. As a schoolgirl of seventeen, she had embraced and kissed a young stranger, Sue Gilbert, and Sue had been as much surprised as flattered. Such a kiss might have startled Emily on this day of sleet and frost; perhaps Kate did kiss her. But two poems of Emily's suggest another explanation of this memorable day. A beginning poet discovered a new and appreciative reader.

"That first day when you praised me, Sweet." So Emily wrote afterwards, remembering that her friend had called her "strong," and had said that she could be "mighty" if she tried. "You said that I was 'great' one day," she began, in another poem, and then playfully rang the changes on the meaning of "great." Did her friend want her to be tall like a stag or small like a wren — rhinoceros or mouse, queen or page? Emily would be each by turns, or none, or anything at all, just so it pleased the other. This poem is a love poem. Emily wrote it to a person who, she was happily certain, loved her and would be entertained by a joking tone. Much of the joke depended on the contrast between their heights. Perhaps Kate was not quite the six feet that one awed friend remembered, but she was tall enough to make the small Emily feel tiny.

Of course Emily would show Kate her poetry. She was much attracted, she wanted to please, and she could have found no better way of interesting a young woman who was, by all the evidence, passionately, extravagantly, fond of poetry. Nor could she have found a better or more private place than her own southwest bedroom, where she kept her poetry in a bureau drawer. Afterwards she would send Kate many poems, two of which have been published as coming from Kate's manuscript copies. Apparently Kate preserved still others and sent copies of them to Lavinia after Emily's death, but if so, they have been published either without acknowledgment of the source or from variant manuscripts already in Lavinia's possession.

To complete the scene described in the first two stanzas of "When I hoped, I recollect," it is necessary to supply only the figure that Emily carefully left blank in all her poetry. Once more the dark head and the auburn are bent over the sheets of poems. Storm rattles the windows and sleet spits against the panes. But Emily, in her merino shawl, is so warm with praise that she scarcely feels the cold of that blustery March day. Afterwards she will remember the exact spot where she stood in "a chamber facing West" — west toward her brother's house and west toward Cooperstown — and hoped that she had at last found the stimulating, affectionate companion for whom she had long searched.

One more incident of Kate's March visit remains to be described. Its history goes back to a disgraceful squabble that

split the South Congregational Church of Amherst. For years
the two divided halves of the congregation had been meeting
separately, one in the basement, one in the main auditorium,
and their warring devotions were a Sunday scandal. Referees
were appointed, a Mr. Hyde of Ware and a Mr. Chapman of
Springfield, who came from their several towns to Amherst in
an effort to settle the matter. According to the *Springfield
Republican* of mid-February, 1859, the quarrel was settled, but
the skirmishing actually went on for some months longer. The
referees made new trips to Amherst, and on March 22, 1859,
apparently after consulting the Dickinson law firm, they advised
legal action.

While the two gentlemen were busy with this church matter,
they called on three successive evenings at the house of Austin
Dickinson. On the third evening Emily was sitting, as usual,
with Sue and Kate. Probably all three women were engaged in
so exciting a conversation that they would especially resent a
business caller. At the sound of the doorbell Kate and Emily
took hands and ran.

> *What was my surprise and shame* [*Emily wrote to Mrs.
> Holland*], *on hearing Mr. Chapman ask for "Mrs. D!"
> K. S.* [*Kate Scott*], *a guest of* [*Sue*]*'s, was my confederate,
> and clinging fast like culprit mice, we opened consulta-
> tion. Since the dead might have heard us scamper, we
> could not allege that we did not run, besides, it was* untrue,
> *which to people so scared as we, was a minor consideration,
> but would have its weight with our seniors. I proposed that
> we ask forgiveness.*
>
> *K. was impenitent and demurred. While we were yet
> deliberating,* [*Sue*] *opened the door, announced that we
> were detected, and invited us in.*
>
> *Overwhelmed with disgrace, I gasped a brief apology,
> but the gentlemen simply looked at us with grave surprise.*

Austin scolded Emily, because the trifling offense had occurred in his house, and she crept home to her "little room,
quite chagrined and wretched." She cared nothing for Mr.
Hyde, but Mr. Chapman had talked with her about her books,
and moreover he was a friend of Mrs. Holland. As Lavinia was
absent, and could not be sought for consolation or advice,
Emily begged Mrs. Holland to intercede with Mr. Chapman,
lest she end in Newgate, "a loving felon, sentenced for a door
bell."

The whole letter is lively, and the penitence is hardly skin-
deep. In the entire correspondence there is no other picture
quite like that of the impudent Katie and of the scarcely more
remorseful Emily "clinging fast like culprit mice." For young
women of twenty-eight, with their dresses down to the floor,
the incident was surprisingly schoolgirlish.

After Kate left Amherst, in late March, 1859, or perhaps
while she was still in the house next door, Emily wrote her a
letter. It is an exercise in poetry rather than a communication
of news.

Amherst [1859]

*. . . Sweet at my door this March night another candi-
date. Go home! We don't like Katies here! Stay! My
heart votes for you, and what am I, indeed, to dispute her
ballot!*

*What are your qualifications? Dare you dwell in the
East where we dwell? Are you afraid of the sun? When you
hear the new violet sucking her way among the sods, shall
you be resolute? All we are strangers, dear, the world is
not acquainted with us, because we are not acquainted with
her; and pilgrims. Do you hesitate? And soldiers, oft —
some of us victors, but those I do not see to-night, owing
to the smoke. We are hungry, and thirsty, sometimes, we
are barefoot and cold — will you still come?*

Then, bright I record you — Kate, gathered in March!

It is a small bouquet, dear, but what it lacks in size it gains in fadelessness. Many can boast a hollyhock, but few can bear a rose! And should new flower smile at limited associates, pray her remember were there many, they were not worn upon the breast, but tilled in the pasture. So I rise wearing her — so I sleep holding, — sleep at last with her fast in my hand, and wake bearing my flower.

EMILIE

The letters to Katie evoke more echoes of the poetry than any similar amount of the correspondence. Emily lavished most of her poetic imagery on this one friend. This March letter, like the other two published letters, is rich in the symbolism that was to reappear in the poems.

In letters and poems Emily's friends are represented as flowers or gems or birds. It is not safe to assume that a bee or a butterfly is real until the possibilities of symbolism are exhausted. In the March letter Kate is identified with the rose; in a subsequent letter she becomes a bird; and throughout the poetry she appears as rose, bird, pearl, bee, butterfly, the setting sun, the sea, and in as many other guises as the poet's ingenuity could supply. Naturally this wealth of symbolism overflowed upon others. The Norcross cousins became birds, Mary Bowles the sea, Maria Whitney a pearl, and even Wadsworth a "dusk gem." But no other single person, except Emily herself, had so many poetic titles as she bestowed on Katie.

The friend who came from the West was asked if she dared "dwell in the East" where Emily made her home. The literal meaning is only a springboard for the symbolic. Emily lived in the East of the poetic mind, and she knew that she had treasures to offer her less gifted friend. The playful catechism is reminiscent of a poem, "I showed her heights she never saw." In this poem Emily describes the wonders of her mental world and appeals to a reluctant friend to share it with her. In a later version beginning "He showed me heights I never saw," she changed the pronouns and reversed the situation. But the delicate imagery became grotesque and clumsy with the introduction of masculine pronouns.

The remaining symbols of the second paragraph — "pilgrim," "soldier," "hungry," "barefoot," "thirsty," "cold" — were Emily's figures for the lonely, introspective life she led. "Hunger" was a word she often used to describe her need for love. The symbol of the weary soldier she had used as early as 1850 in a letter to Abiah Root. She liked to play at being the brave little soldier. The symbolism was natural enough for a person who lived through two wars and whose life was a struggle against a hostile society.

This second paragraph of Emily's letter, which implies that friendship with her would be difficult but rewarding, illuminates the personalities of the two women: warm, vital, lifegiving Katie and the lonely poet, hopelessly estranged from the everyday world, and suffering, in her estrangement, from a painful sense of cold and an insatiable hunger for reassurance and affection. Perhaps it was fortunate for Emily's poetry, though disastrous to her peace of mind, that her friend was drawn to this alien world. While Kate was still under the shadow of her young husband's death, her imperative need to love met Emily's imperative need to be loved. The result was tragic for both.

2

Did Kate return to Amherst in August, 1859? The available clues suggest that she did, and there is nothing improbable in the suggestion. Her attachment to Sue would have been enough to bring her, and Emily's first letter to her witnesses a new and powerful attraction. Certainly Kate was in Amherst during late February or early March of 1860, and again in late October and early November of 1861. Mrs. Bianchi also speaks vaguely of other early visits. Having found her way, Kate apparently came often. She was an incessant traveler, she had neither an occupation nor a family to tie her down, and when she was attracted she would go to extraordinary lengths to see the person who attracted her. Years later, ill and half-frantic, she was to go from the Italian Lakes to England because she could not bear a separation of six weeks from a much-loved young friend, the English girl Florie.

On the supposition that Kate visited Amherst again in August, 1859, it is possible to unite many loose strands in the history of Emily Dickinson. Such a visit would explain Emily's allusion to the significance of August, identify the summer day on which she joined her life to that of a woman friend, introduce Kate and Samuel Bowles to each other, introduce Elizabeth Browning's *Aurora Leigh* to the entire party, and interpret and date some mystifying letters to Bowles and Mrs. Holland.

Once, toward the end of her life, Emily wrote to Mrs. Holland that certain months had been of special significance to her. April had robbed her repeatedly, August had brought her most. Bowles paid his first visit on a summer day, apparently in August, 1859. Was Katie another gift of the same month? Of course, a warm, highly emotional friendship had existed since the preceding March, but would either woman have realized so early that it was more than friendship? On the other hand, several poems attribute to a summer day the beginning of a love relationship between Emily and another woman, most probably Kate Scott.

Only one of these "summer" poems specifically names the month of August. The reference might even be dismissed as a poetic convention if Emily had not stressed the importance of August in her letter to Mrs. Holland. This poem ("In lands I never saw, they say") describes the Alps towering over the meek daisies at their feet. Then comes a turn which identifies the poet with the daisies and the lover with the mountains:

Emily playfully asks her friend to guess which one of them is the daisies and which one the mountains "upon an August day."

The important summer day reappears in another poem, "When diamonds are a legend." No one has ever tried to interpret this poem, for no one has hitherto possessed the facts that might give meaning to it. Briefly, diamonds and diadems have become legendary, but Emily still raises and sells her own jewels. Although her merchandise no longer attracts much notice, she recalls a summer day when she had customers — "once . . . a Queen, and once a Butterfly!" That is the poem. But the symbolism is so complex that it can be interpreted only within the close web of symbolic meaning that knits all the poems together.

"Diamonds" and "diadems" (and other precious objects in the poetry) signify love or a loved person. The jewelry that Emily "sows" and "raises" refers to the flowers of her little conservatory, but it also symbolizes her poems and, more intricately, the love that she continues to express in her poems. "Queen," a word Emily used incessantly, is a borrowing from the symbolism of Elizabeth Browning's *Aurora Leigh*. Here it means little more than a woman whom Emily regarded as far superior to herself; in other poems it means a woman crowned by love. "Queen" and "butterfly" are the same person seen under different aspects. Perhaps Emily had in mind two summer days — one on which the friend had been brilliantly playful like a butterfly and another on which she had been a queenly, even a tragic, figure. Queens and butterflies reappear in the poetry, and they often stand for a woman friend, presumably Kate Scott.

Now the poem can be interpreted. Since the diamonds and diadems have become a legend, the friend has ceased to love. Emily imagines herself at work in her conservatory (another poem begins "I tend my flowers for thee, Bright Absentee!"). That is, she is writing poems which express her continuing love

for her faithless friend. As she works and muses, she recalls a
past summer day (or days) when the friend, now playful, now
tragic, praised the flowers, praised the poems, loved Emily herself. As the friend's attachment has ended, Emily has only the
melancholy pride of remembering that she was once loved.

A closely related poem reads as follows:

> Ourselves were wed one summer, dear,
> Your vision was in June,
> And when your little lifetime failed
> I wearied, too, of mine.
>
> And overtaken in the dark,
> Where you had put me down,
> By some one carrying a light,
> I, too, received the sign.
>
> 'Tis true our futures different lay,
> Your cottage faced the sun,
> While oceans and the north did play
> On every side of mine.
>
> 'Tis true your garden led the bloom,
> For mine in frosts was sown,
> And yet, one summer we were queens,
> But you were crowned in June.

Both persons are women, for both are "queens." In short,
Emily states flatly that one summer she and another woman
were "wed" to each other. (This notion of a symbolic marriage
is echoed in another poem, "Her sweet weight on my heart
a night," in which Emily calls another woman "my bride.")
Then come the puzzling references to June. The friend has a
"vision" in June and is "crowned" in June. Now the word
"crowned," another symbol borrowed from Elizabeth Browning, has a graduated series of meanings in Emily's poetry, rang-

ing from mutual love through betrothal to marriage. In this poem it apparently means betrothal or marriage in the literal sense. If Kate is the person meant, then the allusion is to her second betrothal, which apparently occurred in June, 1864. Incidentally, the manuscript of the poems is in handwriting of about this period. Whatever happened to the other woman in June, it was an event that contrasted sadly with the happy summer that the two women spent together.

According to the third line, the other woman's "little life-time failed," but the meaning would seem to be that she died only as far as Emily was concerned. Few of the "deaths" alluded to in the poetry are real deaths. In the last two stanzas of this poem the unnamed woman goes her separate way toward a very happy future. With a sad glance at her own blighted life, the poet consoles herself with the memory that one summer they were "queens." (In like manner, she finds comfort in the recollection that one summer a "queen" patronized her flower jewelry.)

The second stanza of the poem is mysterious. After her friend repudiates her, Emily is overtaken by "some one carrying a light," and she, too, receives the "sign." There is no present explanation. In several poems Emily imagines that she is crucified; in one poem she describes the friend also as crucified. But it is merely a guess that the "sign" refers to the stigmata and that the person carrying the light is Christ.

In a poem beginning "Like eyes that looked on wastes," the word "queen" is given a stronger meaning than in either of the two poems already examined. Again the lovers are two women, for both are "queens." They face each other in blank misery, unable to renounce their love, but unable to belong wholly to each other. Though in appearance they continue to "reign," neither can be truly a "queen" without the other, and so they die, as far as their emotional life is concerned.

In yet another poem, "So much summer me for showing," Emily begs a smile of the "lady with the guinea" who has given her an "illegitimate" summer of happiness. The word "guinea" is puzzling. In a poem beginning "Sweet, you forgot, but I re-membered," Emily begs

> Just to be rich, to waste my guineas
> On so best a heart!

Perhaps the "guinea" is related to the "amulet" of another poem. In "Forget? The lady with the amulet," Emily accuses a woman friend of treason. Emily herself is the amulet which the other woman once wore against her breast, and perhaps Emily is also the guinea of "So much summer me for showing."

The momentous summer day figures in still another poem, "The Heaven vests for each," which describes feelingly the danger and anguish of this friendship. Knowing that their love is hopeless, the poet half shrinks from the glory she has begged to see. In circumstances like theirs, to appeal for love is to ask a star to descend from the bright ranks of heaven and "enter-tain despair." According to this poem, the mutual avowal took place on a "bashful Summer's day."

In another poem, "Again his voice is at the door," the time and circumstances appear to be stated with great exactness. It is dusk on an evening pleasant enough for a long stroll. Once more the loved friend comes to the door. The voice that is "like a tune," a "silver call," asks the servant for Emily, and Emily feels the old, excited quickening. As she goes silently toward the meeting at the door, she takes a flower from her conservatory. Her friend has never seen her "in this life" and might not recognize her without the flower. They are not in Amherst at all. This is the reunion in heaven which Emily longingly anticipates in many a poem. It is a heaven remark-ably like the familiar earth, with all the well-known surround-ings of the Dickinson house, for Emily was never reconciled to a misty heaven of bodiless spirits.

The lovers meet, recount their experiences, and shyly explore each other's feelings. Then they walk together. With surprising particularity, Emily states that she leaves her dog at home. For a little while the lovers are accompanied by "a tender thoughtful moon," apparently a new moon, for it sets early. Then they are alone. They are angels taking their first flight through the skies.

In the last stanza the pretense of a heavenly reunion, patterned after some earthly walk, breaks down completely, and the poet cries out in anguish. To relive that hour, she would give all the blood in her body, stipulating only that the faithless friend be punished by having to count the drops. This sudden and confusing shift, of course, is one of the many artistic lapses which betray the biographical character of Emily Dickinson's work. The manuscript of the poem is in handwriting of about Emily's thirty-sixth year. It may recall a very real event of her twenty-ninth year — an evening walk in August, 1859.

(In the summer of 1860, about a year after this presumed stroll, Emily Dickinson wrote rhapsodically to Kate Scott: "Oh, dew upon the bloom fall yet again a summer's night!" In poems and letters "dew" was her constant symbol for love.)

On the morning after this declaration of love, apparently, the poet takes stock of her altered self and writes: "I am alive, I guess." The manuscript is an early one (recopied in handwriting of Emily's very early thirties), and the poem describes a summer morning that followed a momentous night. Emily observes that the branches in her hands are "full of morning-glory," that the blood tingles in her fingers, and that her breath blurs a glass — all of these, proofs of life. It is good to be alive, "infinite to be alive twofold" — her initial birth in the flesh and her second birth in love.

All the evidence, taken together, suggests that a woman whom the poet deeply loved was with her on a memorable summer day or evening. To be sure, one poem uses masculine pronouns, another makes a masculine identification with the single word "sir," and two poems avoid pronouns altogether, but the remainder describe a strong, even an anguished, love relation between two women. No woman writes poems about a love affair between herself and an imaginary woman; this relationship is bound to be real. The other poems appear to be equally real and to describe the same tragic event.

In the poem beginning "The Heaven vests for each," Emily offers her unreserved love to her "small Deity" and begs that deity to leave the row of stars and share tragedy with her; but other poems suggest that the friend made the initial avowal. A poem beginning "He fumbles at your spirit" is an account of a love declaration. The poet describes a speaker, perhaps bashful (it was a "bashful Summer's day"), who leads up to the subject, draws away from it, gives the listener a moment's relief from tension, and then

> Deals one imperial thunderbolt
> That scalps your naked soul.

In still other poems the coming of love is described as a thunderbolt or a stroke of lightning. The poem beginning "Many a phrase has the English language" records a love declaration that Emily receives with astonished delight — a "push of joy." In a poem beginning "It did not surprise me," she referred to "God's old-fashioned vows" between herself and another woman. If Kate Scott did take the initiative, the action would have been in character.

In an age when women were supposed to cling, Kate Scott had a vigor, an independence, a decisiveness, which would be called masculine. She liked her nickname "Tommy" and signed many letters "Tommy" or "Thomas." A young English friend, Florie, referred to Kate as "Mr. Pump," called herself "Mrs. Pump," and wrote that "the dear old gentleman" (that is, Kate) had given her a gold ring in token of "his" love. Emily, too, liked to pretend that she was a boy. In her letters she sometimes spoke of her "boyhood" and in many poems she was "boy," "prince," "earl," or "duke." Her friend Bowles, amused by a line in Emily's poem "A narrow fellow in the grass," asked how a girl knew that corn would not grow in a cool soil. Sue Dickinson reminded him that Emily had been a boy.

Both Kate Scott and Emily Dickinson were too self-assertive, too dominant in personality, to be comfortable in a society that forced women into an inferior and often servile rôle. Probably for this reason they envied men and adopted their titles. As for being a man in truth, Emily fiercely repudiated the idea in a poem beginning "Rearrange a wife's affection," and Kate placidly echoed the current diatribes against "strong-minded" women. It did not occur to her that she too was "strong-minded." The two women were, in fact, so dominating that they might not have remained friends under any circumstances. But Kate was the more experienced and the more courageous, and for a time Emily followed her lead.

Emily Dickinson had a natural taste for secrecy, but she was slightly more naïve than her friend, and she did not immediately see the reason for concealing a love that was harmless, beautiful, and necessary to her. "Is bliss, then, such abyss?" she demanded in one poem. Must she be careful where she put her foot for fear of spoiling her shoe? Shoes could be replaced, but bliss was "sold just once." Mabel Loomis Todd, the first editor of the poetry, curtailed this poem of its revealing conclusion:

> Say, foot, decide the point!
> The lady cross, or not?
> Verdict for boot!

On another occasion Emily writes as if she were tying a poetic note to the collar of her dog Carlo and sending him to the house next door:

What shall I do it whimpers so —
This little hound within the heart —
All day and night with bark and start,
And yet it will not go?

Would you untie it were you me?
Would it stop whining if to thee
I sent it, even now?

It should not tease you, by your chair,
Or on the mat, or if it dare
To climb your dizzy knee,

Or sometime at your side to run
When you were willing — shall it come?
Tell Carlo — he'll tell me!

This is a lover's message, and it is directed to someone in the
Austin Dickinson house next door. If Sue Dickinson was the
recipient, then the story becomes unpleasant. Fortunately the
manuscript is in handwriting of about 1859. It may be conjectured that Emily wrote the poem in August, 1859.

3

In the late summer of 1859 Samuel Bowles, editor of the *Springfield Republican,* paid his first visit to the Dickinsons. Emily's
earliest letters to the Bowles family, referring clearly to this
summer visit, were tentatively assigned to the fall of 1858; but
they were dated after a lapse of more than thirty years, and
memories were understandably a little vague. Bowles had had
a slight acquaintance with Mr. Dickinson as early as 1850, following a meeting in the town of Monson, and Emily had long
been intimate with the family of his assistant editor, J. G.

Holland, and had even visited in Springfield. But she did not meet Bowles until he came to Amherst in the late summer of 1859.

Amherst is only about twenty-five miles north of Springfield, and was approached then, as now, most commonly through the gap by way of nearby Northampton. In July, 1859, Bowles made a carriage trip to Northampton and wrote with interest of a countryside that was new to him; he returned directly to Springfield. In August he apparently came again, and this time he drove the remaining distance to Amherst. There was a reason for the trip.

August 11, 1859, was Commencement Day for Amherst College and a very important date for the entire community. On the Wednesday preceding Commencement the Dickinsons customarily gave a tea; Emily presided over the punch bowl, with a good deal of quaking; and everyone of the slightest consequence in Amherst crowded into the house. The *Springfield Republican* always sent a man to report the several days of exercises, and on this occasion the man was probably the editor himself. The newspaper account that appeared two days later sounds not unlike Bowles' editorials and letters:

> *The latent heat of the morning fog developed into sensible heat during the forenoon, and had the town been tightly fenced in an explosion might have occurred. As it was the temperature of the air was very warm, the town full of people, and the shows, candy and whip sellers drove a good business. At the tents most frequented on the green were sold hot oysters and ice cream, which, singly or mixed in proper proportions, were warranted to produce any temperature of the body wished for by the purchasers.*

This mixture of rowdy carnival and commencement probably did not attract Emily or her friend Kate. They would have stayed at home in such coolness as they could find, and would have helped Sue and Mrs. Dickinson entertain Bowles' family, and Bowles himself, during the hours when he was free from his duties. Kate was to see Bowles again the following winter. But slight as their acquaintance must have been, it was evidently based on more than one brief meeting. In late 1861 Bowles sent a new book over to Amherst with the expressed hope that Sue and "Mrs. Kate" would enjoy reading it. Many years after his death Kate Anthon recalled how they had all "loved Mr. Bowles."

Bowles' friendship with Emily Dickinson has been not so much exaggerated as misread. Emily had many filial and sisterly relations with men. It is a little hard that all of them should be read as passionate attachments, when the available evidence suggests that she was remarkably constant — one might almost say, pitiably constant — to one person all her life. Bowles was important to Emily because he knew and liked Kate Scott. On a day of bitter suffering Emily was driven to confide in him, and he helped and comforted her. As a result, her letters to him took on a highly emotional tone that has deceived at least one biographer. She was grateful to him, but she was never in love with him.

At the time of their meeting Bowles was thirty-three years old, tall, shaggy-browed, with luminous dark eyes. He was an intense, vital man, incapable of rest, suffering already from some of the nervous ills that burdened the rest of his life, but still able to give abundant energy to others. On this trip he was accompanied by his family, "elder and minor Mary, Sallie and Sam." In words that must have gratified a mother's heart, Emily wrote afterwards to Mrs. Bowles that "traditions of 'Mamie's' eyes, and little Sallie's virtues and Sam's handsome face" were still current among her family.

In August, 1859, Mary Bowles apparently found Emily Dickinson a charming woman. Emily was happy, and happiness made her attractive. In a poem beginning "It would never be common more, I said," she described feelingly the euphoria of

that brief period. For the only time in her life she was loved,
she felt secure, and she made friends easily. She met everyone
with a "word of gold" and "dowered all the world." Wings
seemed to uphold her body, and though she could not tell her
love, she published the joy of it on her cheek and in her eyes.
Little wonder that Mrs. Bowles was attracted. A common love
of gardening led to the exchange of flowers and plants between
them, and Emily wrote: "You cherished me many times." But
when Emily's suffering began and she turned in desperation to
Mrs. Bowles, it was to find that sorrow was less appealing than
joy.

On that hot August day the group collected in the Dickinson
parlor would discuss ideas and books. Mrs. Bowles was soon to
make Emily a Christmas present of a book by Theodore Parker,
and Emily would be impressed by Parker's religion of love and
good works. But at this moment she was brimming over with
admiration for Elizabeth Browning, an admiration which
Samuel Bowles shared. During the next several years Emily
was to write to him as if they had once discussed Mrs. Browning's *Aurora Leigh*. Bowles quoted Mrs. Browning in letters
or in conversation, and put her works in their entirety at the
head of a little traveling library for his friend Maria Whitney.
Apparently he and Emily were struck by Mrs. Browning's use
of the Book of Revelation, particularly Chapter 21. This "gem
chapter," as Emily called it, describes the building of the New
Jerusalem and the city wall with its twelve courses of jewels:
jasper, sapphire, chalcedony, emerald, sardonyx, sardius,
chrysolyte, beryl, topaz, chrysoprasus, jacinth, and amethyst.

Years later Emily must have recalled this earlier enthusiasm
to Bowles, for after his death she wrote to his wife: "I spoke to
him once of his Gem chapter." In the early winter of 1859, a
few months after the Bowles' visit to Amherst, Emily wrote to
Mary Bowles: "the days turn topaz, like a lady's pin." Some
two years later she wrote to Bowles: "The moon rides like a
girl through a topaz town." Incidentally, one of the characters

in *Aurora Leigh* has "topaz" eyes, a description which would have struck Emily.

In 1861 Emily wrote to Bowles: "To-night looks like 'Jerusalem!' . . . I hope we may all behave so as to reach Jerusalem. . . . You shall find us all at the gate if you come in a hundred years, just as we stood that day. If it become of 'jasper,' previously, you will not object." And a few months later: "Friends are gems, infrequent."

Mrs. Browning ended *Aurora Leigh,* a poem which clearly made a deep impression on Emily Dickinson, with these lines:

> "Jasper, first," I said;
> "And second, sapphire; third, chalcedony;
> The rest in order: — last, an amethyst."

More prodigal than her model, Emily made repeated use of all the celestial jewels except two or three of the least poetic. It was not by chance that she represented the friend whom she had loved so well and so unwisely as a jewel that slipped through her fingers and left only an "amethyst remembrance." The amethyst was the twelfth and most exalted course of the heavenly walls. Moreover, the two young women had read, or reread, *Aurora Leigh* together. "To pile like Thunder to its close," wrote Emily, " . . . would be Poetry: Or Love, — the two coeval came —" The evidence shows that she fell in love with Kate Scott and with Elizabeth Browning's poetry at the same time.

4

The enchanted summer came to an end, and Kate returned to Cooperstown. She left behind her a mixture of happiness, tension, and increasing loneliness. Emily poured herself out in letters. In a poem published in a masculine version (it exists also in a manuscript with feminine pronouns, "Going to her, happy letter. Tell her — "), she described powerfully the anxious joy of writing to her friend. She worked at her letter through the greater part of the night, wrote and rewrote it, sealed it just before daybreak, and then apparently hid it in her nightdress. The recipient was supposed to guess where the letter had rested.

In a companion poem, "The way I read a letter's this," which carefully fails to identify the lover, Emily described how she locked the door of her room, retreated to the farthest corner, carefully drew out the letter and opened it, then once more scanned the room before she dared

> Peruse how infinite I am
> To — no one that you know!
> And sigh for lack of heaven — but not
> The heaven the creeds bestow.

But it was not enough to write to Katie. Emily overflowed in letters to all her friends, old and new. In late August or early September she wrote for the first time to Samuel Bowles. She had received a little pamphlet which she believed to be addressed in Bowles' handwriting, but the wish to thank him was only a pretext for writing. Her friends, wrote Emily, were her "estate." "God is not so wary as we," she added, "else He would give us no friends, lest we forget Him! The charms of the heaven in the bush are superseded, I fear, by the heaven in the hand, occasionally," In the fall of 1859 Emily Dickinson was in love. The "heaven in the bush" seemed very remote and held little attraction.

To Mrs. Holland she wrote: " . . . if God had been here this summer, and seen the things that *I* have seen — I guess that He would think His Paradise superfluous. Don't tell Him, for the world, though," she continued playfully, "for after all He's said about it, I should like to see what He *was* building for us, with no hammer, and no stone, and no journeyman either. Dear Mrs. Holland, I love, to-night — love you and Dr. Holland, and 'time and sense' — and fading things, and things that do *not* fade." This is the letter of a woman in love. It is the superfluity that overflows upon her friends.

Plainly Emily had been rereading Chapter 21 of Revelation. The passage already quoted refers to the building of the New Jerusalem. "Wicked" as she was (the letter to Mrs. Holland begins), she read her Bible sometimes, "and in it as I read to-day, I found a verse like this, where friends should 'go no more out'; and there were 'no tears.' " As often happened, her memory was inexact. The second phrase was an allusion to verse 4 of the "gem chapter": "And God shall wipe away all tears from their eyes; and there shall be no more death, neither sorrow, nor crying, neither shall there be any pain; for the former things are passed away." The phrase "go no more out" appears to be a vague recollection of verse 12 of Chapter 3: "Him that overcometh will I make a pillar in the temple of my God, and he shall go no more out."

Emily almost wished that she could take her place beside Mrs. Holland in that marvelous heaven, where "the 'hundred and forty and four thousand' were chatting pleasantly, yet not disturbing us." The number of the saved, according to Revelation, would be 144,000.

Further on in this same letter, Emily rejoiced that Mrs. Holland was not a rose or a bee or even a robin, for "when the west winds came, you would coolly wink at me, and away, some morning!" Mrs. Holland lived in nearby Springfield, and was expected to pay a visit in September. But Kate Scott, who was rose and bird and bee, had indeed gone (some day there would be a heaven in which friends should "go no more out"), and the west winds blew from distant Cooperstown. In a poem which may have been written at this time (it begins "Because the bee may blameless hum," and has apparently been recopied in handwriting of the eighteen-sixties), Emily herself proposes to become bee, flower, and robin, for none of these would be debarred from seeing the loved friend:

> So wings bestow on me,
>
> Or petals, or a dower of buzz,
> That bee to ride, or flower of furze,
> I that way worship thee.

The letter to Mrs. Holland contains still more allusions which suggest the shadowy presence of Kate in Emily's mind. In the fourth paragraph Emily salutes her friend as "little Mrs. Holland" and "that tiny lady." Mrs. Holland had not shrunk during the six years of their acquaintance; yet there had been no earlier references to her small stature. There were to be many such in the letters that followed Emily's unhappy attachment to a very tall woman. It was as if Emily herself had suddenly been made conscious of size.

"Pardon my sanity, Mrs. Holland," the letter continued gaily, "in a world *in*sane, and love me if you will, for I had rather *be* loved than to be called a king on earth, or a lord in Heaven." There is a reminiscent line in the last published letter from Emily to Kate: "Insanity to the sane seems so unnecessary — but I am only one, and they are 'four and forty,' which little affair of numbers leaves me impotent." Here the "insanity" appears to be playful nonsense: Emily wants summer the year round; insane people want a winter also. The curious "four and forty" may recall the "hundred and forty and four thousand" of the saved. Or perhaps it was intended to remind Kate of a poem ("Glee! the great storm is over!") which tells of four seamen who were saved, forty who were drowned. Kate admired the poem and marked it repeatedly in her copy of Emily's verse.

But was Kate already acquainted with a poem beginning "Much madness is divinest sense"? It may have been written as

early as 1859 or 1860, for it bears a marked resemblance to the
passages quoted from the letters to Mrs. Holland and Kate.
There is a madness that is "divinest sense." On the other hand,
much of the common sense preached by the world is stark madness. Unfortunately in this, as in all other matters, the majority overcome by sheer weight of numbers. The person who con-
forms to the world's madness is reckoned sane; the noncon-
formist is "dangerous, and handled with a chain."

The years 1859–60 were crucial ones for Emily Dickinson. At
no other period of her life would she be so acutely conscious of
a "sanity" that others might consider madness. That she loved
a woman, that she defied convention in so important a matter,
was enough to open her eyes to the arbitrariness of many conventions. She discovered that she was different. To preserve
her own integrity, she was compelled to defend that difference.
Conformity would have meant destruction of herself. The
issue, of course, was much broader than her attachment to Kate.
She must ask herself what life means, whether the inevitableness
of death intensifies or destroys the value of life, and what part
love plays. And she would reach conclusions very different from
those of her neighbors. Late in life, recalling that she had often
misspelled the word "phoebe," Emily observed to Mrs. Holland
that if she spelled everything as she heard it and reported all
the facts as she saw them, "it would send consternation among
more than the 'Fee Bees'!" She did report them in her poems,
but her readers have taken pains to misunderstand her.

In the early winter of 1859 Emily wrote to Mrs. Bowles:
"I have a childish hope to gather all I love together and sit
down beside and smile." The idea reappears still more strongly
in a letter of September, 1859, to her intimate friend Mrs.
Holland: "Indeed, this world is short, and I wish, until I tremble, to touch the ones I love before the hills are red — are gray
— are white — are 'born again'! If we knew how deep the
crocus lay, we never should let her go." In late December,
1859, or early January, 1860, she wrote again to Mrs. Bowles:

"I think there will be no spring this year, the flowers are gone so far." She meant that the snow was very heavy, but she also felt that her friend Kate was far away and might not soon return. Because of the tension and the loneliness of her position, she was now writing so often to Mary Bowles that she apologized shamefacedly.

And how did Katie feel? Apparently she was no happier. On October 21, 1859, as shown by her inscription on the flyleaf of each volume, she bought a two-volume set of Lamb's essays. As she read and marked, she left evidence of a disturbed state of mind. In the style of handwriting characteristic of her at this period, she copied on a blank page at the back of the second volume:

> Adieu, les jours de mon enfance,
> Adieu, mes premiers beaux jours;
> La vie est une morne silence
> Où le coeur appelle toujours!

On a page of Lamb's essay "New Year's Eve," she marked the sentence: "A new state of being staggers me." Perhaps the painfulness of her situation led to the next marking: "Whatsoever thwarts, or puts me out of my way, brings death into my mind." Elsewhere she bracketed these lines: "Methinks it is better that I should have pined away seven of my goldenest years, when I was thrall to the fair hair, and fairer eyes, of Alice W——n, than that so passionate a love adventure should be lost."

Lamb's essay "The Superannuated Man" interested her, and on a page of it she marked the sentence: "For the first day or two I felt stunned, overwhelmed. I could only apprehend my felicity; I was too confused to taste it sincerely. I wandered about, thinking I was happy, and knowing that I was not."

These markings, of course, cannot be dated except by reference to the date on which the books were purchased — October 21, 1859. But in moments of great emotional stress it was

Kate's habit to mark, in any book that she happened to be reading at the time, just those passages that reflected her troubled
state of mind. She can be shown repeatedly doing the same
thing at periods which can be dated with great exactness. Moreover, her books were to remain in storage for nearly thirty
years. When she recovered them in old age, she was not likely
to have a new experience evoking similar feelings. All that can
be said with certainty, however, is that she would have reacted
as these passages suggest.

There is no reason to doubt that Kate suffered — then and
afterwards — because of her intimacy with Emily Dickinson.
Nor would it be just to blame her for a catastrophe toward
which Emily had been driving since the days of her infatuation
with Susan Gilbert, when she had written to a friend: "The
shore is safer, Abiah, but I love to buffet the sea . . . oh, I love
the danger!"

There was to be danger enough, and shameful humiliation,
fear of madness, acid disillusionment. At times Emily would
arraign a God who had brought her into a world where she could
have no hope of fulfillment, and she would write bitterly of the
woman who had injured her; but she never regretted that she
had loved. Love was her coming of age. She was not ignorant
of the usual meaning of words when she referred to her twenty-
fourth year as her "little girlhood" or when she described herself as a child or a schoolgirl up to her twenty-ninth year. Her
method of reckoning was symbolic. Any doubt of her intent is
swept away by the several poems in which she described her
belated emotional and poetic maturing. One of these poems
she sent to Katie, perhaps in this same fall of 1859:

> There are two ripenings, one of sight,
> Whose forces spheric wind,
> Until the velvet product
> Drops spicy to the ground.
> A homelier maturing,

> A process in the burr
> That teeth of frosts alone disclose
> In far October air.

Out of the symbolic context, this poem is nonsense. It is a mere horticultural note: Peaches ripen in summer, nuts in the fall. Originally the poem may have contained another stanza, or the accompanying letter a sentence, that clarified the meaning. At all events, Emily meant Kate to understand that she herself was the chestnut burr — a bit homely, a bit late in maturing, but sound and sweet.

"The gentian is a greedy flower," she wrote to Mrs. Holland in September of that same 1859. The gentian was her personal symbol in another poem that described her late emotional maturing. "God made a little gentian," the poem began. This gentian, unaware of her destiny, tried to become a rose and was the laughingstock of the entire summer. But in the autumn she blossomed into such beauty that mockery was silenced. The last line of the poem is in quotation marks. Perhaps Emily addressed it, not to her Father in Heaven, but to her "small Deity" on earth:

> "Creator! shall I bloom?"

✥ VI ✥

KATE SCOTT returned to Amherst in February or March, 1860. The evidence is in a letter to her from Emily Dickinson. Apparently written about June and dated 1860, it refers to a visit of the preceding winter or early spring. Of course, when Kate attempted to date Emily's letters some thirty years afterwards, she could have made mistakes, but she obviously believed that this summer letter referred to her visit of early 1860. The visit itself she was not likely to forget. It was momentous.

In old age Kate's memory hovered painfully around these wintry days of early 1860. She did not mention Emily in her letters to Sue Dickinson (a curious omission, suggesting a wound too sore to touch or a sensitive knowledge of Sue's jealousy). But the impression is given that Emily's name is barely below the surface.

Longing to be once more in Amherst, Kate wrote to Sue: "I recall those sleigh rides with Austin. How young we were, how happy, how *merry!* How careless! What spirits!

"O world! Oh life! O Time!
On these last steps I climb

143

> Trembling at that where I had stood before
> When will return the glory of your prime?
> No *more* — O *never more!*"

At another time she wrote: "I am thinking of the old precious days, when we were so happy. They seem now like a blissful dream! How joyous we were! I think we laughed all the time! I must not indulge in this strain or the tears will blind my eyes." Troubled by the estrangement between Sue and Lavinia, she wrote to her own sister-in-law, Lila: "It was so sad when I remembered how happy we were all together in years gone by."

After the death of Sue Dickinson, Kate Anthon wrote more freely of Emily. In a long letter of 1914 to Martha Dickinson Bianchi, she recalled tenderly many details of their friendship:

> *Such genius and mysticism as Emily possessed often tran-*
> *scends mortal comprehension. It [the preface to* The
> Single Hound] *carries me back to the old blissful evenings*
> *at Austin's! Rare hours, full of merriment, brilliant wit,*
> *and inexhaustible laughter, Emily with her dog and lantern,*
> *often at the piano playing weird melodies — all from her*
> *own inspiration. Oh, she was a choice spirit!*

With sadness she continued: "Those heavenly nights are gone forever! One can only live on the memory of them!"

On those wintry evenings of early 1860 Bowles and Kate, and indeed the whole party, laid aside their dignity and romped. The tall woman in mourning black and the taller man played a spirited game of battledore and shuttlecock, while from the sidelines Emily kept score in her high, excited voice and interrupted the game with her pranks. Or Emily played the piano for Kate, who was always fatally susceptible to music of any kind. In quieter moments the two friends held hands or sat with their arms around each other's waist.

Time passed without their knowledge. At midnight they were surprised by the rays of Mr. Dickinson's lantern advancing across the snowy lawn. Then Emily made a face at the company and escaped over the snow with her dog Carlo. Safe in her own room, she placed her lantern in the west window to flash a signal to the other house. But at this point the anecdote seems to falter, for Mrs. Bianchi says that a lantern in Sue's east window gave back a "fond response." The gesture seems out of character for Sue. Perhaps Emily's signal was intended to reach Kate, and perhaps it was Kate who responded.

If Kate and Emily actually put lanterns in their windows, they may have taken a hint from the symbolism of another poet. In the early summer of 1860, some months after this visit, Emily wrote to her friend: "Distinctly sweet your face stands in its phantom niche." The word "niche" is reminiscent of Poe's verses "To Helen." But Emily cared little for Poe, and Kate never mentioned him and did not own a copy of his poems. Both women, however, were extravagant admirers of Elizabeth Browning. Emily's allusion is most probably to certain lines of *Aurora Leigh* in which the heroine offers a refuge to her young friend Marian Erle:

> And in my Tuscan home I'll find a niche
> And set thee there, my saint, the child and thee,
> And burn the lights of love before thy face,
> And ever at thy sweet look cross myself
> From mixing with the world's prosperities;
> That so, in gravity and holy calm,
> We two may live on toward the truer life.

The allusion to a "phantom niche" could have been Emily's way of addressing Kate as "my saint," reminding her that the "lights of love" still burned before her face, and recalling a dream of escape to an Italian paradise.

2

On this visit of early 1860 Kate Scott apparently brought with her, or was given by one of her Amherst friends, a copy of Hillard's *Six Months in Italy*. On the flyleaf she wrote "Kate Turner." On the title page, however, appears a brief inscription in another handwriting: "Katie, Feb/60." Afterwards Kate herself appears to have erased those words. Finally, in the shaky hand of old age, she wrote over the erasure in this fashion: "K. T. Feb/60." The original inscription can be made out, but the handwriting has not been identified. Nor is there any explanation of this incident — except that Kate sometimes erased unpleasant reminders from her books and diaries.

On her travels Kate always carried books. In early 1860 she would have had a particular reason for bringing to Amherst Hillard's popular book about Italy. Her Amherst friends were enthusiastic about *Aurora Leigh,* which devotes much space to Italy, and more especially, to Florence. Kate may have read aloud from Hillard's book during her Amherst visit (she was to read aloud from duller books at other times), and Emily may have been impressed anew by the traveler's commonplace of the sudden and dramatic change from Alpine snows to Italian vineyards.

In the summer of 1860 Emily reminded Kate of her recent visit in these words:

> It's but a little past, dear, and yet how far from here it seems, fled with the snow! So through the snow go many loving feet parted by "Alps." How brief, from vineyards and the sun!

The "loving feet" were those of the two friends. The "Alps" may have stood for the practical considerations which separated them. The "vineyards and the sun" were the happiness that they found together.

Perhaps Kate knew the poem "Our lives are Swiss," or it may have accompanied this letter. Poem and letter are identical in meaning. On "some odd afternoon," says the poet, the Alps lift their curtain of mist, and from our cool Swiss heights we glimpse the warm, alluring sensuousness of Italy. But we are debarred from entering paradise; the guardian Alps "forever intervene." In another poem beginning "It always felt to me a wrong," Emily warmly sympathized with Moses, who also was given a glimpse of the promised land and forbidden to enter it.

Like many other poets of northern climes Emily Dickinson was in love with the South. She also valued the cool discipline and the austerity that she associated with the North, and these two sides of her nature warred in her perpetually. The South symbolized escape and sensuous freedom. Just as one stripped off heavy layers of clothing on a tropic island (the poet dreamed of the "spicy isles"), so one stripped off the stifling Puritan taboos against pleasure and lived in the sun of enjoyment. Emily was far from being the cool New England nun of popular fancy; she was a sensuous, passionate woman. In her love of the sun and of the South she could have written with Sappho: "For me richness and beauty belong to the desire of the sunlight." Emily undoubtedly read the fragments of Sapphic verse published by her friend Higginson in 1871, and she herself may have noticed resemblances of temperament. In the driving passion and intensity of her poems she was a Sappho without the informed sensuality.

In her first youth Emily identified Susan Gilbert with the South — "the love South." Sue was "Egypt," and had a "torrid spirit" and "depths of Domingo." Then Kate appeared on the scene, and in a poem ("As the starved maelstrom laps the navies") Emily wrote of hungering for "a berry of Domingo and a torrid eye." With her dark hair and brilliant dark eyes, Kate looked somewhat like Sue, but she had a warmth and a

passion of which Sue gave little evidence. So pronounced was
Kate's longing for the South and sunlight that a friend of later
years made a particular reference to her passion for "brighter
climes." She spent as much of her life as possible on the French
and Italian Rivieras and in other sunny spots of Italy. The
transfer of the southern symbolism to Kate was appropriate,
indeed well-nigh inescapable.

It was made easier by the reading of *Aurora Leigh,* which
speaks fervently of "the white walls, the blue hills, my Italy."
Kate admired the poem no less warmly than Emily. Later on,
in Florence, she made pilgrimages to Mrs. Browning's grave
and home, and even sought out Mrs. Browning's old servant,
Liza Wilson. From the hill of Bellosguardo, where the fictitious
Aurora Leigh had rented a villa, Kate brought away a leaf and
tucked it into her guidebook with this inscription: "Bellosguardo, Florence, March 26th, 1873." During those wintry days
of early 1860 she and Emily dreamed of Italy, and for Kate the
dream came true.

In lines that must have echoed in the minds of her two
devoted readers, Mrs. Browning wrote of the "perfect solitude
of foreign lands":

> A new world all alive with creatures new,
> New sun, new moon, new flowers, new people — ah,
> And be possessed by none of them! . . .
> — Such most surprising riddance of one's life
> Comes next one's death; 'tis disembodiment
> Without the pang.

To Emily, who had once hidden in a wood to avoid being questioned by her neighbors, and who described death as "Escape
from Circumstances, and a Name," Mrs. Browning's Italy must
have seemed very desirable. With Kate she would talk wistfully
of the joy of visiting Florence. Years later Kate Anthon took a

young friend to live with her in Florence, and her first act upon settling young Florie in their new home was to read aloud from *Aurora Leigh*. It was as if she were consummating a dream that she had been unable to realize with her earlier friend.

"My Italy of women" — with these words the lover in Mrs. Browning's poem sums up its heroine. Kate Scott became Emily Dickinson's "Italy of Women." The old southern symbolism fused with the new love for Kate and for the *Aurora Leigh* and the Italy of Mrs. Browning. Kate's Italian journey in 1864 completed the fusion; the blue hills and the bluer seas of Italy set the color; and Kate Scott, or perhaps the love that she stood for, became the "blue peninsula" of Emily's longing imagination.

In the last years of her life Emily Dickinson wrote a poem about two butterflies. Some two-thirds of the way down the manuscript page appears the isolated word "peninsula." Neither Emily nor her editor, Mrs. Bingham, could find any way to use the word, and it disappeared from the printed page. But it had significance for Emily. Kate was the peninsula, and she was also one of the two butterflies. The connection was perfectly clear to Emily, even though she never decided how to employ the word in this particular poem.

At the end of a little note Emily once signed herself "Butterfly." The poem beginning "The butterfly obtains but little sympathy" may be, in part, a sly symbolizing of herself, for she liked to play with the idea that she was a bright, many-colored creature with no time or taste for the homely tasks of drudging mortals. In a poem already discussed, "When diamonds are a legend," she recalled a summer day when she had had customers, a queen and a butterfly, both apparently Kate Scott. Of course, there are many butterflies, bees, and other creatures in the poems, and some of them are real; but it was the nature of this poet to see in symbols. If the butterflies disappear, especially at noontide, or suffer unreasonable punishment, or if any nature poem has a moral that is unduly heavy, there is reason to suspect symbolism. No butterflies ever justified the weight of the moral in the "peninsula" poem.

The poem may be interpreted in this fashion: "Two butter-flies [Emily and her friend] went out at noon." "Noon" is a frequent symbol for the zenith of love. They had an extraordinarily good time gamboling in the sun (again the symbolism of the South and of warmth). At length, "rapture missed her footing": they made a sad mistake. In an alternate line, the butterflies were overcome by "gravitation," which might be interpreted as the strong, centralizing pull of society. "And both were wrecked in noon": they were destroyed at the high point of their happiness. An alternate line, which the editor rejected, is perhaps still clearer: "And they were hurled from noon"; that is, they were thrown down from the zenith of love. The moral is that the butterflies demanded too much happiness from the world and paid a heavy price for their mistake. Emily hopes that their fate will be a lesson to all "surviving butter-flies."

The tone is playful; Emily has outlived the bitterest part of her suffering. The curious circumstance is that in her last years she still meditated about the woman who had been butter-fly and peninsula to her. Yet it is no more surprising than the fact that Kate Anthon mourned Emily three decades longer.

The symbolism of the two butterflies was attractive to Emily Dickinson. She wrote still another version of the poem. Here the butterflies are not wrecked; they are borne away "upon a shining sea" and simply never come back. That is, the two devoted, happy young women disappear; the two sobering women who remain are no longer butterflies.

To believe that so subtle and witty a poet as Emily Dickinson should devote, not merely one, but two poems, to the simple, natural fact that butterflies have short lives, would seem to make light of her intelligence. Either these butterflies have human faces, or the moral is grotesque. But if the poems are interpreted symbolically, the isolated word "peninsula" is explained, and the poems themselves become meaningful and take their place in the intricate web of Emily's symbolism. It remains only to determine why the two butterflies suffered so cruelly.

3

Early in 1860 Lavinia Dickinson paid another long visit to the Norcross cousins in Boston. She left Emily in sole possession of the southwest bedroom, which the two sisters commonly shared. As Emily looked about this room in later years, she wrote sadly:

> Sweet hours have perished here;
>   This is a mighty room;
> Within its precincts hopes have played, —
>   Now shadows in the tomb.

That is, the hopes were in the tomb, not necessarily the person involved in the hopes. Emily herself died too often, rested too often in her grave, for any literal interpretation of poems describing the death of a loved person. Repeatedly she imagined her friend dead; it was the only way she saw of their being together again.

Apparently the two friends slept together in Emily's room on a night of late February or early March, 1860. The ease and naturalness of such an occurrence render it at least plausible. But what happened on that night, as very circumstantially related in the poems, may not be so easily believed.

A poem which survived in a version with feminine pronouns begins with these lines:

> Her sweet weight on my heart a night
> Had scarcely deigned to lie,
> When, stirring for belief's delight,
> My bride had slipped away.

> If 'twas a dream, . . .

And the poet goes on to say very plainly that it was not a dream. The third line, "When, stirring for belief's delight," describes accurately the uneasy sleep of lovers. The fourth line anticipates, not the dawn of that actual day, but the time, much later, when her "bride" did slip away from her.

Another poem, apparently describing the same night, uses masculine pronouns. It begins:

> He was weak and I was strong, then,
> So he let me lead him in.

That is, she persuaded her friend to accompany her into her own house.

> I was weak and he was strong, then,
> So I let him lead me home.

The word "home" is symbolic; it means "toward love." In other words, after the friend is invited into the actual house, the two women spend some moments of indecision, and then the friend suggests that they spend the night together and successfully overcomes Emily's hesitation.

The next stanza describes the tense, wordless excitement in which they climbed the stairs and entered Emily's room. Finally:

> Day knocked, and we must part,
> Neither was strongest now,
> He strove, and I strove too.
> We didn't do it though!

A third poem suggests a confused memory as to who proposed the night together. It may have been decided almost
without words. "He was my host, he was my guest," Emily
wrote. She could not remember who asked the other, but the
interview that followed was "infinite" and "intimate" beyond
her powers to analyze.

Still another poem, "Title divine is mine," unmistakably
indicates that their love was not consummated. It ends on an
uncertain note, with the recollection that women say "my
husband" as if they were "stroking the melody." The reason
for the poet's uncertainty should be obvious. That Emily
Dickinson referred to another woman as her bride and her husband, and described herself as "wed" to this other woman,
may seem fantastic. It is not fantastic at all in the light of
Kate's subsequent history.

A fragmentary poem, which survives in Emily's late handwriting, may be a recollection of the fruitless struggle of this
same night:

> 'Tis seasons since the dimpled war
> In which we each were conqueror
>   And each of us were slain,
>
> And centuries 'twill be and more
> Another massacre before
>   So modest and so vain.
>
> Without a formula we fought,
> Each was to each the pink redoubt

·   ·   ·   ·   ·

The poet was unable to continue. A poem already quoted ("He
was weak and I was strong, then") describes a similarly in-
conclusive struggle: "We didn't do it though!" Was she defend-
ing herself or expressing bitter regret that they had stopped

short? The latter would appear to be true. In the poem "Had I known that the first was the last," she compared the fulfillment of love to drinking from a cup. If she had known that the cup would be offered her only this one time, she would "have mixed it stronger."

Another poem, "One year ago jots what," written apparently a year after the crucial night, reads in part:

> I tasted careless then.
> I did not know the wine
> Came once a world, did you?
> Oh, had you told me so,
> This thirst would blister easier now!

In one poem, "I could suffice for Him, I knew," she describes the proposal as having been made rather quietly. They were aware, she says, that their two fractions would make one whole, but they hesitated before the enormity of the step. Then the friend made the suggestion, and Emily's "syllable rebelled." Significantly it appeared against *nature* and against God. Before Emily could make up her mind, "withdrew the Sun to other Wests," and decision came too late. She often identified Kate with the sun, usually the setting sun.

Other poems manifestly bearing on that night suggest that the interview was stormy. In "One year ago jots what," already mentioned, she wrote that her friend had complained of greater sufferings:

> You said it hurt you most,
> Mine was an acorn's breast . . .

Then follow misleading references to the other's "shaggier vest" and greater maturity. Emily had in mind another maturity than that of age. Although Emily and Kate herself used the name "Kate Scott," it should not be forgotten that the

young woman was actually Kate Turner. A widow might have
called Emily a child, inexperienced in love and incapable of
understanding its pains. In this poem Emily replied, apparently
a year later, that the child had now suffered enough to be considered adult.

In another poem, "I rose because he sank," she described a
contest of wills between them and declared that her moral
strength had proved superior to her lover's. In two interesting
stanzas suppressed by Mrs. Bianchi (afterwards published by
Mrs. Bingham), there is a suggestion that the friend suffered
agony:

> I cheered my fainting prince,
> I sang firm steady chants,
> I stayed his film with hymn.
>
> And when the dews drew off
> That held his forehead stiff,
> I gave him balm for balm.

Although Emily was shocked and frightened by this episode,
it did not destroy her love for Kate. There was a pleasurable
excitement in her alarm, a delightful sense of having ventured
perilously close to the volcanic center of life, plus a large incre-
ment of self-esteem. In "A pit — but heaven over it," she suggested that they were each other's doom.

In the early summer of 1860 Emily wrote to Kate Scott:

> *I touch your hand — my cheek your cheek — I stroke
> your vanished hair. Why did you enter, sister, since you
> must depart? Had not its heart been torn enough but you
> must send your shred?*

The poems make it abundantly clear that the two women
spent only one night together. Either they were too badly
frightened to repeat the experience, or it was the last night of

Kate's stay in Amherst. Otherwise there would have been an
opportunity, for Lavinia did not return to Amherst until late
April or early May. Long before that time Kate had apparently
gone back to Cooperstown.

In the *Springfield Republican* for March 17, 1860, Emily
read that Dr. Holland had just returned to Springfield after a
long lecture tour. Shortly afterwards she wrote to Mrs. Holland
to express her joy that husband and wife were once more together:

> *Vive le fireside! Am told that fasting gives to food
> marvelous Aroma, but by birth a Bachelor, disavow
> Cuisine.*

"Food" was her constant symbol for love, and she had just been
given a notable opportunity for "disavowing Cuisine." The
language was daring, but very likely Mrs. Holland did not
understand it.

The letter continues:

> *Meeting is well worth parting. How kind in some to
> die, adding* impatience *to the rapture of our thought of
> Heaven!*

In the passage just quoted Emily Dickinson mentally buried
her lover and anticipated the joy of their meeting in heaven.
Then followed a poem, "As by the dead we love to sit," which
had little relevance to Mrs. Holland's situation but was
markedly appropriate to her own. The poem suggests that Emily
had just parted with a friend whose value increased in propor-
tion to the distance between them.

In the next paragraph Emily continued this notion of a
heavenly reunion, but she also appeared to give a rueful
thought to the ease with which Kate moved about the country:

People with **Wings** *at option, look loftily at hands and feet, which induces watchfulness! How gay to love one's friends! How passing gay to fancy that they reciprocate the whim, tho' by the Seas divided, tho' by a single Daisy hidden from our eyes!*

The "seas" are evidently symbolic; Emily had not a friend abroad at this time. In the following summer she wrote to Kate of her fear that the latter might die: "Therefore I guard you more." It is understandable that she would not always be consistent in her wish for a reunion in heaven and her wish for a continuance of earthly happiness. As for the "Daisy" that might hide a loved friend from her eye, she must have written at about this time the poem beginning "Here, where the daisies fit my head," in which she imagined that her friend was buried beside her. The poem ends with the statement that the two women made up "a single bloom . . . departed or at home." The line "departed or at home" is also the last line of a poem beginning "The day she goes or day she stays." It is suggested that both poems were first written in March, 1860, while Emily was sorrowing over the departure of Katie and writing to Mrs. Holland of the "single Daisy" that could hide loved friends from the eye.

In the last lines of her letter to Mrs. Holland (March, 1860), Emily gave striking evidence of morbid excitement. Her sister was still in Boston, she wrote, and consequently she was often afraid at night. The furniture seemed to move around the room. Although she wrote gaily, there is no reason to doubt that she spoke the truth. The furniture did seem to move around the room — that "mighty room."

Mrs. Holland was an intimate friend. Perhaps in time she came to know something of the causes which underlay this excitement and the anguish that soon followed. It appears certain that she destroyed every letter from Emily between early

1860 and late 1865. Surviving letters of this period to less intimate friends like Samuel and Mary Bowles suggest the misery that Emily may have poured out to Mrs. Holland. Years later Mrs. Holland seemed to understand Emily's reason for seeking help from the Reverend Charles Wadsworth, and both she and Dr. Holland assisted in carrying on the secret correspondence.

4

Of great significance are the poems in which Emily Dickinson described a momentous moral choice. They have led many readers and some biographers to assume that she was in love with a married man. But the poems are just as applicable in a strong attachment to a woman friend, and certain details are more readily explained by this hypothesis.

In a key poem Emily wrote:

> To make one's toilette, after Death
> Has made the toilette cool
> To only taste we care to please
> Is difficult; and still —
>
> That's easier than braid the hair
> And make the bodice gay,
> When eyes that fondled it are wrenched
> By Decalogues away.

The poet was separated from her lover, not by the ten commandments usually cited, but by unwritten decalogues. As for the details about her dress and hair, an unworldly clergyman was not likely to compliment her. The fastidious, dress-conscious Katie would certainly have done so. Her later Florentine diary and letters were filled with approval of young Florie's appearance. It is true that Kate Scott was attracted to beauty,

but she had the amiable quality of finding beauty where she
was attracted. She would have been the one person to whom
Emily was ever wholly beautiful, for it is certain that she loved
Emily.

"I had not minded walls," wrote Emily Dickinson. She
would tunnel through a universe of solid rock to reach her
lover, but the barrier was a "hair, a filament, a law, a cob-
web" —

> A limit like the veil
> Unto the lady's face,
> But every mesh a citadel
> And dragons in the crease!

In imagination she appeared to be looking directly at the veiled
face of her friend. "The lady" was one of her many ways of
referring to the person she loved.

By her own account Emily Dickinson ransacked history for
sufferings and martyrdoms as cruel as her own. She was attracted by the story of Thermopylae and especially by the last
words of the doomed Spartans: "We die in obedience to law."
Apparently she thought of herself as dying in obedience to the
moral law. The poem " 'Go tell it' — what a message!" ends
with a significant rejection:

> Obeyed a lure, a longing?
> Oh, Nature, none of this!
> "To law," said sweet Thermopylae,
> "Convey my dying kiss."

"God gave a loaf to every bird," wrote Emily Dickinson, but
to her He gave only a crumb. She could "own it, touch it," yet
dared not eat it, though she starved.

In a poem beginning

> I play at riches to appease
> The clamoring for gold

she appeared to say that there had been a time, perhaps more than one time, when she might have stolen a little love. Instead she contented herself with describing what she could not have. Other poems suggest that she was not fully convinced of the value of sublimation. Love was life, and poetry was a barren substitute.

A fervent admirer of Emily Dickinson wrote to Mrs. Bianchi: "With every impulse to go to hell, with the whole lineage of martyrs to passion sanctioning it, from Sappho to Byron, she just didn't. Sappho became Puritan." But Emily Dickinson did not escape martyrdom. The poems are a record of intense suffering.

5 🖙

Much of the imagery is erotic, even consciously erotic. Words like "noon," "sun," "dew," "crowned," "bread," "water," and, in some instances, "home" and "sea" are erotic symbols. Love is represented as climbing mountains, drinking from a well or a cup, flying, sailing on the sea, diving into the sea. The loss of love becomes starvation, suffocation, intolerable thirst, dessication, death. Clearest of all is the symbolism involving bees and flowers.

It began innocently with a long, nonsensical valentine of 1850 to Mr. Bowdoin, a young lawyer in her father's office:

> The bee doth court the flower, the flower his suit receives.

In a letter urging her brother to pay a visit, Emily naïvely likened him to a bee and herself to a garden, but innocence vanished from the later symbolism.

"Bee" was one of Emily Dickinson's favorite words. Many of the bees are doubtless real, but a few are symbolic. Com-

monly the poet is the bee and the friend the rose, although the
pattern shows interesting variations. In the March letter Emily
identified Katie with the rose. In "Here, where the daisies fit
my head," she apparently referred to Kate as "my flower";
indeed both women are flowers and make up "a single bloom."
Incidentally, this poem was written or copied in the early
eighteen-sixties.

As the attachment strengthened, the rôles wavered back and
forth, even in the compass of one poem, with the friend tend-
ing to become the bee by reason of superior aggressiveness. After
the friend withdrew — became alienated and inert — the poet
assumed the active rôle and searched for her vanished rose.
This confusion was probably an unconscious product of changing relationships, but it appears noteworthy that Emily most
commonly assumed the dominant, or masculine, rôle.

The poem beginning "Because the bee may blameless hum"
is early. If there is any sexual symbolism, it is unconscious.
The poet is in love and cannot reveal her love. She proposes
to become not only the bee but also the flower and even a robin,
for none of these need hide or be afraid to see the lover. It has
been suggested, in a previous chapter, that this poem was written
in the late summer of 1859.

A short poem, "Oh, honey of an hour," is marked by a wild
disorder in the symbolism. At first the poet is the bee: never
before had she known the power of this honey. But in the
closing lines she entreats postponement until her "unfre-
quented flower" is worthy. The poem seems to reflect a good
deal of emotional confusion — very natural under the circumstances. It was probably written in early 1860.

A poem beginning "Did the harebell loose her girdle," in
which the poet is the flower and the lover the bee, would seem
to belong to the same period. The symbolism is explicit and
unmistakable. If the harebell admits its bee-lover, will the bee
continue to respect the harebell? If the paradise yields its
defenses,

> Would the Eden be an Eden,
>   Or the earl an earl?

Here the earl stands for the lover; in other poems, for Emily herself.

In a poem beginning "The Flower must not blame the Bee," Emily is the bee and a woman friend is the flower. The poet fears that she may seek her "felicity" too often at the door of her friend. She suggests that the latter instruct "the footman from Vevay" to deny admittance to his mistress. This is the kind of apology that a young woman might make if she feared that her letters or her visits were becoming too numerous. It should be compared with two other poems. In "Is bliss, then, such abyss," Emily playfully anticipates the displeasure of "the lady." In "What shall I do it whimpers so," she apparently begs to be allowed to visit some one in the house next door.

The word "Vevay" of the poem under discussion brings up an interesting problem. Another poem begins:

> Pigmy seraphs gone astray,
> Velvet people from Vevay.

It has been assumed that Emily acquired both her knowledge and her misspelling of Vevey, Switzerland, from the 1862 travels of her friend Samuel Bowles. Yet the spelling "Vevay" was probably the more common at the period, and the little town was a well-known resort. In the spring of 1873 Kate herself was to go to "Vevay" (she corrected her spelling after she arrived), and here she received a letter from Sue Dickinson. Apparently she was interested in Switzerland as early as 1860, and her failure to see it in 1864 was one of the keenest disappointments of her trip abroad. There is no way of knowing all the reading and the interests that she may have shared with Emily as early as 1860. But if the two "Vevay" poems were written after Bowles' trip of 1862, then a question arises as to the possibility, indicated by still other poems, that the friendship between Kate and Emily may have had a brief, disappointing renewal.

The question is raised again by a poem beginning "I envy seas whereon he rides." It looks very much as if it were written at the time of Kate's Italian voyage of 1864. Of course, Kate was now engaged to John Anthon, but in a later chapter it will be shown that she went abroad in a troubled state of mind, perhaps in an effort to reach a decision. That Kate was the person Emily meant seems indicated by the following stanza:

> Yet interdict my blossom
>   And abrogate my bee,
> Lest noon in everlasting night
>   Drop Gabriel and me.

That is, flower and bee long to come together, but fear to be dropped from the "noon" of love to the "everlasting night" of unhappiness and damnation.

But why "Gabriel"? He is the angel of the Annunciation, but in this poem he is also very clearly a pet name for Emily's lover. In 1860–61 Kate was reading (probably, rereading) Longfellow's *Evangeline*. She marked lines which suggest that she was reaching a painful decision, and she enclosed between the pages leaflets from her Shakespeare calendar which strengthen this suggestion (they will be quoted in the following chapter). Twenty years later she read the poem aloud to her young friend Florie. Did it have significance for her and Emily? Did Emily know she was reading the poem in the winter of 1860–61? Probably there will never be any definite answer. But Gabriel, the hero of the poem, disappears into the West, and his patient Evangeline searches vainly for him through a lifetime.

In a poem beginning "It makes no difference abroad," Emily is again the bee in search of her vanished rose. Another poem,

"Come slowly, Eden!" must also have been written after the friend was lost and while Emily drugged her pain with the notion that they would meet in Paradise. Unaccustomed to its jasmines, she must sip bashfully,

> As the fainting bee,
>
> Reaching late his flower,
> Round her chamber hums,
> Counts his nectars — enters,
> And is lost in balms!

It was never clear to Emily why she must be separated from her friend. The problem was one of those that she must take to God. Many poems express her hope that the inexplicable barriers of this world will be absent from the next, and that she will rejoin the person she loves. Among them is a poem beginning "Of all the souls that stand create." It speaks of a time when "subterfuge" will end, and draws an apocalyptic picture of the unveiling of that "atom" which she preferred to all other created souls. Still other poems assert that there was only one person, one lover, one lost paradise in her life. When they are finally dated and arranged in order, they will show that she continued to brood about her lost friend until she died.

There are poems, however, which were not written to Kate or indeed to any real person. They lack reality and appear to be no more than vague wishes. Into this group fall such poems as "I'm ceded; I've stopped being theirs"; "I'm wife; I've finished that"; "She rose to his requirement, dropped"; "I gave myself to him." Apparently the taboo on one relationship drove her to fantasies of an attachment that would meet social approval. How Kate was connected with these fantasies seems indicated by a poem beginning "I learned at least what home could be." Emily writes that she has been taught the meaning of love by

> This pattern of the way
> Whose memory drowns me like the dip
> Of a celestial sea.

Unfortunately the friendly courtesies of men like Higginson, Bowles, and Wadsworth were pallid stuff beside the breathing, vital passion of her knowledge. She was forced back repeatedly to the only real experience that she had ever known. Living in seclusion, she had nothing to cultivate but her memories.

✦ VII ✦

IN THE EARLY SUMMER of 1860 Emily Dickinson wrote another of her many letters to Kate Scott. It is the second, and the most loving and lyrical, of the three afterwards published. Kate valued it so highly that she carried it in her writing portfolio until she died.

[*Amherst. 1860*]

The prettiest of pleas, dear, but with a lynx like me quite unavailable. Finding is slow, facilities for losing so frequent, in a world like this, I hold with extreme caution. A prudence so astute may seem unnecessary, but plenty moves those most dear, who have been in want, and Saviour tells us, Kate, the poor are always with us. Were you ever poor? I have been a beggar, and rich to-night, as by God's leave I believe I am, the "lazzaronis'" faces haunt, pursue me still!

You do not yet "dislimn," Kate. Distinctly sweet your face stands in its phantom niche — I touch your hand —

my cheek your cheek — I stroke your vanished hair. Why did you enter, sister, since you must depart? Had not its heart been torn enough but you must send your shred?

Oh, our condor Kate! Come from your crags again! Oh, dew upon the bloom fall yet again a summer's night! Of such have been the frauds which have vanquished faces, sown plant of flesh the church-yard plats, and occassioned angels.

There is a subject, dear, on which we never touch. Ignorance of its pageantries does not deter me. I too went out to meet the dust early in the morning. I too in daisy mounds possess hid treasure, therefore I guard you more. You did not tell me you had once been a "millionaire." Did my sister think that opulence could be mistaken? Some trinket will remain, some babbling plate or jewel.

I write you from the summer. The murmuring leaves fill up the chinks through which the winter red shone when Kate was here, and Frank was here, and frogs sincerer than our own splash in their Maker's pools. It's but a little past, dear, and yet how far from here it seems, fled with the snow! So through the snow go many loving feet parted by "Alps." How brief, from vineyards and the sun!

Parents and Vinnie request love to be given girl.

EMILIE.

This letter has been in print for almost sixty years without directing attention toward Kate Scott. Apparently the best way of insuring a mystery is to put all the clues in plain sight. If the interpretation is unwelcome, it will not be seen. However, a second, partial explanation must be mentioned.

The letter just quoted is one of strong feeling, but, except for a few lines, it is scarcely more sentimental than many a letter from Emily to Mrs. Holland. The emotion is expressed in figures or by allusion. Some phrases would be meaningful to

Kate alone. In fact, if the letter had been more open, Kate would never have let it be published. As it was, she hesitated.

Emily begs the "dew" of love to fall once more upon a summer night. She speaks of the "Alps" which separate lovers from "vineyards and the sun." She alludes to the "phantom niche" — a very probable reference, as already noted, to lines of high emotional content in Mrs. Browning's *Aurora Leigh*. She describes the poverty of her life prior to her meeting with Kate. She has been a "beggar" for love. "And rich to-night, as by God's leave I believe I am" (words of strong, deep emotion), Emily is still hauntingly afraid that this love will go the way of all the others. In imagination she is pursued by the faces of beggars — "lazzaronis."

One or two puzzles should be noted. In the fourth paragraph Emily alludes to the surprising fact that Kate has never spoken of her dead husband — or, rather, has never indicated that she once loved him and now mourns him. Emily approaches the subject delicately, but her real purpose is to demand emotional usury through the fear of death. In the fifth paragraph she refers to "Frank," as if "Frank" might have been Kate's companion. Sue Dickinson had two brothers, one of them called Frank, but apparently Emily was somewhat formal in speaking of Thomas and Francis Gilbert. Kate had a woman friend, Frank Newton of Flatbush, whom she may have brought with her to Amherst, just as she was to bring another friend later on.

"Our condor Kate" (a striking tribute to the other woman's height and commanding personality) is urged to leave her crags and come again to Amherst. Apparently Kate was then in Cooperstown. However, she was soon to pay a long visit to her sister, Maggie Bartlett, who had recently borne her first child. Kate's "prettiest of pleas" may have been that she could not leave her sister in order to visit Emily.

About this time Emily knitted a pair of garters and sent them to Kate with the following doggerel:

When Katie walks this simple pair accompany her side, —
When Katie runs, unwearied, they travel on the road,
When Katie kneels, their loving bands still clasp her
    pious knee.
Oh Katie, smile at fortune with two so *knit* to thee.

                                     EMILIE

But in the summer of 1860 Katie was not smiling at fortune. Apparently she was much disturbed. By the evidence of the poems, by the evidence of her behavior during this summer and afterwards, and — it may be guessed — because of her greater knowledge of passion, she was now suffering more painfully than Emily Dickinson. She must have been still more shocked and frightened by the compulsiveness of her actions. Nothing else explains so well the violence of the efforts by which she wrenched free of a disastrous attachment. To save herself, it was necessary to be cruel, and she was not by nature a cruel woman.

Emily's allusion to De Quincey's *Suspiria de Profundis* (in the word "dislimn" of her letter to Kate) suggests that both women were then reading this work. Kate marked the passage to which Emily referred. Then, in her Ticknor and Fields edition of the *Suspiria,* she went on to mark still more suggestive passages. If they were marked at this time — or, as is still more probable, shortly after she broke with Emily — assuredly Kate's sighs came from the depths:

But love, which is altogether *holy, like that between two children, will revisit undoubtedly by glimpses the silence and the darkness of old age: and I repeat my belief — that, unless bodily torment should forbid it, that final experience in my sister's bed-room, or some other in which her innocence was concerned, will rise again for me, to illuminate the hours of death.* [Pages 178–79.]

Further down, on page 179, a half-sentence: "but the door was now locked, the key was taken away — and I was shut out forever." On page 197, a long passage ("Sweet becomes the grave") asserting that death will "prove but the brief summer night that had retarded a little, by a refinement of rapture, the heavenly dawn of reunion."

On page 222:

Forever I dallied with some obscure notion, how my sister's love might be made in some dim way available for delivering me from misery, or else how the misery I had suffered and was suffering might be made, in some way equally dim, the ransom for winning back her love.

On page 262: "What I wanted the quarrel for was the luxury of reconciliation."

On page 255 Kate marked a long passage beginning with the statement that God "works by earthquake." And in a footnote to page 210, enclosed with a long pencil mark, she undoubtedly recognized a description of herself:

Some minds stand nearer to the type of the original nature in man, are truer than others to the great magnet in our dark planet. Minds that are impassioned on a more colossal scale than the ordinary, deeper in their vibrations, and more extensive in the scale of their vibrations, whether in other parts of their intellectual system, they had or had not a corresponding compass, will tremble to greater depths from a fearful convulsion, and will come round by a larger curve of undulations.

Kate Scott was neither a poet nor a particularly good writer of prose. She was forced to look in others' works for the expression of her own passsionate nature. But the passages that she selected bear a striking resemblance to the spirit of Emily

Dickinson's poetry. Emily, too, was steeped in the *Suspiria*.
The passage describing the holiness of a love "like that between
two children" may have influenced Emily's poem beginning
"We learned the whole of love." After studying love by alpha-
bet, words, chapter, "then the mighty book," the two lovers
turned to each other,

> And in each other's eyes
> An ignorance beheld
> Diviner than the childhood's,
> And each to each a child
>
> Attempted to expound
> What neither understood.
> Alas, that wisdom is so large
> And truth so manifold!

Kate Scott may not have understood all of this manifold
truth, but she was beginning to be much troubled. In July,
1860, she turned for help to a new friend, Gertrude Vanderbilt.

2

Mrs. Vanderbilt has long been a puzzling but obscure figure in
the Dickinson story. Although she is likely to remain puzzling,
she can no longer escape notice. Emily's first editor, Mrs.
Todd, referred to Mrs. Vanderbilt as a friend of Emily Dickinson. Mrs. Bianchi described her as a friend of Sue Dickinson.
In truth, Mrs. Vanderbilt was — and remained — an intimate,
devoted friend of Kate Scott, and her connection with the Dickinsons was fortuitous and brief. It came, however, at a crucial
period.

Gertrude Lefferts Vanderbilt, then a woman of thirty-six to
Kate's twenty-nine, was the wife of Judge John Vanderbilt of

Kings County, New York, and the mother of a small boy, "Leffy." She was also a member of a proud old Dutch family, descendants of Pieter Leffertse (or Lefferts Pieterse, as the name is sometimes written), who received his large grant from Peter Stuyvesant. Apparently much of Flatbush was built on the old Lefferts grant. In every branch of the family one son bore the name of the founder: there were a Lefferts Vanderbilt, a Lefferts Laidlaw, a Lefferts Brevoort, even a Lefferts Lefferts.

It is impossible to describe Gertrude Vanderbilt. No one remembers whether she was tall or short, plump or slender, fair or dark. Fortunately other qualities have been better preserved. She was a woman of courage, intelligence, generosity, and tenderness — "very active, witty, gentle, vivacious, religious, and sure" (wrote a member of her family). In 1856 she converted an unoccupied cottage on her husband's estate into a Negro mission school, of which she took personal charge for the next forty years (and where Kate was to join in the singing). During the Civil War she organized a society for the benefit of Flatbush Negroes and worked hard in New York sanitary fairs to raise money and needed articles for soldiers. Toward the close of the war she almost lost her life in the courageous defense of a servant against a marauder. In later years she became secretary of the State Board of Charities and of the Brooklyn Industrial School Association, and was active in foreign mission work, and gave large sums to charities.

In the midst of these charitable activities Mrs. Vanderbilt somehow found time to manage a fairly large estate, take care of an invalid husband, and do a great deal of writing. Her *Social History of Flatbush* (1872), a meticulous account of the customs of her Dutch friends and ancestors, is well written and interesting. She also published a book for children and contributed to the *Youth's Companion, Harper's Bazaar,* and other magazines.

A woman of such vitality and charm made herself felt. Even

Emily Dickinson, who apparently came to look upon Mrs. Vanderbilt as a rival, could not entirely resist her. And on Kate
the impression was instant and lasting. She was devoted to
Mrs. Vanderbilt. During many years she wrote to her while
neglecting Sue Dickinson. In old age she noticed with concern
that Mrs. Vanderbilt's inscriptions in two gift volumes of Longfellow were beginning to fade, and she painstakingly retraced
the faded letters. Mrs. Vanderbilt had written them in the
summer of 1860.

On the flyleaf of the second volume appears the following:

> To Kate
> from Gertrude
> July 1860
> — perhaps hereafter
> When she shall learn how heartless is the world
> A voice within her will repeat my name
> And she will say, "This was indeed my friend."

The verses are adapted from *The Spanish Student.*

The flyleaf of the first volume also has an inscription, "To
Kate Turner from Gertrude 1860," followed by a note in Mrs.
Vanderbilt's handwriting: " (see page 164)." On page 164 a
pencil mark encloses a long passage of *The Spanish Student*
beginning:

> Dost thou still doubt? What I most prize in woman
> Is her affections, not her intellect!

There follow several lines in rhapsodic praise of love, and the
marked passage concludes with an emphatic "Art thou convinced?"

Mrs. Vanderbilt's affection and sympathy were expressed in
still another manner. On July 29, 1860, she copied out a long,
sentimentally religious poem entitled "The Call" and gave it

to her friend. For the rest of her life Kate treasured this manuscript, eventually placing it in her writing portfolio along with
the summer letter from Emily Dickinson.

The poem, which would be wearisome in its entirety, begins:

> Thy night is dark; behold the shade was deeper
> In the old garden of Gethsemane . . .

The suffering reader is compared to Christ on the cross and is
exhorted to practice "poverty and self renunciation," "meek
obedience," abhorrence of "the land Egyptian," and endless
patience under earthly sorrows, awaiting "the calm stillness of
regeneration." "What if thou *always* suffer tribulation?" begins one stanza, with the word *always* emphatically underlined.
Death will "gather thee to everlasting peace." Instead of seeking "aid from any human creature," the weary soul must look
to God alone:

> And he will come in his own time and power
> To set his earnest hearted children free;
> Watch only through this dark and painful hour
> And the bright morning yet will break for thee.

Religiosity like this was commonplace in the mid-nineteenth
century. Nevertheless, the poem seems exceptionally pointed,
as if Mrs. Vanderbilt knew that her friend was enduring a truly
"dark and painful hour." It would have been natural for Kate
to turn to a sympathetic older woman and confide — not everything, perhaps (Emily was not to confide everything to her
Norcross cousins the following spring), but enough to secure a
protective tenderness. As for the "dark and painful hour" itself, there is some evidence in Emily's poetry that Kate had just
returned from a visit to Amherst, where she and Emily had
tried to give each other up.

3 🪶

Emily had wanted Kate to come to Amherst, and Kate had apparently begged off with "the prettiest of pleas." But in the end Kate may have found that she could go — or had to go. One of Emily's poems, "I make his crescent fill or lack," suggests a proud knowledge that once in her life she commanded the destinies of another human being. If she ever supposed that she had such influence over her masculine friends, she flattered herself. They admired her, but they never came at her command. On the hapless, emotional Katie (who was to flee, years later, from Lago Maggiore to London because she could not bear a six weeks' separation from young Florie), it is probable that Emily Dickinson exercised a great though shortlived influence.

A poem beginning "There came a day at summer's full" describes a tragic parting in midsummer. The poem tells how the two friends spent their final hours together in a tense, almost wordless misery. At the last moment each "bound the other's crucifix." After Emily's death Kate was to read this poem. She marked it, and then marked two lines within it:

> So faces on two decks look back,
> Bound to opposing lands.

And the red silk bookmark still stands where she left it between the pages of this poem of farewell.

Another poem, beginning "When I hoped, I recollect" and apparently describing this same parting, has already been related to the history of Emily Dickinson and Kate Scott. On a cold, blustery day (March, 1859?), in her southwest bedroom, Emily had sealed a new friendship. Then came a hot summer day (mid-July, 1860?) when she "feared." Although the world outside was swimming in heat, icicles grew upon her soul. Everywhere birds were singing joyously: "Mine alone was still." Apparently "our condor Kate" was now disguised as a singing bird, but with a voice choked by the sorrow of a parting that might well be fateful.

Still another poem, beginning "I got so I could hear his name," clearly describes the separation of devoted friends. Apparently when the visitor turned to go, perhaps with Austin, toward the carriage that would drive her to the train, Emily turned blindly in the opposite direction in search of privacy, and there was created between them "that angle in the floor" which Emily would find difficult to cross. Because of the masculine pronouns this poem has been associated with the Reverend Charles Wadsworth, but Emily alone knew him or was likely to speak of him. His name would not be introduced unexpectedly into a Dickinson conversation. On the other hand, Kate Scott, who had visited often and long in the house next door, and who remained the intimate friend and correspondent of Sue Dickinson, would be mentioned again and again. Emily must often have braced herself against that name.

If there was a parting in midsummer of 1860, it probably took place in the house of Sue Dickinson. Sue would have been an interested spectator, and she would not have been entirely sympathetic. The emotionalism of the other two women must have been a trial to her. Long afterwards her daughter was to write that the partings between Emily Dickinson and some other woman were like those of "desperate final sundered souls." The anecdote has a slight edge of malice, which vouches for its truth, but Mrs. Bianchi attached it, most improbably, to Helen Hunt Jackson.

Emily Dickinson had only a distant and rather literary acquaintance with Mrs. Jackson. By her own account, she saw Mrs. Jackson only three times in her life, and all three visits were brief and formal. As a young woman, Mrs. Jackson had come with her first husband, Major Hunt, to a crowded reception at the Dickinson house. On a brief morning visit, years later, she came with her second husband, William S. Jackson. The only remaining visit was also a brief morning call. In 1876, while touring New England to gather literary material, Mrs. Jackson spent an hour or two with Emily Dickinson and tried vainly to persuade Emily to write for the *No Name Series*. At the end of this visit (according to Mrs. Bianchi) Mrs. Jackson ran down the steps toward her waiting carriage, with a wave of her hand and a laughing threat to the woman who had refused her. Furthermore, Mrs. Jackson was not the kind of woman to have desperate, final sunderings from any other woman (Katie was to have many such in the future of her "dreadful partings" from young Florie). Presumably Mrs. Bianchi was repeating a faintly malicious story that she had got from her mother. Attached to Mrs. Jackson, it did no harm.

A poem beginning "Like eyes that looked on wastes" appears to belong to this summer of 1860. Although it does not name the season or mention a parting, it describes a tense, anguished situation which can only be read as a parting. The two women — they are women and "queens" in this poem — face each other in blank misery. Emily can offer no help to the other woman, because they are equally involved —

> The misery a compact
> As hopeless as divine.

The reference to a compact between them is of interest. The poem beginning "There came a day at summer's full" states that they merely bound each other's crucifix — "we gave no other bond." Other poems tell a different story. In "Up life's hill with my little bundle," Emily absolves from blame

> Heart that proposed, as heart that accepted,
> Homelessness for home.

In "While it is alive, until death touches it," she declares that
they "dwell in one blood under one sacrament." Perhaps there
was no formal oath between them, but there must have been
at least an impulsive promise to love each other forever.

Another poem which may belong to this period begins with
the lines

> Because that you are going
> And never coming back . . .

The three known manuscripts are all in a fairly late handwriting, but Emily copied and revised many early poems toward
the end of her life. In length, subject matter, and frantic, despairing tone, the poem would seem to be early. The sex of the
other person is not indicated; the poet addresses her friend
directly. The significance of their lives, she writes, is that they
have lived to "detect" each other — a discovery that even God
could not "annihilate." In the last stanza, however, she begs
God to restore her own "confiscated god."

In April, 1862, some twenty-one months after this presumed
summer parting, Emily wrote to her new friend Higginson,
giving some of her background and concluding her brief emotional history with these words: "Then I found one more, but
he was not contented I be his scholar, so he left the land." With
this letter she sent a poem, "Your riches taught me poverty,"
which describes separation from a loved person (at other times
Higginson also received "There came a day at summer's full"
and "Because that you are going"). But a few weeks later Emily
wrote to him, more circumspectly: "When I state myself, as
the representative of the verse, it does not mean me, but a supposed person." Did she repent the statement that she had let
slip in the earlier letter?

It must be pointed out that all of Kate's first four visits to
Amherst have not been fully documented, and they may never
be. Much of the present evidence is in the poems, and poems

of very different tenor could have been inspired by events of
the same visit, or Emily's "summers" might be symbols for the
warm happiness of a wintry season. But the following sequence
would seem to be clear and plausible. In March, 1859, the two
young women undoubtedly met for the first time and were
strongly attached to each other. In August, 1859, they recognized that the attraction was love. During a visit of late February or early March, 1860, a growing passion and the opportunity of spending a night together precipitated a situation
which was bound to terrify both women. If Kate returned in
July, 1860, with a proposal that they find some way of sharing
their lives — but what could she propose? Neither woman had
any money or independence. The situation was hopeless; they
could only try to break it off, and apparently they did try. Kate
then went to Flatbush and enlisted the sympathy of Mrs. Vanderbilt, who seemed both touched and concerned. There is
evidence, however, that Mrs. Vanderbilt's advice was not immediately effective, and that Emily and Kate resumed their
warm correspondence.

4

During the fall of 1860 Emily Dickinson appeared unusually
happy. In September she wrote to her Norcross cousins, thanking Lou for a cape:

> Do you think I am going "upon the boards" that I wish so
> smart attire? Such are my designs, though. I beg you not to
> disclose them! May I not secure Lou for drama, and Fanny
> for comedy! You are a brace of darlings, and it would give
> me joy to see you both in any capacity.

Referring to her father's nomination as lieutenant governor
(announced in the Amherst paper of September 14), Emily

begged young Fanny Norcross to give her insincere respects to the "Bell and Everett party." "Were they cats," she added, "I would pull their tails, but as they are only patriots, I must forego the bliss."

The letter is warm, affectionate, even joyful at times. There is healthy sympathy without a trace of morbidness in a reference to the recent death of the young girls' mother. The letter offers, in fact, a remarkable contrast to the style in which Emily would write to the Norcross cousins a few months later.

Is it fantastic to suppose that about September 14, 1860, Emily received a letter from Kate Scott, and that all was well again? The final blow was still some months in the future.

In a poem beginning

> The whole of it came not at once,
> 'Twas murder by degrees,

Emily would write bitterly that her friend had treated her as a cat treats a mouse, teasing it with an apparent reprieve before she "mashes it to death." Emily would have preferred dying just once to

> . . . dying half, then rallying
> For consciouser eclipse.

In the early winter of 1860 Emily wrote again to her cousins, still quite blithely, reporting the doing of an errand for Lou: "'Is there nothing else,' as the clerk says?" This quotation is reminiscent of a poem, "I asked no other thing," which may have been written at this time. The poet offers her whole existence for the possession of her love, symbolized as an unattainable "Brazil." God, "the mighty merchant," simply smiles at her, twirls a button, and asks indifferently:

> "But, madam, is there nothing else
> That we can show to-day?"

Emily wrote several versions of this unanswered prayer: "I meant to have but modest needs," "Of course I prayed," "There comes an hour when begging stops," and "Just once! Oh, least request!" It is interesting to note that she was able to use the last-named poem in the fall of 1861 to persuade Samuel Bowles to accept a basket of her mother's apples. Fortunately for her sanity, when the tragic emotion had been discharged in verse, Emily could use a poem almost lightheartedly for other purposes. On another occasion she sent Bowles the noncommittal last stanza of a poem of tragic meaning, "Sweet, you forgot, but I remembered," which had, of course, nothing to do with Bowles. To Higginson she sent a revised last stanza of a poem, "The Stars are old, that stood for me," which, in its original form, accused some woman of cruelty. Undoubtedly many a friend of Emily Dickinson received poems not written to him.

If the poem using the word "Brazil" ("I asked no other thing") was written late in 1860, it is additional evidence that Emily's Latin-American symbolism began in 1860–61. Why she was particularly attracted to Mexico and South America is not clear. The family library contained Prescott's *Conquest of Peru* and *Conquest of Mexico* and Stephens' works on Yucatan. During the early eighteen-sixties the *New York Times,* a newspaper which Emily read, devoted a large amount of front-page space to news items from Latin-American countries. But perhaps some lost book, affecting Emily much as *Aurora Leigh* had done, was responsible for this imagery.

The Latin-American symbolism, as in the "Brazil" poem already mentioned, was consistently associated with the unattainable beloved. In a poem "As the starved maelstrom laps the navies," which clearly indicates another woman, Emily begs for "a berry of Domingo and a torrid eye." The poem "I envy seas whereon he rides" declares that the "earrings of Pizarro" would not buy her a look at her beloved's face. In "What would I give to see his face?" she offers "purple from Peru." In "Reverse cannot befall that fine Prosperity" she refers to "far

Bolivian ground." In "Some such butterfly be seen," which is
related to the butterfly symbolism, she speaks of a butterfly
disporting himself on "Brazilian Pampas" precisely at noontide; after that, "sweet license closes" (the butterfly's happiness
ends at the high noon of love). The poem "More life went out
when he went" mentions Popocatepetl. A two-line fragment
reads:

> Brother of ingots — ah, Peru,
> . Empty the hearts that purchased you!

In the summer of 1860 Emily wrote rhapsodically to her
"condor Kate." A year later she wrote to Bowles: "Friends are
gems, infrequent. Potosi is a care, sir." (The silver mines of
Bolivia's Potosí recall "far Bolivian ground.") In June, 1862,
she wrote to Higginson: "Domingo comes but once." It would
almost appear that Emily had read some interesting book on
Latin America in the summer of 1860.

In April, 1862, she sent to Higginson a poem entitled "Your
riches taught me poverty," which linked her unattainable beloved with Peru and "Buenos Ayre." This poem has been attributed to the influence of Ben Newton, with the implication
that it was written as early as 1852 or 1853. But the poem is
in Emily's 1860 manner and is far superior to the few youthful
poems that have been preserved. Besides, Emily was most unlikely to send a youthful poem to Higginson in 1862, when she
was particularly anxious to impress her new critic; she would
choose her newest and best. Nor is there any evidence that she
was interested in Latin-American symbolism prior to the summer of 1860. Finally, significant lines read:

> Of mines I little know, myself,
> But just the names of gems, —
> The colors of the commonest;
> And scarce of diadems

> So much that, did I meet the queen,
> Her glory I should know . . .

Gems, diadems, and queens became of particular interest to Emily after she read *Aurora Leigh*. Yet the last stanza speaks of a pearl that slipped through her fingers "while just a girl at school."

Emily Dickinson's "school days" ended with her tragic love. Students of the poetry have tripped over her symbols in trying to relate to her "little girlhood" events that clearly took place much later. In one of her "school poems" Emily speaks of her long study of Greek, a language with which she was totally unacquainted. The poem begins:

> Knows how to forget!
> But could she teach it?

During the late eighteen-sixties Emily rewrote this poem in order to disguise the woman:

> Knows how to forget!
> But could it teach it?

Although she had gone to school, Emily continued, she "was not wiser." Neither globe nor logarithm had taught her how to deal with the sufferings of unrequited love. The word "logarithm" is a borrowing from *Aurora Leigh*. The symbolic "Greek" of the first version is also a borrowing, for Elizabeth Browning and her fictitious Aurora Leigh were both students of Greek.

Another of the "school poems" begins:

> Let us play yesterday —
> I the girl at school . . .

Emily had "logarithm" to drink; it was a "dry wine." She tried to ease the hunger for love by poring over her "lexicon." Then the beloved touched Emily's shell, and Emily broke from her "egg-life" and was free and happy. Now love has ended, and as Emily once more faces her manacles and dungeon, she begs God not to take her liberty from her.

In a letter of April 25, 1862, to Higginson, Emily gave the story of this poem as her own life history: "Soon after, my tutor died, and for several years my lexicon was my only companion. Then I found one more, but he was not contented I be his scholar, so he left the land." In other words, after Newton's death, in March, 1853, Emily went through a long, dry period of reading and study. These were her school days. Then came the loved friend — not a man, as the passage to Higginson was intended to suggest, but the woman of the "school poems" who knew how to forget but could not teach it.

The first hint of Emily's coming unhappiness may be detected in December, 1860, in a letter to Lou Norcross beginning "Dear Peacock." As the letter stands, there is nothing to date it except Emily's reference to December and to the recent death of Lou's mother. Some material has been deleted. Emily wrote: "There is something fine and something sad in the year's toilet." Then follow the dots of elision so familiar and so exasperating to readers of Emily Dickinson's letters. Few letters to the Norcross cousins were printed in their entirety, and the baffled reader is left wondering whether the delicate cousins omitted references to Kate or to their own affairs. Nor will the problem ever be solved, for the cousins furnished their own copies for publication and burned the originals. They were, incidentally, very careless editors of the letters entrusted to them, even misdating their own father's death. Whatever the omission in this instance, the whole tone of the letter is opposed to the idea that it was written in December, 1861, as the Norcross cousins thought.

In a letter correctly dated December, 1861, Emily Dickinson wrote that she was weeping constantly. She referred guardedly to her personal tragedy, grieved over the death of two young soldiers, and in the words "Ah! the dreamless sleep!" seemed to express her own need and fear of death. She was disappointed of an expected visit from Lou Norcross, was writing to the cousins several times a week, and was alarmed by the fear that her letters had miscarried.

On the other hand, the "Peacock" letter shows clearly that no visit was expected or given up during that December (1860?), although Emily spoke vaguely of seeing the cousins next spring. In referring to the recent death of Mrs. Norcross, Emily wrote, "We often talk of you and your father these new winter days," as if the first snows might be falling on the grave of a woman who had died in April, 1860. The letter is fairly cheerful and makes no reference to the war or to Emily's own sufferings. The following passage recalls markedly her joking letter of September, 1860, regarding her clothes:

> *You seem to take a smiling view of my finery. If you knew how solemn it was to me, you might be induced to curtail your jests. My sphere is doubtless calicoes, nevertheless I thought it meet to sport a little wool. The mirth it has occasioned will deter me from further exhibitions! Won't you tell "the public" that at present I wear a brown dress with a cape if possible browner, and carry a parasol of the same!*

The reference to the brown cape may be a way of again thanking Lou Norcross for the cape received in September, 1860. The quoted words "the public" seem to refer to her earlier joke about needing fine clothes to go on the stage. In short, the "Peacock" letter is cheerful, as Emily herself was cheerful in the early winter of 1860. The following lines alone seem to indicate the beginning of alarm and confusion:

> *I believe it is several hundred years since I met you and*
> *Fanny, yet I am pleased to say, you do not become dim; I*
> *think you rather brighten as the hours fly. I should love*
> *to see you dearly, girls; perhaps I may, before south winds,*
> *but I feel rather confused to-day, and the future looks*
> *"higglety-pigglety."*

It is a guess — but a guess supported by several indications
— that about December, 1860, without a word of explanation,
Kate Scott ceased to write, and Emily began to worry.

Early in 1861 Emily wrote the last of her three published
letters to Kate Scott:

[1861?]

> *Katie, — Last year at this time I did not miss you, but*
> *positions shifted, until I hold your black in strong hal-*
> *lowed remembrance, and trust my colors are to you tints*
> *slightly beloved.*
>
> *You cease, indeed, to talk, which is a custom prevalent*
> *among things parted and torn, but shall I class this, dear,*
> *among elect exceptions, and bear you just as usual unto*
> *the kind Lord?*
>
> *We dignify our faith when we can cross the ocean with*
> *it, though most prefer ships.*
>
> *How do you do this year? ... How many years, I wonder,*
> *will sow the moss upon them, before we bind again, a little*
> *altered, it may be, elder a little it will be, and yet the*
> *same, as suns which shine between our lives and loss, and*
> *violets — not last year's, but having the mother's eyes.*
>
> *Do you find plenty of food at home? Famine is un-*
> *pleasant.*
>
> *It is too late for "frogs" — or what pleases me better,*
> *dear, not quite early enough! The pools were full of you*

*for a brief period, but that brief period blew away, leaving
me with many stems, and but a few foliage! Gentlemen
here have a way of plucking the tops of the trees, and putting the fields in their cellars annually, which in point of
taste is execrable, and would they please omit, I should
have fine vegetation and foliage all the year round, and
never a winter month. Insanity to the sane seems so unnecessary, but I am only one, and they are "four and
forty," which little affair of numbers leaves me impotent.
Aside from this, dear Katie, inducements to visit Amherst
are as they were — I am pleasantly located in the deep sea,
but love will row you out, if her hands are strong, and
don't wait till I land, for I'm going ashore on the other
side.*

                                                    EMILIE.

The exact date of this letter is the most difficult problem
that it offers. In the third paragraph Emily suggests that her
letter must cross the ocean. Kate did go abroad in the fall of
1864, but neither Emily nor Sue knew her foreign address.
By that time Emily had dropped her youthful vagary of
"Emilie" and her style of writing had changed markedly. This
letter is in the style of 1860. In the fifth paragraph Emily demands pointedly: "Do you find plenty of food at home?" Kate
is in Cooperstown, not Europe. The "ocean" that Emily's letter crosses is as symbolic as the "deep sea" in which Emily herself is located. It is an ocean of silence no longer bridged by
Kate's own letters.

The first sentence offers another clue: "Last year at this time
I did not miss you, but positions shifted . . ." Kate was in
Amherst in late February or early March of 1860, and the
passage just quoted suggests that Emily's letter was written a
year later, in late February or early March of 1861. But the
last paragraph begins: "It is too late for 'frogs' — or what
pleases me better, dear, not quite early enough!" Then follow

allusions to the recent autumn. Emily's letter was written in a season midway between frogs. The fourth paragraph opens with the words: "How do you do this year?" After an elision, Emily wonders "how many years" will pass before they meet again, and refers to "violets — not last year's, but having the mother's eyes." In short, Emily is writing her first letter of the new year to Kate, and the date must be January 1, 1861, or very shortly thereafterwards. That "positions shifted" would be Emily's way of saying that they are no longer united by the lively correspondence of the preceding year. She is reproachful.

This letter apparently contains several allusions to Emily's poems. For example, it was suggested in Chapter V that the curious sentence "Insanity to the sane seems so unnecessary" was intended to remind Katie of a poem beginning "Much madness is divinest sense," and that the phrase "four and forty" (in Emily's own quotation marks) might recall to Katie a poem beginning "Glee! the great storm is over!" This poem is undoubtedly early, and Kate may have seen and praised it during the period of their intimate friendship. In her own copy of Emily's poetry Kate marked this poem more extensively than any other.

The "frogs" of this and the preceding (summer, 1860) letter, which clearly are not frogs, suggest that there was a joke between them. Kate may have seen, in manuscript, the humorous "I'm nobody! Who are you?" The poem has a warm, intimate tone, as if the two persons who admit to being nobodies might be real. There need not have been any particular model for the pompous frog who tells his name to "an admiring bog." Kate had praised Emily extravagantly. The poem would have been a suitable — and amusing — reply.

The fourth paragraph is as significant as it is brief: "Do you find plenty of food at home? Famine is unpleasant." Emily did not need to enlarge on this idea; Kate understood her symbolism well enough to know what "famine" meant. The lines suggest a jealous fear that Kate might indeed be finding "plenty of food at home." As late as 1874, Emily wrote to her Norcross cousins:

> . . . *How short it takes to go, dear, but afterward to come so many weary years — and yet 'tis done as cool as a general trifle. Affection is like bread, unnoticed till we starve, and then we dream of it, and sing of it, and paint it, when every urchin in the street has more than he can eat. We turn not older with years, but newer every day.*

Kate did not answer Emily's letter. The silence which had apparently begun in early December, 1860, remained unbroken for four months. The evidence is in the poems, in Emily's letters and behavior, and in Kate's behavior also. Afterwards Emily would describe this period as one of racking suspense. She suffered cruelly.

Emily was to write a poem, "Two swimmers wrestled on the spar," in which two persons are described as clinging desperately all night to the same spar. In the morning, however, one of the swimmers is able to turn "smiling to the land." In view of Kate Scott's life, the word "smiling" seems cruel. Again and again she was to struggle out of the shipwreck of her hopes and stubbornly build new relationships to replace those that had failed her. In no other respect was her life happier than Emily Dickinson's, and her personal losses were far greater and more calamitous. Admittedly, however, there was in this instance the advantage of being the jilter rather than the jilted. The pain of rejection is probably the severest that any person ever suffers; a sensitive ego, wounded in its tenderest part, stings endlessly. The saddest of partings would affect Emily Dickinson less cruelly than a silence which suggested that she was not worthy to be loved.

Many poems, apparently written after the event, describe the months of tension that Emily suffered during her friend's silence. The anguished "One year ago jots what" was apparently written in the early spring of 1861. In another poem, "The most pathetic thing I do" (it is in a late handwriting, but may be a recollection of this time), Emily described the pathos of pretending that her friend still writes to her. She almost persuades her heart, then breaks it by admitting the pretense, then wishes she had not broken it: "Goliah — so would you." "Goliah," by which she meant Goliath, could have been her tall and faithless friend, the "condor" who now remained silent on her far western crags.

And what of Katie? She had been reading *Evangeline* in Mrs. Vanderbilt's gift volumes of Longfellow, and must have been trying to decide what to do about Emily's pleading letters. In *Evangeline* she marked the following line:

> Something within her said, — "At length thy trials are ended";

and the concluding lines:

> All was ended now, the hope and the fear, and the sorrow,
> All the aching of heart, the restless, unsatisfied longing,
> All the dull, deep pain, and constant anguish of patience!

On Tuesday, March 19, she discovered an appropriate quotation in her daily Shakespeare calendar, and she inserted the leaf between the pages of *Evangeline*:

> Repent what's past; avoid what is to come;
> And do not spread the compost on the weeds,
> To make them ranker.
> *Hamlet,* iii.4.

What would Emily have felt if she had known that her life ended in the pages of *Evangeline?* Why did she apparently call Kate "Gabriel," the name not only of the angel of the Annunciation but also of Longfellow's hero who wandered in the West while Evangeline sought him vainly through a lifetime?

In April, 1861, the Civil War began, and Kate Scott apparently broke her long silence with a letter to Emily terminating their two years' attachment. Was it coincidence? In the tragic excitement of war Kate may have felt that all personal tragedies should be sunk and forgotten.

The existence of this letter can never be proved (after Emily's death Lavinia destroyed all letters from other persons), but it can be demonstrated with a fair degree of probability. Kate was much agitated in the spring of 1861, as if she were deciding upon a course of action and justifying her decision. After two happy years Emily suddenly became desperate in this same spring. Years later she wrote to Mrs. Holland that April had robbed her repeatedly. In May, 1861, Emily apparently saw her Norcross cousins and confided in them, for in December, 1861, she reminded them of this same May (a month, as she wrote to them, that stood "next April"), and years afterwards she thanked them for their kindness to her during some particular May. In many poems she described feelingly a long period of suspense terminated by a feared and dreadful blow. A poem in the handwriting of this period begins, "He scanned it, staggered, dropped the loop." Then "he" (that is, Emily herself) felt that his mind was "going blind," and failing to find God, "he" killed himself. The poem describes the receipt of bad news and ends with a suicide-wish. In a poem beginning "Death-warrants are supposed to be," Emily remembered bitterly that "a pencil in an idol's hand" has often sent a devotee to "crucifix or block." The crucifix was her personal symbol of suffering. A poem beginning "Did we disobey him" states that her lover has specifically charged her "to forget him."

From these indications Kate's letter may be restored. She

was not unkind in begging Emily to forget her. She pointed out the dangers of their attachment, the wisdom of putting an end to their mutual suffering, and the necessity of turning to religion. Had not Mrs. Vanderbilt urged her to such a course as early as July 29, 1860? But Kate did not find the letter easy or painless to write. For months Emily would cling to the belief, in part justified, that Kate was suffering as she herself suffered.

On Saturday, May 18, at about the time when Emily must have broken down to her Norcross cousins, Kate discovered another suitable quotation in her Shakespeare calendar. Apparently she had finished *Evangeline,* and was now reading the next poem, *The Golden Legend,* and marking in it lines that speak of "a loud perpetual wail, as of souls in pain," and of a heart "that aches and bleeds with the stigma of pain." Between the pages of *The Golden Legend* she inserted the leaf from her Shakespeare calendar for May 18, 1861. With these words Lady Macbeth exhorted her husband to forget the murder of Duncan:

Things without all remedy
Should be without regard: what's done is done.
Macbeth, iii. 2.

 VIII

THE LETTER from Kate was a cruel blow to Emily Dickinson. For months she had endured a painful suspense. She was even to insist that the period of waiting had been worse than the final blow, but it is clear that her sick hopes died violently. In a poem beginning "The first day's night had come," much of which Mrs. Bianchi prudently suppressed, Emily described the night and the day that followed. She had hoped that her grief would spend itself with the first night, but the second day dawned as horrible as "yesterday in pairs." Then her "brain began to laugh," she "mumbled like a fool," and down through the years her brain kept on "giggling":

> And something's odd within.
> That person that I was,
> And this one, do not feel the same —
> Could it be madness, this?

Even in its emasculated form, Mrs. Bianchi dared not print this poem until Kate Anthon was dead.

Emily shut herself up to wrestle with pain. In a poem, "My

first well day, since many ill," describing a respite toward the
end of summer, she recalled that the flowers were just beginning to blossom when she "went in to take [her] chance with
Pain." Several poems emphasize the loneliness of this struggle
with herself. They are, in fact, an accurate description of a
mind that came near to breaking. When the first wave of pain
was at its crest, in May, 1861, the Norcross cousins visited Amherst. Plainly they were in the Dickinson house, for the confidence that they received and the comfort that they admin-
istered were not of a kind to be given by letter.

Lou and Fanny Norcross were very young, a mere nineteen
and fourteen, but they were generous and tender, and they
helped her. She was to be lastingly grateful for the comfort that
they gave. If the pain were not so grim, there would be absurdity in the picture of the young girls hovering over the
woman of thirty (probably in the southwest bedroom), while
she unburdened herself of the suffering inflicted by another
woman. She did not, of course, tell them everything. Several
poems speak of a secret that must be kept for the ears of God.
The secret was apparently the strong moral temptation which
she had resisted on the night spent with her friend.

Although the Norcross cousins were to be Emily's kindest,
most dependable confidantes, others were not ignorant. A
young woman could not disappear from her familiar circle and
spend much of her time in painful solitude without attracting
some notice and speculation. Emily's sister Lavinia would have
noticed that Kate no longer wrote and that Emily suffered.
There are also faint but perceptible signs that Sue Dickinson
was uncomfortably aware of the situation.

Emily had loved Sue, and the milder attachment of their sisterly years had not yet worn thin. Sue was also Kate's intimate
friend, and Emily could not help asking, by distressed looks if
not words, for some explanation of Kate's behavior. On one
occasion Emily thanked Sue for being "subtle," and then
quoted the first four lines of a poem, "The farthest thunder

that I heard," in which she described her unhappy love affair as a stroke of lightning. The reader is left wondering how much Sue Dickinson knew and in what subtle ways she spared Emily's feelings.

The position of buffer between Emily and Kate was not an easy one. Sue must have wearied of Emily's unhappy face or notes or poems. There are indications that she did grow weary. In the spring of 1861 she was expecting her first confinement. She could make an excuse of that. After young Edward Dickinson was born, Sue had many excuses for avoiding painful interviews. Emily would be well aware that the baby was a pretext and would feel pain and even resentment.

It is interesting that Mrs. Bianchi should refer gingerly to the year 1861 as one of distress for Emily. Sue Dickinson was too preoccupied with the child, said her daughter, to give Emily the usual amount of companionship. As evidence Mrs. Bianchi quoted a little note in which Sue apparently denied herself because of the weariness of sewing for the baby. But a suggestion that the agony of 1861 resulted from jealousy of a child does little credit to the heart or mind of Emily Dickinson. Though heart and mind were obviously troubled, they were not petty. There is, however, some indication that Emily did resent Sue's hiding behind the baby.

2

In the second week of July, 1861, Samuel Bowles, in the company of his friend Charles Allen, took a vacation by carriage through the Connecticut Valley to the White Mountains. On the way he stopped in Amherst to visit the Dickinsons. Emily was then recovering from her first severe grief and was able to see him. Shortly afterwards she sent him a rather emotional letter, which has been cut by the editor. In this same July, 1861, Bowles himself wrote a curious letter, published in *The*

Life and Times of Samuel Bowles by George S. Merriam. The recipient is not named. However, Bowles wrote the letter in the month when he saw Emily, and it is strikingly appropriate to her situation at that time. After Bowles' death Merriam consulted the Dickinson family about letters and memories, and Emily may well have given him, under proper safeguards, a letter from Bowles which she would have had reason to cherish.

The letter itself is addressed in blank, and the first sentences or paragraphs have been excised. All that remains is warm, sensible advice to a person who has been hurt by the coldness of an intimate friend.

July, 1861.

My dear —— : . . . You must give if you expect to receive — give happiness, friendship, love, joy, and you will find them floating back to you. Sometimes you will give more than you receive. We all do that in some of our relations, but it is as true a pleasure often to give without return as life can afford us. We must not make bargains with the heart, as we would with the butcher for his meat. Our business is to give what we have to give — what we can get to give. The return we have nothing to do with. It will all come in due time — in this world or another. We shall have our dues. One will not give us what we give them — others will more than we can or do give them — and so the accounts will balance themselves. It is so with my loves and friendships — it is so with everybody's. There is no call for any of us to humble *ourselves before each other. To do right, to be generous, forgiving, kind, charitable, and loving, is not humility — it is only justice and truth to the God in us.*

The remainder of the letter speaks of other persons who might neglect friendly ties because of overzealous attention to duties. For example, no mother should spend twenty-four hours taking care of her baby when four hours would do; she owed some consideration to her friends.

That this letter was addressed to Emily appears very probable. It fits her circumstances at the time of Bowles' visit and explains her behavior toward him for many months to come. Bowles knew and liked Kate. It would be natural for him to ask Emily about her old friend, but he could scarcely anticipate the scene that would follow. It must have been distressing and embarrassing. The strong advice not to *humble* oneself suggests that it was. If Bowles then spoke of Sue as a friendly solace, he would meet another woeful admission. Sue was too preoccupied with baby Ned to see Emily. After Bowles escaped from this interview, he evidently took the first opportunity available to amplify by letter the advice that he had given awkwardly face to face.

Emily was to be very grateful to Bowles for some unspecified service at about this time. She was to write to him as if he knew the cause of her misery and would offer comfort, and her grateful letters were highly emotional. Several of her poems (among them, poems sent to Bowles) reflect the generous, disinterested philosophy outlined in Bowles' letter.

The warmth of Bowles' kindness made itself felt, but the wound that had been dealt by a woman could be healed only by another woman. Emily turned to Mary Bowles with the intensity of a lost child in search of a mother. Mrs. Bowles had shown a flattering interest in her as early as the summer of 1859, and from the beginning Emily's letters had been warm, but not as they were to be in the summer of 1861 and for many months afterwards.

In August, 1861, Emily sent Mrs. Bowles a rather childlike letter, looking her "heart in the eye," striving for an intimacy that Mary Bowles had permitted to languish, and ending: "Please remember me, because I remember you — always." Then followed a love poem, "My river runs to thee." On another occasion she sent Mrs. Bowles a poem beginning "Her

198

198198

breast is fit for pearls." These poems, like some of those sent to Bowles, may not have been written with the actual recipient in mind. When Bowles went abroad in 1862, Emily wrote consolingly to his wife, but out of her own bitter knowledge, "Not to see what we love is very terrible, and talking doesn't ease it, and nothing does but just itself." In another letter to Mrs. Bowles of about this period, Emily enclosed her heart: "A little one, sunburnt, half broken sometimes, yet close as the spaniel to its friends."

The "spaniel," incidentally, appears to be another borrowing from Elizabeth Browning, who used the word to describe the pathetic Marian Erle of *Aurora Leigh*. Emily called herself a spaniel in a poem, "If he dissolve, then there is nothing more," which may have been written at this time. In stanzas suppressed by Mrs. Bianchi, the poet begs "some god" to tell the vanished lover that she is dying:

> Say that a little life for his is leaking red —
> His little spaniel, tell him! Will he heed?

The letters to Mary Bowles are remarkable, but like most of the supposedly inexplicable behavior of Emily Dickinson, they have a plausible explanation. If Emily confided part of her grief and perplexity to Bowles in July, 1861, and assumed, or knew, that he had spoken to his wife about it, she had some warrant for entrusting her half-broken heart to Mary Bowles. "You wonder why I write so," said Emily, vaguely conscious that her letters transgressed all customary emotional bounds. "Because I cannot help." Perhaps they both knew that Mary Bowles was not entirely in the dark. Emily was desperately seeking comfort from any source, and she was in no state of mind to understand that such letters would embarrass or annoy.

Mrs. Bowles is reported to have said, with an attempt at kindness, that Emily Dickinson was her own worst enemy. Mrs. Bowles made no effort to respond, and the artificial intimacy withered away. At the end of some three years of one-sided correspondence, Emily was still begging for a *first* letter. Long afterwards she apparently referred to Mary Bowles as "ungracious soil." In a poem, "A shady friend for torrid days," she recorded the sad discovery that women were fair-weather friends; men were more dependable. The truth is that her demands upon men were less exorbitant.

Apparently Mrs. Holland was more understanding, or perhaps she was not asked to fill so completely the position vacated by Kate Scott. There was no diminishing of her friendship with Emily, although she did Emily the service, and biographers the disservice, of destroying all letters received at this time — the only significant gap in their long correspondence. She had long been the elder sister, the consoler, the maternal friend, and need only intensify her kindness during the crucial period of 1861–64. On the other hand, it is not surprising that Mary Bowles, a woman little older than Emily and a recent and slight acquaintance, should decline the role thrust upon her. It is easier to pity a genius after she is dead than to live with her comfortably.

"Think Emily lost her wits," wrote Emily to the Norcross cousins about July or August of 1861. The fear of madness was recurrent, but she was now entering her brief respite from suffering, and felt weakly convalescent.

This letter, dated "Spring, 1861," by the Norcross cousins, could not have been written before mid-July. In the last paragraph Emily referred sorrowfully to Mrs. Browning and George Sand: "Women, now, queens, now! And one in the Eden of God." Mrs. Browning died June 29, 1861, and the news that she was now "in the Eden of God" would have taken some two weeks to cross the Atlantic and appear in a newspaper.

As the letter stands, it is tragic enough, but it must originally have been far more revealing. Every paragraph opens with marks of elision. Emily wrote:

> . . . *The seeing pain one can't relieve makes a demon of one. If angels have the heart beneath their silver jackets, I*

*think such things could make them weep, but Heaven is
so cold! It will never look kind to me that God, who causes
all, denies such little wishes. It could not hurt His glory,
unless it were a lonesome kind. I 'most conclude it is.*

Mutilated as this paragraph is, it is impossible to tell whether
Emily was consoling the Norcross cousins for some disappointment of their own or interpreting to them their distress at not
being able to relieve her suffering. The latter is at least plausible. The cousins had seen Emily during the preceding May,
and she had confided some part of her distress to them. Other
parts of this letter undoubtedly reflect Emily's own pain.

After an excision by the cousins, Emily wrote:

*. . . I'm afraid that home is almost done, but do not say
I fear so. Perhaps God will be better. They're so happy,
you know. That makes it doubtful. Heaven hunts round
for those that find itself below, and then it snatches.*

The thought of this paragraph is tortuously expressed; it cannot
be analyzed in a few words. Emily fears that "home is almost
done"; that is, she expects to die shortly, either from illness
(her mental conflicts are felt, and often expressed, as unbearable
physical suffering) or by suicide. There are, in fact, several
"suicide" poems. Perhaps death will be a happy solution; the
dead are reported to be in bliss. But — "that makes it doubtful." The reported happiness of the dead, the reported good-
ness of God, makes heaven itself doubtful. Life is cruel, Emily
adds; earthly happiness is snatched away, without reason or
justice, as if by some malignant agent. Can a power that is
malignant to the living become beneficent to the dead? To
Emily's rational, non-mystical mind, the manifest evil and
misery of the world are incompatible with the idea of an
omnipotent, benevolent God. But she does not quite dare write
this answer, for the abused, suppressed life in her needs the
redress of heaven.

Earlier in this letter to the Norcross cousins, Emily wrote: "Thank you for the daisy. With nature in my ruche I shall not miss the spring." Perhaps for this reason the letter was assigned to spring rather than midsummer of 1861. But Emily meant that spring had already passed her by, while she was locked up in her struggle with pain. At the end of the letter she asked vaguely: "When did the war really begin?" It had begun on April 12, 1861, with the bombardment of Fort Sumter.

The war disturbed Emily; it intruded upon her private grief. "Sorrow seems more general than it did," she wrote to the cousins in April of the following year, "and not the estate of a few persons, since the war began; and if the anguish of others helped with one's own, now would be many medicines." Although Emily wrote some poems about the war, it never became real to her. In the egoism of pain she concentrated on her private war.

In September, after the respite of late summer, there was a renewal of Emily's anguish. The following spring she wrote to Higginson: "I had a terror since September, I could tell to none." It was the fear of madness. The immediate provocation may have been slight — perhaps a letter from Kate to Sue or a rumor that Kate might return to Amherst or even a minor illness which weakened Emily's power of resistance.

Unfortunately there was nothing favorable in her circumstances. A meager round of housework, which could not occupy her mind, was varied only by reading that increased her suffering. If she had had the duties and occupations of a Samuel Bowles, she could have profited more readily by his advice. Her age — she had recently turned thirty — was critical for a single woman. Then the nature of her jilting (a jilting for which she could not claim the sympathy of her intimates) was a peculiar aggravation. There was no one to tell her that the fear, shame, and moral suffering were unnecessary. Altogether, her position was one to insure repeated struggles with pain.

The course of one day might witness changes of mood from intense suffering to elation. She wrote, "I sometimes drop it"

(that is, her anguish) for the "anonymous delight" of knowing
herself alive. If so terrible a woe had torn at her throughout
the day, she added, death would have seemed priceless. "Three
times we parted, Breath and I," she wrote, comparing her
struggles with those of a drowning person; and elsewhere:

> Drowning is not so pitiful
> As the attempt to rise.
> Three times, 'tis said, a sinking man
> Comes up to face the skies . . .

But three was only a convenient number. "I many times
thought peace had come," she wrote, remembering that she had
often slackened her efforts, only to discover that the peaceful
shore was a mirage.

Sometimes her agony was likened to a storm. "It struck me
every day" (she wrote) that the lightning was as fresh as if it
had just that moment flared in the sky. It "burned" in her
sleep, "blistered" her dreams, "sickened" her vision every
morning. The first brief storm was followed by one that threatened to be perpetual. There were, however, lengthening intervals of calm. Sometimes she could write that she had outgrown
love and laid it on the shelf. With renewed suffering, she
admitted that time had merely proved the reality of her pain.

Although the exact period will not be known until all the
poems can be dated, it is obvious that she was morbidly affected
for years. In her early forties she still wrote to the Norcross
cousins of an unconquerable sorrow; and in manuscripts of her
fifties she recurred to the old grief. At an undetermined period,
however, there came a real lifting of the cloud that had hung
over her ("I should not dare to be so sad"), and she saw with
astonishment and terror the weight of suffering she had borne.
Elsewhere she wrote: "It ceased to hurt me, though so slow."
Something had obscured the track of pain, and now it was
"almost Peace."

Consistently she wrote that she had been jilted, mistreated, hurt. She had been struck by a sword, lashed with a whip, pierced by an arrow, a dirk, a cannon ball; her grave had been dug and the spade (Kate's letter?) remained in memory; she had got a bomb — and yet she continued to love the friend who had cruelly wounded her. "Most I love the cause that slew me," she wrote ("Struck was I, nor yet by lightning"). In "Not with a club the heart is broken," she declared that it was magnanimous of a bird, an Emily, "to sing unto the stone of which it died." Further on, in a stanza suppressed by Mrs. Todd, she cried out that "Shame need not crouch" — it might stand erect in a universe given over to shame.

She was "forgot." Many are the poems of this tenor, and they accord ill with the theory of an attachment to a married clergyman who was demonstrably kind and generous all his life. Indeed five of the poems clearly refer to a woman. The connection between the feminine and the neuter versions of "Knows how to forget" is perfectly obvious. "Precious to me she still shall be" and "It did not surprise me" will be mentioned again later on. The fifth poem, "That she forgot me was the least," again strikes the note of shame, for Emily was ashamed to love the woman who had forgotten her. "He forgot, and I remembered," she wrote, comparing her friend's behavior to Peter's denial of Christ. Hate, love, shame, arrogance — all had their turn.

" 'Twas love, not me," wrote Emily. Both were guilty, they looked much alike, and yet Emily had the guilt of loving most and should be forgiven last. "The court is far away" — she had offended her sovereign and could find no one to plead for her. The day would come, however, when the friend must beg forgiveness of God, and on that day Emily would intercede. In "Elizabeth told Essex," Kate became an unforgiving Elizabeth who condemned her Essex-Emily to death; Elizabeth-Katie was reminded that she must eventually sue God for a pardon that she herself had refused to give.

Naturally Emily would torture herself with wondering how she had offended. Two related poems are particularly clear. The first, "Why make it doubt — it hurts it so — ," employs a weird jumble of pronouns and other devices, apparently to obscure the sex of the other person, although it concludes with the words "Oh, Master!" Emily, on her deathbed, recalls the last words spoken to her by the dear "Vision," and fears that she has done or dared something which has offended her beloved. The second poem, "Not probable — the merest chance," suggests that "a smile too few — a word too much — " has alienated the friend just as Emily herself was "close on Paradise." It ends with the frank and despairing cry "oh phantom Queen!"

If Emily were free of blame, was it not probable that someone else had come between them? The poem "I shall not murmur if at last" speaks of a strong and dangerous attachment brought to a close by the friend's alienation and Emily's seclusion from the world. It concludes:

> Why, Katie, treason has a voice,
> But mine dispels in tears.

In "Forget? The lady with the amulet," Emily is the "amulet" that the lady had worn at her breast. Had "treason" come between them? "When the astronomer stops seeking" (a poem in Emily's handwriting of the early eighteen-sixties) recites a list of impossible conditions. After these are fulfilled, Emily will find it early enough to "ask what treason means."

To a person in Emily's morbid state of mind, a plausible traitor was near at hand. Sue Dickinson was Kate's intimate friend as well as Emily's sister-in-law. What would be more natural than to suppose that Sue had in some manner alienated Kate from Emily? If Sue was trying to keep Emily at arm's length during 1861 — and Mrs. Bianchi's testimony suggests that she was — the suspicion would be strengthened. It need have no basis in fact.

There is, however, some probability in the suggestion that

Sue would have thrown her weight on the side of common
sense. A cool, unemotional woman, she would have looked
askance at the neurotic intensity of this attachment, and she
was never to like Emily's love poems. Sue was also a jealous,
possessive woman. She had enjoyed the devotion paid to her
by both Kate and Emily, and she would not have been pleased
with an attachment that excluded her. If Kate showed a tendency to recover from the sickness of romantic love, Sue would
have supported her. It was something to be got over, and the
only pity of it was that Emily too did not succeed.

What pressures were brought to bear on Katie, aside from
Mrs. Vanderbilt's anxiety for her, will never be known. Time,
absence, and new interests had done much. Yet Kate was not
wholly easy, and she was not to be easy for years — perhaps,
never. Emily was not completely deceived in supposing that
she had made a lasting impression. In a suppressed stanza of
"Proud of my broken heart since thou didst break it," she assumed that Kate was suffering equally:

> Thou canst not boast, like Jesus! Drunken without
>   companion
> Was the strong cup of anguish brewed for the Nazarene.
> Thou canst not pierce tradition with the peerless
>   puncture!
> See! I usurped thy crucifix to honor mine.

The lines marked by Kate in *The Golden Legend* suggest a
like feeling. She thought of herself as wearing the stigmata of
pain and carrying her cross. Probably she was hearing from
Emily, who would not easily give up a connection that had
meant everything to her. Perhaps for this reason Kate decided
to return to Amherst and try to bring Emily to a common-sense
reduction of their attachment. But if she made an earnest,
feeling attempt to rescue Emily from suffering (and in view of
her character, it is highly probable), her own record is lost,
and Emily witnessed only for Emily.

On Tuesday, October 22, 1861, Kate was struck by another

quotation in her Shakespeare calendar, and she thoughtfully enclosed it between the pages of her Longfellow:

> Give sorrow words: the grief that does not speak
> Whispers the o'er-fraught heart and bids it break.
> *Macbeth,* iv. 3.

Nine days later she was in Amherst. She came to visit Sue Dickinson, and she was accompanied by Gertrude Vanderbilt.

The fact is certain, but the interpretation is difficult. If she sought even a partial reconciliation with Emily, why did she complicate matters by introducing a new friend? It is true that she disliked traveling alone, and Mrs. Vanderbilt would have been a very pleasant companion. Perhaps the most reasonable assumption is that she hoped, under the protection of Mrs. Vanderbilt, to show Emily that they could still be friends in the ordinary sense of the word. There is evidence in Emily's poems that the two women continued to meet with civility and outward kindness, and Mrs. Bianchi stated that Emily always interrupted her seclusion to see Katie. But beneath the quiet surface Emily was seething. She complained that "they" had shut her out, "they" had left her in the cold, and she begged God to forgive them. She was as unwilling to take second place with Kate Scott as she had been years earlier with Susan Gilbert.

From one activity she was certainly excluded — by her own choice or by that of the three women in the house next door. Kate began a manuscript cook book, the very book in which she first wrote her name "Kate Turner" and then changed it to "Kate Scott." Sue wrote a motto and some miscellaneous details, and Mrs. Vanderbilt copied many recipes into the book, often in amusing detail. Neither Emily nor her sister Lavinia wrote a word in a book which was evidently a very pleasant joint entertainment of the other three women. "Emily's fruit cake" and "Vinnie's gingerbread" are recorded, but in Kate's handwriting and probably from Sue's recollection. They are simply

bare notes of ingredients and quantities, without the directions
and elaborations that the inventors of the recipes would surely
have given.

A poem, "Now I knew I lost her," points to a woman visiting in the house next door. Lest the first line mislead, Emily
was careful to explain that the other woman was not yet gone.

> But remoteness traveled
> On her face and tongue.

Even though the visitor stayed in the "adjoining" house, she
was "alien," and "though pausing" (that is, physically present
for a short while), in spirit she was already crossing "latitudeless
place." Recalling the day which the poet "had paid so much
for," Emily wept over her lost idol. All summer she had deceived herself with the notion that her friend was suffering
equally. Now that she saw Kate's laughing face again, it was
obviously no such matter.

A poem of similar meter and tone, "It did not surprise me,"
is in handwriting of this period. Emily told herself that she had
always expected her friend to forget "the nest" —

> Traverse broader forests,
> Build in gayer boughs,
> Breathe in ear more modern
> God's old-fashioned vows.

What she thought of Kate's warm intimacy with Mrs. Vanderbilt seems to be reflected in this poem. Although Kate might
change attachments lightly, the poem continued, Emily's own
heart was a "coffin." The loss of her friend was often described
as her own death.

Jealousy broods over another poem. In June of the following
year (1862) — that is, about seven months after Kate's visit to
Amherst — Emily used the odd word "Saxon" in a letter to
Higginson: "I have no Saxon now." In a poem, "Many a phrase

has the English language," she used the same unexplained word to refer to Katie. Recalling the one phrase (obviously, "I love you") which had meant so much to her, Emily begs the "Saxon" to repeat the magic words, but adds jealously, "Hush — only to me!"

During the late fall of 1861 Samuel Bowles was once more in the neighborhood of Amherst. His trip to the White Mountains having done him no good, he placed himself in the hands of a doctor in Northampton. One day he wrote of seeing "A —— " (probably Austin Dickinson), and added: "The elder Mrs. D —— gave me a fine basket full of big apples, which are a great treat for me." This must have been the time when Emily wrote a note to Bowles, accompanied by the strained "Just once — oh! least request!" begging him to accept "a little barrel of apples" from her mother. It was the first favor, she continued, that her mother had ever asked of him. In her disordered state of mind she was unable to see the contrast between her letter and the highly emotional poem that accompanied it.

On another day Bowles came to Amherst, and Emily refused to see him. Kate was now in the house next door, and Emily may have been unwilling to let Bowles see how little she had profited by his well-meant advice. At least she was in no condition to endure even the gentlest reminder of her distress. Bowles evidently called on Sue and her friends, for after his return to Northampton or Springfield, he sent over a new book, *Great Expectations,* with the pleasant hope that Sue and "Mrs. Kate" would have pleasure in reading it. He had also a kind word for the sister in the house next door who never forgot his "spiritual" needs. In her letter of apology to Bowles Emily had offered to send a flower and a bottle of wine that she had prepared for him.

Kate left Amherst — how soon is not known, but evidently sometime in November. Emily wrote, "How happy I was if I could forget," adding that "the recollecting of bloom Keeps making November difficult." In late December she wrote to the Norcross cousins that she was weeping constantly. Kate's visit and apparent indifference had deepened the wound.

After an elision made by the Norcross cousins, Emily's letter continued: "Odd, that I, who say 'no' so much, cannot bear it from others. Odd, that I, who run from so many, cannot brook that one turn from me."

Mrs. Bianchi, whose awareness of the true history was always a piece of awkward knowledge, could not let this rest in the safe obscurity of its context, but dragged it out with a view of explaining it away. "Once she seemed puzzled," wrote Mrs. Bianchi, quoting the second of these two sentences, "by some slight coldness on the part of a friend." The "coldness" is indubitable. Whether it was slight or whether Emily was puzzled is another matter.

But if Mrs. Bianchi was well informed, the Norcross cousins were still better informed, and a brief review of relations between Emily and her cousins might prove helpful. Early in 1859 Emily wrote the first in her long series of letters to them. Throughout 1859 and 1860 she was always cheerful, sometimes elated. Even these letters, however, have been slightly edited. Perhaps the cousins removed references to Katie.

About mid-July, 1861, Emily sent her cousins an anguished letter (discussed earlier in this chapter), every paragraph of which begins with elision marks. In late December, 1861, she wrote them the letter mentioned two paragraphs earlier. In this letter she alluded to still other letters that have perished, described her suffering, and referred to some friend who had turned away from her (a reference to which Mrs. Bianchi was to react sensitively). Emily's letter continues: "I don't remember 'May.' Is that the one that stands next April?"

In May, 1863, she wrote to the Norcross cousins, recalling her pain in these words: "that old nail in my breast pricked me." Years later (apparently in May, 1870) she wrote to them: "I always think of you peculiarly in May, as it is the peculiar anniversary of your loving kindness to me." It is clear that something happened to Emily Dickinson, very probably in April, of which the cousins were informed in May, 1861.

Over the years Emily continued to write to her Norcross cousins more freely than to any other correspondents. She trusted them, and they were fiercely loyal to their trust. Marked resemblances of temperament between Emily and Lou made confidence still easier. Although Lou never achieved anything, she dreamed of being "great." She could sympathize with Emily's ambitions. Apparently she suffered a rather similar emotional injury, and like Emily she withdrew from the world. The letters do not always make clear whether Emily is referring to her own disappointment or consoling Lou. Perhaps both. After Emily died, the question of publishing her letters arose, and the cousins reacted with great anxiety and alarm. Lavinia Dickinson did not particularly like them, but she was annoyed by their reticence and perhaps by a feeling that Lou was giving an inferior imitation of Emily. The cousins were not necessarily "geese." They had an alarming secret, and they did not know what to do with it. Who would understand and continue to love Emily as well as they did?

Although they refused to let anyone see Emily's letters to them and made sure that the letters would be burned after their death, they agreed to copy them — and copied material that even Mrs. Todd thought almost "too personal" to print. What the Norcross cousins permitted to stand in Emily's letters is almost more astonishing than their persistent secretiveness. Plainly they had a sincere desire to publish every word that was not a telltale name or an obvious clue. They believed that no reader would understand the allusion to their visit to Emily in May, 1861, or to the black April that preceded it. And their confidence was almost justified.

IX

THE NEW YEAR of 1862 dawned without hope for Emily or Kate or a nation rent with conflict. In the margin of Lamb's essays, Kate wrote: "Feb. 20th 1862. bells all ringing for the victory in Tennessee! — Cooperstown — Thursday — " But a few pages further back she had gloomily marked a line in "The Superannuated Man": "Those eternal bells depress me." There were doubtless many bells — triumphant, victorious bells, tolling bells, and the regular call to worship and to penitence.

For Emily Dickinson, the year 1862 was one of profound change. Her handwriting altered from a small, rather delicate script to a bold, disconnected one, and she dropped the girlish "Emilie" of her signature for an uncompromising "Emily." She manifested interest in the symbolism of white garments, and may have begun to wear white as a conscious symbol. With the walls of her prison closing around her, she made a brave but ineffectual attempt to break out by means of her poetry.

"As early as 1862" wrote Mrs. Bianchi, "she had visibly withdrawn from the outside world, even humoring her moods until those she professed to love saw her less often when they came to the house." Flagrantly careless in all other matters, Mrs. Bianchi was, as usual, remarkably accurate where Emily's relations with Kate Scott were concerned. The poem to Katie, quoted at the outset of this book, and indeed the whole story of this attachment, strongly support Mrs. Bianchi's statement that from the beginning of 1862, probably a few months earlier, Emily found herself unable to meet a world that had treated her cruelly.

One path was open to her, and she tried to take it. If she had been unusually fortunate, or strong enough to withstand initial disappointment, she might have made her way back into society through her poetry. In June, 1862, Emily wrote proudly to Higginson: "Two editors of journals came to my father's house this winter, and asked me for my mind." The two were probably Bowles and J. G. Holland. The latter was now a free-lance writer and lecturer but had recently been one of the editors of the *Springfield Republican*. Holland's opinion of her poetry is known. At the end of many years he still considered it unsuitable for publication. Very likely both men were more impressed by her letters, and asked that she contribute prose essays. "They shut me up in prose," wrote Emily resentfully in one of her poems. Neither man was to give her a real outlet, although Bowles did use two of her poems.

In January, 1862, Emily began a letter to Bowles with these words: "Are you willing? I am so far from land. To offer *you* the cup, it might some Sabbath come *my* turn." Bowles was not mystified; he knew what she meant: Do me the kindness to listen and perhaps reply to me; I have not yet recovered from that grief of which you know. Evidently he answered her kindly, for her next letter to him began with the simple words: "Thank you." The idea of death, she added, was worrying her incessantly.

By February (if a letter to the Norcross cousins is correctly dated), Emily was recovering from her midwinter storm of suffering. She had been very ill, she wrote, and had "feared one

day our little brothers would see us no more, but God was not
so hard. Now health looks so beautiful." She was waiting impatiently for spring and summer. Nevertheless, she was not
well, for when Bowles came in March, she once more refused
to see him and apologized in these words:

> *Perhaps you thought I didn't care — because I stayed out*
> *yesterday. I did care, Mr. Bowles. I pray for your sweet*
> *health to Allah every morning, but something troubled*
> *me, and I knew you needed light and air, so I didn't come.*

On March 1 Bowles published two stanzas of her poem "Safe
in their alabaster chambers." There is no record that he was
deeply impressed or that he asked for more poems. However,
the experience of seeing herself in print must have been salu-
tary for Emily. She began to hope. In the April *Atlantic Monthly*
appeared an article by Thomas Wentworth Higginson entitled
"Letter to a Young Contributor." Emily resolved to ask this
understanding stranger for criticism of her work. On April 15
she sent him an odd little letter, touchingly sincere, asking if
her poetry "breathed." It was accompanied by four poems. For
some reason Emily refused to sign the letter but enclosed a
card bearing her name.

2

It has been suggested — and the suggestion is plausible — that
Emily wrote some of her "gambling" poems during the period
of suspense that preceded Higginson's answer. Every new
writer gambles with his hopes and his very tender self-esteem
when he meets his first professional audience, and for Emily
the hazard was far greater. Of course, she was well acquainted
with the history of the Brontës, who had tried the same experiment of sending poems to well-known writers. They had been

younger, however, and had weathered discouraging criticism.
Emily was making a late start. When Higginson wanted to
know her age, she adroitly turned the question aside with the
untruthful statement that she had "made no verse, but one or
two, until this winter." Moreover, she was so obsessively preoccupied with her disastrous love for Kate that only a remarkable understanding on Higginson's part could have drawn her
out. Years later she thanked Higginson for saving her life, but
it is plain that he kept her in a state of prolonged invalidism.

Although he answered with kind promptness, his criticism
was harsh. Emily thanked him for the "surgery" and admitted
that he had "bled" her. Like the other professional writers
who saw her work in manuscript, he had a mind worn smooth
by much reading, and he was offended by her off-rhymes and
disturbed by her originality. The correct mediocrity of his
friend Helen Hunt Jackson was more to his taste. In his rôle
of preceptor to the young, he inquired about Emily's age,
books, and companions, and suggested that she drop her poor
attempt at rhyme and imitate the free verse of the newly famous
Walt Whitman. But Emily had heard that Whitman was disgraceful. With an echo of *Aurora Leigh* she answered that she
"could not drop the bells whose jingling cooled [her] tramp."

There is a subtle difference in Emily's second letter which
suggests that she had taken Higginson's measure. If she could
not win him with her poetry, she would catch him with her
prose, and the letter scintillated. She flattered, mystified, and
dumbfounded him. The two poems enclosed were exactly like
the preceding four, but her prose conquered him, and he overflowed with praise. Higginson had found his place in her life.
He could not return her balls, but they bounced off his solid
surface and afforded her game of a sort. She was a witty woman,
and he was a good-natured pomposity. But she was also a suffering woman, who placed a lasting value on his kindness to her
at a difficult period. She was, in fact, altogether too dependent
on his kindness.

Unwisely Higginson urged Emily to delay publishing her work — a hint that may have chagrined her but fell in too dangerously well with her own tendency to withdraw. The idea of publishing, she told him, was as "foreign to [her] thought as firmament to fin." Yet among the first four poems sent to him was "Safe in their alabaster chambers," which had appeared in Bowles' newspaper six weeks earlier. Emily now hastily disavowed the very circumstance which apparently had encouraged her to write to Higginson. She was to be curiously bound by his advice. In 1866 Sue Dickinson enabled Bowles to publish a second poem, and Emily was annoyed with Sue and apologetic to Higginson. In spite of the officiousness, Sue was the better friend.

Years later Emily apparently sought a lifting of the ban. Her approach was so oblique, however, that Higginson might easily have misunderstood. Helen Hunt Jackson wanted some poems, and Emily begged Higginson's permission to *refuse*. Wistfully she pursued the subject in three more letters. Mrs. Jackson did publish one of Emily's poems in *A Masque of Poets* (1878), and it is by no means certain that she acted without permission. That Emily was often devious in her letters to Higginson appears in another instance. On March 12, 1864, she permitted her Sweetser cousins to publish "Some keep the Sabbath going to church" in their paper, *The Round Table,* and she said nothing to Higginson about it. On another occasion she promised three poems to a charity. Apparently she had already copied them out, when she thought to ask Higginson's approval. He did not approve. In her next letter she thanked him for his advice, thanked him repeatedly, but stressed the nature of the ensnaring cause by which she had been misled.

Higginson never understood her, but he enjoyed her flattery, when he was not made uncomfortable by her exaggerated deference. Quite apart from his very real doubt of the merits of her poetry, he had apparently no wish to share her with a larger public. She was "my eccentric poetess who . . . sees only me and a few others." Although he wrote to her with respect and admiration, he laughed about her to others and enjoyed his friends' parlor game of imitating her letters to him. In a sense he relished and encouraged her eccentricities.

Doubtless Higginson believed that he answered her wish. He would have shown more understanding if he had urged her to publish whenever and wherever possible and learn from the experience. Emily was caught between her own scruples and Higginson's enjoyment of them. She wrote disdainfully of publication but wistfully of fame. At intervals she revised her work and assembled much of it in a painstaking manner. Late in life, according to her sister, she sent many packages to an editor of *The Century,* and she continued to place poems in the hands of Higginson, Bowles, Holland, and Thomas Niles, all of them connected with the business of publishing. After Emily's death Niles would be reluctant to associate his firm, Roberts Brothers, with her poems, which he considered "quite as remarkable for defects as for beauties" and "generally devoid of true poetic qualities." This was the unanimous verdict of the men to whom Emily submitted her poems. She did not realize that she had to persist. Hungry for fame but harassed by repeated failure and by the knowledge that much of her poetry dealt with Katie, she was driven more deeply into herself.

For any understanding of Emily Dickinson, it is necessary to distinguish between what she said and what she did — more accurately, between what she believed about herself at any particular moment and what the persistent, unconscious direction of her life shows that she was. Nowhere is the contradiction more apparent than in her letters to Higginson. The first few are sincere; they tell a great deal about herself. The remaining letters are marked by a strained euphuism, behind which she effectively concealed her real personality. In her poems, however, as an examination of the manuscripts will show, she remained the same passionate, demanding, fearfully torn woman that she had always been. Although she called

Higginson "Master" and herself "Pupil," she never altered a word of her poems to please him. They were her real life, and Higginson had little to do with her real life. Once she acknowledged a spelling mistake; Higginson was permitted to tutor her in spelling. He was a friend rather than a teacher, and she valued him because his kindly human voice, all unconsciously, had recalled her from the brink of madness or suicide. With a little understanding, he could have been a great deal more.

Harvard graduate, schoolteacher, Unitarian minister, colonel in the Civil War, essayist, poet, and novelist, Higginson was a man of broad rather than deep sympathies. The one exception seems to have been a passionate attachment to a college friend named William Hurlburt. Their letters, according to Higginson's widow, were like those between a man and a woman. In spite of contemptuous neglect, Higginson wrote faithfully to Hurlburt for many years, and his final disillusionment was bitter. To an unnamed younger friend, who had timidly introduced the subject of such attachments, Higginson wrote a letter relating his unhappy experience with Hurlburt, but the unnamed person was probably a young man. Higginson and Emily apparently never knew each other well enough to exchange confidences about their similar misfortunes.

On April 15, 1862, the date of Emily's first letter to him, Higginson was thirty-eight to her thirty-one. He was preparing to enter the army, and he had just written an article of advice to young writers which had deluged him with unprintable effusions. The wonder is that he found time to write to Emily, and evidently he was not very encouraging. Her second letter arrested his attention. For some time he was interested and wrote often, but he was soon willing to let the correspondence lapse. Emily revived it, not once but many times. In like manner an Oriental who has rescued someone from death is ever afterwards considered responsible for the person he has saved.

Higginson was not always happy about his responsibility. He

made fun of Emily and once echoed his wife's plaint, "Oh, why do the insane so cling to you?" But Emily was as brilliant as she was peculiar, and she held him. He made inquiries about her, first to an uncle of hers in Worcester and then to Helen Hunt (afterwards Mrs. Jackson) at Newport. In August, 1870, he found time to visit Emily, and in December, 1873, he came again. (After her death, however, he could not remember whether he had seen her once or twice — a forgetfulness which suggests that the impression was not indelible.) When his invalid wife died in 1877, Lavinia entertained a wild hope that he would marry Emily. It is hard to say which of the two principals would have been more astonished or dismayed by this suggestion. For his second wife Higginson chose a younger, better-looking, and more conventional woman. Higginson's last visit to Amherst, in May, 1886, was for the purpose of assisting in the burial services of Emily Dickinson.

After Emily's death Lavinia turned to Higginson, among others, for help in editing the poems. He was courteous but scarcely encouraging. When Mrs. Todd assumed the editorship, she too saw the advantage of securing a well-known writer for launching an unknown poet, and she was more successful than Lavinia. Young, handsome, intelligent, and enthusiastic, Mrs. Todd obviously did more to convince Higginson of the value of Emily Dickinson than Emily had done in twenty-two years of correspondence. Mrs. Todd did most of the work of editing. Higginson lent his name, wrote an article introducing the poems and a preface to the first volume, smoothed out irregularities and contributed titles which are in themselves strong evidence of ineptness and misunderstanding. He was not fully convinced of the merit of the undertaking until it was crowned with public success. In her forthright manner, Alice James, sister of William and Henry James, noted in her journal that her only doubt of Emily's genius arose from the fact that it was "sicklied o'er" with Thomas Wentworth Higginson. Yet he was probably kinder and more helpful than any other man Emily was likely to have found.

Higginson did Emily one service which might have been a great one. He introduced her to Helen Hunt Jackson. If Mrs. Jackson had lived longer, if she had not been distracted by many other interests, and if she had been an intimate friend, she might have drawn Emily out of her prison. For she recognized the talent to which Emily's masculine friends were blind. Unfortunately her efforts remained sporadic. They are interesting only as a "might-have-been" and as the genesis of a curious biographical legend.

According to this legend, Emily related her love story to Helen and encouraged Helen to use it in poems and prose. The works of Helen Hunt Jackson were considered source material for Emily's life, and biographers who wanted "evidence" of Emily's attachment to a Hunt or a Gould or a Wadsworth succeeded in finding it. But they built upon a mythical intimacy between the two women and ignored Emily's reticent nature. Emily did not entrust to a woman whom she scarcely knew the details of love affairs which never occurred.

3

In her second letter (April 25, 1862) to Higginson, Emily remarked that she had Sir Thomas Browne "for prose." The influence of Browne's *Religio Medici* upon Emily Dickinson is now well known. She was especially influenced by one page, which has been identified with "the leaf at love turned back" in a poem beginning " 'Twas the old road through pain." One student of Emily Dickinson has even noticed a resemblance in temperament between Emily and Browne. But no one has studied thoughtfully the page to which Emily turned for her lessons in love. Browne wrote (and Emily echoed him in several poems):

I hope I do not break the fifth Commandment, if I conceive I may love my friend before the nearest of my blood,

even those to whom I owe the principles of life. I never
yet cast a true affection on a woman; but I have loved my
friend as I do virtue, my soul, my God. From hence me
thinks I do conceive how God loves man, what happiness
there is in the love of God. Omitting all other, there are
three most mystical unions: 1. two natures in one person;
2. three persons in one nature; 3. one soul in two bodies;
for though indeed they be really divided, yet are they so
united, as they seem but one, and make rather a duality
than two distinct souls.

There are wonders in true affection: it is a body of
Enigma's, mysteries, and riddles; wherein two so become
one, as they both become two. I love my friend before my
self, and yet methinks I do not love him enough: some few
months hence my multiplied affection will make me believe
I have not loved him at all. When I am from him, I am
dead till I be with him; when I am with him, I am not
satisfied, but would still be nearer him. United souls are
not satisfied with imbraces, but desire to be truly each
other; which being impossible, their desires are infinite,
and must proceed without a possibility of satisfaction. . . .
This noble affection falls not on vulgar and common con-
stitutions, but on such as are mark'd for virtue: he that can
love his friend with this noble ardour, will in a competent
degree affect all.

Browne had no very high opinion of women, whom he regarded as "the Rib and crooked piece of man." He could have
wished "that we might procreate like trees, without conjunc-
tion, or that there were any way to perpetuate the World without this trivial and vulgar way of union." Although Browne
eventually married, it was apparently for the benefit of posterity
rather than with a view of pleasing himself; his opinion of
women remained unchanged. Nothing further need be said
except that Higginson had warmly recommended Browne in

his "Letter to a Young Contributor." Emily, of course, was already acquainted with Browne and looked upon Higginson's recommendation as a bond of sympathy. She may have heard of the *Religio Medici* through Kate, who always read far more widely than Emily, but the only copy surviving in Kate's library was a gift from young Florie many years later.

In the same letter of April 25, 1862, Emily gave Higginson her most tantalizing piece of information, the short account of her emotional history already quoted in part:

> *When a little girl, I had a friend who taught me Immortality; but venturing too near, himself, he never returned. Soon after, my tutor died, and for several years my lexicon was my only companion. Then I found one more, but he was not contented I be his scholar, so he left the land.*

In her next letter to Higginson she remarked: "My dying tutor told me that he would like to live till I had been a poet, but Death was much of mob as I could master, then." She had not forgotten her preceding letter. The "dying tutor" and the tutor who died are one person, and presumably Ben Newton. All the circumstances agree. But who was the friend 'who taught her Immortality'?

In a strict sense, one cannot be *taught* immortality, but Emily's grammar is not always reducible to logic. Frequently, however, she used the word "immortality" to describe the mystical sense of the annihilation of time which is experienced in passion. Under this interpretation, she was telling Higginson, without any intention of his understanding: In my youth I was taught the meaning of love by some one who fell in love with another person and never returned to me.

To Sue Dickinson, Emily wrote: "Love is immortality." If she omitted Sue from any account of her emotional history, then she purposely distorted the picture. No attentive reader of Emily's letters, notes, and poems can dismiss as wholly incredible the suggestion that Susan Gilbert taught her the immortality of love but fell in love with Austin Dickinson and never returned. The chronology is correct, for Sue turned from Emily to Austin some time before Newton died.

There remains the "one more" who "left the land." At the time of Emily's letter only one of her close friends was literally gone from the land. In mid-April, 1862, Samuel Bowles had sailed on the *China* for a summer of rest and recuperation in Europe. Although Emily wrote very emotionally to Bowles, she was not in love with him, and if he loved any woman other than his wife, it was certainly not Emily Dickinson. In fact, during the years of his closest friendship with Emily, Bowles was plainly very much disturbed by a highly emotional attachment to a Northampton woman named Maria Whitney, and of this, too, Emily was aware.

In the early summer of 1862 the Reverend Charles Wadsworth was expecting to leave Philadelphia for California. This would not be a literal departure from the land, and in any case the event was still in the future. Emily rarely saw him, and though she may have sorrowed over the removal of a kind friend from a distant city to one still more distant, it was not enough to account for the violent emotional upheaval of the preceding twelve months. Even poets do not go distracted and think of suicide because a friend has moved from one city to another, unless they are the direct cause of the friend's leaving. If Wadsworth was in love with Emily, if their passion came to a tragic climax about April, 1861, then, and not otherwise, he may be identified with the "one more." Emily meant the land of her heart, and there is no reason to believe that Wadsworth had occupied it.

Although the person may not be identified, the meaning of the sentence is perfectly clear. Emily found one more person who absorbed all her attention, but the other demanded something more than a relationship of mere friendliness, and when Emily refused, abandoned her. That is the plain meaning of

the words "he was not contented I be his scholar, *so* he left . . ."
Emily was in no state of mind to be just, and the word "so" is
bitter. According to the evidence, her friend retreated, not in
anger, but in blind panic over a situation that had got out of
hand. For this other person was assuredly Kate. This was the
"bride" of the poem "Her sweet weight on my heart a night"
and the disguised woman of other poems referring to the same
night. This was the Kate who vanished beyond an "ocean" of
silence and refused to answer Emily's letters. And this was the
loved, lost friend of the poem "I've none to tell me to but
thee," who now remained silent on "some unanswering shore."

4

The published works of Emily Dickinson contain some forty
poems which are addressed, without subterfuge, to another
woman. They are of greater biographical importance than a
hundred employing masculine pronouns. A woman might con-
ceivably write love poems to an imaginary man (it is probable
that many do), and she might sometimes, but not habitually,
imagine the love affair from the viewpoint of the man involved.
But no woman ever wrote poems describing a love affair between herself and an imaginary woman. Only the strong compulsion of truth would dictate poems so opposed to convention.

Another point must be made. Volume after volume of
Emily's poetry was issued without any poems that directed
attention toward a woman. In an early collection, as already
noted, Mrs. Todd included the poem "Is bliss, then, such
abyss," but omitted the three last lines showing that the bliss
involved another woman. When Mrs. Bianchi assumed the
editorship, she began cautiously to publish one or two feminine
poems in each new collection, but they were not strikingly
pointed. They could be interpreted — and were interpreted —
as relating to Sue Dickinson. Consequently most of the signifi-

cant poems dealing with a woman, as well as the majority of the
"forgot" poems and the frantic accusations, were reserved for
the final collection published by Mrs. Todd's daughter, Millicent Bingham. A careful screening of the poems had been employed, and the biographers of Emily Dickinson were thrown
hopelessly off the track.

Not all of the feminine poems are of equal weight — or
necessarily to the same person. An unimportant little poem
was apparently written to Emily Fowler Ford, and some four
or five may have been written to Sue. The three "Dollie"
poems, which witness an unhappy dependence on some woman,
are very much in point. Mrs. Bianchi referred to her mother,
Sue Dickinson, by the pet name "Dollie." But it would be
dangerous, and discreditable to both women, to assign all of the
remaining poems to Sue's influence. The betrayal of a brother
was not one of the problems that arose in the tragic but honorable attachment between Emily and her friend.

Only one of the poems is addressed to Katie, but the information that it gives is astonishing — nothing less than the explanation of Emily's withdrawal from the world. Probably
Emily felt the danger of harboring too many manuscripts con-
taining personal names, even though she had considerable
privacy and an honorable and incurious family. In a manuscript in the handwriting of the eighteen-sixties, "Distrustful
of the gentian," she used a long dash to represent a name:

> Weary for my ——
> I will singing go.

The meter requires a disyllabic name. Either "Dollie" or
"Katie" would suffice, but the latter appears more probable.
Emily is searching for some beloved person, who flees from her
like "the phantom meadow before the breathless bee."

The poem to Katie accused someone of treason. It is related

to another "treason" poem beginning "Forget? The lady with the amulet," in which Emily herself is the amulet. It is highly probable that Kate is "the lady" of other poems. In "So much summer me for showing," Emily thanks "the lady with the guinea" for showing her an "illegitimate" summer. In "Is bliss, then, such abyss," Emily fears that "the lady" will be cross with her on account of her indiscreet conduct. One poem declares that "The lady feeds her little bird [Emily] at rarer intervals." In another poem ("The bird must sing to earn the crumb") Emily complains that "the lady" comes only "once a century." In the poem "I had not minded walls," which clearly defines the moral problem between them, Emily appears to be looking into "the lady's" veiled face.

A visit to Amherst is the subject of a poem, "The day she goes or day she stays," which refers to the other woman as Emily's "existence." The last line, "Departed or at home," is identical with the last line of another poem, "Here, where the daisies fit my head," in which Emily calls her friend, "my flower" and declares that the two women form "a single bloom."

The two women were "wed one summer," and the other woman was the poet's "bride." She was also the "queen" and the "butterfly" who came on a summer's day, and though identifying clues are carefully avoided, she must also have been the "small Deity" of the "bashful Summer's day" who is implored to leave heaven and "entertain despair!"

At last the affair reaches its tragic climax ("Like eyes that looked on wastes"), and the two women face each other, anguished, unwilling to be "queens" but equally unwilling to renounce each other. Nevertheless the other woman breaks away and Emily is "forgot."

> Knows how to forget!
> But could she teach it?

wrote Emily in bitter anguish. "That she forgot me was the least," wrote Emily elsewhere, describing the shame of continuing to love the woman who had forsaken her. In kinder mood she wrote:

> Precious to me she still shall be,
> Though she forget the name I bear . . .

With renewed proof of her friend's indifference, she wrote: "Now I knew I lost her." In "Frigid and sweet her parting face," Emily affirmed that every clime was "alien and vain," every fate was "acrid." Who was this woman that dared "withhold from me Hemisphere and home?"

Nothing was left but memory, and memory was stimulated by the visits that Kate continued to pay to her old friend Sue. Emily could not stay away, but she looked at the other woman across an impassable gulf. "Unworthy of her breast," she wrote sadly, but doubted that any soul was worthy. "To see her is a picture," she declared generously; yet the other woman, by failing to give Emily "Redemption,"

> Makes mockery of melody
> It might have been to live.

An interesting poem, "I years had been from home," which belongs with this group, has bewildered a good many readers. The poet stands in front of her lost home, tries desperately for courage to open the door and ask if the life she has left is still dwelling there, fears that the answer will be against her, and runs away in panic. The explanation is simple. During one of Kate's later visits Emily was left alone with her for some minutes. She was strongly tempted to ask if the old tenderness still lingered in her friend's heart, but in the end she dared not put the question. According to Mrs. Bianchi, Emily always interrupted her seclusion to visit Sue's house when Kate was there. Sue Dickinson would have mentioned this to Mrs. Bianchi as one of the painful absurdities of the affair.

It is unreasonable, and quite unnecessary, to suppose that Emily repeated this whole tragic experience with a man. Under any circumstances, once was enough. In a seclusion that protected a vulnerable heart, she turned into poetry the one brief event of her life. But here a difficulty arose: she could not publish love poems to a woman. Of course, Shakespeare's sonnets to a young man had been printed during his lifetime (Emily was well acquainted with the sonnets and much influenced by them), and Anna Seward, the forgotten Swan of Lichfield, had written elegies and a centenary of sonnets commemorating her unhappy attachment to a young woman. But notions of propriety had changed, and the poet who now braved such a taboo would be silenced in life and in death. "Tell all the truth but tell it slant," wrote Emily Dickinson.

If Emily had consistently disguised the sex of the person she loved, she would have done no more than many another modern writer has done, but the truth was too strong in her. It tore her apart. "I felt a cleavage in my mind," she wrote, "as if my brain had split." Her sense of unreality was great and painful; she could overcome it only by separating herself from the world. She withdrew into seclusion because she could not live as society demanded and was not permitted to live as her own nature demanded. In a terrible isolation she debated the problem with God. Although she suspected that her sufferings were not unique, she had no other help than her young cousins, the *Religio Medici,* and Shakespeare's sonnets. Sometimes she put her poetry into acceptable form and took hesitant steps toward publishing it — that is, toward rejoining society under a mask. And again she defied the world and wrote for herself and truth alone.

Consistency in the handling of her poems is not to be expected. As early as her thirtieth year, she used masculine pronouns in a love poem, "Heart! We will forget him!" Some love poems of this period were undoubtedly written with feminine pronouns, still others with a careful avoidance of identifying clues. Kate's visit of late 1861 apparently excited new poems with feminine pronouns, for the grief of this new rejection was immediate and very real. The following spring, in a letter to Higginson, Emily disguised her friend as a man, and yet some of the feminine poems were undoubtedly written long afterwards. A great deal would depend on the mood of the moment and the intensity and nature of the feeling to be expressed. Toward the end of her life she again dealt very frankly with Katie. With life failing, she seemed in haste to tell the truth.

Some poems were rewritten to make them more acceptable. Two poems, "Going to him! Happy letter!" and "I showed her heights she never saw," exist in both masculine and feminine versions. There were probably others, but Emily destroyed many early manuscripts in the ceaseless revision of her work. Another poem, "The Stars are old, that stood for me —" was partially rewritten to serve another purpose. In the original Emily wrote that time had passed, the "West" had grown older, and yet the only gold she had ever wanted to earn looked newer to her every day. The last four lines arraign the other woman for her "infinite disdain" and tell her that her apparent victory is really defeat for both women. When Emily sent these four lines to Higginson to describe her meeting with a bird, she carefully changed the pronouns from feminine to masculine. Yet Higginson would have been satisfied with a female robin.

It is true that Emily was lawless with pronouns. She often referred to herself in the plural or under a masculine disguise, and she spoke of Newton's spirit as "it" and "itself" and asked Higginson: "Would it teach me now?" Yet certain poems suggest that the employment of neuter pronouns was another attempt to escape from the telltale feminine. The poem "Knows how to forget! But could she teach it?" was rewritten with a neuter pronoun. The poem "Like eyes that looked on wastes" refers to the other person as "it" and "itself"; yet the line "Neither would be a queen" betrays the fact that both were women. This poem speaks of a compact between them "as hopeless as divine," and is related to another poem, "While it is alive, until death touches it," which uses neuter pronouns and affirms that the lovers "dwell in one blood under one sacrament." Still another poem, "If I may have it when it's dead," begins by calling the lover "it" and ends with a direct "thee."

The identity of subject matter in two poems, "Not probable — the merest chance —" and "Why make it doubt — it hurts it so —," has already been pointed out. The first poem ends with the frank cry "oh phantom Queen!" The second poem is a good illustration of the poet's struggle to find an acceptable way of presenting her lover. The lost friend is referred to as "they," a "dear, distant, dangerous sake," a "Vision," "it," "They," and finally "Master."

The use of "they" to describe a single person can be illustrated by another poem, "Though I get home how late, how late!" First it is "they" who will have given up expecting her in heaven, and then "they" will hear her knock, and at the end she wonders what "itself" will say to her. The plural may conceal a single person in still other poems: "They won't frown always — some sweet day," "Why do they shut me out of Heaven," " 'Tis true they shut me in the cold," and "If I could bribe them by a Rose." On the other hand, these poems may reflect her belief that she had been excluded from the partnership of Kate and Sue — or Kate and Mrs. Vanderbilt.

The use of neuters and plurals is at least suggestive. If Emily had been in love with a man, surely she would have had less difficulty with pronouns. Her problem was very real, and her behavior, often dismissed as irrational and lawless, was exactly proportioned to the terms of her problem.

The poems using neuter or plural pronouns to describe a woman are, of course, in the minority. Masculine pronouns, though they cost her an effort, were undeniably simpler. Even more satisfactory was direct address, and if she feared that her readers might still see through a "you" which must have appeared transparent to her, she could always replace a "sweet" or a "beloved" with an odd but masculine "Sir," "Signor," "Master," and the like.

An example may be given. In the poem "Sweet, you forgot, but I remembered," she reproaches her friend for abandoning her, wonders how she has "erred," but promises to love twice as much in order to make up for the friend's default. The poem belongs, of course, to the "forgot" group. The last stanza is generous:

> Just to be rich, to waste my guineas
> On so best a heart!
> Just to be poor, for barefoot vision
> You, sweet, shut me out!

With a change of "best" to "broad" and "sweet" to "Sir," she sent this final stanza to Bowles, who obviously was not the subject of the orginal poem.

To her friend Mrs. Holland she sent a copy of the poem beginning "To see her is a picture," but here again she made significant changes. She dropped the lines that speak of "Redemption" and of another woman as the cause of her misery. It was Katie to whom she looked for redemption, and it was Katie who had caused her anguish — not Mrs. Holland.

One version of "Oh, shadow on the grass!" has a first stanza beginning "We can but follow to the sun." As the sun goes down, the poet is left hopelessly following. In the next two stanzas a shadow approaches, and Emily prepares her "nominated heart," only to find that she has waited too long ("delayed to guess"); the lover has consecrated someone else. Late in her life Emily sent a version of this poem to a new friend, Mabel Loomis Todd. As Mrs. Todd was not a setting sun, the first stanza was dropped, and the tense of the last stanza was changed, so that the poem became merely a playful anticipation of a visit. In its original form it was tragically serious.

The symbolism of this poem illustrates Emily's last and favorite means of disguising her friend. The bee-rose symbolism has already been described. The friend also appears as butterfly, sun, sea, gem, bird, the West, home; Emily herself is gentian, rose, leopard, peacock, butterfly, and so forth. With the clues given, any attentive student of Emily Dickinson's work may read as he runs.

5

In a letter of July, 1862, to Higginson, Emily sent the poem "Of tribulation these are they." The interesting point is that "they" are "denoted by the white." In words much too subtle for Higginson to understand, Emily was telling him that she had won through death to a kind of austere triumph.

"God's dead, who afford to walk in white," wrote Mrs. Browning, whose *Aurora Leigh* was Emily's Bible in those days. *Aurora Leigh* also directed Emily to the Bible itself, and in the Book of Revelation she read:

> *3.5. He that overcometh, the same shall be clothed in white raiment.*
>
> *4.4. . . . I saw four and twenty elders sitting, clothed in white raiment; and they had on their heads crowns of gold.*
>
> *6.11. And white robes were given unto every one of them.*

*7.13. And one of the elders answered, saying unto me,
What are these which are arrayed in white robes? and
whence came they?*

*7.14. And I said unto him, Sir, thou knowest. And he
said to me, These are they which came out of great tribulation, and have washed their robes, and made them white
in the blood of the Lamb.*

There is no certain knowledge of the date on which Emily
Dickinson began to wear white. John W. Burgess remembered
her as an apparition in white. These memories undoubtedly
belong to his student days in the mid-sixties (Emily was then
in her middle thirties), for he associated them with Emily's
cousin, Perez Cowan, a fellow student in those days. When
Burgess returned to Amherst in the mid-seventies, Emily was
entirely secluded. Her niece could not recall ever seeing her in
anything but white. Higginson noticed a white dress during
his first visit of August, 1870, and she was in white when he
came again, in December, 1873. She may have begun to wear
white tentatively, perhaps only in the summer, as early as 1862.
The poem sent to Higginson in midsummer, 1862 ("Of tribulation these are they"), certainly indicates that she was already
beginning to consider the symbolic value of white. She herself
wrote that she did not wear it exclusively.

In a poem, "Unworthy of her breast," which commemorates
one of Kate's visits after the rupture of their friendship, Emily
wrote:

> By her exacting light
> How counterfeit the white
> We chiefly have!

The manuscript of this poem is a clean copy in Emily's last
handwriting. It may have been a revision, for Emily was prob-

ably refurbishing old poems as well as writing new ones about Katie in her last years.

In a letter to Kate (quoted earlier and tentatively dated about January 1, 1861) Emily wrote: "I hold your black in strong hallowed remembrance, and trust my colors are to you tints slightly beloved." It has already been suggested that Emily began to wear white only after passing through her midwinter storm of suffering (1861–62) and emerging into the bitter triumph of summer, 1862. The passage just quoted, however, raises a question as to whether Kate's perpetual black may not have influenced Emily as powerfully as the Book of Revelation. Emily was much impressed by her friend's mourning; she may have wished to set herself apart in a similar manner. Her white was a shroud, not a bridal garment. Recalling the bitter April of 1861, she wrote, "Somehow myself survived the night," but added that she was "dated with the dead." Some two dozen poems describe her continued existence as a death in life.

But white was also her symbol of victory, for she wrote that she had overcome great tribulation. That is the meaning of the poem sent to Higginson in July, 1862. The date of this poem, the fresh memory of Kate's black, and the combined influences of *Aurora Leigh* and the Book of Revelation, which were especially strong at this time, all suggest that as early as the summer of 1862 Emily had begun to consider wearing white, or even to wear it part of the time, as a symbol of death and victory.

6

During 1863 Emily's life would be almost a blank if it were not for letters to the Norcross cousins. Mrs. Holland preserved none. The Bowleses preserved a short letter and perhaps some poems, and Higginson a letter. They are not very informative. The correspondence with Lou and Fanny Norcross is fairly large, but, as usual, it has been severely edited by the cousins. Emily seemed more comfortable, but she was not happy. In May, during her sister's absence, she wrote to her cousins, describing new nightmare terrors in the darkness of her lonely room and adding: "that old nail in my breast pricked me." In the autumn she wrote to them simply: "Nothing has happened but loneliness, perhaps too daily to relate."

Part Two

 X

In the spring of 1864 Gertrude Vanderbilt was shot, Emily Dickinson went to Boston for treatment of strained eyes and strained nerves, and Kate Scott Turner became engaged to be married.

Mrs. Vanderbilt was accidentally shot — she received a bullet intended for someone else — but it was well-nigh as fatal as if it had been done on purpose. About ten o'clock on the night of March 20, 1864, she was aroused by screams of "murder" and the sound of pistol shots. Running to the back of the house to admit her terrified maid, she opened the door just in time to be shot by the girl's crazed lover.

The housemaid fell across the doorstep, bleeding from a bad wound in the hip, and the man disappeared into the shrubbery and got safely away. In the excitement of rescuing and attending to the injured girl, Mrs. Vanderbilt did not feel the pain of her own wound. Even when she was forced to lie down on the sofa, she thought her weakness was due to nervous strain. It was some time before anyone noticed the blood seeping through her dress. Still her wound was believed to be slight — the news-

paper next day reported a flesh wound — and the housemaid
received more attention.

On the morning of March 22 Mrs. Vanderbilt's condition
was acknowledged to be critical. Cautious probing had failed
to locate the bullet, which was buried deep in the intestines,
and the danger of infection was very great. The four attending
physicians, among them Kate's brother-in-law, Homer Bartlett,
agreed that there was little hope of recovery. The housemaid,
who was improving (but with a pessimistic medical opinion
that she would be a cripple), forgot her own pain in anxiety
for Mrs. Vanderbilt and suffered more for her mistress than
for herself. Mixed with excitement over an event so rare in
the peaceful little community, there was general regret for the
expected death of a kind, generous woman.

Two days later, according to the Brooklyn *Daily Eagle,* her
physicians were more hopeful of Mrs. Vanderbilt's recovery.
The bullet had not yet been found, nor had the man who fired
it. On March 25 the Brooklyn *Daily Union* reported that
"Mrs. Judge Vanderbilt" would almost certainly be well again.
From that day onward the newspapers were silent. Whether
the mad lover was caught, whether the maid was permanently
crippled, no one ever said, but it is certain that Mrs. Vanderbilt made a complete recovery and lived until 1902.

If Kate was not in Flatbush at the time, she was fully informed by her sister or her brother-in-law, and from her the
news went to Sue Dickinson. Sue must have been interested
in the near-fatal accident to a woman who had visited her and
whom she was to visit in Flatbush some years later. From Sue
the information went to Emily.

In April, 1864, Emily Dickinson was in Boston, or rather in
neighboring Cambridge, where she stayed with her Norcross
cousins and underwent a long series of treatments for her eyes.
Whatever jealousy Emily may once have felt regarding Kate's
attachment to Mrs. Vanderbilt, she could not help being impressed by the circumstances of the accident. Mrs. Vanderbilt's

gallantry in rescuing her maid and attending to the girl's wound before her own, would certainly impress. Emily would also remember that she was a charming woman, altogether deserving of Kate's admiration; and death, or a near escape from death, struck deep in Emily's sensitive imagination. It was returning to this world "with a tingle of that" other world. She wrote a poem congratulating Mrs. Vanderbilt on her recovery, and to Sue she wrote still more warmly that Kate's friend was "worthy of life." The note was headed "At Centre of the Sea."

In her last published letter to Kate (January, 1861), Emily had written: "I am pleasantly located in the deep sea, but love will row you out, if her hands are strong." What she meant by the "deep sea" is certainly not clear, although it is plain enough that she was beginning to doubt the strength of Kate's love. The little note to Sue, with the heading "At Centre of the Sea," was intended to be a reminder. She expected, or hoped, that Kate would see her note.

Emily compared her months in Cambridge to a stay in the wilderness. She wrote to her sister that she was like Elijah. Some months after her return to Amherst she wrote to her Norcross cousins: "Every day in the desert, Ishmael counts his tents." There was wilderness in Cambridge and desert in Amherst, and everywhere Emily was an outcast. But in a poem, "You know that portrait in the moon," her friend became the outcast Ishmael, for Emily believed that both of them were lost. Looking at the moon, she tried to trace in it the features of her vanished friend:

> But Ishmael, since *we* met 'tis long —
> And fashions intervene..

In the spring of 1864 the lost Ishmael engaged herself to John Hone Anthon and was lost indeed. The exact date is unknown. In a poem of this period ("Ourselves were wed one summer, dear") Emily wrote that her friend was "crowned in June." The phrase might refer to a June engagement. Whatever the crowning signified, it was destructive to the "wedding" between Emily and her friend. In May, 1864, John Anthon joined the church, and on May 28 he gave his photograph to Kate. There is at least a suggestion that he was expecting some change in his life. A few months later he spoke of his claims upon Kate as still recent.

Kate was now thirty-three and had been a widow for seven years. John Anthon, born October 25, 1832, was thirty-one and a bachelor. He was a tall man, about five feet eleven, slender and graceful, with sharp features, black eyes, dark brown hair, and long, drooping mustaches. His friends described him as a natural orator and spoke with pride of his deep, sonorous voice and of his self-possession and poise in arguing a lawsuit or making a political speech. They would have liked to make him district attorney of New York or even governor of the state, and if he had lived longer, they might have done so.

The sharp features and the somber black or professional iron-grey suit concealed a warmly emotional personality. The loss of his first big murder trial affected him so profoundly that he never again tried a criminal case. He turned to politics, built up a large civil practice, taught medical jurisprudence, and took a leading part in the Masonic Lodge. "Our gifted John Anthon," Mrs. Scott called him, for he had many interests and a turn for many things. His brother Charles, a professor at Columbia, dedicated a classical dictionary to him in affectionate admiration of his scholarship; but the Greek quotations in his commonplace books gave way to absurd epitaphs picked up from tombstones here and there. He was a pleasant young man, lively, talkative, engaging in his manners. In short, he was a good match, and he came of a good family.

The record of the Anthons fills several columns in the *Dictionary of American Biography*. The elder John Anthon was a well-known New York lawyer, author of several legal books, and founder and president of the Law Institute. He was considered the ablest member of the New York bar in his generation. His brother Charles was a well-known classical scholar at Columbia, and his brother Henry was rector of St. Mark's in the Bowery. His wife, Judith Hone, was the daughter of a wealthy New York merchant and niece to Philip Hone, mayor of New York. She was a gentle, devout woman, a faithful worker in the Protestant Episcopal Church, and a charitable First Directress of the New York Orphan Asylum.

Of their children, two sons achieved some distinction. Charles Edward, already mentioned, was named for his uncle and was only a little less eminent as a classics professor at Columbia. Another son, General William H. Anthon, was a well-known lawyer. There were two unmarried daughters, Bessie and Joanna. A third daughter married the Reverend George Houghton, founder and rector of the Church of the Transfiguration, better known as the "Little Church around the Corner." Kate said he was the best man she had ever known. During the Civil War Houghton invited Negroes into his church, and in spite of great personal risk, protected them from the excesses of the draft riots. Years later the actor Jefferson, who had solicited in vain for the burial of a fellow actor in a large Fifth Avenue church, was directed to try the "little church around the corner." Houghton welcomed him, and the Church of the Transfiguration became the actors' church.

The Anthons were not wealthy, and young lawyers were far from prosperous during the Civil War. This might explain the long engagement between John Hone Anthon and Kate Scott Turner, if there were not strong indications that Kate herself was reluctant to marry. Perhaps she marked at this time the passages in Lamb's essays which suggest a doubt regarding some step she had taken, a fear that the happiness which she had promised herself was not happiness. Her father gave her a thousand dollars, which would have made a handsome wedding present, but she chose to use it for another purpose. In the fall of 1864, shortly after her engagement, she went abroad, and she was in no hurry to return.

On October 5, 1864, according to an announcement in the *New York Times*, Mrs. C. M. Turner of New York, in the company of the Edward Clarks of Cooperstown, sailed for Europe aboard the Cunard liner *Persia*. It may have been this voyage which Emily had in mind when she wrote "I envy seas whereon he rides." She need not have envied Kate herself, who was miserably seasick.

The voyage was like all other voyages of that period — extremely uncomfortable. Yet in her day the *Persia* was a proud ship. At the time of her launching in 1856 she was the largest ship on the Atlantic, with the most magnificent appointments. These appointments included swinging oil lanterns, a small, stuffy saloon, no deck space for passengers, uncomfortable little staterooms in the bowels of the ship, two latrines to be shared among 250 first-class passengers, and long benches in the dining saloon, where the Cunard officials served rigidly prescribed meals at rigidly prescribed hours. The only picturesque element was the billowing spread of white canvas which the ship carried in a favoring wind. With her sails, her two big side wheels, giant engines, eight boilers, and forty furnaces, the *Persia* made surprisingly good time — almost fourteen knots — and on a summer voyage of 1856 she captured the blue ribbon for an Atlantic crossing of nine days and five hours. But the Cunard company sold safety, not speed or comfort, and all the wealth of Edward Clark could not have bought a more comfortable passage in those days. This Edward Clark, incidentally, was the father of Kate's good friend Alfred Corning Clark, who was to gather some twenty-five million dollars from the Singer sewing machine industry founded by his father.

Emily Dickinson knew that Kate was abroad in the closing months of the Civil War. She continued to receive news of all important events in Kate's life by way of Sue Dickinson, and clearly Sue knew that Kate was in Europe, even though Kate made a point of telling her family, toward the close of her trip, that she had not written to Amherst from Europe. Several of Emily's poems seem directed toward a person who was, or had been, abroad. One has already been mentioned, "I envy seas whereon he rides." Of course, Emily's "seas" are so characteristically symbolic that the poem cannot be safely dated on the strength of this one word. Nevertheless, it seems to describe a European journey. The poet envies not merely "seas" but also "spokes of wheels" in the carriages that convey her friend and hills that look upon her friend's "journey"; and the poem closes with the familiar bee-rose symbolism.

Another poem begins "I had a guinea golden" (reminiscent of the "lady with the guinea" in "So much summer me for showing"). The second stanza speaks of a "robin," and the third stanza of a Pleiad (one of Emily's "treason" poems, "When the astronomer stops seeking," in handwriting of the period of Kate's trip abroad, speaks of a lost Pleiad). "My story has a moral," Emily continues explicitly. Her "missing friend" is named Pleiad, robin, and guinea. If her unhappy poem reaches the "eye of traitor in country far from here," she hopes the friend will repent.

A poem beginning "The sunrise runs for both" suggests that when one of the two friends (presumably Kate) is in the bosom of midnight, the other (Emily) is upon its hem. In short, they are separated by a time interval of some five or six hours. A poem beginning "I knew that I had gained" speaks of a suffering relieved only by the knowledge that her friend is suffering equally "in other continent." A poem already mentioned, "I've none to tell me to but thee," refers unquestionably to a love relationship broken by the friend's choice. Once the two were together, but now the other's "sweet face has spilled" beyond Emily's "boundary." And Emily speaks of "some unanswering shore" from which her friend's voice no longer returns to her.

Most interesting is a poem beginning "They put us far apart." The two friends are separated like the sea and its "unsown peninsula" (a symbol deriving from Mrs. Browning's Italy, where Kate lived during the winter of 1864–65). "They" (that is, the inimical world) have separated the two lovers, but still the latter communicate with each other by "telegraphic signs." During the Civil War there was an intense interest in the laying of the Atlantic cable, commonly referred to as a "telegraph." According to this poem, the lovers are separated "with guns." The word "guns" suggests the Civil War, which raged upon the Atlantic as well as upon the land, although Emily surely knew that Cunard ships, bearing the British flag, were inviolate to both sides. Of course, nothing can be proved, but this poem and the others described are certainly more applicable to a Katie going abroad than to a Wadsworth going to California during the period of the Civil War. No matter that Kate had turned away from Emily. She had loved once (she was still uneasy), and Wadsworth had never done so. Emily was intelligent enough to know the difference.

2

After some ten days in London, the Clarks and their young companion went to Paris, where they remained for five weeks. It was the Paris of Louis Napoleon and the Second Empire — corrupt and brilliant. Kate was always expecting to catch a glimpse of the imperial family. When the Clarks' carriage entered the Bois de Boulogne or neared the Tuileries, the dark eyes gleamed beneath the black veil, but for some reason Kate never saw the emperor or the empress or even the young prince. It was strange, for by the testimony of other American travelers they were easily the most visible royalty in Europe.

In the absence of such a spectacle, Kate found her pleasure in the modern Paris which Louis Napoleon had created — miles of slate-grey uniformity, wide avenues illumined by flaring gaslights, green breathing-places like the Bois de Boulogne

— and in the ancient Paris of art and civilization on which the
Second Empire was a temporary gilding.

Kate was never quite sure how well she liked Paris, and she
had no wish to live there. Enjoy it she would, and derive every
possible benefit from the shops, museums, and luxurious restaurants, but the Puritan in her could never wholly approve.
Paris, she thought, "must be the most beautiful city in the
world, with its spacious avenues and gates and bridges and
splendid monuments and churches." But she was surprised and
disapproving when several boarders at Miss Ellis' *pension* on
the Champs Elysées attended a Sunday opera, and High Mass
at St. Roche provoked the exclamation, "Oh, the mummery
we did witness!" The levity of a Parisian Sunday never failed
to astonish her, and after a tour of the Palais Royale she cried
out, "Oh, what a 'Vanity Fair'!" It is pleasant to note, however, that the bill for her dresses, bonnet, hat, crinoline, gloves,
and lingerie was rather more than twice the cost of board and
lodging during her five weeks in Paris.

Sightseeing was the main business of the day, and Kate went
at it with a seriousness tempered by amusement. She called it
"work." She saw everything and reported everything — in a
mixture of naïve surprise and good humor, subtly colored by
the unannounced conviction that she was having her last fling.
The war and the family at home were often in her thoughts
and on her paper, but she had little to say about her fiancé.
Once she remarked that John Anthon was working too hard in
the campaign for the re-election of Abraham Lincoln and she
wished he would stop. Another day she spoke of her disappointment in finding no other mail at the banker's than a letter
from John, but added hastily that of course she felt repaid for
her walk. Although she liked him and became in time very
fond of him, there is at least a suggestion that in the beginning
she was not passionately in love with him.

"We are longing to know about the election," she wrote on
November 15, 1864. "I suppose it is Lincoln, of course. I read

the 'Galignani' every day, and it is not very favorable to our Federal cause." On November 21 she wrote gleefully that the news had just reached them by telegraph. "Lincoln elected! Great excitement at dinner among the Americans and much champagne drinking. The English very glum and quiet. The London papers are in an awful wrath at Lincoln's re-election. The 'Standard' this morning furious and abusive."

In late November the Clarks made plans for their Italian journey, and Kate began reluctantly to pack. "Paris is so beautiful," she wrote wistfully. "We drove all through the Boulevards the other evening and through the long Rue de Rivoli with its interminable rows of lights, and the shop windows are so gay and brilliant. Paris is in a blaze at night, and I often look out of my window in the evening so fascinated with the miles of lights all up and down the beautiful Champs Elysées." The city of light was harder to leave than she had imagined.

"Mr. Clark is perfectly disgusted with us," she wrote, "for having so many traps." She was "tired to death — been packing all day," and feared they could hardly read her scrawl. "Wait till I get to the 'Eternal City.' It is hard to realize I am going to — Rome! Goodnight, dear Father and Mother. God bless you both. Ever your loving Katie."

The party went by rail to Nice, which Kate was persuaded must be the earthly paradise, and then hired a carriage to take them by the Corniche road to Genoa.

The four-day trip from Nice to Genoa was all adventure and intoxication. Even an uncomfortable stop at Oneglia ("poor inn and a funny time generally") became part of the excitement. With an Italian *vetturino,* a great carriage, and four horses, the journey had a color and a magnificence hardly to be recaptured in days of swifter travel. Hour after hour, on their left, the rocky cliffs rose in grandeur, and on their right, often as much as two thousand feet below, lay the intense blue Mediterranean, from time to time giving way to "fertile valleys with their terraced gardens filled with dense groves of olives and figs and orange trees." In the distance the snow-covered Alps blocked the horizon. Kate had never seen anything like it — "so novel, so wild and romantic," and of course she was in "perfect raptures the whole time."

After a day in Genoa the party embarked on a Mediterranean steamer for Leghorn and Civita Vecchia. Among the company, Kate reported, was the German ambassador to Rome with his wife and children, and the lady was so beautiful that the American could hardly take her eyes from her.

"Rome! Rome! Here we are!" she exclaimed on the evening of December 11, 1864.

It was Rome of the papal state, of Pius IX and his unpopular secretary of state, Cardinal Antonelli — the Eternal City of magnificence and poverty, of ancient corruption and new reaction, of decayed grandeur and modern filth unspeakable. Even in palaces, as Hillard noted, ladies must lift their skirts and not be overmodest about exposing their ankles. "Too true!" Kate was to write in the margin of his guidebook. But in this first hour it was enchantment, "and all seemed like a dream, as we looked at the old walls and the Tiber and the Castle of St. Angelo and the Dome of St. Peters."

"The white walls, the blue hills, my Italy." So Mrs. Browning had written, and Kate could not help remembering. She had come, in sober fact, to the blue peninsula of Emily Dickinson's dreams.

"Thou piercing silence of ecstatic graves," said Aurora Leigh. Almost at the outset Kate discovered a grave. On a day that was, for a change, warm and sunny, she went with Mrs. Clark to the Protestant Cemetery. While the older woman paused at the grave of her son (victim of an earlier trip to Rome), Kate "wandered on deeply impressed with the quiet and beauty of the spot, and finally came upon the grave of *Shelley!*" He was always, and characteristically, her favorite poet. In later years she would use quotations from Shelley and leave marginal notes in his books which would throw light on some unusual chapters of her own life.

Soon after their arrival the party moved from the Hotel di Roma on the Corso to a pleasant apartment "in the Via Condotti (one of the best streets), very near the Piazza di Spagna, and close by the Spanish Stairs, a splendid flight of 135 steps leading directly up to the famous Pincian Hill, the favorite resort of all the Romans every afternoon for walking or driving." Here they settled down in great comfort for the winter — a winter of hard "work," by Kate's definition.

The first several days were rather too gloomy and damp for much sightseeing, and in preparation for the work to come Kate read and marked in her copy of Hillard's *Six Months in Italy*. One passage is tantalizing evidence that her letters were not always to be trusted for the state of her mind. Diaries were to be more reliable, but she destroyed the journal that she kept during this first trip, and even in diaries she never felt so secure as in the margins of her books. The sight of the young nuns in the Trinita de' Monti had moved Hillard to write:

> *That man lives to little purpose, in my judgment, who does not gather, from increasing years and enlarged observation, a stronger sense of the peculiar perils to which woman is exposed — of her unequal chances in the lottery of happiness, and of the sterner sentence passed upon her wrong-doings. In thoughts like these there was a power that lifted the heart above the atmosphere of sect, and I never omitted to offer a silent prayer that these fair, young creatures might be shielded from the snares that everywhere lurk in the path of woman, and, if they failed of happiness, at least, not part with peace.*

Kate marked the entire passage, and then underlined the word "peace." Like Emily Dickinson, she was wandering in the desert and the wilderness. But she left even more striking evidence of her uneasiness in another book that she carried with her. This was Ik Marvel's *Reveries of a Bachelor,* beloved by Emily and Austin Dickinson, by Susan Gilbert, and by many another romantic adolescent of the early nineteenth century. Why Kate brought this book with her is not clear, except that it contained several vivid descriptions of Rome and the Apennine region and recorded a bachelor's perplexities about marriage.

Of course Kate marked every passage that dealt with the Rome she was then seeing, and she underlined the words *Via Condotti,* the name of the street in which she was living. But, oddly, she marked also every passage referring to the unpleasantness of in-law relationships, and she marked Johnson's famous lines (which Marvel mistakenly ascribed to Lyttleton or Shaftesbury) that "marriages would be happier if they were all arranged by the Lord Chancellor." "Unfortunately [Marvel added, and Kate marked the lines], we have no Lord Chancellor to make this commutation of our misery."

Further on in Marvel's book, Kate bracketed three lines of poetry quoted from a play by Davenport:

> And if you hear hereafter
> That I am dead, inquire but my last words
> And you shall know that to the last I loved you.

She also marked passages describing a loved woman, as in the following examples:

> *. . . a sweet-faced girl, with a pretty little foot lying out upon the hearth — a bit of lace running round the swelling throat — the hair parted to a charm over a forehead fair as any of your dreams; — and if you could reach an arm around that chair back, without fear of giving offense, and suffer your fingers to play idly with those curls that escape down the neck; and if you could clasp with your*

*other hand those little white, taper fingers of hers, which
lie so temptingly within reach . . .*

*Her smile would illumine the blackest of corroding
cares; and darkness that now seats you despondent, in your
solitary chair for days together, weaving bitter dreams,
would grow light and thin, and spread, and float away, —
chased by that beloved smile.*

It might be rash to suggest that these passages recall Emily
Dickinson (although a passionate attachment of some two years
must have left its traces), but assuredly they do not recall John
Anthon.

3

The idleness of Kate's first days in Rome brought on an
attack of homesickness. She had been to the apartment of Dr.
Gould, physician to the American colony, and the party had
ended with the singing of hymns, "all those sweet hymns we
used to sing at Maggie's and at Gertrude's Mission School! I
felt like crying. And, oh, how I thought of you all. Sometimes
I feel that I cannot stay here four long months. I must see you
and Father and dear Maggie and the Doctor and those blessed
children. Do tell me if Harry Bartlett [her sister Maggie's oldest son] is well and if he remembers his '*Annie* Katie.' I would
give anything on earth to see that beautiful boy. I stop and cry
a little. Alas! alas! Rome is a dark, grand, dingy old place. You
must detach yourself from the present and live in the past.
Crumbling ruins, mossy fountains, ruined arches, ancient gate-
ways meet you at every turn. I have seen nothing as yet — been
twice to St. Peters and driven on the Pincian Hill. It will clear
soon, and then we will begin to work."

On Christmas Eve the fit had by no means worn itself out.
"I think of you all at home, so busy, dressing the dear old

church. I am longing to see you all. Feel a little homesick (yes, a good deal)." She had gone to Mrs. Gould's to help with preparations for the children's Christmas party at the American Legation. "It did seem so queer making candy bags here in Rome!" But the Christmas celebration at St. Peter's brought forth the "raving epistle" that she had warned her family to expect.

"Christmas Day! Oh, my dear Mother, here you have me just home from St. Peters! I am very tired and ought to lie down, but feel too excited to sleep or do anything but talk of all I have seen on this great Festival." They had gone early, without bonnets and with black veils on their heads, as the church had prescribed, but were still unable to find seats. With awe and excitement Kate watched the Pope being carried in, "followed by his own guard in their splendid uniforms." Then came High Mass, with responses by the choir stationed above one of the great piers of the dome.

"But the most solemn, the most impressive and overpowering ceremony of all was the tinkling of the bell announcing the Elevation of the Host. Simultaneously the whole assembly dropped on their knees — Cardinals, Priests, Officers, Soldiers, people, all fell prostrate! The marble pavement suddenly rang with the clash of arms. Then a silence as of death pervaded the vast audience, broken by a burst of music from a full military band accompanied by silver trumpets. It lasted but a few seconds. Never, never did I hear or dream of strains of such angelic sweetness. For the moment you were carried to the very gates of Heaven. As the last notes died away, I drew a long breath, and choked back an involuntary flood of tears."

When the Pope was carried out, Kate stood near enough to receive his benediction. He looked, she thought, like a benevolent, good old man, but she craned her neck in vain for a glimpse of "that wicked old Cardinal Antonelli."

Outside the great church there was an animated scene — "the vast concourse of people, the immense number of carriages, and the general confusion and excitement. I stood on the steps and gazed at the motley crowd, the beautiful fountains, the long colonnades, the grand obelisk, the noble bridge across the Tiber, and the flags flying from the Castle of St. Angelo! It was a wonderful day. It seemed not like Christmas, or Sunday, or anything else I had ever conceived of."

Fatigue and excitement left her even more vulnerable than usual, and she flamed into a passion of homesickness. "I have thought of you all so much. My heart is with you all the time. Oh, I trust you are well and happy. Tell me if any of you get sick. Sometimes I am dreadfully depressed, thinking something may happen. Write me *instantly* if you or Father or Maggie or Henry or those blessed children get sick and I will come right home. It is a terrible thing to be so far away! Do tell me if Harry Bartlett keeps well this winter. If anything happens to that beautiful boy while I am gone, it will utterly ruin all my happiness. I often think of him at night and cry to see him and hear him say 'Annie Katie.' I will tell him stories all the time when I come back!" And she added impulsively, "I am crying now like a fool."

The sharpest edge of her homesickness was now dulled by a new friendship. She became acquainted with a Miss Brasher, who was traveling with an American family named De Forest. The two women attended concerts, dined together, shared their sightseeing. On St. John's Day they were caught in a pouring rain outside St. John Lateran and were unable to find a carriage. "We had a world of fun," wrote Kate. Sharing an umbrella, the two young women set off down the wet, narrow streets, Miss Brasher with a reckless disregard for traffic. Again and again, between warning cries and fits of laughter, Kate rescued her from a passing cart or carriage. In high good humor they reached the Coliseum and resolved to walk through it. When they emerged, the wintry evening was already closing in, and Kate grew nervous, remembering that she had promised Mrs. Clark hours ago to be home in a few minutes. For-

tunately she was at last able to hail a cab driver. "He drove
so fast," wrote Kate, "I thought we should be dashed to pieces.
We laughed all the way home." A few days later she referred
to Miss Brasher in these words: "We are *desperate* friends."

Shortly afterwards, however, Miss Brasher disappeared
from the story, and new names chequered the letters. Kate became acquainted with the American actress, Charlotte Cushman, who was living in retirement in Rome with her young
protégée, the sculptor Harriet Hosmer. Meetings at the American church led to a very pleasant evening in Miss Cushman's
house, and a few days later Kate was invited to witness a hunt
on the Campagna, where she had the pleasure of watching Miss
Cushman and Miss Hosmer "chasing the hounds furiously."
Then there was Mary Chapman, daughter of an American
painter, to whose efforts, assisted by Miss Chapman's "French
beaux," Kate was indebted for a seat in St. Gesu on the Feast
of St. Silvester. Maggie Knapp, an old acquaintance, turned up
in the party of the James Averells, and it was almost settled that
Kate would return to America with them in the spring.

The American colony in Rome — artists, writers, the professional men who kept it in health and religion, as well as parties
of well-to-do tourists — was by now engulfing her, and plainly
she was having a very good time. She even revived tentatively
the hope that her family would somehow find money to provide a summer in Switzerland, but it was with the expectation
of disappointment. The wartime inflation of the currency
made foreign travel very expensive for Americans. "To multi-
ply every dollar by two and a half," wrote Kate, "is *rather too
much!* I cannot afford to travel through the summer with gold
so high." Resignedly she added, "Well, it has done me a world
of good and I should be very thankful for so much!"

In mid-February, 1865, Kate joined the Averell party and
accompanied them to Naples. Her enjoyment of the city was
heightened by the discovery that Vesuvius was *smoking.* Night
after night she dashed into the street to watch the red flames

streaming from the volcano, and the memorable voice went up
and down the scales with excitement. Dared she make the ascent? She was very anxious to go, and so was Maggie Knapp,
but then it was very fatiguing. Abandoning the subject one
moment, she returned to it in the next, painfully torn between
timidity and her ambition to do everything that was to be done.
"I am crazy to do it, but I presume Mr. Averell will protest
against it. I shall not wish to go if we continue to see these
flames issuing from the top every night."

The ascent itself she found as hilarious as it was tiring.
"Took a carriage as far as Resina, close by Herculaneum, and
then for six miles ascended on horseback — great fun, great
merriment, but very fatiguing. I could hardly keep my seat
coming down — such vast beds of lava — seas of lava! I was
frightened sometimes — so steep and rough. Magnificent view
all the way. The carriage road was buried by the eruption of
1861, so we were forced to take horses and donkeys. Such a
time! Guides screaming to the horses in Italian, boys following
us, beggars importuning for alms. I laughed and I screamed,
and I shouted to my guide not to leave me, and he only replied, Allons, Madame, *Courage! Courage!*" Four days later,
in closing her letter, she added at the top: "All alive and well,
but very *stiff* and *sore*."

Shortly afterwards she was writing in more than her usual
state of rapture about their trip to Sorrento. She had never
seen anything "so utterly fascinating, so dreamy, so romantic!"
Rome was a gloomy tomb by comparison. It was "delightful to
get somewhere where there is nothing to do — no palaces to
visit, no churches, no tiresome museums! No trouble of any
kind! Only long rambles by the seaside over the cliffs, through
the loveliest ravines, with the grandest views everywhere before
your eyes." Tenderly she concluded: "Good night, dear
Mother. How my heart aches to think you cannot see this
lovely Sorrento!"

On February 27 she returned to Rome to take leave of the

Clarks. A severe cold was aggravated by the depressing news that a friend at home had died, and for several days she was very ill. Mrs. Clark was concerned, and the doctor was discouraging, but over their protests she insisted on going ahead with the Averells. On March 5, at noon, she embarked in the steamer for Marseilles, and she was very miserable. "Mrs. Averell, Maggie Knapp & I had a state room together, & three *sicker* creatures you never beheld! It was pitiable! It was heart-rending! It was ludicrous! I tumbled down out of my high berth & could by no means get back, so I fell upon Maggie's berth & we lay there together. Such a muss, such a confusion! I was really very ill, & Mr. Averell at last called in the surgeon on board, I was in such violent pain. He gave me powerful doses of opium. If that surgeon had any sense of the ludicrous he must have nearly died at the scene before him. I couldn't laugh then, but I have since!"

In Paris the days passed uneventfully. Except for a few afternoons at the Louvre the sightseeing was over. The Averells and Maggie Knapp had gone on to England, where Kate could not immediately afford to follow them, and she had no companion in the serious business of the tourist. The ladies at Miss Ellis' *pension* — the company was mostly ladies — were by now all her friends, but they were more interested in shopping than in works of art. Kate accompanied them, unable to purchase but fascinated as always by the profusion and splendor. "It is hard to realize it is Lent, or anything else but fashion and gaiety and glare and glitter. I do not see how one could live in Paris and not become perfectly worldly and given up to the 'pomp and vanities' of life!"

While she waited in Paris for the sailing date of the *Scotia*, Kate Turner mended and sorted her clothes, and perhaps her thoughts as well. Beneath the froth of comment and description, of exclamation and tears for home, strong currents were flowing, but the drift is hard to determine. Why she went abroad when she did, so soon after her engagement and for so many months is nowhere explained. In the feverishness with which she explored an alien environment there is a confessed fear that this would be her last chance. Henceforth she must be sober and domestic and tied to home. She said that the trip had done her good, and in spite of the very real homesickness, she was in no hurry to end it. Apparently she had needed a respite.

Throughout this winter of 1864–65, and on later trips, Kate lived, to a surprising degree, the life that Emily Dickinson was writing about. If Emily mentioned Sèvres china in her poetry, Kate had been to Sèvres and inspected acres of china. If Emily was preoccupied with the idea of volcanoes, Kate had ascended one. Emily wrote of Vevey and the Alps, and her lost friend spent a summer in one and many seasons in the shadow of the other; and of the "South, the love South," which Emily described with longing, Kate was an inhabitant for many years and, figuratively, all of her life.

Obviously Kate was not a learned woman or even a very clever one. "I showed her heights she never saw," wrote Emily with truth. On the other hand, Kate marked a passage in De Quincey's *Opium-Eater* suggesting that she thought herself far more clever than the woman she loved — but magnanimously overlooked the difference. It need not surprise that Emily proposed to be her "scholar" and once referred to her bitterly as "learned waters." Kate learned to speak French fluently and acquired a smattering of German and Italian. She read far more widely than Emily found either time or opportunity to read, and her memory was phenomenal. She had an immense curiosity and a communicable enthusiasm which influenced many people. The young English girl Florie described her as a teacher, and her niece wrote enthusiastically of her skill. In a passion for miscellaneous information she filled pages of her diaries with random jottings of the height of cathedrals, the number of pillars and statues, or the events in the lives of famous writers. Her commonplace books are a record of wide and incessant reading. In the margins of her astronomy books there are many notes, and she wrote down the date of the next transit of Venus, in the year 2004, as if it were of great importance even to eyes that would not see it. In old age she regretted that she was not near a good telescope, and eighty-six years were far too short to see all the places that must be seen and to read all the books that must be read.

Emily herself was not a learned woman and was not attracted to scholarship. Her niece remembered her unflattering description of one Amherst professor, and on another occasion Emily described professors in general as "manikins." Of some intellectual friend, perhaps Maria Whitney, she observed lightly that there was learning but not the "phosphorescence of learning." What Emily wanted was life, and in the art of living her friend was as clearly superior to her as in other things she was inferior. Kate was a passionate woman, with a vitality and a warmth that attracted the less vital and the cold; in her presence they were more alive, and in this sense only was Emily her "scholar." If other attraction had been wanting, Kate was the first to fall in love; and this flattery was irresistible. "Given to me without the suit," wrote Emily with bitterness in a poem beginning "Frigid and sweet her parting face."

Toward the end of this second stay in Paris, there is at least an indication that Kate was making up her mind. She wondered how New York would look to her. A friend suggested that the buildings would appear very low in comparison with those of Rome. Another added that New York would seem dark after Paris, and Kate answered stoutly: "I think it will look *perfectly lovely*. New York is a good enough place for me. Paris is very fine to be sure! but who cares when one's whole heart is somewhere else. I love New York better than any place on earth (and Cooperstown in summer)." She did not mention John Anthon, but she must have had him in mind.

The *Scotia* sailed from Liverpool on April 22, 1865. At Queenstown, where the ship halted to pick up letters, there was wonderful news. Lee had surrendered, and the long, bloody, fratricidal war was at an end. The rejoicing lasted until they reached New York. On May 1 the pilot came aboard with news of the assassination of President Lincoln, and the company was plunged into gloom. "Alas! alas!" wrote Kate tenderly, but no sadness could long withstand a boisterous welcome from her sister and brother-in-law, their young children, her friend Eliza Synnott, and of course John Anthon, who had given up all business for the day and had been waiting for her since early in the morning.

Their marriage was delayed another year, but at last, on September 5, 1866, the *New York Times* carried a brief announcement:

Anthon–Turner. — At Christ Church, Cooperstown, on Aug. 30, by Rev. S. H. Synnott, John H. Anthon, of this city, to Catherine S. Turner, daughter of Henry Scott, of the former place.

4

Emily Dickinson wrote a poem, "The Malay took the pearl." It is an odd little poem and has been oddly interpreted. According to one student, it is clearly "drawn from the mines of stoicism." (Mrs. Bianchi, who suppressed it, did not think highly of its stoical content.) There are three persons or objects in the poem — an earl, a Malay, and the pearl which both desire. The Malay, under this interpretation, represents the stoic ideal, because he cares little or nothing for the prize. There is obviously nothing stoic about the despairing earl, and the poem as a whole suggests the danger of interpreting the poetry of Emily Dickinson without some knowledge of her life.

Emily herself is the earl in a poem beginning:

> No matter now, sweet,
> But when I'm earl,
> Won't you wish you'd spoken
> To that dull girl?

Her friend is as clearly the pearl in a poem (among the first four sent to Higginson, on April 15, 1862) which begins:

> We play at paste,
> Till qualified for pearl.

In another poem, "I'll clutch and clutch," Emily describes herself as diving for a jewel, obviously a person, which she will wear on her breast, show at court, and carry to heaven.

In the poem under discussion, the Malay takes the jewel that should have belonged to the earl. The latter has "feared the sea too much, Unsanctified to touch," and has waited and prayed to be "worthy the destiny." The Malay, on the other hand, is not "unsanctified" to touch this particular sea, for he plunges fearlessly, and now wears on his "dusky breast" a gem that was too precious for a "vest of amber." The poem ends with these unflattering lines:

> The Negro never knew
> I wooed it too.
> To gain or be undone
> Alike to him, one.

It was natural that Emily should think so. Perhaps she was drawing conclusions from Kate's prolonged engagement.

The word "unsanctified" is clear proof that Emily was concerned with a taboo — which was not a taboo to the Malay.

The poem has nothing to do with stoic philosophy, but it might be profitably compared with a poem by Sappho:

> Peer of gods he seemeth to me, that man who sits before thee, and close beside thee listens to thy sweet voice and thy lovely laughter — this, this indeed, causes the heart in my breast to tremble. . . . But now, since I must lack, I must endure all.

Neither Sappho nor Emily Dickinson was stoical under a great disappointment.

The use of the word "Negro" is a reminder of *Othello*. Emily's copy of the play is well marked, presumably by herself, and she cited it more frequently than any other play. Senator Brabantio, the Moor (or Negro) Othello, and the fair Desdemona form a triangle which has some resemblance to that of the earl, the Malay, and the pearl. Brabantio calls his daughter "jewel," and in the final scene, lamenting the murder of Desdemona, Othello says that his hand

> (Like the base Indian) threw a pearl away
> Richer than all his tribe.

When Brabantio reluctantly yields his daughter to the Moor, he uses words which Emily quoted repeatedly:

> I here do give thee that with all my heart
> Which, but thou hast already, with all my heart
> I would keep from thee.

Elsewhere Emily herself would appear to be Desdemona ("O falsely, falsely murder'd!"), and Kate, the Moor, an identification which may owe something to height, dark coloring, and superior aggressiveness, as well as to the status of being a stranger. In a poem beginning "All forgot for recollecting," Emily wrote that she had given up everything for the sake of a stran-

ger. Rank, fortune, home, family, even fate, were all sub-
merged in the other's "bolder sea." The elopement of Desdemona was reported in these words:

> Your daughter . . . hath made a gross revolt,
> Tying her duty, beauty, wit, and fortunes
> In an extravagant and wheeling stranger
> Of here and everywhere.

Emily's bitter poem beginning "Good night! which put the
candle out?" may be a reminiscence of Othello's "Put out the
light, and then put out the light." Once Emily identified herself with Desdemona by signing a note to some friends: "Nobody. Myself. Desdemona." How far these identifications were
conscious — that is, how consciously Emily realized that she
was equating herself with Desdemona and Kate with Othello,
or herself with Brabantio, Kate with Desdemona, and John
Anthon with Othello — is, of course, an unanswerable question.

After Kate's marriage Emily seemed to enter upon a long
period of barrenness and creative poverty. Many of her love
poems, however, were written (or, at least, revised) during the
late eighteen-sixties. A poem of this period, "Crumbling is not
an instant's act," describes the slow wasting of her spirit. At
a later time she wrote, "The mind lives on the heart." If the
heart was empty, then the wit became "emaciate." The barrenness is reflected in her correspondence, which was very scanty
between 1866 and 1870. Of course, no one — not even Fanny
and Lou Norcross — saved more than a fraction of the letters
written to him, but where the published correspondence to all
Emily's friends is negligible, it may be presumed that the letters
actually written were proportionately fewer. During this period
few letters to the Norcross cousins, Samuel Bowles, the Hollands, or Higginson were preserved, and probably few were
written.

In August, 1870, Higginson paid his first visit, was much impressed, and came again in December, 1873. In the latter year an old school friend, Abby Wood Bliss, came home from Syria and received an ambiguous welcome. Emily proposed to talk with her from an adjoining room, but when Abby flatly refused, Emily agreed to meet her face to face. There were no other events.

The life of Kate Anthon was probably more active, but the record is still blanker. Every summer she returned to Cooperstown, where her husband joined her for their wedding anniversary. During the rest of the year she supervised her household and found what entertainment she could in New York society. It was not much. To a young friend she described feelingly the tedium of paying calls and going to teas. At some period she had cancer of the breast and underwent a disfiguring operation. It was probably during these years, for after 1874 her life is well recorded. There were no children, although there is a recollection of at least one miscarriage. This was unfortunate, for she loved and needed children. She was a devoted aunt to her sister Maggie's children and to the growing family of her brother Henry, who had married her old friend Eliza Synnott and settled in New York.

In the absence of positive ties to home, Kate traveled a good deal with her husband, and very likely came at times to Amherst. Probably she was with John Anthon on June 24, 1871, when, as Grand Master of the Masonic Lodge of New York, he laid the cornerstone of the state capitol at Albany. One thing is certain, and that is that she moved incessantly from one house to another. She began her married life in a two-story house on 30th Street, which apparently is still standing, not a hundred yards from the site of the Empire State Building and within a block of her brother-in-law's Church of the Transfiguration. Thereafter she moved restlessly, once a year on the average, but within a narrow circuit. She was living on 32d Street when this comfortable, if somewhat monotonous, part of her life came to an end.

Meanwhile John Anthon had been prospering. After the Civil War he built up a good practice and a comfortable estate in a rather short period of time. In 1867 he was nominated for the mayoralty of New York, but declined and supported the candidacy of John T. Hoffman, who won the election and went on to become governor of New York. In 1869 he was defeated for district attorney by a rather narrow margin. During the following two years he was Grand Master of the Masonic Lodge for the state of New York.

The year 1871 marked the turning of John Anthon's luck. Hurrying to a business appointment, he pitched headlong down a flight of iron steps to the pavement on Broadway. He picked himself up, apparently not much the worse for his fall, but the mischief was done. After his fall he became markedly nervous and irritable, lost his vigorous self-reliance, and became cold and withdrawn. Then his eyesight began to fail, and he had difficulty in speaking and walking. Apparently he was suffering from a brain tumor, but no one realized it. As his condition worsened, the New York doctors admitted their helplessness and urged him to go abroad. Kate's brother Henry was now showing alarming signs of tuberculosis, and it was decided that Kate, John, and Henry should all go abroad together.

On October 17, 1872, the three sailed for Europe aboard the *Russia*. And with this date the life of Kate Scott Anthon comes once more into the light.

 XI

In a hotel "way down in the south of Europe — 4000 miles from home," Kate sat with her husband in front of their foreign hearth, mournfully recalling their last cozy Sunday evening tea. "How suddenly our happiness seemed to slip away from us! In a twinkling, almost, I am set down in a strange country with two invalids!"

An inquiry in another letter, touching in its homeliness, reflects still more strongly the haste and panic of departure. Upon the breaking up of their home on 32d Street, Kate's Swiss maid Julie had gone to work in the Flatbush home of Maggie Bartlett. When Kate found time to remember some of the omissions of her last day in New York, she wrote to her stepmother: "Please ask Mag if Julie had a satchel of mine carried to Flatbush with her trunk. She promised to attend to it on that last *distracting* morning. There were clean clothes and soiled all thrust in anyhow and the key tied on the handle. Will Mag open it and see that all is right? I think some of my nice nightgowns were thrown in. I was *nearly* crazy, and don't know what I did."

Although John Anthon's illness had come on slowly, the

decision to go abroad was sudden and panic-stricken. There
was not even time to return to Cooperstown for leavetaking.
Kate consoled herself by remembering that her parents had
been spared the sight of her own alarm.

The day of their sailing, she wrote in her diary, was "a fair,
lovely day. Many friends came out in the tug to see us off. I
was too utterly worn out bodily and mentally to realize anything, even the sad parting with my dear sister, and the terrible
possibility that I might never again see my beloved Father, already so advanced in years! My husband's health was fatally
threatened, and every means must be attempted towards a
restoration."

To her parents, however, she wrote cheerfully, and with
some humor, of her inevitable seasickness and painful headaches. "Mrs. Nelson, the stewardess (whom I at once recognized as stewardess on board the *Persia* when I crossed before),
immediately came and did everything for me — said she remembered me (which was probably a pleasant little fiction on
her part), rubbed my head with her large strong hands and advanced the most extraordinary theories in regard to headaches
— how the bones of the head separated, and how she (suiting
the action to the word) squeezed them together again!"

The steward knocked at the door to ask what they would
have for supper.

" 'Oh, nothing,' we cried.

" 'Ah! but that will never do. No, sir, just let me get you
a fried sardine!'

" 'A fried sardine!' shrieked John. 'I never heard of such a
thing.'

" 'Oh, yes, sir, just the thing to settle the stomach.'

" 'For mercie's sake, then get one,' I said." The steward
soon returned with his fried sardine on toast and a cup of good
tea, and the effect (according to Kate) was miraculous.

The weather improving, their health improved likewise, and
Kate wrote cheerfully: "We have made 343 miles since yester-

day at twelve o'clock and are now steaming along at the rate of 14 knots — sails all set." But a day or two from Liverpool they ran into gales and rainstorms, and the letter ended hastily in a burst of inquiries, affectionate messages, and maledictions against the sea: "Tell Mag, Henry's bag was on board — only put in the opposite state room. He soon found it. Ask her if I gave Julie the key of the parlor closet. Oh, how I long for land — I *hate* the sea. Oh! how we roll! It is fearful! Everybody is writing letters, and the inkstands are dancing up and down the whole length of the table. Good bye, dear Mother. Best love to dear Father. Oh! what a gale!"

Their stay in London was short and disappointing. The London specialist merely echoed the diagnosis of the New York doctors: "Nervous prostration and loss of strength." Since there was nothing more to be gained in London, they decided, for Henry's sake, to push on southward.

Without any particular plan, they came at last, on the evening of November 8, 1872, to Mentone, and found that Henry liked it, and that it was considered a good place for tubercular patients. John Anthon liked it too, and as he was in need of rest, the whole party moved from their large hotel to cheaper and more permanent lodgings in the Splendide. "We are not as *splendid* as the name would indicate," wrote Kate. But it was an excellent hotel, with a magnificent view of the Maritime Alps from the back windows, and the Mediterranean almost at the front door. All around them were groves of orange and lemon trees, figs and olives, and the air was scented with roses.

Mentone had few distractions for two invalids and an anxious woman, and they soon exhausted all of them. There were such walks as John Anthon could manage, donkey trips to Cap Martin, up the Gorbio Valley, and to the oldest olive tree in the region, and carriage drives to Nice and to Monaco. Kate spent most of her time reading to her husband, walking with him, and striving in every way to banish the irritable sadness that clung to him. She had little time for writing letters, even

to her family, and closed her portfolio instantly when John
Anthon came halting into the room with flowers for her in his
outstretched hand.

When the mild news of walks and drives and the beauty of
their surroundings were exhausted, Kate fell back on the
trifling pleasures of hotel life for the material of her letters.
"We drive and we walk and we sit in the sunshine," she wrote
to her family, "and we lounge around at Mrs. Taylor's and
read very stale New York papers, and in the evening have I not
two fires to punch and poke!" It was interesting to her that
their fires were lighted, not with kindling wood, but with pine
cones, and the cones became the means of a spirited game. Before sending for a fresh basket of wood, they carefully hid all
remaining cones, and thus were never in arrears. John hid
cones everywhere; she was always coming across them in odd
places, and fully expected to find them someday among her
collars and cuffs. "A stupid letter," she added hastily, "but
what can I say?" She drew a picture of the bellows with which
they blew their fires, and devoted paragraphs to its patient,
resigned expression and to John's and Henry's attempts to improve her drawing.

On another occasion, when she had been trying, in much the
same manner, to enliven her letters, she added desperately,
"Well! well! We *try* to be jolly!" But of course she was far
from jolly, although she contrived to keep her gravest anxieties
to herself.

The local doctor discovered an inflammation of the throat
and larynx which might account for John Anthon's difficult
speech. The sick man submitted to weeks of painful cauteriza-
tion, and Kate wrote: "I begin now for the first time to have
some hopes of John's recovery." Later on, in Rome, she was to
think less highly of Dr. Bennett, but at this moment of renewed
hope she was thankful they had stopped at such a health-giving
place and fallen into the hands of so clever a doctor. Surely
rest and a good climate would do much, and she rejoiced at

every drive or walk that cheered her husband.

"My impetuous temperament," she admitted, "would demand a miracle to be performed, but that age has passed away, and the healing process must be essentially slow. I hope in my next letter to record a decided improvement. Perhaps not the very next — but soon — soon."

When the treatments ended, she tried hard to see an improvement. "Is it not a very tedious, trying disease, and John is *so patient* — never complains and is never even irritable under it." As her letters are often to be read by contraries, it is not necessary — or even reasonable — to suppose that John Anthon was always in an angelic temper. He was as patient as a man could be in his circumstances, but his wife had more to bear than she ever admitted to her family.

Storms lashed the Riviera and buried the Alps in mist. The Mediterranean at their door became a seething cauldron, washing away hedges and embankments and deafening them with its incessant roar. John Anthon was fascinated.

"I *must* go out and look at it," he exclaimed again and again. "I never saw anything so grand and terrible." While his wife and her brother remained in the hotel, shrouded in weariness and melancholy, he opened the door, walked with uncertain steps to the edge of the promenade, and remained there for many minutes.

It was not all gloom, however, for with the ease that never deserted her, Kate very early made friends of her fellow lodgers. After a siege of illness she reported gratefully, and with amusement, that Mrs. Lees of Scotland had poured hot water on her lame shoulder, Mrs. Baker of Bristol had made arrowroot, Mrs. Parks of Dover had brought soothing liniments, Mrs. Armitage of Devonshire, brandy, and Miss Fowlis of Norfolk, medicated wool. Other friends from outside the hotel had come to cheer her up or to bring help. With such a multitude of nurses, Kate wrote, she had been almost killed with kindness. Best liked of the new friends were the Bakers of Bristol, who were soon to show their kindness still more feelingly.

Months of inaction and very dubious improvement wore upon the sick man's nerves, and the Anthons decided to proceed to Rome, leaving Henry at Mentone to complete his cure. But here a difficulty arose. With the intention of giving them pleasure, their brother-in-law, Dr. Houghton, sent ten pounds for the hire of a carriage from Mentone to Genoa. The sum had grown hopelessly inadequate since his own European travels, and Kate was embarrassed by the necessity of refusing the gift or going still more deeply into their shrinking funds. At this point the Bakers came forward with a generous proposal to leave their children in Mentone, share the expenses of the carriage journey, make all the arrangements, and help with the care of the invalid. After satisfying herself that the Bakers really wished to make the trip, Kate cautioned her family never to let a word slip to Dr. Houghton and then gave herself up to the pleasure of anticipation.

"I feel so excited to think we are going over the Cornice road I can hardly write. I told John it did not seem right that I should be permitted to go over the whole road *twice*."

On the morning of February 25, 1873, Henry was up early to bid them good-bye; indeed the whole hotel were at the door and windows to see them off, for a large *veltura*, with its four horses, bells, and whip-cracking Italian coachman, always produced a great excitement. It was more than a casual excitement. The Splendide was much like a sanatarium, catering to the ill, the dying, and the anxious families who served as attendants. The foreign cemetery was filling with the unlucky, and Kate had already attended, with painful consequences to her nerves, the funeral of a young woman who had come too late. As his companions helped John Anthon to his seat, and the great carriage got under way amid a tremendous bustle and a volley of Italian, and the four horses stepped off smartly to the crack of the whip and the jingling of bells, there were some half-envious faces at the windows. Here surely was one party escaping from the dreary tedium and the fears of the sickroom into the healthy, hopeful world outside.

The Roman holiday that ensued has an air of grimness, tempered by the recollection that John Anthon had not yet consented to die, and that his wife did not know he was dying. She wanted very much to show him all the things which had given her pleasure eight years before. Eagerness was succeeded by a fear that she had tired him too much. They drove on the Pincian Hill and glanced into St. Peter's, and for a few hours John Anthon felt a reviving glow of interest in the classical studies which he had pursued at Columbia under his uncle Charles Anthon. On the last day of their visit they went to the Vatican, but the sick man grew weary.

"I regretted he could not get into the picture gallery to see the Transfiguration," wrote Kate, "but he was not equal to the stairs, so we gave it up. All the pictures and statuary in the world would not compensate if they made John ill."

The Roman doctor destroyed the hopes fostered by the Mentone doctor but offered none of his own. He advised rest and removal to a less enervating climate.

On March 22, 1873, Kate wrote from Florence, outlining plans for tours of Venice and of the Italian lakes and adding: "We shall tarry here till we are rested and well acquainted with lovely Florence." Years later the city of the Duomo and the Campanile, of Savonarola and Fra Angelico, of the spreading green Cascine and the winding, many-bridged Arno, was to be the scene of the happiest, most extraordinary winter of her life. In her present situation there was little to recommend the place. She wrote to her family of drives in the Cascine, of a trip to Fiesole, of an ascent of the Campanile. The journal, however, was frankly desolate: "I felt very nervous and sad. After John fell asleep I sat and *cried* to my heart's content."

Kate could not be in Florence without thinking of Elizabeth Browning. She made pilgrimages to the grave in the Protestant cemetery, to Casa Guidi, and to Bellosguardo, where Aurora Leigh had rented a villa. With a friend she groped her way by candlelight up many flights of stairs to the garret room of the former Liza Wilson, trusted servant of Elizabeth Browning. "She told us a great many interesting things," Kate wrote to her family, "and showed us some of Mrs. Browning's letters to her. We told her to keep them very carefully as they would bring a good price as time rolled on." Kate still had many letters and poems from Emily Dickinson. Did she think of them now? But she no longer had reason to suppose that Emily would become a poet.

Henry Scott joined them, to Kate's delight and relief, and the three made a brief trip to Venice. In a thorough romantic mood Kate saw and did everything considered necessary for a tourist, but with an admission that the city appeared to have decayed. Apparently she never saw Venice again, and she was regretful, for some years later she made an earnest attempt to return. The party journeyed together as far as Verona, where Henry left them, to return home and die more wretchedly another day. Henry was grieved at their parting, and his sister sobbed openly. He had been well enough all along to help her, and even the knowledge of his presence in Europe had been a comfort to her. Now all the responsibility came upon her alone.

The doctor in Florence had first directed the Anthons' hopes toward the baths of Gastein in Austria, to be followed by a long rest and another course of baths at St. Moritz in Switzerland. No sooner were their plans set than he decided on the hot baths of Wildbad in the Black Forest. Kate listened and consented. All their hopes were now pinned on the miraculous effects of Wildbad. She gave up the Italian Lakes (but filed them away at the back of her mind) and surrendered Switzerland. The trip to Venice was only a diversion until the baths opened at

Wildbad, and on April 24 the Anthons proceeded to Munich, while Kate studied the currency and tried to learn enough German to get along.

The Munich doctor whom they consulted flatly contradicted the doctor in Florence and pronounced the hot baths too "exciting," even dangerous, for a man in John Anthon's condition. There was to be no miracle. Instead they were directed to go to a cool climate, preferably Switzerland, and trust to the slow effects of rest and a better atmosphere. After some hesitation, for she had had a desperate faith in the baths, the unhappy woman accepted the new opinion and made plans for their Swiss journey.

On May 12, 1873, the Anthons arrived in Vevey, and Kate promptly called in a new doctor. It was here, and on this day, that she learned the hopelessness of their long pilgrimage through Europe. In her diary she wrote simply: "Dr. Muret called in the evening. Not a very agreeable man. Did *not cheer me at all.*" Of the same day she reported: "I passed a sleepless night." Much tragedy was concealed, not to be openly manifested until the last heartbroken entries in her diary; but the tone of the diary now altered perceptibly, and even in her letters she could not wholly subdue the note of despondency and abandoned hope.

Four days later she wrote to her family: "Oh, if I could only see him get decidedly better here in this heavenly place. He remains about the same. I see no great change as yet. His recovery is very, very slow. What the summer may do for him, God only knows. I have consulted six different physicians, all eminent men. They say time alone can bring about a cure. He must be kept quiet, with a pure air and nourishing diet. He seems very happy here. I feel at times very much alone. What a blessed thing it is I keep well to take care of John. I do not know what would become of him if anything should happen to me."

It was a very creditable effort, but she had much to bear, **in** her self-imposed silence, during the next several months. With more open sadness she wrote: "I want to see you all so much. I can hardly keep the tears from my eyes as I write. Europe is very beautiful, but I never care to come again. Every place is associated with John's illness and full of sadness for me. I think when one is not well the best place is *home*, among your own relatives and friends." And again: "Home! Home! I long for home!"

When the weather grew too warm at Vevey, they moved higher up to a quiet, pleasant hotel above Chexbres, overlooking Lake Geneva; and Kate gave herself wholly to the task of making the dying man as happy and comfortable as possible. The unmeasured tenderness and devotion of this period are revealed in many a casual remark. There is sweetness in her account of the pleasure her husband found in their Swiss garden or in feeding the pigeons or stroking the cows. She read to him constantly, took him for drives or for such walks as he could manage on her arm, and with a tenderness that far exceeded patience played with him countless games of backgammon. When he was strongest, they rowed on Lake Geneva and were carried back in painful memory to earlier, happier days on Lake Otsego. But their greatest resource, during these weeks in Switzerland, was a stroll in the pine woods adjoining the hotel, with books or backgammon board ready in Kate's hand whenever the sick man had to stop and rest. She rarely left him, even to write a letter, unless a friend was ready to entertain him.

Except for the weekly accounts to her own family and to her husband's mother, the vast correspondence was given over. She was not writing to Sue Dickinson at this time, but her stepmother sent news of Kate to Sue. On June 28 Kate wrote gratefully: "Your letter of June 12th with Sue Dickinson's enclosed just received. So delighted was I to see them both. You are very good to write so regularly, dear Mother, but if you knew the joy with which your letters are received you would never mind the trouble of writing them. How good in you to write to Sue Dickinson! Thank you *very much*."

Although John Anthon did not know the doctor's verdict, the strain of long illness told on his courage. To her family Kate insisted that her husband was always cheerful with her, but in her diary she wrote of constant efforts to overcome his depression. He worried about his law practice, about the expense of their long stay in Europe, about her future without him, and she had often more than she could do to comfort him. June 18, a wet, miserable day, was black in her diary. The gloom outside intensified the gloom within. Her husband was wretchedly unhappy, and she had never felt sadder in her life.

"My days are dark indeed! When will light come? Oh, for home and friends and sympathy! This loneliness is dreadful — *insupportable and overwhelming!*"

In early July the heat drove the two Americans from Lake Geneva to the little mountain resort of Grindelwald high up in the Bernese Oberland. Kate Anthon was finally among the great mountains, and they frightened her. At night, after she had watched her husband asleep, she walked softly to their bedroom window and looked out. The brawling Lutschine, to her excited fancy, sounded like a full-throated Niagara, but there was no other sound and no warmth of human lights. High in the unclouded sky the stars shone with cold brilliance, and the Wetterhorn lifted its icy crest toward the moon.

By daylight the scene was hardly more reassuring. At that time Grindelwald consisted of one or two big hotels, a few chalets, and some herdsmen's huts. There was little to do except listen to the roar of an occasional avalanche and note the fresh snow that made dazzling white sheets on the Eiger. Kate threw back her head to look at the mighty crests, and her hair came loose and tumbled down about her shoulders. She felt oppressed, shut in — "as if I never, *never* should, or could, by any possibility see any of you again." The mountains, she complained, were *too near;* they threatened to fall and crush her;

and though she grew accustomed to the sight of the great walls, she seemed a prisoner still.

An absurd incident brightened one letter. The English chaplain ("a very prosy old gentleman, who, to tell the truth, proved to be an ineffable bore") sent a large book up to her room. When it turned out to be *The Evangelization of the Syrian Females,* Kate was justly annoyed. It was a species of literature distasteful to her under any circumstances, and it seemed particularly uncalled for at such a period of loneliness and depression. Though she trusted that the Syrian females would become evangelized, she hoped Heaven would forgive her if she omitted going into the details at that stage of her life. Shortly afterwards she met the chaplain, who told her seriously that he had thought Mr. Anthon would enjoy a little "light reading." Controlling her face with an effort, Kate bowed her thanks, backed into her room, and there enjoyed the only good laugh she had had in many a day.

The change of climate brought a temporary illusion of strength, and John Anthon took a few horseback rides. He was soon fit for nothing more than a *chaise-à-porteur,* borne on the backs of two strong men, while his wife walked beside him. In this fashion they visited the lower Mettenberg glacier, and walked carefully and shiveringly through the ice grotto. Kate wrote to her family that it had been a very pleasant walk. In her diary she reported, more truthfully, that it had been much too long and hard for her, and that she was exhausted and ill. It was much pleasanter to go by carriage to the Staubbach Falls in the Lauterbrunnen Valley.

In these mild amusements the season wore away, and Kate began to think seriously and forbodingly of the long trip to Paris. It was no light undertaking. To spare the sick man's strength, she was obliged to plan short daily journeys and many stops. All the business of making reservations, engaging carriages and porters, registering their luggage, worrying with the change of currency, and seeing that they got on and off at the

right stops fell upon her shoulders, which were already burdened enough by an invalid who could not walk without her
arm. When the effort seemed beyond her strength, she cried
out, "I can do it, I can do it!" But after it was over, and she saw
that she had done it, she wondered how.

They reached Paris on August 27, 1873, and found a new
difficulty. Their hotel room was up four flights of polished
stairs, and Kate had dreadful visions of her husband's falling.
After two days of tiring effort she found better lodgings.

August 30 was their wedding anniversary — "a nasty rainy
day," she observed in her diary, but to her stepmother she
wrote: "A year ago today we parted with you and dear Father.
Oh! how much has happened since! This is the first year we
have not spent with you on our wedding anniversary. John says
it is the first time he has missed the Sunday school picnic. You
know how hard he used to work on those occasions."

As their ship would not sail until mid-October, Kate's chief
concern was to find a comfortable place for her husband during
the next several weeks. The Isle of Wight was decided on, and
in her diary she wrote: "Packed all day — tired to death, and
feeling dreadfully discouraged. Dread the journey to England
and the Isle of Wight so much. John can do nothing. I am
alone — alone." On a trip to the banker's to get money, John
Anthon was unable to sign his name, and she signed it for him,
with terror at this evidence of his weakness.

Of the Channel crossing, which was hideous, she wrote to
her stepmother, in a halfhearted attempt to be amusing: "The
boat was perfectly packed, and not even seats enough. I managed by hard work to secure a camp stool for John, who was
very tired, and finally a lady offered me a seat on her port-
manteau. The wind was blowing somewhat when we started,
but it increased to a real gale, with a furious rain storm — wind
and tide dead against us. John was not sick at all, but I *was*,
fearfully! At last I could endure it no longer, and stretched
myself out on the floor. A lady near, allowed me to rest my

head on her lunch basket. God bless her! It was a fearful and disgusting scene. When nearly over, I called out to a sailor who was ministering to my necessities (wash bowls etc.!), how much longer before we would reach Dover?

" 'Seven minutes,' he replied.

" 'I cannot stand it seven minutes longer,' I said.

" 'Well,' he answered, 'I *rather* think you'll have to, Ma'am!' And so I did, but it was dreadful."

Wet, sick, and disgusted, she arrived in Dover and dragged her husband up the steps to the pier and into shelter at the Lord Warden Hotel. She had now crossed the detestable English Channel four times, she wrote, and trusted she would never do it again. She was to cross it many times.

Their sojourn in the Isle of Wight was wretched. They remained at Ventnor for three weeks, and John Anthon went steadily downhill in strength and spirit. On the morning of September 25 he had a serious attack. Fearing that it was the paralysis of which the Swiss doctor had warned her, Kate sent in panic for a physician. To her brother Henry she wrote openly of her distress but begged him to keep the letter from their parents. On September 29 the Anthons left the Isle of Wight, and she had great trouble getting him on and off the boat. In London she learned that their ship, the *Wyoming*, would not sail. For several days she tried frantically, but without success, to get passage on another ship. Once more the Bakers came to her assistance and invited the two Americans to Bristol. On October 12 word came that repairs had been made and the *Wyoming* would sail after all. If it had only been a Cunarder! Kate thought desperately, for her patriotism stopped short at the water's edge, and she did not trust American ships.

During the last tedious hours at Liverpool she thought of the earlier and happier period of waiting for the *Scotia* to take her back to John Anthon. She would give anything to have him as well and strong as he had been in those days. It was dreadful to take John home so sick — so changed. What if he should die at sea? She begged God to have mercy on her and to help her through this affliction, even as she wondered what she had done to deserve such a crushing blow. They had been a year in Europe, homesick, isolated from all they loved, spending money they could ill afford — all to no purpose. She longed for her father and mother and Maggie's children and John's sisters. But would they know her with her grey hair?

"For months," the diary concluded, "I have carried the knowledge of John's illness (the real nature of the illness) in my mind and spoken to *no one* on the subject! The 12th of May in Vevey Dr. Muret told me candidly the nature of the brain disease. Never can I forget that night! Since that moment the world has been dark, dark to me. I never had the heart to write the naked truth to the dear ones in Cooperstown or 29th Street. I could *not* do it. I cannot endure this much longer. My own brain fairly staggers under all this weight of sorrow and anguish - - - - - -"

The *Wyoming* was met quietly in New York, as she had directed. For the next several months she tried to care for her husband in New York lodgings and at the house of her sister Maggie in Flatbush. Her father died on December 19, 1873 — an anniversary that she never failed to mourn — and shortly afterwards she went with her husband to Cooperstown to stay with her widowed stepmother. For the last five months of his life John Anthon was bedridden and helpless. There were day and night nurses, and Kate worked without stopping. On October 29, 1874, he died, and she buried him.

2

The following January Kate's little niece Margaret Bartlett died, and her sister Maggie was stricken with tuberculosis. In late 1875 Maggie Bartlett was persuaded to go abroad, but the time was already past. It would have been kinder to spare her the needless suffering of separation from her husband and children. On November 10, 1875, she sailed for Europe aboard the *Scythia,* and Kate went with her as companion and nurse. In this winter of 1875–76 Kate was nearly forty-five, her sister, forty-two.

To Kate Anthon, her sister was already doomed. She tried to hope, but she had already seen the failure of many hopes. When the issue was clear beyond a doubt, she wrote pleadingly to her brother to come and take Maggie home. She was worn out with struggle and suffering and wanted to hide for a few months in Switzerland. Nevertheless, she was compelled to go through with it.

After a rough passage and a short stay in London, the two sisters went to Mentone and lodged at the Splendide. Kate had not expected to return to the Splendide, but involuntarily walked in that direction. The manager, who was lolling in the doorway, smirked and grinned his welcome. And where were her brother and her husband? After a moment Kate was able to tell him that one had recovered, "and the other, gone — gone."

The two women remained in Mentone for four months, and all was as it had been in 1872. They ate off the same green and white china, poked their little fires, slept on the same good beds, had their little breakfasts in their own rooms, ate the same good lunches, and then went out to bask in the garden under the hot sun. The surf came tumbling in as mightily as of old, and the manager and the concierge still lounged hatless around the garden or stood in the gate looking up and down the street. Presently came Maggie's "dragowoman" with the bath chair, and there was a general rush to help Mrs. Bartlett into the chair and adjust rugs and shawls. Then Kate and her friends scattered to the valleys around Mentone or strolled on the Promenade du Midi.

It was so much the same story that only two things need be mentioned — Kate's struggle to live again and Maggie's gallant humor as she died. Maggie Bartlett was a woman very much like her sister. She had a magnetic charm which collected people even around a sickbed. They filled her room with flowers and helped Kate prepare food for her. And she entertained them with a humor that grew wilder and more exuberant the closer she came to death. She never complained, was grateful for every attention, and tried to match Kate's pretense that they were taking a pleasure trip to Europe. The bitter homesickness escaped only in an incessant letter-writing and in a fanatical determination to return to America. Kate warned her family not to be deceived by the cheerfulness of Maggie's letters, and was almost distracted by the problem of transporting a woman who had grown too weak to move. In self-defense she turned feverishly to new interests.

Because of her sister's illness Kate was even more rigidly confined than she had been in 1872. Often she was weary and bored. In a moment of discouragement she wrote in her diary: "Oh! how depressing to be ever in a sick room!" Once she broke out irrepressibly that it was a pity to be so near Milan and yet fail to see the great cathedral. Another day she regretted that her sister was unfit even for the short drive to Monte Carlo, where they could have heard an orchestra reckoned almost the best in Europe. It was not heartlessness. In the midst of death she was struggling toward life.

There were, as usual, many new friends. One in particular, a young English girl named Clara Gardner, received a good deal of notice in letters and diary. She was a very handsome girl (wrote Kate), very sweet and lovely, spent a great deal of time with them, and appeared to have taken a "violent fancy" to Kate herself. Miss Gardner was neither the first nor the last young woman to do so. Without effort on her part, and throughout her lifetime, Kate Anthon exerted an immediate and powerful influence on many young people. During these months at Mentone she was besieged with letters from a young Cooperstown girl, who wrote of her loneliness now that Mrs.

Anthon was gone and begged Kate to take her abroad.

"Miss Gardner and I," wrote Kate in mid-December, "walked an immense distance up the Cabrole Valley, and it was just heavenly! A luxury to breathe. One of those calm, *windless* days, with all harshness removed from the atmosphere. The earth, the sea, the sky — in perfect harmony! I quite abandoned myself to the scene, and tried to forget everything sorrowful, and with this sweet English girl on my arm, wandered on, wishing the walk might never end. Miss Gardner is exceedingly pretty — beautiful, I might almost say — and fond of Americans."

For weeks, in her diary and in letters to her brother Henry, Kate quoted Miss Gardner, celebrated her birthday, and reported many walks and constant meetings. Then a young Irish brother and sister came to stay at the Splendide. After the first meeting Kate changed her place at table to a seat near theirs. Young O'Flaherty took charge of her and had much to say about the natural sympathies between Irish and American temperaments and about the coldness of the English.

"*C'est vrai,*" said Mrs. Anthon, who was half-Irish herself. May O'Flaherty became a lasting friend, and Miss Gardner, without being entirely neglected, sank to a subordinate position and finally disappeared from the story.

On April 17, 1876, Kate and her sister went to Montreux on Lake Geneva, partly to escape the growing heat and partly to be near Mrs. Anthon's old friend Mrs. Osler. Maggie Bartlett was now plainly in the last stages of illness. She could no longer walk or eat, and her coughing was incessant. To tempt an appetite that refused to be tempted, Kate spent much time cooking over a spirit lamp — with a rueful side glance at the entrancing, unattainable Castle of Chillon.

Poor Maggie was "so ill," she wrote, in her last letter (May 15, 1876) to her brother Henry. The sick woman now had to be carried up and down the stairs by two porters, and Kate was sorely troubled how to bring her home. The Oslers thought Kate could not possibly take care of her sister alone on the journey to England and urged her to engage a courier, but she was worried about the expense. Would Henry be on hand to receive them? She hardly knew whether her sister would survive the trip, but so great was Maggie's determination to see her husband and children that the resolve alone might keep her alive until they reached New York. "If we are *stopped on the way*," the letter concluded, "I will at once cable. In much sadness and trouble, Your loving sister, Kate Anthon."

The courier was engaged, and with his help the two sisters reached England. They sailed for America aboard the *Scythia* in late May. The dying woman had almost two months with her husband and children. In her last days she gave away her books, and the hand with which she wrote the inscriptions was firm and unfaltering. On July 27, 1876, Margaret Scott Bartlett died.

3

Meanwhile the eventless life of Emily Dickinson had been troubled by three events. On June 16, 1874, her father died very suddenly in the Tremont House at Boston. It was her first real bereavement, and she felt that the props of her world had given way. A year later Mrs. Dickinson was paralyzed, and Emily began the seven-year period of nursing which reconciled her with her mother. In the fall of 1876 Austin Dickinson was very ill, and about this time, according to the uneasy recollection of Mrs. Bianchi, Emily herself was once more in violent upheaval.

Mrs. Bianchi's allusion to this period is curious. When Sue Dickinson was preoccupied with family duties, said her daughter, "Emily felt herself without sympathetic comprehension, as she once wrote during the first months of Ned's babyhood, and again during that siege of malarial fever through which Sue took Austin."

Although Mrs. Bianchi implied that the fall of 1876 marked only a slight disturbance of mutually cordial relations, the evidence suggests that Emily had long been estranged from Sue. In January, 1875, Emily had written with obvious relief that "Austin's family" (by which she meant Sue and the two children, Ned and Martha) had gone to Geneva for a month and that Austin had spent those weeks with his sisters. In the fall of 1876 the alienation was so profound that Emily would not enter Sue's house even to see a brother believed to be dying. Once she came to the window to ask if Austin were better, and this was apparently her closest approach to the house in years. A few months later she remarked scornfully that Sue was "busy with scintillation." In a letter of late 1878 to Higginson she referred to her sister-in-law as her "pseudo-sister," and the word was intended to characterize.

Plainly Emily's alienation from Sue was not limited to the fall of 1876. Nor is there anything pleasant or admirable in Mrs. Bianchi's suggestion that Emily resented her sister-in-law's preoccupation with a sick husband, any more than with a new baby years before. But it is interesting that Mrs. Bianchi bracketed the two incidents. In 1861 Emily was not jealous of her infant nephew; she was suffering because she had been jilted by Kate Scott. Did Mrs. Bianchi fear that something might focus attention on the years 1876–77? Was this the time when Kate Anthon returned to Amherst and tried to renew her friendship with Emily?

At present there is little external evidence. Mrs. Bianchi stated, probably with no more than her usual accuracy, that Mrs. Anthon always visited Amherst between trips abroad. In 1892 Kate spoke of Sue's youngest child, Gilbert, as if she had actually seen the little boy, whose short life began in August, 1875, and ended in October, 1883. If she ever saw little Gilbert,

it was most probably in late 1876 or in 1877, for soon afterwards she went abroad again and did not return until six
months after Gilbert's death. The most suggestive evidence for
this visit to Amherst, however, is in the poetry of Emily Dickinson and in the circumstances of Mrs. Anthon's life.

Kate Anthon had recently gone through a period of suffering
and bereavement. Her behavior during the next several years
makes clear that she was actively searching for new interests
and attachments. She had not forgotten Emily, although she
had given her up and had tried to make a new life for herself
by marrying a very worthy young man. It was the only sane
solution, and whatever Emily thought (and Emily was bitter),
no sensible person would have proposed that Kate remain
isolated and suffering in an unrealizable attachment. Kate was
so constituted that she had to be in love with a real person,
not an idea; and if she was not caring for a husband or mother-
ing some young girl or schoolboy, then she was restlessly hunt-
ing a person to love. Now that she was once more alone, and
grievously distressed, she would turn naturally to a woman whom
she had never ceased to love.

When the two women came together, there was evidently a
dramatic and painful scene. It had been a long parting, and
the interview was not at all what Emily had anticipated in
many a poem, nor was the atmosphere heavenly. Kate must
have sought Emily out, for the latter no longer interrupted her
seclusion even so far as to cross the lawn. And they did not exchange messages through the hall door, as was now Emily's
habit in receiving guests. They met face to face, and probably
for the last time.   .

Both women were forty-six. Kate's ivory skin was lined, her
dark eyes were worn with tears, and her grey head (no longer
dark) was bowed with suffering. Emily's own auburn hair
never greyed, and she was sensitive to the signs of age in her
acquaintance. "Mine enemy is growing old," she wrote in one
poem. There was sweet revenge in observing the aging face

of the hated beloved. Yet, even in the moment of triumph, Emily found that she had lost the taste for vengeance; the anger that had grown fat on starvation died when it was appeased (the tone of these lines is clear proof to the contrary!). Of course, this poem might have been addressed to Sue, but it is hard to believe that continued slights and pinpricks from Sue — or indeed anything less than a betrayed love — would evoke so deep a hatred. As Emily penned this vindictive poem, was she recalling the grey hair of which Kate had written despondently in her diary at Liverpool?

In a manuscript of the late eighteen-seventies (that is, about the time of this supposed meeting), Emily related her two crucial experiences with Kate under the figure of a sea and a brook. The first stanza deals with the period of 1859–61. "The sea said 'Come' to the brook," but the little brook begs to be allowed to grow. The sea answers that it wants a brook, not another sea, and again urges the little brook to "come now." In the second stanza Kate comes again and renews the invitation, but — "The sea said 'Go' to the sea." (Assuming that there had been a slip of the pen, the editor changed this line to read, "The *brook* said 'Go' to the sea." It is possible, however, that in 1876–77 Emily wanted to say that she too was now a mighty sea confronting the other.) With desperate tactlessness the original sea (Kate) reminds the erstwhile brook, You loved me once, and the poet answers disdainfully:

> "Learned waters,
> Wisdom is stale to me."

"When we have ceased to crave," wrote Emily, in an undated manuscript quoted by Mrs. Bianchi — in short, when she no longer cared, she was at last offered the gift for which she had once surrendered the earth and even "mortgaged heaven."

Another poem, "We see comparatively," in the abridged version published by Mrs. Bianchi, reads like a general commentary on youthful disillusionment and the wisdom of age. Suppressed stanzas suggest that it had a very personal and bitter application. Perhaps God had been good to her, Emily wrote, in depriving her of the thing that had once belonged to her. She had been spared the chagrin of

> . . . waking in a gnat's embrace,
> Our giants further on.

"It came his turn to beg," she wrote elsewhere. The other person, according to a significant line, was begging for life itself; but Emily merely looked at his "narrow realm" and gave him a very cold pardon, "lest gratitude revive the snake."

Years earlier, apparently, she had written, "Not with a club the heart is broken." Love was lashed to death by a whip too small to be seen; it was slain by a stone. Yet the magnanimous bird continued "singing unto the stone of which it died." In a manuscript of the late seventies Emily added this stanza:

> Shame need not crouch
> In such an earth as ours;
> Shame, stand erect,
> The universe is yours!

Was this stanza written after she had witnessed the painful humiliation of her former friend?

In a manuscript of the latest handwriting, "Art thou the thing I wanted," Emily was still powerfully and cruelly agitated by the return of her lost love. She told the lover to try some person who had not "starved so long." During her own ghastly famine "the mystery of food" had so increased that she had given up hoping for love and had learned to exist in isolation, "like God."

These several poems ("Mine enemy is growing old," "The

sea said 'Come' to the brook," "When we have ceased to crave."
"We see comparatively," "It came his turn to beg," "Not with
a club the heart is broken," and "Art thou the thing I wanted?")
appear to relate to one experience and to one person. Indeed
it would have been difficult for Emily, who had isolated herself
from the possibility of new experiences and new attachments,
to go through a series of bitter disillusionments with different
persons. Four of the poems are known to survive in late manuscripts — that is, from about 1877 to 1884. The person to
whom they refer could hardly have been Sue Dickinson. For
what had Sue to offer Emily? At best she could have asked forgiveness of earlier slights and promised kinder behavior, but
she could not have offered an exclusive devotion. These poems
are not concerned with an ordinary friendship but with the one-
to-one relationship of lovers. Almost certainly they apply to
Kate, who, in 1876–77, was once more free and searching for a
person to love.

No paraphrase does more than suggest the hatred and bitterness of these poems. Emily could hate as lustily as she had
loved. In justice, she had suffered a great provocation. However, these poems reflected her in only one mood; during the
same general period she wrote poems expressing a kinder feeling toward Kate. In the ceaseless agitation of her soul she was,
by turns, in many moods, and the conflict of passions wore her
out. After the first attack of her fatal illness, she wrote to a
friend: "The crisis of the sorrow of so many years is all that
tires me." Although the context shows that she was referring to
the death of parents and friends, the statement was true in a
sense that she did not intend her correspondent to understand.

In returning to Amherst Kate may have hoped to persuade
Emily to become her traveling companion. As early as 1873,
despite her preoccupation with John Anthon, she was beginning to enjoy the carefree life of European hotels and *pensions*.
In early 1876 she begged to be allowed to stay in Europe. "I
want very much to see you all," she wrote to her brother Henry

and his wife, "but I do not want to go home (especially as I have no home). I like life on the Continent." Now that Kate had her own income, and Emily (by reason of her father's death) was less dependent than she had been, there was no practical reason why they should not have gone abroad. But Emily felt bound to her mother, and like the prisoner of Chillon (to whom she once compared herself), she no longer wished to leave her prison. Liberty had come too late, and the "learned waters" had grown distasteful to the former scholar.

Not long after this presumed visit to Amherst, Kate Anthon copied into her diary these revealing lines from a letter of Shelley:

> *I think one is always in love with something or other. The error, and I confess it is not easy for spirits cased in flesh and blood to avoid it, consists in seeking in a mortal image the likeness of what is perhaps eternal.*
>
> *I stand, as it were, upon a precipice, wh. I have ascended with great, & cannot descend without greater peril, & I am content if the heaven above me is calm for the passing moment.*

Kate had arrived, by a different route, at much the same way-station as Emily Dickinson, but neither of them was content to rest in so impersonal a conclusion. Warm, passionate, deeply emotional women, they both felt, as Emily wrote, that "each of us gives or takes heaven in corporeal person." The pilgrimage on which Kate was now engaged, perhaps all unconsciously, was directed toward a renewed embodiment of the eternal.

4

On April 10, 1878, Kate sailed aboard the *Bothnia* to make her permanent home in Europe, if indeed she could ever be said to have a home again. Emily had called her Ishmael, and

Ishmael she was. More homeless than Emily herself, undomiciled in flesh or in spirit, Kate wandered restlessly to and fro upon the face of the earth. For a few months she traveled through England and Ireland, renewing old acquaintances and struggling with an overpowering homesickness. By late fall she was once more in Mentone, with spirits not improved by the memory of earlier scenes.

Loneliness precipitated her into an intimacy which she soon regretted. A lively French party at the hotel engaged her attention, and for some days she spent a great deal of time with her new friends. She accompanied Madame M— to Monaco, and she lent young Monsieur C— some of her books and gave him a few lessons in English. (Mrs. Anthon wrote their full names, which are here suppressed.) All this was recorded in the diary, then erased, and written over in a most complicated manner. For example, Kate wrote, "I went to Monte Carlo in the evening with Madame M—. Returned late. *She* won 30 francs. I did not play." (The last was unnecessary. She was always careful with her small income and never gambled with anything except her heart.) Later on she erased this entry and wrote over it: "I went to my room early. Read and studied and felt rather lonely." References to walks with Monsieur C— up the Cabrole Valley or to Cap Martin were rewritten to omit his name or to substitute, quite fallaciously, the name of her French instructor, Mlle. Brecka. The original records of gaiety were revised to read: "I felt greatly dissatisfied with everybody and everything"; or, "stupid evening in the salon."

It would almost appear that Monsieur C— presumed on the friendliness of the lonely widow. Having erased him from her life, she tried, with unequal success, to erase him from her diary. Shortly afterwards she left the hotel and reported that she was glad to leave it.

Whatever her new society lacked in other attractions, it was certainly prim enough. The *pension La soeur ainée* was inhabited by middle-aged spinsters, or widows like herself, and by

German families of certifiable domesticity and dullness. Kate read and studied French or astronomy during the day, and evening after evening played whist with three other women until bedtime. Her life during this period sounds rather dreary, and apparently she found it so.

The old year — "this troublesome year," she called it in her diary — went out on a note of profound despondency. With the emphasis of much underlining and many exclamation marks, she wrote on December 31:

"This is New Years eve. The last day of *1878*. LET IT GO!! Next year God grant me *peace* and *happiness!*"

ﾟ XII ﾟ

Dᴜʀɪɴɢ the next year Kate Anthon's long, homesick pilgrimage came to an end, or more exactly, to another way-station of remarkable and delicate complexity. A whimsical destiny chose to grant, most certainly not peace, but an astonishing measure of happiness. The place was a small mountain resort in Switzerland, and the time was most probably June 6, 1879.

The evidence for the date is inferential. The diary which Kate Anthon began with the sailing of the *Bothnia* on April 10, 1878, ended in mid-sentence on May 26, 1879. Meanwhile she had at last seen Milan Cathedral and had paid her long-deferred visit to the Italian Lakes. On May 22 she was still at Luino on Lago Maggiore, disappointed in her hopes and involved in one of her frequent moods of anxious indecision. "At lunch," she wrote, "was told the St. Gothard would be impassable owing to the deep snow for another month. Felt discouraged and unhappy, not knowing what to do." On May 26 she wrote despondently: "Still raining. I was uncertain what to do. Went out and found an eye-glass — "

The diary broke off at this point, and the succeeding diary

was destroyed. When the story was resumed (in mid-sentence), the time was March 5, 1880. On June 6 following, however, Kate wrote: "A year ago today I crossed the Simplon"; and on June 6, 1881: "Two years ago tonight we had just reached Brigue crossing the Simplon." Obviously an anniversary was being commemorated, and later events permit an almost certain identification. Nothing else in her life, with one possible exception, was of greater importance to Kate Anthon than her meeting with Florence Eliot.

Basically it was a mother-daughter attachment. On the part of the young girl, it may never have been, with full consciousness, anything else. There were reasons why Florie would seek a mother, although her own mother was living, and Mrs. Anthon loved and needed children. The relationship was approved by the family of the young girl, and afterwards, with some reservations, by the man she married. The interest of this attachment lies in the intense emotionalism that it engendered and in the parallel that it suggests with the emotionalism of Emily Dickinson's poetry.

Florence Eliot, born in 1856 in a medium-sized Indian town on the bank of the Ganges, was the youngest child in a large family of Anglo-Indians. Her mother was then approaching forty-five and was an elderly woman almost before Florie was out of her childhood. The older woman leaned heavily, too heavily, on her latest-born child, and from a very early age Florie became mother to her own mother.

At the outbreak of the Indian Mutiny, when Florie was only a few months old, Mrs. Eliot performed her last decisive action. The older children were apparently in England, the father was isolated in a besieged town, and the mother and baby were surrounded by untrustworthy Indians. Taking young Florie, her *amah,* and a male servant, Mrs. Eliot set out through a hostile countryside. On the way she heard rumors that the Indians were planning to kill them, and she confronted her servants and awed them into leading her to a place of safety.

Shortly afterwards Mr. Eliot died, and his wife returned to England with her baby. Florie celebrated her fourth birthday in Egypt at about the time when the thirty-year-old Emily Dickinson began to wonder why her friend Kate no longer wrote to her. In England mother and daughter lived much like other retired Anglo-Indians. There were wanderings from one lodging place to another, visits with the older children, and a season of French studies in Boulogne when Florie was twelve years old. Already Florie was beginning to assume much responsibility.

The Eliots were a handsome family. An older sister attracted the notice of the Prince of Wales and had to tell him that she did not go out to dinner without her husband. And Florie herself was almost as handsome as Mrs. Anthon was to think. She had blue eyes, fair hair, and a strong, aquiline nose contradicted by a soft, childlike chin. Dressed as Mary Queen of Scots, she looks solemnly, almost poutingly, but with adolescent charm, from an ancient photograph; and portraits made of her in old age have a serene beauty that is beyond description. She had a fine singing voice, to which Mrs. Anthon was to listen with rapture, but her other talents, to judge from surviving water colors and drawings, were not unusual. Even Kate adopted the slightly apologetic tone of a fond mother in sending some of these productions to her family. For the rest, Florie was a tender, very generous girl, given to harmless, impractical enthusiasms, with a discerning eye for beauty, a quick mind, and a spirit of fun that blossomed notably during her tutelage to Mrs. Anthon.

In extreme old age Florence tried to gather up the tangled skein of her life for the benefit of her children. She began to write her memoirs, but a stroke interrupted her writing at a point shortly after she recorded the event which effectually separated her from Mrs. Anthon. It is hard to tell what is

most important in the life of any person, but even though
Florie married, brought up a large family, and spent her old
age in the social-service work which she had long wanted, it is
probable that she had already related the most significant part
of her life. Youth comes but once, and if it is spent in the
company of a person deeply loved, it is rich beyond any succeeding period.

In the fall of 1878 Florie persuaded her mother to go to
Switzerland. The era of winter sports had not yet begun, and
a Swiss winter was a rare and perilous undertaking even to the
much-traveled English. Probably the two women spent the
winter months in the comparative warmth of Lake Geneva,
but with the coming of pleasant weather they moved to a little
resort high up in the mountains overlooking the valley of the
Rhone. Not long after they arrived Florie was tempted to join
a party making a steep Alpine ascent, but was stayed by the
thought of her mother's helplessness if she should be injured.
"I always felt I was in charge of mother," she wrote, "and it
would not do for me to become incapacitated."

The little resort is now popular, but in those days it consisted only of some chalets and two hotels, in the smaller of
which the two Englishwomen stayed. "We found several
pleasant visitors in the Hotel," wrote Florie, "among them an
American lady, a Mrs. Anthon."

There is nothing more, and the diary in which Mrs. Anthon
recorded their meeting has been destroyed, but the scene can
be readily imagined. They sat together at the *table d'hôte* and
encountered each other in the garden or on their separate
walks. There must also have been a piano in the salon. The
tall, handsome young English girl, even fresher and more childlike than her twenty-two years, had only to raise her beautiful
voice in song. The woman of forty-eight had found her
daughter, the only child she was ever to have. And if the events
of the succeeding months and years should appear, as they

must, imprudently extravagant, and the language wildly emotional beyond anything to be met outside the poems of Emily Dickinson, it must be remembered that Kate Anthon had endured a long period of unhappiness.

Toward the close of the season Mrs. Anthon proposed a change of scene. "She had travelled in Italy a great deal," wrote Florence, "and she suggested that we should go together to the Italian Lakes. There was a Mr. Waters, a geologist, who also wanted to go to Italy, so we decided to join forces and hire a carriage to take us across the Simplon Pass. I think the village where we hired our vehicle was Brigue. I knew nothing about the charge and should have paid whatever was asked, but Mr. Waters was an experienced traveller and knew that it was necessary to bargain. Mr. Waters, Mrs. Anthon and I spent the afternoon walking about asking the drivers what they would charge to take us to Italy."

William George Waters was the author of several long, sentimental Victorian novels. Mrs. Anthon had met him at Mentone in 1876. During a visit of 1878 to his home in Norfolk, she read the first of his novels in manuscript. They often encountered each other in their travels from one watering place to another.

On the second day of the Italian journey Florie and Mrs. Anthon decided to leave the carriage and overtake it by a shorter route across the meadows. They had not considered the heavy morning dew, and Florence recalled that shoes were wet and skirts bedraggled when they rejoined the carriage. Still it had been pleasant to walk in the sun and breathe the crisp mountain air. Sixty years later Florence remembered how pleasant it had been.

When the carriage came down into Italy, the girl was disappointed by her first sight of the olive terraces. She had expected big trees, and they were small and drably grey. Under the guidance of a lover of the olive, however, she soon learned

to admire them properly. Kate Anthon's tastes were to direct
her own for many years; and in a copy of Shelley's poems Mrs.
Anthon would mark these lines:

> And this belovèd child thus felt the sway
> Of my conceptions, gathering like a cloud
> The very wind on which it rolls away.

In later years Florence spoke with reverence of her indebtedness to Kate Anthon's teaching. A whole world — history, literature, art — was opened up or revivified for her during this
exciting period of tutelage. As for Mrs. Anthon, she renewed
her study of French and astronomy with a zeal that now had a
purpose, and she had a willing pupil in these subjects.

On the margin of Kate's French astronomy book, at the
chapter entitled "La Lune," a new and youthful hand has
written: "Oct 1st 1879 — Rose on Lago Maggiore, Baveno,
6.30 P.M. F.E.E." Below, in Mrs. Anthon's bolder, more
vigorous hand, appears the phrase "Italian Lakes."

The words are like a sudden, dazzling glimpse into a dead
world. The full moon rises, a rim of brilliance, then a great,
swelling coppery disk. It appears to leap from the dark mass
of the Borromean islands into the paler darkness of sky; and
all the cypress trees are edged with light. Did they see it from
their hotel window? Were they engaged in their favorite pas-
time of strolling arm in arm along a path beside the lake? Was
this moonrise memorable above all others? But just as a curtain
may be rung up before the stage is set, and hastily let down
again, so the penciled note is only a precursor of the real drama.
Darkness prevails again, and the moment's glimpse, as by a
startled opening and shutting of the eyes or by a lightning
flash in the heart of night, stands forever isolated and strangely
compelling in its isolation.

Of their whereabouts in the next several months there is
only one faded memory. They went to Cadenabbia on Lake

Como and had an adventure. It was a place for adventure of the most picturesque kind — this soft, sensuous lake fringed with pink-walled villas and hung round with shimmering mountains. Unfortunately the adventure itself is meagerly recorded. One morning Mrs. Anthon and her young friend hired a boat, with a boatman resplendent in white blouse and broad crimson sash, to take them across the lake. They almost failed to get back. When they at last won through the sudden and severe storm, they found Mrs. Eliot waiting anxiously at the boat landing. Her grateful fee to the boatman was so large that every morning for a week he brought them a basket of fresh figs.

By March, 1880, the three women were in Mentone, where they had evidently been for several weeks and perhaps months. It is also evident that Mrs. Anthon was still in charge of the expedition. Kate Anthon's new diary begins abruptly in the middle of a sentence: "[Mrs. Eliot] out in her bath chair. Florie passed a wretched afternoon."

The curtain is up at last, but only on the front part of the stage. There is an inner drama being played, of which there will be scarcely a hint for many weeks. The diary is noncommittal — dry and factual like all of Mrs. Anthon's diaries — and it is only after the unfolding of the story that one returns to the earlier pages with an enlightened perception of the emphasis upon young Florie. Kate Anthon was always associated with people; she was incapable of being alone. The records of walks, drives, and tea-drinkings in the new diary sound precisely like all those in earlier diaries. Even the grateful note that "after lunch Florrie bathed my head" is reminiscent only of the sympathy and interest that Mrs. Anthon's slightest illnesses invariably aroused in those about her. But when the references to Florie are disengaged from a welter of notes concerning the weather, correspondence, letters of credit, and other miscellanea, they do indeed loom large.

The life at Mentone was idle and charming. Constance

Fenimore Woolson, Cooper's grandniece, was there, and they saw something of her. One day they went to Monte Carlo, but Florie refused to enter the gambling casino. Much impressed by a recent sermon on the evils of gambling, she had taken to heart the clergyman's warning that even the curiosity of the strong might lead weaker persons into temptation. Perhaps it was at this time that Kate erased from her 1878 diary the account of her visit to the casino with her French friend.

Florie read Kate's diaries. Sometimes she took the pencil herself and added comments in an amusing mimicry of Kate's laconic style. Mrs. Anthon wrote: "Sunday March 21st (Palm Sunday). Beautiful day." Florie took the pencil from her and added, in a lighter, rounder hand: "Went to church at 10:30. All decorated with palms. Mr. Woodhouse officiated. Made a great deal of noise."

Another day Florie was ill, and Mrs. Anthon "read aloud in *Roman Days*." (This was a Swedish book on ancient Rome translated by Mrs. Anthon's friend Alfred Corning Clark.) The young girl reached for the pencil and wrote with affectionate whimsy: "& made myself as sweet as a Bouf (written by F. E. E.). Lovely evening. Florie dined in her room. Put on my thinner dress and looked lovely. So says F. E. E." Her friend added, more prosaically: "A large party of noisy Americans here all night." The word "bouf" is baby-talk. What it meant to them they never said.

In mid-March, 1880, the party moved to Bordighera, and Kate became very fond of the little town. With Mrs. Eliot and Florie (Kate sometimes wrote the name "Florrie"), she rambled up one of the valleys and reported: "Very pretty walk. Found violets and anemones, came home very hungry, enjoyed our lunch immensely. Florrie and I then sat and read a long time in the salon. Tea at four o'clock. I opened my trunk and got things in good order before dinner. In the evening Florrie played on the piano. Germans much delighted with Florrie's touch, execution, etc. We had tea at nine o'clock.

Florrie very tired and ready for bed at ten o'clock."

One entry is pretty much like another, varied only by the direction of their walks or their differing aches and pains, or the people they met and the sermons they heard. It was all delightful and idle and, of course, inexcusable, since they were doing nothing more important than living, but undoubtedly they felt that they were very busy and useful. The girl was tied to the care of her mother; in her free hours she busied herself with French and Italian lessons, reading and music. Mrs. Anthon charged herself with the welfare of both mother and daughter. In her copy of Shelley she marked the following lines:

> Do I not live
> That thou mayst have less bitter cause to grieve?

Although Kate never allowed herself the luxury of a single criticism, she undoubtedly saw that the care of the elderly woman fell with unnecessary heaviness on the shoulders of the young girl. There were older children who might have shared the responsibility, but Mrs. Eliot clung to Florie. Nor was she quite so helpless as she imagined. Since she was able to walk, surely she could have dressed herself, but she declined to do so. At times she had spells of moodiness and depression, from which the united efforts of Kate and Florie could hardly reclaim her, but she imperiously forbade anyone else to have moods. Fortunately Mrs. Anthon was a woman of great tact and gentleness, and with the almost uniform good spirits that recommended her to every one, she made Florie's life more bearable.

Mrs. Eliot always liked the American woman, and liked having her around. To the end of her days (and Mrs. Eliot survived all her complaints, to become a nonagenarian), she continued to urge Mrs. Anthon to visit her. Sometimes she forgot her own troubles and was solicitous for the health of her companion. During the Mentone stay Kate once reported: "I wished to go forth and gaze at the stars, but Mrs. E. said 'No,' I would take cold." It was an odd trio, admittedly, with a curious mixture of mutual sentiments, but all three seemed well pleased with the arrangement.

Toward the end of May the party went to Cornighano and did a little sightseeing in Genoa. By June 1 they were in Luino at a little hotel close to the lake, with a garden at the back (as Florence remembered many years later), "where the fireflies lit up every brick at night." Kate secured a pass to a silk factory in Milan and took her young friend to see the silk manufacture. (In her memoirs Florence recalled that the cocoons were dipped in boiling water. She hoped that the moths did not suffer too much.) The manager gave the young girl two cocoons, which she took carefully home and placed on the table of her hotel room. Not long afterwards, coming into the room on an errand, she saw with delighted surprise that the moths had cut through the silk and were resting on the gutted cocoons.

By the middle of July they were beginning to suffer with the heat, and were anxious to proceed to Switzerland, but here a perplexity arose. Mrs. Eliot received a letter from a son who was returning to Europe after several years in Australia. His ship was expected to reach Venice late in July, and they debated the wisdom of remaining in Italy to meet him. Apparently they decided that he could be persuaded to visit his mother in Switzerland, for on July 15 they went to Locarno and thence to Hospenthal.

On July 26 Kate wrote anxiously in her diary that they had not heard from Venice and were afraid that Mr. Eliot and his wife had gone directly to England. Next day the reason for her disturbance became clear, and the inner drama burst into flame. "Florie had a talk with her mother about remaining in Europe or returning to England. Had a good cry. We both felt dreadfully sad, fearing a parting this autumn." For several days Florie continued to plead with her mother and to cry stormily in Mrs. Anthon's room. There were records of "dreadful headaches," and both were "nearly frantic at the thought of a separation." But when the vacillating mind of the elderly woman came to rest, it was with a decision to return to England and take her daughter with her.

Although Mrs. Eliot wished to see her son, she had only a mild feeling for the older children as compared with her possessive attachment to her youngest child. The plain fact would seem to be that she was tired of the rootless wandering that enchanted the other two. It was much to be feared that if she returned to England, she would not be got out of it again. The two other women were forced to desperate scheming. At last they persuaded Mrs. Eliot to let her daughter come to Europe again in October, Mrs. Anthon remaining meanwhile at Luino. "We could think of nothing else," the latter wrote. And she added that she "retired early, all sad and blue."

The month of August was filled with excursions and alarms. They went from Hospenthal to Airolo and were much interested in the blasting of the St. Gotthard tunnel. From Airolo they went to Faido ("six diligences in all," wrote Kate, "three ahead of us, two behind. Great time!"), and were annoyed by the rudeness of a St. Gotthard miner. He placed his dirty boots in Mrs. Eliot's lap, and with all their efforts, could not be ejected from the carriage. But when he consented to take his boots down, he became an entertaining companion and proudly showed them his medal for work on the tunnel.

Vague notes of unhappiness disturbed the serenity of the diary for the next month. Mrs. Eliot was "very dull and low spirited," Kate had many sleepless nights, and Florie was much worried about plans for the long, fatiguing trip to England — and with fears that she might not be permitted to return. "We shall be inexpressibly relieved," read the diary, "when all is settled." There was good reason to fear that Mrs. Eliot might again change her mind.

Another perplexity of this month was the engagement of

Mrs. Anthon's twenty-year-old nephew Harry Bartlett. Harry was still as dear to Kate as in the days of his childhood, when she had wept to see him and hear him call her "Annie Katie." She was much concerned about his rash engagement. There were emphatic letters to her stepmother and to Harry himself. On August 20 she "received a latter from Harry (from Amherst)," where he had been visiting her friends, the Dickinsons. Perhaps he had been sent there for distraction. Months later it appeared that Mrs. Anthon had been instrumental in getting Harry to Leipzig to study music. During the next year she pared her income to assist him and worried and fretted over him in much the same manner as she did over Florie.

Toward the end of the month the two older women had a serious fright. One day the young girl had a short but severe illness, which required a doctor, and the handwriting of the diary became painfully agitated. Next day Florie was better, and Mrs. Anthon read to her. In the evening came a letter from Kate's stepmother with music for Florie. The title, "Abide with Me," must have been especially meaningful to them at this time. Immediately after the words "Abide with Me" in the diary, Florie wrote affectionately: *Mud and Bab. She is the most beautiful thing I have ever seen, and far sweeter than any Pup.*" "Mud" and "Bab" are clearly pet words for "mother" and "baby." The identity of "pups," as well as "boufs," remains a mystery, but a reference to them later on suggests that they were cakes.

On August 30 the three women returned to Luino and busied themselves with preparations for the journey to England. Mrs. Anthon trimmed a traveling hat for her young friend and sewed a pocket in Florie's petticoat to hold her French gold, then altered a parasol ribbon and made ruffles for Mrs. Eliot. In the evening the two friends walked beside the lake and grieved over the approaching separation. They had little hope of accomplishing their desire, which was to spend the winter together in Florence. Mrs. Eliot was "so opposed to the scheme."

Not that the mother had any objection, then or later, to Mrs. Anthon's chaperonage. She was reluctant only to give up her daughter's companionship.

As the day of parting drew near — "that dreadful day!" — they became increasingly unhappy. On the last Sunday the two walked for a long time. "We felt so sad," the diary reported, "but tried to keep up. Came home, read the service in Mrs. E.'s room. F. very tired and sad. In the evening sat by the lake. We retired early, but could not sleep a wink and hearts *so heavy.*"

Monday, September 6, 1880, received the emphasis of double underlining and a tragic entry in the diary: "This has been a long sad day. My darling Florrie left me this morning at five o'clock for England. We said good bye in the clear starlit morning. I felt nearly heartbroken, even when I knew she was to return to me in six weeks. *Six long weary weeks!* Will they ever pass?" The bereaved woman "retired early, sad, so sad, looked at the stars a long time, thinking constantly of my darling. Alas! alas!"

All the entries for the succeeding days were much alike. "Went a little way on our lovely walk, but was so oppressed with the thought that dear Florrie was going farther and farther from me, I *could not* go on." She returned to the hotel and tried to read in the salon, but her head throbbed with pain, and she crept wretchedly upstairs to her room and threw herself on the bed in despair and loneliness, "when to my joy (at three o'clock) Florie's blessed Post card arrived. Oh! how thankful I was to get it, read it again and again. Blessed child!"

In imagination she followed every step of their progress, grieved for them in the terrible heat, wondered if they had reached Macon — if they had reached Paris — if they were nearing London. What would she not give to know!

"Oh! Florie, how can I live six weeks without seeing you!"

And the sequel proved that she could not.

The loneliness was eased, or aggravated, by an industrious

correspondence, all of which was destroyed on both sides. They exchanged postcards or letters, newspapers or ribbons or other trifles, at least every other day during this period of separation. And Mrs. Anthon walked and walked, "thinking of dear Florie all the time."

By the middle of September she was beginning to worry about her stepmother. Anxious notes regarding the health of Mrs. Scott alternated with longing remembrances of her young friend. She was already making herself ill when a letter from Alfred Clark of Cooperstown brought alarming news of her mother. The first panicky reaction was to write a note to Florie. The next morning, after a sleepless night, she wrote to Mrs. Scott and to her brother, saying that she would wait for a letter before doing anything. Then she cried terribly for a long time.

The unhappy woman, as always, attracted the sympathetic notice of strangers. Moved by her obvious distress over her step-mother, they took her for walks and drives and suggested remedies, none of which proved helpful. For several days she was unable to eat, and the diary read distractedly: "Could eat nothing, only drink a cup of tea. Wrote to Mrs. Cooper, as well as I could for my tears. Wrote a post card to dear Florie. Lunch in my room. Could eat nothing. Long dreary day — so unhappy and wretched. Mrs. S — (the English lady) came up and stayed with me in the evening."

On September 28 her gravest anxieties were put to rest by a reassuring letter from a young friend in Cooperstown. She at once sent a postcard to Florie, and the next day wrote at greater length about her stepmother's improvement. In the evening she received Florie's answer to her first letter: "She urges me to come on at once, nobly urges it, is perfectly unselfish in regard to giving up Florence. Blessed darling! Oh! what shall I do? Slept not a wink the entire night." In other words, Florie resigned herself to the loss of the winter in Florence and urged Kate to come to England and take ship for America. Torn between duty to her mother and love for Florie, Kate became seriously ill. Apparently she then forgot her mother, the winter in Italy, and everything else in her frantic desire to reach Florie.

Thursday, September 30, was a "lovely day, but how black to me! Went out and packed all day, thinking it possible I may go tomorrow. Or shall I wait for Florie's answer, which will come on Monday?" The following day she was very unwell. In the evening she received another letter from Florie, and sent a postcard telling of her own illness. But apparently she was unable to wait until Monday. On Saturday she wrote in desperation: "Nearly frantic. Must go tomorrow. Cannot endure this another day. Very ill all the morning. Took more arrowroot and brandy. Packed the last things. Will *go if alive* in the morning."

A blank in the diary is summed up in these words: "A long interval of a *sad weary month,* in which I made the journey to London, and returned to the Continent."

What took place in England may be guessed from other events. It appears likely that Mrs. Eliot had once more changed her mind, and that the combined efforts of the two other women were necessary to persuade her that she could manage comfortably with a hired companion in the house of an older daughter and thus allow Florie to return to Italy. Financial matters had also to be arranged. As early as the preceding summer Florie had written to a brother in India, asking for seven pounds to pay her traveling expenses, and her mother allowed her enough money for her other expenses. She was wholly independent of her companion.

Mrs. Anthon did not have a large fortune. She had inherited about sixteen thousand dollars, which, at the high rates of interest current in the nineteenth century, brought her a yearly income of between nine hundred and a thousand dollars — in terms of modern purchasing power, perhaps as much as three or four thousand dollars. It was enough to pay for second-class hotels, a moderate amount of travel, and a few good clothes, but it did not leave much room for extravagance. Toward the end of her life her income declined precipitously, but she was then confined to one place and needed less money. Although she felt poor in relation to her friends, she was, of course, rich in comparison with most of the world.

The diary resumed briskly: "Oct. 28th 1880. Arrived in Florence. Came to Miss Godkins Saturday afternoon October 30th. Oct 31st Sunday. Wrote to Mother. Told her to direct to this Palazzo. F. in bed all day — very tired. Everything in confusion." The next day they went to the Annunziata and heard some very fine music.

The *pension* Godkin was conducted by a widowed English-woman and her two unmarried daughters. With these women Mrs. Anthon and her young friend were soon on the best terms. Sometimes they helped Mrs. Godkin cut up oranges for marma-lade, and they advised each other about their sewing problems and went together, in their best clothes, to the English church around the corner on the Via Maggio. One Sunday the younger Miss Godkin had her purse stolen so neatly that she did not immediately discover its loss, but when the thief saw that he was detected, he returned it to her with a graceful bow.

"Ah, even our thieves are polite," said an Italian, to whom this was reported.

Mrs. Anthon had a similar experience, although the rascal was less courteous and required more persuasion. While she was strolling with Florie on the Lungarno Guicciardini, a man darted out of one of the narrow side streets and clutched her hand and purse. She tightened her grip and waved her um-brella in his face, shouting so vigorously, "Go away, you wretch!" that he was dismayed and slunk back into the shad-ows from which he had come.

The *pension* occupied the fourth and topmost floor of the massive, grey-white Palazzo Leonitti. Florie could not remem-ber how many stone steps they had to climb every day, or how many times a day they climbed them, to reach their two rooms under the roof. The pension itself was comfortable and plain and thoroughly English, a homelike island from which they fared forth into the exotic seas around them. The lower floors, retained by the owner, were more elaborate and were ornamented by fine frescoes (which the guests on the fourth floor were sometimes invited to see); and the stairway, though wearisome to climb, was very handsome.

Florie remembered that the view was not very good. They could look down on the yellow Arno, almost below their windows, and at the beggars in the square and the man who clipped French poodles, or they could look across the river at the roofs of houses. But the Pitti Palace nearby and the Duomo and the Campanile on the other side of the river were shut off by other buildings. Undoubtedly they could see the clumsy, curious Ponte Vecchio with its row of shops and covered passage from the Uffizi to the Pitti Palace. And the delicate, silvery Ponte Santa Trinità was almost at their feet. The *palazzo* faced the Lungarno Guicciardini, where they often walked in the sun, and was only a few steps from the dusky Via Maggio, on which Elizabeth Browning had lived two decades before. Sometimes they walked to Casa Guidi, for Mrs. Anthon had friends occupying the Brownings' old rooms.

Shortly after their arrival Kate began to read to Florie from Mrs. Browning's *Aurora Leigh*. It was very appropriate, for it described the life of a woman who invited a younger friend to share her home in Florence. As she read, surely Kate Anthon remembered Emily Dickinson. About the same time she read to Florie the whole of *Evangeline*. They also went seriously through Ruskin's *Mornings in Florence,* the Misses Horners' *Walks in Florence,* and biographies of Michelangelo, the Medici, and Savonarola. They were determined to make their winter in Florence as profitable as it was delightful.

"I loved Florence," wrote Florie in her old age, "and was well coached in the history by Mrs. Anthon. When I went there I knew nothing of Dante or Savonarola, Fra Angelico and the other painters, the architects and sculptors." It was a rare combination of good pupil and good teacher.

The lover of fantasy might try the experiment of placing Emily Dickinson in Florie's stead, for it is a reasonable guess that Kate had gone to Amherst in 1876 or 1877 with the hope of persuading Emily to become her traveling companion. That she failed was understandable, perhaps desirable. By the late eighteen-seventies, Emily was too crippled emotionally to deal with any life situation except through the hall door or, even more distantly, through letters. It is impossible to picture her on the fourth floor of the Palazzo Leonitti.

Even in Kate's laconic diary there is a charm diffused over these winter months in Florence. It was not all work and study, even though, with the aid of her memories of the city and the conscientious reading of many histories, biographies, and books of art, she put her young friend through as strenuous a course of sightseeing as she herself had enjoyed in Rome. The diary records morning after morning spent in the Uffizi, the Pitti Palace, the Baptistery, the Duomo, the churches of Santa Croce, San Lorenzo, Santo Spirito, and Santa Maria Novella.

The two women read a history of the monastery of San Marco and spent a morning strolling through the quiet cloisters and the cells ornamented by Fra Angelico and his pupils. On the second floor they were shown the dusky corner in which Savonarola was arrested, and in his cell, fragments of his clothes, hair shirt, rosary, and books. Savonarola became very real to Florie, but the angry friar attracted her less than the gentle painter. She fell in love with the suave little angels, so brightly and perfectly executed yet so tiny, that enamel the margins of one painting by Fra Angelico. Twenty years later Mrs. Anthon bought some garish copies of these angels and recalled with wistful tenderness how much Florie had loved the originals.

In lighter moments (but it was all fun) they drove in the Cascine or climbed the steep, graveled paths of the Boboli gardens or strolled through the narrow streets, stopping for coffee and ices in one or other of the many good restaurants. There were longer excursions to San Miniato, Fiesole, and La Certosa, and once more Kate hunted out the fictitious Aurora Leigh's villa on Bellosguardo. Once they went to the circus with their landlady and a pleasant young Italian: "Very funny time." They saw plays at the theater and heard *Don Giovanni* at the opera and visited every church that promised good music. They shopped and sewed and dawdled happily in the salon — or escaped quickly if the evening game was "Proverbs." When her young friend was ill, Mrs. Anthon "bought Florie a pup and a 'bouf'!" Another day they went to the photographer's, and "Florie was *executed*."

A copy of the photograph went home to Cooperstown, and acquaintances wrote that "they could see, with the coloring, that her young friend would be very beautiful." The attachment, of course, was well known to Kate's family and close friends. Certain hints and reservations would suggest that the family were uncomfortable about it. Not that they openly disapproved. They were too fond of Kate, and too understanding, yet they were also conventional people. Affection was all right in its place, but its place was rather narrowly circumscribed.

A fairly large part of the diary was concerned with Florie's music lessons. A piano was rented and tuned, and the young girl played and sang. "F. in good voice." But later on: "Short lesson because Florie could not get her voice up — not feeling strong." Mrs. Anthon was always present to hear her young friend sing. Later on, in her copy of Shelley, she would leave evidence of the effect that the lovely young voice had upon her.

One day they met Constance Woolson, who called soon afterwards at the *palazzo*. Mr. Waters also called, and there were other visitors. Once they dressed for company which failed to appear, but Kate noted that "F. looked lovely in her buff dress."

The holiday season was joyful. In later years Kate would be melancholy at Christmas time, but there was no melancholy now. She remembered Florie's twenty-fourth birthday with appropriate underlining in her diary (her own fiftieth birthday the following March would be passed over in discreet silence), and they bought presents for each other. "Such a happy Christmas Eve!" And on Christmas day: "Spent the afternoon in our own room *very* happy."

On the last day of 1878, it will be remembered, Kate Anthon had been thoroughly miserable. With passionate vehemence she had said farewell to the old year and had begged God to send her peace and happiness. On this last day of 1880 she was tranquil and serene: "Went out for a short walk in the afternoon. Came home, and read aloud to the *Pigeon*." A few days later, in the midst of a severe cold, she reported gratefully: "The Pigeon would not allow me to go out of my room or to use my voice." Undoubtedly Mrs. Anthon had reason to be careful. Perilously thin, susceptible to chest diseases, and with a family history of tuberculosis, she clung prudently to warm, sunny climates, though she was also a lover of the South for its own sake.

Shortly afterwards, the note of distress, long absent from the diary, was heard again. January 11, 1881, was a "cold, horrid day," and the two women spent it very unhappily, "talking over our dreaded separation in the spring — blue sort of a day. Florie very low-spirited." Ten days later even the prospect of spending the spring together appeared doubtful. The girl received a letter from her sister, telling her that Mrs. Eliot was ill and needed her. "We were greatly annoyed at the idea of her being asked to make the journey to England in this severe weather." In the evening Florie wrote to her sister, "expressing her mind pretty freely. She has felt so hurt about being sent for in such a summary way." During the next several days they were "nearly frantic" under a bombardment of letters, all demanding Florie's return. "Blue time," read the diary. "We are in despair about this summons to England. Alas!" But they held their ground and awaited developments. The imperious woman in England, as they well knew, was capable of recalling her daughter through a thousand miles of wintry travel for nothing more than an attack of low spirits. At length the storm blew itself out. It was apparently of no more consequence than the two in Florence had supposed it to be.

On April 3 they "felt very blue over Mrs. Eliot's letter telling us she intended to go to housekeeping. F. had a good cry." This proposal, always reappearing in the mind of the elderly woman, was a source of distress. As long as Mrs. Eliot remained in lodgings, Kate Anthon could take a room in the same house. If Mrs. Eliot took a house of her own, it would be a different matter. A long lease would also defeat a plan for transporting Mrs. Eliot once more to the Continent.

A week later they were hopeful that the mother might be persuaded to let Florie stay a fortnight longer and go to Venice, a city that Mrs. Anthon had not exhausted in her brief visit of 1873. While they waited for an answer from Mrs. Eliot, they "both felt blue and unhappy at the terrible thought of the near separation." A favorable reply brought a wild excitement, but on painful second thought they decided that a delay would not be fair to Mrs. Eliot, and they wired her that Florie would be in London on April 30.

Their last days in Florence were excited, hurried, and not very happy. Mrs. Anthon spent a morning tearing up "letters, etc.," and they paid their final visits to the Uffizi and to the Pitti Palace. "Walked in the Boboli gardens till five — lovely! lovely! Our *last walk* there. We felt very sad."

The following day they visited the National Museum and then finished their packing. "I did not sleep," wrote Mrs. Anthon.

On April 27 there was a "terrific thunder shower early in the morning. I went in Florie's room. Florie took her last

singing lesson at half past one. The weather cleared. Our last,
last day in dear Florence."

At this point her young friend took the pencil from her
and wrote tenderly, and for the last time, in the amazing diary:

> *The Bab of the Mud. loves the Mud of the Bab. Mr.*
> *Pump is a great Bouf, and Mrs. Pump has, and always will*
> *have, the greatest respect and love for the dear old gentle-*
> *man. Mr. Pump has given Mrs. Pump a gold ring in*
> *token of his love. This is written by me (My Peccious).*
> *Make yourself very small. Florence E. Pump.*

Together they journeyed through Italy and France until
their ways divided, one to Lausanne, the other to Paris and
England.

"At Culvy — at five o'clock — came the *dreadful parting*
with my darling Florie!"

Succeeding entries were marked by a quiet desolation in contrast with the frantic tone of the autumn before. Not that Kate
was resigned. On the contrary, she seemed to feel that all was
settled between them, that they must be together, and that the
only question was the length of the weary interval. At Lausanne,
fortunately for her peace of mind, she was with an old friend
and the latter's young children and could take a warm interest
in their activities. Other friends were also comfortingly near
at hand, with teas and drives to beguile her. Also the troubles
of her nephew Harry were at least a distracting worry. The
young man was out of funds, had exhausted himself in a tramp
from Leipzig to Berlin, and was anxious about his prospects
for remaining in Europe. To Harry she sent money and a
scolding for his long walk. To her stepmother she wrote, with
vexation, of Dr. Bartlett's reluctance to give his son another
year at Leipzig. The usual vast correspondence (in addition
to these and the three or four letters weekly to Florie) filled
the remainder of her time.

There were records of an incessant exchange of letters between the two women, and an occasional half-cry: "*So* lonely without the *Pigeon*." More despondently Kate wrote: "Felt very miserably unhappy and dreadfully lonely and sad without Florie." Still the passionate language of May 8 is exceptional:

"What is dear Florie doing? I am afraid she is ill. Oh! if I could only see her — I *cannot* stand this separation!"

Toward the end of the month she was much concerned over the illness of her nephew Harry and still more worried about Florie. On May 31: "Last day of this long, weary, dreary month. Thank God it is over. The first month from dear Florie! Sad and worried about Harry and Florie and everything." Apparently Florie was bearing the separation no better than she, perhaps not so well, and was distressing her with piteous, homesick letters. In desperation Mrs. Anthon wrote to some English friends, begging them to call on Florie and alleviate some of the miserable loneliness.

On June 4 she wrote in her diary: "Felt blue and depressed thinking about Florie and wondering when I can see her again. God grant it may be soon." On June 10: "Six weeks today since I parted with my dear Florie." The following day: "I wrote to Florie, sent a list of prices (Montreux), posted the letter at ten o'clock." For the past week she had been looking at lodgings in Montreux and Vevey, and apparently the plan was to share an apartment in Switzerland with Florie and her mother, but it came to nothing.

With the entry for June 13 the book was filled. The succeeding diary or diaries (the purchase of a new blank book was reported) were most carefully destroyed. Kate preserved this diary (as she had kept, for remembrance, some of her many letters from Emily Dickinson) and read and reread it to the end of her life, until its pages were stained and the binding was weakened, because it recorded that most happy winter in Florence. She was never to have such another.

⟆⟆⟆ XIII ⟆⟆⟆

On August 17, 1881, Kate Anthon was in Château d'Oex, Switzerland, where she had evidently been staying for some weeks. She had persuaded her nephew to come from Germany, and she was gratified by his improvement in health and proud of his fluent German. Her concern for Harry was so great that she entertained briefly the idea of going to Berlin for the winter to take care of him. A friend, Mary Osler, chided her gently for the notion that any young man would wish to be so closely supervised even by the most devoted aunt. The plan came to nothing and may never have been very serious. Her strongest desire was in another direction.

"I do not yet know what I shall do," Kate wrote to her brother Henry, "but am almost sure I shall pass the winter in England. Florie is most impatient for me to join her. They will go to some warm sheltered place — probably Clevedon, not far from Bristol. They will either go into lodgings or take a house, and I shall be with them." Another friend was begging her to spend the winter in Montreux, "but my desire to see Florie is *so* strong and she is *so* unhappy away from me."

Henry Scott was not well, and Kate was worried about him.

314

If he would come to England for the winter, she would take the best care of him. Nor was she easy about her stepmother. Always in the back of her mind was the realization that Cooperstown expected her to return and take care of the aging woman, and she was divided between family loyalties and her engrossing passion for Florie.

"I *earnestly* hope nothing will call me back to America," she wrote to Henry. "Is mother getting on all right? Oh! I should be so UNHAPPY to leave Europe. I have many friends here. I cannot, *cannot* return to America. Perhaps you will say 'Nobody has asked you to return'! I know it, but I am always thinking *ought* I to go to Mother. Oh! am I very selfish? Dear, *dear* Henry, God knows I would give worlds to see you and dear, darling Lila, but I have had *so much* trouble in America, and this is such a relief — such a radical change — and after all I am not much good to my family. I seem so powerless to help."

Château d'Oex, she told her brother, was not so pretty as other places in Switzerland where she had stayed, but it was *"very* cheap, which is a great consideration." Another attraction was the presence of some old friends, Mary Osler and her husband, who lived in Switzerland for their health. There was also a new friend, a girl of twenty visiting Switzerland with a brother and an invalid aunt.

"Here I was interrupted," wrote Kate Anthon, "by Helen coming in. Helen is a lovely girl — a strong splendid looking English girl with a magnificent physique. She has just returned from a mountain ascension. She ascended the lesser Matterhorn and crossed a glacier, and went up the Riffel, to the infinite delight of her brother and other members of the Alpine Club! They are *such nice* people. Helen is a great friend of mine."

A few years earlier Kate had written contemptuously of women who engaged in such masculine sports as mountain-climbing, but Florie had wanted to climb a mountain, and Helen did climb. In the same manner Kate had dismissed the strong-minded women who were clamoring for higher education. Then she discovered that Helen and her sisters were unusually well educated for women of the late nineteenth century. One sister became a physician, and Kate was proud of her. Her real convictions were those of the persons she loved, and Helen was to be a lifelong friend. At some period in their history the young girl sent Mrs. Anthon the following verses from a poem by Bulwer-Lytton:

> Absent yet Present
> As the flight of a river that flows to the sea,
> My soul rushes ever in tumult to thee
> A twofold existence I am where thou art
> My heart in the distance beats close to thy heart.
> Look up I am near thee I gaze on thy face
> I see thee, I hear thee, I feel thy embrace
> And absence but brightens the eyes that I miss
> And custom but heightens the spell of thy kiss
> It is not from duty, though that may be owed
> It is not from beauty, though that be bestowed
> But all that I care for and all that I know
> Is that without wherefore I worship thee so.

Mrs. Anthon turned the page over and wrote on the back, "My dear, my dear dear, My —," but she used the rest of the space to record a joke. Although she was very fond of Helen and spent many pleasant years in her young friend's neighborhood, Helen never took the place that Florie or Emily had occupied.

2

On December 8, 1881, Kate wrote from Clevedon, near Bristol, to her sister-in-law, Lila. She apologized for the brevity of her letter. In a moment she was going into the kitchen with Florie to make a pudding. They had done a great deal of cooking and were planning to make a cake for Florie's birthday. "She is as sweet as ever," wrote Kate, "has suffered a good deal from sore throat and unable to sing, which has been a great grief to her."

Over the Christmas holidays Kate went alone to Clifton to see her old friends, the Bakers. They urged her to prolong her visit, but she wrote to her stepmother that she could not: "Florie is very lonely without me, and I promised to return at the end of ten days. I was so sorry Florie could not have been here. She would have enjoyed it so much, but she could not leave her Mama." In this same letter Kate thanked Mrs. Scott for remembering Florie with a Christmas card: "She is much pleased with it, thinks it *so* pretty, and so kind in you to think of her."

Both women took pains to win Mrs. Scott's approval of their friendship, but Mrs. Scott remained jealous and mistrustful of any influence that kept her stepdaughter abroad. "Katie will probably not return during my life time," she wrote resignedly to Henry's wife, Lila, but immediately added, "I can discover that the life in England is not quite satisfactory, even with Florie. She says she lies awake so much at night."

Another letter from Kate to her stepmother, dated January 15, 1882, gives a cheerful picture of life in Clevedon. However, there are undercurrents of distress (apparently with regard to Mrs. Eliot) which might explain Kate's insomnia. "We find it extremely quiet," Kate wrote, "and miss the gaiety and freedom of life which one meets on the Continent. Still it is very pleasant." After a late breakfast she and Florie went to market or did errands. On their return Florie practiced her music, and Kate brought her book or her sewing and sat near the piano. After their two o'clock dinner they went out for a walk, and Kate spoke rapturously of the blackbirds' singing. (Long afterwards Florence remembered that their favorite walk had been to the grave of Tennyson's friend Arthur Hallam.) Mrs. Eliot coddled her health and refused to join them, although, as Kate added, with some impatience, "during all this exquisite weather she might have walked out every day, and it would have done her good." At five o'clock they had afternoon tea, and Kate read aloud, or Florie played and sang. After supper "Florie plays bezique with her Mama, or I play backgammon with her till ten o'clock, when we retire."

It was a great change from their life in Florence, Kate added regretfully, but they were very comfortable. Mrs. Eliot talked of getting a house in the spring, much to the disgust of Florie, who longed only to return to the Continent. Kate was troubled about her own position in such an event. "Now we are in lodgings it is a very different thing, but I do not think it would be wise for me to board with them if they rented a whole house, do you? I should not care to live always in Clevedon. It is *too quiet*. I am spoilt for it by my life on the Continent. Still I am *so fond* of Florie I am happy anywhere with her." In later years the winter at Clevedon joined the winter in Florence as the happiest seasons of her life.

Florie attended a party, and Kate Anthon wrote: "I dressed her myself — all in pure white. There is so much style about her. She is so tall and magnificently formed. So distinguished looking. *Such a neck and shoulders!*"

On January 18 Mrs. Scott wrote tartly to her daughter-in-law, Lila: "I suppose we shall hear constantly of Florrie this winter and I seem to be expected to send *love* to the family in all my letters. I don't know *why* we need feel so particularly grateful to them for stealing Katie's affections away from her own family. I sometimes think Katie feels conscious of it when she is writing — and that she tries to disguise it. It often looks so to me. At any rate, I think she loves Florrie better than any one in the world."

Kate's old friend Mary Osler wrote with more gentleness and understanding, tacitly accepting the unusual relationship. She was well acquainted with Florie and had known Kate since the days of Kate's desperate pilgrimage with John Anthon. They had met at the Hotel du Signal in Chexbres during the late spring of 1873, and the friendship so swiftly formed was life-long. On February 27, 1882, Mrs. Osler wrote from the Hotel Anglo-Americano in Florence:

> *My dear Mrs. Anthon, I was more glad of your letter than I ought to have been, for I don't think you were a nice woman to spend all September at Montreux, and never come to see us, or let us know you were there. Them's my sentiments.*
>
> *No, dear, I was not surprised to find you settled down for a time in England, feeling with all your love for brighter climes, that your love for your friend Miss Eliot would at any rate for a time keep you in our dear but foggy isle. Years ago I knew Clevedon. What a lovely little place it is, and its drives and walks delightful.*
>
> *I do hope you may be coming to these parts again. How very glad we should be to see Miss Eliot pouring out the Tea whilst we all talk and laugh together. Is there a chance of such a thing? I am glad to hear such a good account of Mrs. Eliot and her daughter. I do think Miss Eliot should come and finish her singing lessons. Do tell her so with my love. My husband is out, or he would send his kindest regards or a still warmer message to you all.*
>
> *Believe me, dearest Mrs. Anthon, Yours affectionately, Mary Osler.*
>
> *I am glad to hear good news of your beloved Harry Bartlett. I don't think you could have done him good but certainly yourself harm in wintering in Berlin. Young men hate the idea of being looked after!*
>
> *My love to Mrs. Eliot, please, and very much to yourself, dear. I shall expect to hear before long that you are ashamed of your conduct at Montreux, and will never do so no more.*

With this tender, joking letter, Mary Osler passed out of the history of Kate Anthon. She was a woman of fragile health and had not long to live. The letter itself is evidence of the deep and lasting affection that Mrs. Anthon created in many intelligent, sensitive women. Kate was no writer; she could suffer the emotional storms of an Emily Dickinson without the gift of making her readers participate imaginatively in her sufferings. Her letters are a pale reflection of the great vitality, the quick sympathy with other persons, and the wit that sparkled in conversation but could never be reduced to writing. Face to face she was a remarkable woman. Her talent was in actual living, where Emily Dickinson was manifestly so deficient.

Without doubt Kate would have liked nothing better than to return to Florence with her young friend, but they could not manage events. They were forced to be apart for long intervals, undoubtedly because of some whim of Florie's mother. Of course there was never anything so vulgar as a quarrel; Mrs. Anthon saw to that. But Mrs. Eliot grew restive, wanted change, carried Florie off where Kate could not follow, and then, upon a new whim, recalled her useful companion. Mrs. Anthon never complained — she was in no position to debate terms — but afterwards she was to show a lively desire not to become Mrs. Eliot's companion when Florie was gone.

Apparently the two friends were separated during the summer of 1882. In late 1882 and early 1883, however, they spent six months together at Tunbridge Wells. It is difficult to see what they expected. They could never plan with any assurance for more than a few months ahead, and apparently they lived from day to day, trusting that the dreaded final parting would never come.

On May 3, 1883, Kate Anthon wrote from Tunbridge Wells to her brother Henry. She was uncertain about her plans for the summer, but thought she might go to Scotland "with Florie and her mother, and possibly go to Switzerland. I have never seen Scotland, and it is *so beautiful*." On July 10 she wrote to her brother from Callander. She liked the Highlands very much and found that the air agreed with her. Florie was in the neighborhood, but apparently they were in separate parties. "We are quite in the country — nine miles from the Trossachs and Loch Katrine. When Florie comes, we all go to Loch Katrine to spend the day."

As often happened in her wandering life, Kate was concerned about her possessions stored here and there with friends. "I often think I ought to come home, and get what I have together and take care of things myself and not bother anybody. This will become more and more imperative as I grow older. [In this summer of 1883 she was fifty-two.] If it were not for Mother and you and Lila, I would settle down here, but I cannot tear away from you all. The desire to see your dear, loved faces is very *very* strong, but as you say, '*Let things rest quiet for the present.*' Good bye, dear old boy. How many *years* we have been separated! I suppose I should not feel at home in America."

In late autumn Kate went to Switzerland. Her explanation was that she wanted to retrench in a cheaper country. She wished also to look after her niece, Lily Bartlett. "And all things considered," it had seemed best to spend the winter on the Continent. Among the things considered may well have been fresh difficulties with Mrs. Eliot. However, there is at least a suggestion that she and Florie were working at a desperate plan, and that this was at the back of her desire to save money and to collect her possessions and make a home. It is certain that she never left Florie willingly and that Florie never willingly let her go. Whatever Kate's motives, however, she was soon to regret that she was away from England.

3

In November, 1883, at Lausanne, Kate received word that her much-loved younger brother had broken under the strain of long-continued ill health and overwork. Her sister, her father, her own mother, were long since dead. Henry was the last of her immediate family, and now he too, a man of forty-seven, with a dependent young family, was doomed. Faced by this calamity, the unhappy woman longed for the unfailing comfort of Florie: "She would have taken *such* care of me."

The extent of the catastrophe was at first minimized, and Kate could think only of getting Henry to Europe and caring for him there. As the truth was forced home by successive letters, she became frantic. What she could do to help financially, she immediately promised. She signed away a good half of her year's income to her sister-in-law and promised more — and gave more. But should she come at once or wait for better sailing weather? And could she bear to leave Florie for so long and indefinite a period? The letters were anguished.

As Mrs. Scott was to observe, Kate's grief-stricken letters were not very consoling. On December 16 the elderly woman wrote to her daughter-in-law: "It is dreadful to read Katie's letters. Poor child, I wish she could control herself a little. She makes herself so miserable. She ought to take example from you, dearie." But poor Kate could never control herself. It was the penalty of a temperament that in sunny weather made her the liveliest, most delightful of companions.

On January 7, 1884, Mrs. Scott wrote again to her daughter-in-law: "Kate's letter has not yet come to hand. I am very sorry for her, but I wish she could control her nervous system a little more. I fear she will get *too excited* herself." In the next paragraph came a warning note: "If my eyesight is going

to fail me, it will be *necessary* for her to come back to America."
This was probably the point of decision. Henry's illness alone,
for which Kate could do nothing at home that she could not
have done abroad, might have failed to recall her, but the imminent, helpless blindness of her stepmother was a claim that
could not be denied. Afterwards she was to be somewhat annoyed by Mrs. Scott's persistent abuse of this failing eyesight.

The struggle continued, however, throughout Kate's winter
at Lausanne. She did not readily surrender the rest of her life
in order to take up her old duties as nurse; and Mrs. Scott put
very little pressure on her. In a letter which showed no intention of returning to America, Kate spoke of going to
Montreux for a change of air, and her stepmother quietly approved. Meanwhile there was a constant exchange of letters
between Kate and Florie. These letters have perished, no
diary of this period has survived, and yet it is possible to guess
the plan on which the two friends must have been working
when the news of Henry's illness broke upon them.

Kate had gone to Switzerland to save money — all the money
that she could. At the same time Florie had gone to London to
study music. A legacy of two hundred pounds had temporarily
freed her from her mother, and apparently she hoped to make
her independence permanent by means of her voice. If this
was indeed the hope on which the two women were building
— and they could have had no other — it was certainly a slender
one. The old county family to which Florie belonged would
not have welcomed a professional singer, and though Florie had
a mind of her own, they could still exert great pressure on her.
Years earlier they had discouraged her interest in the talented
musician whom she eventually married, and afterwards they
seemed to think that singing at the parties given by her sister,
Lady Russell, was *éclat* enough. The most serious obstacle,
however, was that Florie had only a very pleasant voice, not a
great one. In old age she recalled that she had sung once with

an orchestra, at many charities, and in a "sort of opera," in which she wore a Turkish costume. The lasting effect of her musical training was to reintroduce her to her future husband.

Florie wrote to Mrs. Anthon from Bath, where she had gone to sing, and wrote again on returning to her studies in London. And Kate wept — not altogether for her unhappy brother and her stepmother. It was the situation of September, 1880, all over again, when Mrs. Scott had been ill, and Kate, at Luino, had been torn between her need for Florie and the call from home. This time the call would be decisive. In late January Mrs. Scott apparently wrote with some urgency and then reconsidered and sent a cable to Lausanne. But Kate had already made her decision and had gone to London.

"You will be surprised at my dating from England," she wrote to Mrs. Scott on February 16, 1884. "I left Lausanne Thursday Feb 14th travelled all night & crossed the next day, arriving here last eveg. I am staying with Florie in Norwood. I have come on to make my preparations for sailing as soon as possible."

In bewilderment Mrs. Scott wrote to her daughter-in-law, Lila: "I do not know what to think about Katie. The despatch may have been recd after this letter was written. We can do nothing but WAIT. At any rate I am thankful she is in England."

The cousins with whom Florie was boarding insisted that Kate stay with them. Florie's next older sister, who had just returned from India, also met Kate at this time, and a warm lifelong friendship sprang up between Kate and Lady Bertram. All of them helped Kate prepare for her trip, and of course Florie was untiring. There was last-minute shopping to be done. Alfred Clark had to be notified to meet Kate in New York, for she would have no American money and would not know what to do. Three trunks came out of storage to be packed, and reservations had to be made and a ticket bought.

On a visit to the Cunard office Kate met and charmed Mr.
Cunard, who smoothed out difficulties and gave her a letter to
the captain of her ship.

Meanwhile Mrs. Scott's cable was received in England, but
Kate answered firmly: "My berth is engaged & paid for & I
shall *certainly* come in the 'Gallia.' *Nothing* could possibly
deter me from coming to you." And Mrs. Scott wrote to her
daughter-in-law: "Oh Lila. Isn't it joyful? No matter about
the despatch if she only gets here safely."

On March 1, 1884, Kate sailed on the *Gallia* for the homeland
from which she had long been absent. It was not a joyful home-
coming, for the final scene with Florie had been anguished.
"My heart was torn in pieces," Kate wrote to her sister-in-law.
"Florie was really ill at the parting." And in her copy of Shelley
she was to mark these lines:

> Something within that interval which bore
> The stamp of *why* they parted, *how* they met.

.   .   .   .   .

> Her voice did quiver as we parted,
>   Yet knew I not that heart was broken
> From which it came, and I departed
>   Heeding not the words then spoken.

But if Kate left heartbreak in London, she brought joy to
the half-blind old woman in Cooperstown. "It seems so almost
past belief," wrote Mrs. Scott to Lila, "to think she is here —
even when I *see* her before me — and she seems in good spirits
excepting when she gets dwelling upon poor Henry." Then,
half-jealously, "I am afraid she will *pine* for Florrie — "

On March 25, 1884, Kate wrote from Cooperstown to Lila:
"Your letter with Edith's note to Miss Eliot was received. It
was such a nice little letter, and I have sent it on to England.

It has been such a confusion, my getting home, my seeing
Mother, and trying to keep up seeing all these Cooperstown
people, when my heart is like lead. *Never, never* in all my
troubled life (and God knows it *has* been one) have I suffered
as at present. There has been no agony like this."

Belatedly she remembered her husband and added that
John's illness had come on more slowly and that she had been
in a measure prepared for it. Of course her suffering was intensified by her separation from Florie, but she believed that she
wept for Henry, whom she deeply loved. The immediate crisis
seemed always the most desperate. It was fortunate for her that
her mind worked in this fashion; otherwise she could not have
borne her calamitous life. Once she remarked thoughtfully that
in the space of a very few years she had lost husband, parents,
brother, sister, six nephews and nieces, and many friends. By
comparison, the life of Emily Dickinson was serene and un-
troubled.

During March and April Kate wrote incessantly to her sister-
in-law, pouring out advice, sympathy, and personal anguish.
With silent misgiving Mrs. Scott looked on. At last she resolved
to take a hand. On March 28 she wrote to Lila:

> You and Katie have kept up such a rapid exchange of
> letters that it has seemed unnecessary for me to write —
> and yet I feel as if I wanted to put in a word. You need
> not think I am unmindful of our great sorrow, tho' I keep
> composed, and try to look upon the trial with proper sub-
> mission. It is the all-absorbing subject with Katie and she
> cannot control herself — but weeps and agitates herself —
> until my heart aches for her. Poor child, she overflows with
> love and affection. She is bent upon getting Henry at
> liberty, but this is a matter upon which I am not willing to
> give my advice. I feel as if I dare not trust myself or my
> failing judgment, where there is such frightful responsi-
> bility involved.

A letter from the hospital physician put an end to any hopes of Henry's recovery but did not relieve Kate of the feeling that she must personally take charge of him. On April 5 she wrote again to Lila, offering every penny of her income to provide for Henry in a private hospital. In depression and annoyance she added: "What a climate!! We are buried deep in snow, ice a foot thick in the Lake! Mother is very well and *insists* upon writing letters every day. She is *mad* on writing! and will soon get her eyes weak again."

A letter of April 9 is full of the same project of getting Henry out of the hospital. "Oh! I sit by the hour thinking, thinking, hoping, praying for a ray of light. Never — *never* in all my troubled life has anything made me so profoundly wretched. It is so hard to keep up and see all these people in Cooperstown, whom I don't know nor care to know. Last week I felt so ill — cold, I suppose. The climate is awful, and I have *been*, and am all the time so homesick for dear England. Oh! Lila, *when will* I get back again?"

On April 12 she was delighted to hear that her brother had enjoyed an outing. She wanted to pay for the carriage as often as he could take such drives, but she was still woefully depressed. "The weather is horrible — cold and dreary. I never felt so low-spirited and unhappy in my life. Mother seems quite well, and *will write letters!* She seems mad on the subject of writing! She has been sending off her Easter cards. I don't see how she can have the heart for it. I cannot send one to a human being!"

In late April Mrs. Scott suffered a slight stroke, from which she gradually recovered. Kate too was in very bad plight. Her right arm was so rheumatic that she was compelled to write with her left. This painful inconvenience did not stop the flow of her letters, although it made them very hard to read. She was now busy with a scheme for getting Henry into a rented house in Cooperstown. Lila's brother and the hospital doctor were strongly opposed. Even Alfred Clark seemed to think the responsibility too grave, for his habitual kindness to Kate stopped short at renting her his cottage "Fenimore." He did not refuse outright, but he shuffled and evaded until Kate, in exasperation, rented other quarters for her brother and his family. For the experiment was tried. On July 19, 1884, Lila's sister-in-law, Alice Synnott, wrote of seeing Kate out for a walk with her brother and his little boys. Mrs. Synnott was much struck by Kate's changed appearance: "Mrs. Anthon looks quite bent and old — her hair is almost white."

4

Meanwhile Emily Dickinson had been grievously stricken. In the spring of 1884, shortly after Kate's return to America, she suffered the first attack of her fatal illness. She fainted one noon and was unconscious until late at night. The doctor, Emily reported, called it "revenge of the nerves." Elsewhere she spoke of her illness as "nervous prostration." It was Bright's disease. After some days she was able to sit in a chair and even get about her room, but she was never well again.

Apparently she did not see Kate during this 1884–86 visit to America. Kate did not stir from Cooperstown until after her stepmother died in late 1885. The small remainder of her time is pretty well accounted for, and it did not include a trip to Amherst. But Emily undoubtedly knew that Kate had returned to America. Even though Kate's friendship with Sue Dickinson was rather casual at this time, Kate would have written Sue to announce her return. She may also have written to Emily. There is a late letter from Emily to Kate (not yet available) which may have been sent at this time in answer to one from Kate.

Certain poems in Emily's latest handwriting (that is, about 1884–85) suggest some kind of renewed intercourse with Kate

Anthon. A letter alone would have been enough to start Emily on a tour of memory. There is evidence in the poems that Emily was much occupied with the idea of Katie in these last few years of her life. One poem speaks of Katie by name. Emily was still agitated by the recollection of Kate's "treason," and on occasion she wrote savagely. Still other poems, however, appear to have been written in a generous, forgiving mood.

In a poem beginning "The smouldering embers blush," Emily wonders that the fire of love should survive so many years at the core of ashes that were apparently dead. In a companion poem, "Long years apart can make no breach," she wrote that a second's time (Kate's letter, perhaps?) could fill the gap:

> The absence of the witch does not
> Invalidate the spell.

If love that had been coals for a thousand years (the poem continues) should be uncovered by the person who had "fondled them when they were fire," the embers would live again.

Surely Kate Anthon was the subject of these poems. The language is very strong; the poems do not record a mere friendship. Kate could have been the "witch" (Emily took the word, in this affectionate sense, from Elizabeth Browning's *Aurora Leigh*), the "fondling" was clearly indicated in Emily's letters to her of 1859–61, and Kate had returned after a long absence. Also Emily was in correspondence with her at a fairly late date. The problem will not be settled until all of Emily Dickinson's poems are dated and made accessible, but there is already sufficient evidence for believing that in the last years of her own life Emily was again busy with the idea of a woman who had been "witch," "queen," "butterfly," and "peninsula" to her.

5   ❧

In the summer of 1885 Kate Anthon received a final, overwhelming blow. The nature of this blow is apparent from the following letter:

London, Aug. 3 [1885]

My dear Mrs. Anthon,

I thank you with all my heart for your kind note. I little thought when I met you at Mr. Charles', what a ground of sympathy there would be between us one day. You knew Florence then, you see, I didn't. In fact, I did not really know her till after we were engaged, and I shall perhaps not fully know her for many years yet, seeing that there seem to be deeps of tenderness in her that are not soon fathomed.

From her account, she owes much to you, and I am quite willing to believe her. You have a right to settle that between yourselves. I was a little jealous of you at first: I thought you must be so thoroughly in love with her that you would never give her up. I hope we shall meet again.

Of course I am not good enough for her; but she doesn't know that, and you must not try to enlighten her.

I call her "Florence" because there is a "Florie" already in the family: her cousin, who married my brother. And I think the full name "Florence" has a fine stately sound that sits well upon her. Not that she is "stately" to me, bless her!

There seems to be something very unusual in the love between you and her. I feel that I must love you a little too.

Sincerely yours,

HENRY LAYTON

In her memoirs, long afterwards, Florie was to write that she had been interested in Mr. Layton as early as about 1878. Perhaps she exaggerated in retrospect, or the interest may have been entirely on her side. At all events her family put a stop to the acquaintance, and Mr. Layton apparently forgot all about it. In late February, 1884, he called at the house of the Charleses, the cousins with whom Florie was boarding, in order to see the family of his brother's wife, not to renew a forgotten acquaintance with Florie. On this same visit he met Kate Anthon, who was staying with Florie's cousins while preparing for her return to America. The three principals came face to face without any suspicion of the intricate relationship that would some day bind them together. Kate was fifty-three, Mr. Layton about forty-seven, Florie twenty-seven. The close, emotional tie between Kate and Florie had now endured some five years.

After Kate Anthon sailed for America, Florie was in a difficult position. There was no prospect of Kate's return until Mrs. Scott died — a very problematical date. Even then there would be no security and no predictable future. Probably the dream of becoming a singer was already fading. In these circumstances Florie accepted Mr. Layton. Then she reacted much as Kate had done after becoming engaged to John Anthon. Apparently she described her attachment to Mrs. Anthon and asked for her freedom. If so, her fiancé persuaded her to change her mind. His generosity in overlooking the past may have excited a hysterical reaction in his favor. So much is implicit in the letter from Mr. Layton to Mrs. Anthon.

There is no better place to record the subsequent history of Florence Layton. For she did marry after a long and vacillating engagement. Responsibility sobered her. The exuberant, emotional girl become a quiet, reserved woman, and the music which had once been her most joyful way of expressing herself was almost forgotten. Her husband, though a generous man, was too good a musician himself to be the rapt, uncritical

listener that Mrs. Anthon had been. On the rare occasions
when Florie still played and sang for her children, she stopped
upon his coming into the room. Then the babies came so fast
that for many years she was almost exhausted with child-bear-
ing. She was a conscientious mother. Apparently she tried to
interest her children in the museum-visiting and the amateur-
ish nature studies which she had enjoyed with Mrs. Anthon.
During the war she was almost crushed by the death of two
sons. For years she showed little desire to continue living. After
her husband's death, however, she resolved to live once more
as she chose. Taking a small house in a village near London,
she lived alone and devoted herself to helping others. The
serene beauty of her last portraits has already been mentioned.
She was happier in the end of her life than she had been for
many years. She died in her early eighties. Her last act was
an attempt to write her memoirs, but she was unable to carry
them beyond the crucial period of 1885–87.

In the summer of 1885 Kate Anthon wrote a generous letter
to Florie's fiancé, but she felt like Brabantio — like Emily
Dickinson:

> I here do give thee that with all my heart
> Which, but thou hast already, with all my heart
> I would keep from thee.

She was no happier than Emily had been on a like occasion in
1864. If she had been a poet, she could now have written the
entire canon of Emily Dickinson. Without talent, she nevertheless made her feelings known by means of poetry.

In February, 1885, as she noted on the flyleaf with her customary methodicalness, this true child of Shelley bought a new
edition of her favorite poet. During the next several months
she read through the two volumes and bracketed favorite passages. The markings are undated, but the pencil used through-

out appears to be the same. Also the marked passages hang together in a manner that cannot be explained as coincidence. With trivial exceptions, they deal with a remarkable and beloved woman, the value of friendship, a painful separation with hints of threat and treason, reminiscences of an Italian paradise, a beautiful singing voice, a pair of blue eyes, and finally the anguish of loss and loneliness.

It is impossible to quote all the marked passages. Representative specimens are given, however, in the conviction that they record Kate's feelings during this summer of crisis as truly as the poetry of Emily Dickinson reflected her own anguish upon a similar occasion.

The "Epipsychidion" was a favorite poem, and many lines were marked. The following passage is an interesting example:

> As smoke by fire, and in her beauty's glow
> I stood, and felt the dawn of my long night
> Was penetrating me with living light:
> I knew it was the Vision veiled from me
> So many years — that it was Emily.

On the strength of Emily Dickinson's late poems and renewed correspondence with Kate, there is a temptation to suggest that this marked passage recalled Emily to Kate Anthon. But Kate's real anguish over Emily Dickinson was still to come. Almost certainly she substituted the name of Florie, although she did tend to confuse and identify the two women — just as she occasionally identified Emily with Campbell Turner and Florie with John Anthon. These confusions will be illustrated in a succeeding chapter.

It is to be expected that a man's poetry should contain many beautiful descriptions of a woman. That a woman should persistently seek out and mark these passages is another matter. The following lines are an example:

> Under the grey beak of some promontory
> She met me, robed in such exceeding glory,
> That I beheld her not. In solitudes
> Her voice came to me through the whispering woods,
> And from the fountains, and the odours deep
> Of flowers, which, like lips murmuring in their sleep
> Of the sweet kisses which had lulled them there,
> Breathed but of *her* to the enamoured air.

Again Kate marked:

> Her Spirit was the harmony of truth.

In two passages she brooded upon the inequalities between herself and her young friend:

.   .   .   .   .

> 'I know
> That Love makes all things equal: I have heard
> By mine own heart this glorious truth averred.

.   .   .   .   .

> I love thee; yes, I feel
> That on the fountain of my heart a seal
> Is set to keep its waters pure and bright
> For thee, since in those *tears* thou hast delight.
> We — are we not formed, as notes of music are,
> For one another, though dissimilar.

Elsewhere she marked:

> A woman; such as it has been my doom
> To meet with few, — a wonder of this earth,
> Where there is little of transcendent worth, —
> Like one of Shakespeare's women; kindly she,
> And, with a manner beyond courtesy . . .

In several passages she dwelt upon the beauty of friendship. Passages already quoted described their painful separation. Kate had gone to America, "heeding not the words then spoken." Still other passages suggest that Mrs. Anthon, like Emily Dickinson on an earlier occasion, believed that she had been dealt with treasonably:

> And some were fair — but beauty dies away:
> Others were wise — but honeyed words betray:
> And One was true — oh! why not true to me?
>
> .   .   .   .   .
>
> And we agreed his was some dreadful ill
> Wrought on him boldly, yet unspeakable,
> By a dear friend; some deadly change in love,
> Of one vowed deeply which he dreamed not of.
>
> .   .   .   .   .
>
> And having stamped this canker on his youth
> She had abandoned him.
>
> .   .   .   .   .
>
> And women too, ugliest of all things evil.

This last bitter line is of special significance, for in a tenderer mood Kate went back and erased the mark beside it. Elsewhere she marked the following lines:

> It doth repent me: words are quick and vain,
> Grief for awhile is blind, and so was mine.
> I wish no living thing to suffer pain.

With painful knowledge she bracketed the following line:

> Love sometimes leads astray to misery.

And again:

> My secret groans must be unheard by thee,
> Thou wouldst weep tears bitter as blood to know
> Thy lost friend's incommunicable woe.

Shelley might almost have written his poems to serve as a record of Kate's deepest feelings. Several long passages describing Italy were indicated, and four marked lines from a poem "To William Shelley" were found to be especially appropriate:

> Come thou belovèd as thou art . . . .
>
> Be a dream of days forgotten long.
> We soon shall dwell by the azure sea
> Of serene and golden Italy.

Elsewhere:

> Thy little footsteps on the sands
> Of a remote and lonely shore.

Florie had a lovely voice, to which Kate had often listened, enraptured, and the following passages were marked:

> My spirit like a charmèd bark doth swim
> Upon the liquid waves of thy sweet singing,
> Far far away into the regions dim
>
> Of rapture — as a boat, with swift sails winging
> Its way adown some many-winding river,
> Speeds through dark forests o'er the waters swinging.
>
>   .   .   .   .   .
>
> Though the sound overpowers,
> Sing again, with your dear voice revealing
> A tone
> Of some world far from ours,
> Where music and moonlight and feeling
> Are one.

Florie had blue eyes:

> Oh speak not of her eyes! — which seem
> Twin mirrors of Italian Heaven, yet gleam
> With such deep meaning.
>
> .   .   .   .   .
>
> Thine eyes are like the deep, blue, boundless heaven
> Contracted to two circles underneath
> Their long, fine lashes; dark, far, measureless.

In the preface to *Laon and Cynthia* Kate was struck by this typical Shelleyan line: "Love is celebrated everywhere as the sole law which should govern the moral world." It was her own faith as well. The following marked passages tell their own story:

> At sunrise thou shouldst come, sweet sister mine,
> Too long desired, too long delaying, come!
>
> .   .   .   .   .
>
> Life of Life! thy lips enkindle . . .
> As twilight to the western star,
> Thou, belovèd, art to me.
>
> .   .   .   .   .
>
> My heart beats loud and fast; —
> Oh! press it to thine own again,
> Where it will break at last.
>
> .   .   .   .   .
>
> Like the ghost of a dear friend dead
>   Is Time long past.
> A tone which is now forever fled,
> A hope which is now forever past,
> A love so sweet it could not last,
>   Was Time long past.

Where revelation is complete, there is no need to interpret. These passages are as plain and unmistakable as autobiography. They are, in fact, a deeper, more personal record than any writer gives of himself, for Kate marked as she felt, and not as she would have presented herself to any conceivable audience. If the entire history of Florie had vanished, if diary and letters had been destroyed, it would still be possible, from these marked passages, to reconstruct two personalities and the unlucky course of their attachment.

6

In the autumn of 1885 Mrs. Scott died, and for the next several months Kate Anthon went to and fro upon the Atlantic seaboard. A relative of Lila Scott was shocked by a rumor that Mrs. Anthon was planning to return to England while her brother was still alive. Undoubtedly many people in Cooperstown felt the same way, and for a while the unhappy woman gave up planning. With greater sensitivity and humaneness, Alfred Clark and his wife saw no reason why Kate should be sacrificed to her brother. She was plainly breaking down, and in December they sent her to Atlantic City with a niece of theirs. Then they learned that her brother was failing and must return to a hospital, and they made a trip to Atlantic City to break the news to Kate as gently as possible.

In February, 1886, Kate wrote from the Clarks' house in New York. She was "unsettled and worried and unhappy." On March 3 she almost thought she would "go to England for a radical change. My health is so broken. But please say not a word on this subject to a human being in C. Cooperstown is a terrible place for gossip." The next day she thanked her sister-in-law for some "English letters," which must have been responsible for a slight change in her plans. Florie was calling to her, and she soon wrote: "If there is no change in Henry, my friends *all* advise my going to Scotland to try and restore my shattered health." A few days later she wrote again to Lila: "I cannot help it. I cannot help what any one says, what any one feels. I am sick. I am tired. I am heartbroken and utterly worn out, body and mind. I can do no more for any one. *Rest* I must have— or *die*."

On April 19, 1886, Kate wrote from aboard the steamship *Elbe*. Already her health and spirits seemed much improved, although she had not thrown off her severe winter cold. In closing her letter on Easter Sunday she added: "We shall reach Southampton tomorrow afternoon. Oh! *tomorrow* I shall see England!"

A few days later, on May 15, 1886, her long-lost Emily Dickinson died in Amherst across the width of the salt, estranging sea.

XIV

WHEN KATE ANTHON reached England in late April, 1886, she went at once to the house in suburban London occupied by Florie and Mrs. Eliot. Here she stayed; this was the goal of her journey. Once more she met Mr. Layton, Florie's fiancé, who now called regularly on Sundays. "I do not feel that I know him at all," Kate wrote to Lila. "He is a very reserved man, and I get on very slowly with him."

That Kate had any hope of winning Mr. Layton's real friendship may seem surprising. In his letter to her of August, 1885, he had admitted his jealousy and his fear that she would not give Florie up. Referring to the past, he had written cautiously, "You have a right to settle that between yourselves." But he had expressed a slight hope that he and Kate would meet again, and the concluding sentence of his letter had been wholly generous: "I feel that I must love you a little too." Kate had kept his letter (she was to keep it all her life) as an admission of her claims upon Florie and as a promise that they would not be entirely separated. The ages of all three at this time should be remembered. Even Florie, who was now approaching thirty, could no longer be called young. Kate was fifty-five, and Mr.

Layton was about fifty. Of course the aging do not necessarily love less passionately than the young, but they have become a little more resigned to compromise.

For Kate Anthon, nevertheless, this summer of 1886 was bleak and terrible. Blow followed blow upon an expectant yet defenseless head — and among these strokes the death of Emily Dickinson. Certainly Kate would hear, for Sue would get word to her of a loss that concerned them both, and certainly Kate would feel. The death of the least of our friends takes something from us, and Emily had been more than a friend. Yet if Kate mourned for Emily, she buried her grief beyond finding. Indeed her silence about Emily was surprising, for she habitually lamented the death of even casual acquaintances and of people she had known only through newspaper accounts. She dared not mourn too openly for Florie, who was to be married in a few weeks — a few months — sometime. But on June 6 Henry Scott died, and Kate could heap up about his name not only her real sorrow for his death but all the not-to-be-mentioned suffering that anticipated the loss of Florie or harked back to that part of her younger years which had been Emily Dickinson.

In the early summer of 1886 Mrs. Eliot took a cottage in the Scottish Highlands for herself and her daughter, and Mrs. Anthon accompanied them. Florie was not well, and apparently Kate had the largest share in persuading her to defer her marriage until she could build up her strength. The reasons were sound, whatever the unconscious motive. The three women spent the summer in Scotland, and all improved in health.

The appearance of their cottage is preserved in a pen-and-ink drawing by Florence Eliot. Kate Anthon, in her severe black mourning, occupies the foreground of the picture, and Florie pleased herself with the notion that she had caught her friend's likeness. It is difficult to see: a woman in black, with a round black hat and a black umbrella. Nothing is clear except the pains of the devoted artist. "When you next write," Kate begged Lila, "do enclose a little note to Florie, as she is very anxious to know how you like me in front of the house — and do praise these artistic efforts." Of their surroundings she wrote: "The hay scents the whole house — so sweet, and Oh! the roses! They climb high up (red and white) into our very bedroom windows."

Even in the midst of her despair over Henry's death, over Florie's coming marriage (and over Emily's death?), Kate planned an escape into new interests. On August 9 she wrote to Lila, begging for the loan of Lila's daughter, Edith: "I have been thinking ever since I first came to England last April that I would like very much to have Edith come over and stay with me, at least for a while, or as long as you could spare her. I shall be very lonely this winter." She listed the advantages for Edith but admitted frankly her own need of companionship. She added: "I know you won't let this be breathed to a soul. You would hate the talking about it as much as I would. Let us do it with the greatest secrecy."

Florie entered warmly into the scheme. She knew — no one better — what Kate was suffering, and seconded the attempt to secure Edith as a distraction and a heart-warming influence. "It would give me more interest in life," wrote Kate to Edith's mother. "I have never been so utterly depressed. This child would raise me up." In late August she wrote again: "I feel my grief for Henry's loss increasing. I could not realize it at first. It is more and more acute. Oh! sometimes I cannot bear it. I wish you would consent to Edith's coming to me." Further on in her letter she added: "Edith would rouse me from this deep depression. *Never — never — never* has any sorrow taken such hold upon me."

On their long walks Florie comforted her and tried to divert her from a grief that was becoming morbid. But what could this tenderness avail against Henry's death, Emily's death, and the coming loss of Florie herself — a loss which (it may be conjectured) raked open the never-healed wound of Kate's separation from Emily Dickinson? In the company of Mrs. Eliot, however, Kate was forced to be silent. The aged woman would not hear of any sorrow or affliction except her own.

Lila Scott knew her sister-in-law, warmly and tenderly, and she consented to part with Edith. It was not self-interest, even though Kate was devoting a substantial part of her income — then and throughout her life — to the support of her brother's widow and his three young children. Lila had reason to love Kate, and she knew that Edith would be well looked after and would learn more with her aunt than at a boarding school. This confidence was not misplaced. Edith flourished in England and came to love her aunt almost as well as her own mother. Incidentally, the seventeen-year-old girl was to provide an interesting sidelight on the drama enacting before her eyes.

When Edith reached England, Florie was absent from home on a visit to a sister in Bath, but Kate immediately took her niece to call on Mrs. Eliot. The young American went with much trepidation, but the elderly woman was gracious, and Edith breathed a sigh of relief. Then Florie returned, and Edith's education (her aunt read history and French with her and directed her other studies) was temporarily suspended. Without complaint the young girl wrote that her aunt had left her in order to attend Florie's birthday party and that for days at a time Mrs. Anthon was busy with Florie's wedding clothes (among them, in all likelihood, the white wedding dress which was to have a curious history). Without complaint the tall, dark, handsome seventeen-year-old tried, as she was urged, to imitate the superior neatness and the distinguished air and carriage of the tall, fair, handsome woman of thirty who was Mrs. Anthon's own particular child. Young Edith was awed by the Eliots and captivated by Florie's generosity, but she retained an observant eye.

Mrs. Anthon had taken lodgings for herself and her niece in a London suburb at no great distance from the Eliots. There was much coming and going. "Here interrupted by Florie coming in," wrote Kate. "She said we must be sure and come in this evening. We were there to supper last night. She and Mrs. Eliot love to have us come often." In the absence of the cook, Florie, Edith, and Mrs. Anthon took over the kitchen, scrambled eggs, and mulled claret. These evenings were companionable and amusing, and Edith enjoyed them very much. She did not get to bed so early as at home, she admitted, but then she got up still later in the morning. "Not a word of this when you write, please," she cautioned her mother hastily.

Edith wanted no letter of hers interpreted as criticism of her aunt. Probably she stood in some awe of that charming but imperious woman, who had been to her, during much of her life, a kind of fairy godmother over the seas. But her devotion was still greater than her awe. "Aunt Kate looks awfully sweet this evening," she wrote to her mother. "She has on a velvet bodice and a black skirt and a pretty light blue cap." Elsewhere she wrote with great respect of Mrs. Anthon's ability as a teacher, and she found her aunt a delightful companion on their trips through England and Wales.

Toward Edith Mrs. Anthon assumed the privileges of a mother. She criticized, exhorted, and advised. Edith's shyness was especially disturbing. "I tell her it is nothing but morbid *self consciousness*," Kate wrote to Lila, "and she must get rid of it if she ever wishes to succeed in life or do any good to others. For it is a selfish unhealthy life to take no share in the social chain." The language sounds almost as if Mrs. Anthon had an example in mind. Was she thinking of Emily Dickinson, who had recently died after twenty-five years of seclusion?

2

Florie was to be married in February, 1887, and in January Kate wrote: "I shall miss her *awfully*. It makes me blue to think of it." Young Edith dutifully echoed her aunt's belief that Florie could not get married with her mother ill and the cook gone, and Florie exclaimed aloud that she began to feel "as if she would *never* be married." A diary at this time would have been helpful in elucidating what must have been a very painful situation for at least one person, perhaps two, perhaps three. If any diary was kept, however, it was destroyed.

On one January morning Edith was all alone in the house and had been alone for many hours. Her aunt had spent the preceding night with Miss Eliot, and in the morning the two had come to Mrs. Anthon's lodgings for a scant five or ten minutes before going on to London. Opposite this piece of information, in a letter to Lila Scott, young Edith added a caution: "Of course you will not say anything about Miss Eliot to *anybody*."

According to her memoirs, written more than fifty years later, Florence had a mournful wedding day. Only members of her own family (and very few of them) were invited to attend — her mother and a brother and a sister living in London. The weather was damp, cheerless, adding to the general gloom. Mrs. Eliot was ill and depressed (Mrs. Anthon, on the other hand, was to think that Mrs. Eliot had not been sufficiently grieved). But some member of the wedding party threw roses after the bride, and as Kate had written of another occasion years before, they *tried* to be jolly. Florie refused to wear her white wedding dress. There was no one to put it on her, she wrote long afterwards, although she did not explain why her sister could not have helped her. Involuntarily one is carried back to an evening at Clevedon, when Kate had dressed her, "all in pure white," and had exclaimed over her neck and shoulders. Florie wore her white dress (according to her memoirs) only after she returned from her wedding trip.

The married couple spent their honeymoon at Ventnor in the Isle of Wight. The association was not lost on Kate. She immediately began to recall the terrible weeks of 1873 at Ventnor with her dying husband. Until this spring of 1887 she had scarcely mentioned John Anthon since his death. Now her let-

ters were full of him. "Oh! the anguish of the past," she wrote
to Lila. It was wonderful, she added, that she had preserved
her reason. "I still have many sleepless nights, and lie thinking
of all that has happened, but it is *wrong, very wrong.*" For
some inscrutable reason God had chosen to afflict her, and she
tried to repeat Longfellow's lines: "Look not mournfully into
the Past. It comes not back again. Wisely improve the Present.
It is thine. Go forth to meet the Shadowy future without fear
and with a manly heart."

"I miss Florie awfully," Kate wrote to Lila. "She writes
often." At the time of this letter Florie had been gone on her
honeymoon exactly nine days. How often is "often" within
that length of time must be left to conjecture. Mrs. Anthon
added that she felt very unwell. She thought a change would
do her good and was half-inclined to go to Ventnor. Still hesitant and undecided, however, she took her niece to Tunbridge
Wells, where she had spent the winter of 1882–83 with Florie.

In Tunbridge Wells Edith met an elderly woman named
Mrs. Boutein, a friend of Kate's earlier visit. "I like Mrs. Boutein *very* much," Edith wrote to her mother. "She has a way
of saying every minute '*Poor* Mrs. Anthon, *poor* Florie.'"
Clearly Edith and her mother, as well as Mrs. Boutein, understood the source of Kate's suffering and were moved by tender,
helpless sympathy. Lila expressed a hope that Kate would find
distraction in traveling. And Edith wrote diplomatically, "I
think Aunt Kate misunderstands your meaning when you said
in yesterday's letter, you thought it 'best for her to move from
place to place.' She says she wants to stay in one place for the
rest of her life. I thought I had better tell you this." In fact, at
this time Kate was arranging for the shipping of some of her
stored possessions from America (mostly things that had belonged to her husband), and she was soon to be pitifully stirred
by opening boxes that had moldered undisturbed since 1874.
With her last desperate hope collapsing around her, she seemed
driven by a need to renew the memory of her old life.

On March 21, 1887, Kate and her niece went to Ventnor. As Edith was careful to tell her mother, Florie and Mr. Layton had already returned to London. In Ventnor the young girl and the middle-aged widow walked or drove to every spot that recalled John Anthon. It was an attempt to exorcise one ghost by means of another. In much the same manner, during the winter of 1891–92, Kate Anthon was to call desperately on the memory of Campbell Turner to quiet the reviving ghost of Emily Dickinson.

During this week at Ventnor Kate received word from Florie that the Laytons would be "at home" on Fridays: "Come and call on her — do — !!" The paraphrase of Florie's message is, of course, young Edith's. There are many hints throughout Edith's letters (for example, quotation marks around the words "happy pair" or "happy man") that the young girl's sympathies were all with her aunt. Yet Edith must have been saddened and perplexed by the necessity of Kate Anthon's loss and suffering. Her reason approved, and still she grieved.

Upon returning to their lodgings, they were in no haste to accept Florie's invitation, and Florie came to see them. This was the period, according to Florie's memoirs, when she wore her white wedding dress. Edith studied the bride attentively and reported, "She seems very happy indeed." Florie urged them to lunch with her on the following Tuesday, but Edith wrote that they were undecided. Indeed a casual visit was not easily managed. Florie's new home was in the heart of the city, and Kate still lodged in the distant suburb where Mrs. Eliot likewise had her lodgings. It was easier for Florie to see Kate during the visits that must be paid to the elderly Mrs. Eliot. Certainly there was no diminishing of Kate's affection.

In early April Edith wrote with pleasure that Florie was spending several days with her mother. "Aunt Kate is *very* pleased. She misses her so much." They were expecting Florie to tea. Aunt Kate had bought a pot of yellow flowers for her and had run out to get cream for their tea. "There goes the bell!! It is Aunt Kate with the cream." Mr. Layton came down for a day and called with his wife on Mrs. Anthon. On Easter Sunday Edith went to St. Philip's Church with some friends of her own, but Aunt Kate and Mrs. Layton (it seemed strange, wrote Edith, to call Florie "Mrs. Layton") went to Christ Church alone.

This spring of 1887 must have witnessed one of the last two events recorded in Florie's memoirs. Florie herself did not date it, but she associated it with another event which can be dated. Shortly after her marriage she decided to work with the poor people of London's slums. The rector of her new parish, who of course did not know her very well, assigned her a visitor's duties in one of the miserable quarters of the city. Florie was already pregnant. She had hardly recovered from her illness of the preceding summer, and she suffered almost unbearably in the squalor and misery that she forced herself to visit. The fact is not mentioned in Florie's memoirs, but Mrs. Anthon must have remonstrated with her before taking more decisive action. As Florie persisted in self-immolation, Mrs. Anthon then went to the young woman's pastor — and this fact was recorded by Florence herself — and told him that her friend's health was not equal to the strain imposed upon it. The district visiting came to an end.

During the summer of 1887 Florie and her husband spent their holidays at a fishing village on the east coast. "We had rooms over the one little shop," wrote Florence in her memoirs. "Mrs. Anthon and her niece who had come from America, also had rooms in the same house. It was a primitive place then, just a row of fishermen's cottages and the one little shop." With a few words describing her husband's pleasure in the resort, the memoirs of Florence Layton came to a close. The remainder of her long life unrolled without record.

But the event was not quite so simple. In July Kate and her niece were at Clevedon, hoping that Florie and Mrs. Eliot would share with them the house Kate and the Eliots had occupied during the winter of 1881–82. Kate took her niece over all the ground that she had once covered with Florie. But Mrs. Eliot preferred a cooler climate, and it was agreed that all four would spend the month of August on the east coast. "Florie is very anxious to get out of London for a few weeks," wrote Kate to Lila, "and I do so long to see her. She is expecting her confinement in December. We are all *so sorry* to have the babies begin quite so soon, but it can't be helped!" (This was to be a recurring plaint in her letters for many years.)

At the last moment Mrs. Eliot felt unwell. "Florie was dreadfully disappointed," wrote Kate. "She met us at the Liverpool Street Station and saw us off. She hopes her mother will rally in a few days and that they will yet come." Mrs. Eliot declined to rally. After exhausting her daughter's strength, she called in two trained nurses and settled down for a month's illness, during which she was *"terribly* depressed." The attending doctor clearly thought that a great deal of fuss was being made over very little, but Florie could not be released until her mother decided to take herself off to Eastbourne with the nurses. The hoped-for month was now almost gone. At last Mr. Layton found time to bring Florie himself, and the party of four spent an enjoyable week together — with some agitation on the part of Kate, who now had "a gentleman" to cater for. The ice was broken between Mrs. Anthon and Mr. Layton. Although he had never made any objection to the intimacy between the two women, there was to be henceforth more positive kindliness on his side. He wrote pleasantly to Edith and sent her Christmas cards of his own designing, and he welcomed Mrs. Anthon's visits. Incidentally, Kate never uttered a word of criticism of Mr. Layton, unless a good deal is read into a remark that one of his Christmas cards was unintelligible to her or into a later statement that Florie looked unwell (she was pregnant again, and they were *"so sorry"*) but Mr. Layton looked as robust as ever.

In the fall of 1887 Edith Scott returned to America, and

Mrs. Anthon employed herself in "regulating" her things. She wrote to her niece that she was too busy to be unhappy. In the late fall she spent several days in London with old Mentone friends, the Tipples, who were also acquainted with Florie. (They were, in fact, the friends whom Kate had begged to visit Florie during the unhappy summer following the separation of 1881.) Mr. Layton was absent from London, and Florie, lonesome and uncomfortable in her last month of pregnancy, called so often on Kate at the Tipples' house that they invited her to stay until her husband returned.

Kate Anthon took winter lodgings in London around the corner from Florie's home. She once wrote that she had been spending every evening with the Laytons, until a severe cold ended her visits, and that Mr. Layton *liked* to have her come. During her illness Florie called to inquire about her and doctored the cold, and Mrs. Anthon was full of gratitude to her "blessed child." Their relationship was more adjustable than the old tragic entanglement between Kate Scott and Emily Dickinson.

Edith came again to England. She was much at home with her aunt, who now became "Aunt Tommy." Between the summer of 1886 and the fall of 1890 Edith made three long visits and saw much of England in her aunt's company. On the last visit they went together to Wales and inspected the villa of the "Llangollen ladies." During this summer Kate was apparently deciding on a change in her way of life. Perhaps she had come to realize the futility and the loneliness of her existence in London, forever tantalized by glimpses of her lost "child" and as constantly reminded that the bond between them was severed. The recent widowhood of her old friend Mrs. Baker offered a pretext for moving to Bristol, and in early October, 1890, she took lodgings within walking distance of the Bakers.

The change agreed with her expectations. She was thoroughly happy during the autumn and winter of 1890–91. The letters for this period are unusually full, and all of them witness a constant and happy interchange of visits with the Bakers. Kate read French with one of the daughters and entered warmly and sympathetically into all the family concerns. Long afterwards young Gertrude Baker sent a book to her "darling Auntie Kate" with a note affirming that the book would have no existence until Mrs. Anthon read it.

Florie paid a visit, and Kate proudly introduced her. "The Bakers all admired her so much," she wrote to Lila, "and thought she carried herself with such grace and dignity."

During this period Kate had nothing to say about Sue Dickinson, although a few months later she was to mention Sue repeatedly. As far as the record is concerned, Sue disappeared from Kate's diaries and letters on December 7, 1878 (on that date, in a diary begun the preceding April, Kate mentioned finally writing to Sue), and did not reappear until the summer of 1891. Doubtless there was some communication (it has already been suggested that Kate wrote to Sue, or perhaps to Emily, at least once during 1884–86, and that Sue would have sent her word of Emily's death), but their correspondence must have been casual and infrequent. Apparently this friendship had long since entered on a period of quiet desuetude, from which only an extraordinary event would revive it. This event would seem to be the publishing of Emily Dickinson's poems in November, 1890.

3

How soon and in what manner Kate Anthon learned about Emily's poems cannot be determined. She was certainly informed, and profoundly interested, before she returned to America in July, 1891. Her first act upon reaching New York was to commission her friend Albert Matthews to get her a copy of the poems. Her behavior suggests that she first learned about Emily's poems through English reviews of the American edition. After her interest had been aroused, she probably wrote to Sue Dickinson.

On January 2, 1891, a review in the London *Daily News* attacked the work of an upstart, ungrammatical American poet. On January 17 Kate wrote to her sister-in-law as if she might be considering a trip to America. Lila responded with warm encouragement, but Kate's answer was noncommittal.   On March 7 Andrew Lang renewed the attack on Emily Dickinson in the *Illustrated London News,* a paper which Mrs. Anthon always read. On March 26 Kate wrote ambiguously to her sister-in-law: "I cannot yet say, dear Lila, what I may do about crossing the Atlantic. I want to come, and yet dread the journey — and all the sadness." But she had already written to John Anthon's family, with whom she had kept in touch all these years, asking whether they could receive her in New York.

On April 15 Kate wrote again to Lila: "I have almost decided to go to America for a visit." Her sister-in-law, Sallie Anthon (widow of General W. H. Anthon and mother of Mrs. Stuyvesant Fish), had written that they had room for her and would be happy to entertain her. But Kate was depressed by the thought of all the packing she must do and the seasickness she must endure. "Perhaps you better not tell any one I have fully decided to come until my next letter," she wrote to Lila. "I cannot do shopping. Don't let any one know I am coming — I mean, not until it is too late for me to buy *blanket shawls* &c &c &c!!" From this date onward her excitement ran away with her.

Florie had just had her third baby (it was Mrs. Anthon's opinion, not wholly unshared by the younger woman, that Florie had too many babies too fast), and Kate went up to London on a May morning to see the new child and bid her friend good-bye. At the door she was stopped by the nurse, who peremptorily refused to let her enter without the doctor's consent. For a few moments Kate stood uncertainly on the steps, a handsome, white-haired woman of sixty, dressed in stately black, somewhat bent with rheumatism, but holding herself painfully erect — then turned away in bitter disappointment. When the nurse reported this incident, Florie wept.

Instead of sailing for America on May 10, as she had planned, Kate Anthon went to Ventnor to hire lodgings for Lila Scott and Lila's youngest child, Fred. At the last moment a cablegram had informed Kate that they were coming to England for the boy's health, and all her plans gave way before a family emergency. While she was still arranging matters, she received an urgent letter from Mr. Layton. At Florie's request, he had written immediately after Kate's cool reception at his door, describing his wife's grief and her anger at the officious nurse and begging Kate to come again to London. Kate answered pleasantly that she would try to pay a visit before she left England. There is no record that she went, but the painful quiver in her deepest feelings must have been eased by this letter.

On May 18, 1891, Lila wrote from the Isle of Wight to Edith and young Henry, the children she had left at home: "Aunt Kate looks so tired and jaded. I am *very* sorry that we had to interrupt her plans. She would have arrived in New York now but for us." During their six weeks at Ventnor Kate Anthon did appear to roam around unquietly like a caged animal, but she was her usual attentive, charming self to her unexpected guests.

"Aunt Kate is so good and kind to us," wrote Lila Scott on June 1. "I don't know what we should have done without her. She is entertaining as ever. We do a great deal of talking over old times, and many a laugh do we have." Lila reminded Edith and Henry that there were still many little things to do before their aunt's arrival. Edith must get the furniture polish and rub out two scratches on Grandmother Scott's writing desk in the parlor. "Aunt K. might think we did not take care of it." Henry must get some one to put the face of the Swiss clock to rights, and Edith must be sure to have stale bread for her aunt and the very best butter. Mr. Pell Clark's butter would just suit their aunt, Lila thought anxiously.

Kate Anthon sailed for America on June 24, 1891, aboard the *Havel*. Her sister-in-law and her nephew, much improved in health, followed in the *Trave* on July 1. Kate did not immediately go to Cooperstown with them. She had a good deal of business to attend to in New York, and she was having a very good time. Her old friend Albert Matthews called, and came again with a second edition of the *Poems* of Emily Dickinson. It may have been his own copy, for the book was already in its sixth edition.

Kate spent some three weeks in Cooperstown and then went to Utica to visit her foster cousins, the Derings. It will become apparent that Fanny Dering was aware of some connection between Kate and Emily Dickinson, although her reference to it was guarded. Perhaps Kate talked of Emily during this visit, or Fanny may have been in her confidence as early as the painful attachment some thirty years before. The two women were intimate, lifelong friends, and in spite of an occasional endeavor at secretiveness, Kate was never able to hide her most agitating concerns.

In a letter of August 12 from Utica, Kate Anthon spoke of Sue Dickinson. It was the first mention of Sue (as far as the evidence shows) in almost thirteen years. Kate may have written to Sue when she first decided to return to America, but any arrangements made at that time were upset by the postponement of Kate's sailing. Now Kate wrote to Lila, "Mrs. Dickinson urges my coming to her in September." Indeed so many friends were pressing for visits that she hardly knew how she would get around to them all, but some few she was determined to see — Sue Dickinson, the Derings, and Gertrude Vanderbilt. "If any one asks *when* I am going," she told her sister-in-law, "just say my plans are not yet definitely made (you will understand)."

On September 20, 1891, Kate reached Amherst and plunged

into the beginning, or the renewal, of a very painful experience.

Unquestionably Sue Dickinson now told her a great deal. Sue was bursting with grievances, real or fancied, and Kate Anthon was her oldest friend. Kate was also an outsider to Amherst, which made confidence easier and safer — and Kate was so deeply involved that confidence became inevitable. Sue forbade her friend to go to Emily's sister Lavinia in the house next door. Kate would not have slighted a manifest duty on Sue's bare assertion that Lavinia had been unpleasant. She was never carelessly negligent of the feelings of others, and her conscience was to be tender for months at the memory of Lavinia's pleading note and gift of flowers. There would have to be an explanation from Sue; and as each fact was inseparably linked with another, the whole story would at length unroll. And Kate would suffer.

Sue's chief concern must have been the intolerable situation in which Lavinia had involved them all. Lavinia had taken the poems away from Sue and had placed them in the hands of Mabel Loomis Todd, an action which would make talk in itself. Then Lavinia and Mrs. Todd were publishing just such poems, and in just such a manner, as would arouse unpleasant conjectures. Sue herself had never cared for the love poems and had always thought Emily's "metaphysical" poems her surest title to fame. A selected volume, made up of the "metaphysical" poems and the harmless nature poetry, privately printed and limited in circulation — that was Sue's avowed plan for presenting Emily's poetry. Such a collection, paid for by the Dickinson family and circulated only among friends, would not have been reviewed and would have aroused no public interest. Mrs. Todd and Lavinia were boldly submitting Emily to the world at large, inviting criticism and comparison, stimulating conjecture and gossip.

Already (Sue would continue) the newspaper reviews were

full of objectionable personal detail. Everybody was gossiping and speculating and demanding the name of Emily's lover, while Sue and her friend knew very well that there had been no lover at all — only a highly emotional attachment to Kate herself. It was a little hard that they must all suffer because of Emily's peculiarities.

The woman who spoke and the woman who listened have been dead for many years. No one took notes of their conversations, and they were careful never to refer to the matter themselves. Any reconstruction is guesswork. Yet Kate was to suffer agonies during the next year, and Sue was to suppress Emily's poetry to the end of her life — and Sue's daughter was to lie about it to the end of her own. The words must be guessed, but the discussion took place.

More shaken and torn than she cared to admit, Kate left Amherst and returned to New York. With Emily's poems in her hands, she sailed once more for England.

4

"Poor Katy," wrote Fanny Dering to Lila Scott, "I hope her sails are sunlit ones, and this storm does not attend her on her way to the haven where she would be. I hope she will come soon again, and that I may be able to see more of her — though I am profoundly grateful for having seen her at all." Fanny Dering was a woman of superior ability and intelligence, although she left only a quiet and local fame. Her devotion to her stormy, emotional friend must be ranked with that of Gertrude Vanderbilt, Mary Osler, Florence Eliot, Sue Dickinson, Martha Bianchi, and many others, among them Emily Dickinson. Without comment Fanny Dering added: "Have you seen the article by Col. Higginson in the October *Atlantic* about Miss Emily Dickinson, giving some of her letters?"

Kate Anthon's sails were not sunlit. The *Havel* tossed in

wild seas — Kate wrote that she was black and blue from the
crossing — and her mind tossed in seas still wilder. As she sat
on deck in gentler weather, the book of poems in her lap, or
struggled through sleepless nights in her berth, the waters rolled
over her head. She had had the genius to recognize genius, and
though she had given Emily up — had been forced to give her
up precisely because she had loved her too much — the volume
of poetry in her hands renewed the old spell and the old suffering. Restlessly her pencil marked remembered lines, or lines
that called up memory.

There were several early poems, some of them highly sentimental, which Kate could have seen and admired in manuscript. "Glee! the great storm is over!" was probably one of the
poems that Kate had seen long ago — perhaps the first that had
given her an awed conviction that her friend was marked for
greatness. Another began "If I can stop one heart from breaking." Pages further on were other poems that she might have
seen in manuscript, the playful "The grass so little has to do"
and the young and delightful "Some keep the Sabbath going
to church." Beside all of these poems Kate placed a cross.

An honest woman, Kate bracketed the following stanza:

> I like a look of agony,
> Because I know it's true;
> Men do not sham convulsion,
> Nor simulate a throe.

And she liked "I've seen a dying eye" (she had seen many),
"The bustle in a house/The morning after death," "The sun
kept setting, setting still," and "Because I could not stop for
Death." She marked with a cross the poem beginning "The
last night that she lived" and enclosed the last two stanzas with
her pencil. From someone's letter she tore a long strip of
paper and placed it between the poems "A wounded deer leaps
highest" and "The heart asks pleasure first."

A long, wavering pencil mark enclosed the whole of "The brain within its groove," which declares that a brain, turned aside by the swerving of a splinter, can never be put right again. Now at last came the anguish of knowing that she had irreparably damaged another human being. And Emily was gone beyond reach of an act of contrition (how often the poems had anticipated just this!), had died hating or loving her — or both together. In her copy of Emily's poetry she placed a cross beside "To know just how he suffered would be dear."

It was one of the many poems in which Emily anticipated the death of the beloved friend. Was "he" patient, content, hopeful? Did "he" think of God or home, and what were "his" last wishes? Just a sigh, accented, would have been intelligible to the poet. What name was best and first and last upon the dying lips? Kate's pencil marked the line: "And if he spoke, what name was best." She had loved four persons, two of whom, Campbell Turner and John Anthon, had died in her presence. She could not have wondered how her husbands died or what they said in their last moments. Florie long outlived her. Emily alone died far away and in estrangement. Perhaps Kate wanted to believe that at the last moment Emily had forgiven her.

In the section entitled "Love" Kate marked the last stanza of "Elysium is as far as to." Another poem read, "If you were coming in the fall. . . . If I could see you in a year. . . . If only centuries delayed. . . . If certain, when this life was out. . . ." But there was no certainty that they would ever meet again, and Kate could only mark the poem.

"I cannot live with you." That would be life indeed, and true life, they knew, must be deferred beyond the grave. The poet could not die with her beloved, for one must remain to close the other's eyes, and the friend was too tender for such an office. Emily could not rise with her lover, for that face "would put out Jesus'." God would judge them, but with more leniency toward the loved and lost friend, who "served Heaven

. . . or sought to," when Emily could not. Kate marked the poem and then marked these three lines:

> And I condemned to be
> Where you were not,
> That self were hell to me.

On the next page the pencil marked "There came a day at summer's full" and signaled out two lines that would impress most feelingly the passenger on the storm-tossed *Havel*:

> So faces on two decks look back,
> Bound to opposing lands.

And to register the significance of that emotional parting on a hot summer day, Kate left the red silk marker standing between the pages of this poem.

Not all the ironies are reserved for fiction.

Kate suffered. She wrote that she suffered, although she could not tell why, and that she endured many sleepless nights and wept to exhaustion. It was not for Emily alone, or even chiefly, that she wept, but for herself. The trip to America, the visit with Sue, and the poems themselves reopened the book of anguish which she had thought closed, and she was forced to review every blotted page of her life. Sometimes the writing blurred, and Emily seemed to be Florie, and Florie Emily, or Emily merged into Campbell Turner. But there was grief on every page, and as often as she tried to shut the book, something opened it again. Sue Dickinson wrote or Lavinia wrote or some relative died, and the suffering threatened to be perpetual. It lasted — with, toward the end, growing intervals of calm — until the summer of 1893. Emily was avenged.

On October 30, 1891, Kate wrote from the lodgings near Bristol, where she had been very happy and comfortable the year before. She had had a pleasant visit with her friend Helen, at Harrow, had sat for her photograph (it looks sober but not tragic), and had seen a good deal of Florie and Florie's sister, Lady Bertram. Now she was tired, she admitted, and wanted to be very quiet for a while.

On this same October 30 Lavinia Dickinson addressed a letter to England:

> *My dear Mrs. "Kate"*
>
> *I was sorry you did not come to Emilies house. My memory of you was so warm that I was sure you would gratify me. It would have been a great pleasure for me to have talked with you about mutual interests, but I could not do this in the presence of others. I hope you are well and find life some satisfaction.*
>
> *Austin tells me you have in your possession still notes and poems from Emily. I am gathering together all scattering manuscripts and would be grateful if you would send me copies of anything you may have. Should you not care for the copy labor yourself, please hold me responsible for any expense and I promise to be a prompt paymaster.*
>
> *Perhaps you would say if these words reach you before many days — then attend to my wish at your leisure.*
>
> > *Lovingly*
> >
> > LAVINIA DICKINSON

Kate did not answer, but she was torn. She believed wholly in Lavinia's flattering words, and they may even have been sincere. During the long years of smoldering resentment against Sue Dickinson, the enemy next door, Lavinia would have come to minimize Kate's wounding rebuff to Emily, then to forget it, and at last to recall only, as Kate wrote, "how happy we were all together in years gone by." Whatever Lavinia knew or conjectured about this old attachment, her behavior makes plain that she wanted to shut her eyes to it and imagine that Emily was a conventional woman who might have had a happy marriage with a Higginson or a George Gould. In any case, it would be pleasant to detach Kate from Sue and bind her to herself, and she wanted the manuscripts. After a suitable interval Lavinia would write again.

If Kate had not already begun to review her letters from Emily, Lavinia's request would have started her, and the reading would be pain. She hated to offend Sue, and she did not wish to see the closest secret of her life paraded in print. On the other hand, she wanted to gratify Lavinia, and deep in her heart she was proud of Emily's attachment to her and would have liked to see their names together. It was a confusing problem, and she compromised by doing nothing at all.

On November 23 she wrote briefly to her niece: "Thank you for sending the newspaper cutting from Mrs. Clark about Emily Dickinson. When I write to Mrs. C., of course I will speak of it. The photograph of Mrs. Layton . . . ," and a reference to Florie, as if of necessity, trod upon the heels of a reference to Emily.

During these late fall days Kate was being badgered with reminders of Emily Dickinson. Not only did Lavinia, Mrs. Clark, and Edith Scott thrust upon her a memory that she wanted to forget. Someone (most probably, Fanny Dering) sent her the pages of Higginson's article about Emily Dickinson in the October *Atlantic Monthly*. This article is made up of letters and poems sent by Emily to Higginson, together with his comments. Kate read it, not once but repeatedly: the pages are worn and crumpled and much marked. In this fall of 1891 she bracketed passage after passage with her pencil. In February, 1892, she went over the article again, marking it with ink. The pencil markings are especially interesting.

Some marked passages, of course, are relatively insignificant. For example, at this time Kate was reading Moncure Conway's life of Hawthorne, and accordingly she checked Emily's reference to Hawthorne's death. She also bracketed a paragraph of Higginson's referring to the death of Samuel Bowles, whom she had known, and underlined the words "of the Springfield Republican." And she marked with appreciation the poem "As imperceptibly as grief," with which Higginson closed his article.

Every instance of Emily's peculiarities, in the letters themselves or in Higginson's comments, interested Kate very much. She marked Higginson's long description of Emily (the "faint and pattering footstep like that of a child," the "plain, shy little person," and the "smooth bands of reddish chestnut hair"). Kate was aware that Emily had not been pretty; but she had once marked, in De Quincey's "Visit to Laxton," these revealing lines: "It is unintelligibly but mesmerically potent, this secret fascination attached to features oftentimes that are absolutely plain." Kate had been more susceptible than Higginson to the charm of Emily Dickinson.

Higginson's report of Emily's conversation struck Kate, and she marked: "Forgive me if I am frightened; I never see strangers, and hardly know what I say." Again Kate marked: " 'And people must have puddings,' this very timidly and suggestively, as if they were meteors or comets." At this point Kate must have smiled, for she understood Emily's drollery far better than Higginson ever understood. When Emily apologized for misspelling the word "ankle," Kate checked the passage. Kate also marked every passage in which Higginson referred to the oddities of Emily's style — the "defiance of form," the "fracture of grammar." And she marked Emily's references to the dog Carlo and to Mr. Dickinson's distrust of books. It was as if Kate herself were renewing acquaintance with Emily.

Higginson had wanted to know Emily's age, and Emily had replied: "You asked how old I was? I made no verse, but one or two, until this winter, sir." Kate marked this passage: she was either amused by Emily's evasiveness or astonished by so downright an untruth.

Emily's first letter to Higginson, with its appeal for truthful criticism of her poems, impressed Kate very much, and she marked several passages. Further on she placed a cross beside Emily's "I had no monarch in my life, and cannot rule myself." But if Kate now realized that Emily had been suffering from the withdrawal of her own support, she knew also that she would have failed Emily as Higginson had done. She marked every passage in which Higginson described Emily as "enigmatical." It was a confession that she too had not understood her. Even Kate's last known reference to Emily (in a letter of 1914 to Martha Bianchi) was to repeat this note of bewilderment: Emily's "mysticism . . . often transcends mortal comprehension." Certainly it had transcended Kate's understanding. She had not guessed, until this winter of 1891–92, that under a mask of indifference Emily had continued to love her. The knowledge was very painful.

Kate did not overlook the passage in which Emily informed Higginson of her emotional history. It is marked repeatedly, and in the following manner. A long pencil mark encloses the entire paragraph. Inside this long mark there is a short one, and within the short mark, another line shorter still. The two short lines signal out the following words: "Soon after my tutor died, and for several years my lexicon was my only companion. Then I found one more, but he was not contented I be his scholar, so he left the land." It should be remembered that this letter to Higginson was written on April 25, 1862, one year after Kate had sent a letter to Emily breaking off their friendship. Obviously Kate now understood; otherwise she would not have suffered so bitterly throughout this winter of 1891–92.

In mid-December Kate received a letter from Sue Dickinson which disturbed her so much that she was long in answering it or even mentioning it. It overhung her like a cloud when she wrote to Lila on December 19: "It is 18. years today since my dear, dear Father died. I have thought of it so much. These Christmas holidays are laden with sadness. I am relieved when they are ended. It can only be a merry season to the young.

As life broadens and deepens it can bring only sorrow. I have felt all day as if I could cry my eyes out. I know this is wrong, and I struggle against it."

During this winter she was overwhelmed by repeated waves of pain, lasting a few days or even a week or two at a time. Then she would struggle up once more and, in a new letter to Lila, confess that she had been much depressed but now felt more cheerful. She could not tell Lila why she was miserable; she had no plausible pretext to which she could attach her anguish. No friend had died; nothing in her circumstances had changed. The Bakers were as kind and devoted as ever. In fact, their kindness worried and annoyed Kate; she wished they would leave her alone with her misery. Her lodgings were comfortable, and she had pleasant friends, a widow and her young daughter, in the room upstairs. She was not in bad health (there were the usual winter colds), but she was rapidly making herself ill. Habitual weeping and habitual sleeplessness were inducing an excessive reliance on sleeping draughts. Apparently Emily had used sleeping draughts, too, in the winter of 1861–62. It was much the same.

On January 2, 1892, Kate wrote to Lila: "I have been feeling so depressed lately." On January 3: "I was very reluctant to go to Mrs. Baker this year. Not at all in the humour for it." On January 24: "It was a forlorn Christmas altogether. I don't know when I have felt so depressed." General mourning had been ordered for the death of the Duke of Clarence, and Kate remarked listlessly, "I am always in black, so it matters not to me." She was afraid that she was writing "a very dull letter, but it is hard work to be cheerful."

In early February, 1892, Kate Anthon began to read and to mark one of Campbell Turner's old theology books, *A Rational Illustration of the Book of Common Prayer.* By her own admission she was now much occupied with the memory of Campbell Turner. She had even a semi-rational excuse — a premonition that Campbell's aged mother would soon die. This was not the true explanation. She had fallen in love with Emily Dickinson while still mourning for Campbell Turner; in her mind the two were associated with each other and with her own youth. It will be remembered that in February, 1887, at the time of Florie's marriage, she had seized upon the connection between Florie's honeymoon in Ventnor and her own earlier stay with John Anthon. She had then mourned for John Anthon until she became tolerably adjusted to the loss of Florie.

During 1892 she was to speak often of Campbell Turner (never of John Anthon) — and only during 1892. In the half-million words of her preserved diaries and letters there is no earlier or later mention of her first husband. Undoubtedly she often remembered him, especially on the anniversary of his death, but only in 1892 was her memory of him so compelling that it burst forth irrepressibly in her letters.

In this same February of 1892 Kate was once more reading and marking Higginson's *Atlantic Monthly* article on Emily Dickinson. Apparently she had Higginson's article and Campbell Turner's religious book in front of her at the same time, for when she had finished marking the article about Emily she tucked it between the pages of Campbell's *Rational Illustration.*

The new markings are less extensive and less interesting than those of the previous fall. Kate marked Emily's poem "The nearest dream recedes unrealized." As Higginson noted, it had come to him with Emily's first letter of April 15, 1862. Kate probably saw the connection between this poem and her own rupture with Emily in April, 1861. She liked Emily's definition of poetry and Emily's "How do most people live without any thoughts?" Again she marked (in ink over the earlier pencil) Emily's shy apology to Higginson, "Forgive me if I am frightened . . . " And she almost covered with ink an earlier pencil mark beside a sentence of Emily's beginning, "A letter always feels to me like immortality." Kate, like Emily, depended much upon letters. Perhaps she also remembered that Emily had originally got this notion from a book which they both loved, Ik Marvel's *Reveries of a Bachelor*. Finally, Kate was much impressed by the success of Emily's poems and marked Higginson's statement: " . . . yet the outcome of it is that six editions of the volume have been sold within six months, a suddenness of success almost without parallel in American literature." This piece of information immediately went into a letter from Kate to Lila.

On February 13 Kate wrote to Lila: "I have really been miserable all winter. I long for spring and sunshine. It has been the most depressing winter — take it all in all." Yet she felt a momentary lifting of the gloom and believed that she could now handle the matter of answering Sue's two-months-old letter. For the first time she wrote in some detail of her visit to Amherst, speaking distressfully of the quarrel and cautioning her sister-in-law: "Don't let any one know I have said anything in regard to this estrangement between Sue & Vinnie." Apparently there was enough connection between Amherst and Cooperstown to make her fear that an unguarded word might somehow reach Sue.

Vinnie had written to her, Kate continued, but she did not like to answer. "The second Vol. of Emily's poems are published," she added. (Sue's letter of mid-December, 1891, which disturbed Kate very much, may have contained an indignant report of this fact.) "I have not yet seen them. I have the first, which went through six editions in six months! The poems created a regular furore. Emily, you know, died in May, 1886."

The restraint and coldness of these few references to "Emily, the poetess," concealed a powerful agitation. Kate dared not write more openly. Yet every action for many months — the marking of Emily's poems and Higginson's article, the copying of Emily's manuscripts for Lavinia, the constant, sorrowful plaining, the recall of youth, the frantic search for relief in different scenes and among different persons — is clear evidence that Emily was seldom far from her mind. It is true that she was ill and old, but she was only one year older than she had been during her enjoyable winter with the Bakers, and the illness was apparently the result of her continued depression and inability to sleep.

On February 20 she wrote to her niece that she had "never passed such a stupid winter. Oh, how I long for spring. Winter is terrible." On March 1 she thought that she was "emerging from the dark clouds," and was thankful that the winter had ended. A few days later, however, she fled to Clevedon — into the very house which she had shared with Florie and Mrs. Eliot during a winter of happy memory. Once more she was attempting to exorcise one ghost by means of another.

5

To Lila, Kate wrote cheerfully of her "sweet associations" with the house in Clevedon, and she exulted in the coming of spring. "The birds are singing, oh! so sweetly. I walk every evening at a certain hour to hear the blackbirds, thrushes, linnets, starlings & cuckoos. All the way over to the old church the blackbirds sing beyond anything to be described!" It was the walk that she had often taken with Florie to the grave of Tennyson's friend Hallam, and the blackbirds were the descendants of those which had delighted the two women years ago. With a grateful upwelling of the old spirit, Kate exclaimed, "Oh! is there anything like Spring! I thank God each year that I have lived to see another!"

Yet she had not attained peace. Restlessly she recalled a half-formed scheme of this winter — to return to America and spend her last years with her Utica friends — only to dismiss it as impractical. The Easter season brought back vivid memories of the dead whom she had loved, and she wrote sadly: "Not one would I ever wish back in this sad and disappointing world. We long to see them. A few more years and God grant we may."

It was April, the anniversary of her rupture with Emily
Dickinson, and undoubtedly she remembered. The letters
from Sue and Lavinia prodded memory, and she may have gone
to Clevedon with some hope of finding courage to answer
Lavinia's request. For she did eventually send copies of Emily's
poems and letters — more letters, apparently, than either
Lavinia or Mrs. Todd thought wise to use (this question will
be settled when the Dickinson papers become accessible). What
Kate felt about the pressure that Lavinia and Sue had exerted
upon her may have been expressed in the following odd communication to Lila:

"I hope . . . [at this point two-thirds of the sheet was torn
away, and the top of the next page began:] . . . the strictest confidence. Not for worlds would I have them know how I feel
about it . . . [torn] I don't [kno]w . . . [torn]. I also love *you,*
so you will understand, but oh! be sure and burn what I have
written." And unhappily Lila did. But certainly Lila would
have understood. She had been gentle and tender during Kate's
suffering over the loss of Florie. As young Eliza Synnott, a girl
of eighteen, she had moved to Cooperstown in 1858, and she
had been Kate's close friend during the period of Kate's intimacy with Emily Dickinson.

In mid-May, 1892, Kate learned that Campbell Turner's
mother was dying. Mrs. Turner, a woman in her eighties, had
had a useful, happy life, and was dying without undue pain.
Under the circumstances the grief that Kate displayed was
excessive. But she had discovered an outlet for the intense
misery which had filled her all winter.

"I cannot realize this terrible sorrow," she wrote. "All my
life I have known and loved Mrs. Turner. She has been more
like an own mother to me, & I forever associate her with my
youth and marriage to Campbell and those sweet sad days. Oh!
what a world of grief and parting! It is a mystery, and we must
have faith to believe it is for the best. I have thought so much,
so much of Mrs. Turner for weeks past as if I had a presentiment of coming sorrow. I always live over every spring each

day and hour of that trip to Boston and that dying scene at the Tremont House."

Doubtless she was sincere, but she was also sincerely absurd. No woman spends a month out of every year for thirty-five years (during the course of which she has had at least three additional love affairs), minutely and sorrowfully recalling the details of an earlier love. Kate Anthon always deceived herself more thoroughly than she deceived those who knew her.

Her letter to Lila continued: "I do not much care where I go. The summer will be a sad one. I feel as if the life had gone out of it. I really do not think I can fill my sheet. I have not slept for several nights and feel very nervous and unstrung." Immediately afterwards she went to Devonshire to visit an old friend.

On June 9, 1892, Kate wrote to Edith that she had at last had a night's rest without a sleeping draught, but she was still wretched. In late July she wrote to Lila, proposing that on her next trip to America they should visit the graves of all their dead. "Oh, these terrible losses! These bitter trials! How could we live through them if it were not for the sweet hope that we shall all meet again in a bright world where joy and peace will be unbroken." Three days later she learned that John Anthon's nephew had died suddenly, on the eve of a trip to England, and she at once fled to Harrow, where her friend Helen was now living. She was also once more close to Florie. She was to spend her winters at Harrow for the next fourteen years.

In late August she wrote to Lila: "I am feeling better since coming here (but not well). I have shed too many tears, and weeping always makes one so weak. I have dwelt so constantly on the sad events, the fearful losses of the last few months, it seems as if I should never rally. The 17th was your dear Mother's birthday, was it not? Oh! Lila, to see her again, to see Mother, Mrs. Turner, all — all. Some days I cannot bear it." Two lines below she wrote that she had just received a letter from Sue Dickinson.

On September 15 she wrote again to Lila, sorrowfully recalling their youth and her own dear father. "In looking back upon those days I can think of nothing but joy and happiness. Oh! Lila, a year ago I was with you, getting ready to leave for Amherst."

A year of intense suffering had passed, equaling, recalling in many of its details, the year of anguish that had begun for Emily Dickinson in April, 1861. Gradually Kate's spirits improved. The periods of grief became shorter, less severe, and the intervals of comfort lengthened. Even her handwriting witnessed the improvement, and she signed her letters with Lila's old pet name for her, "Katie Ann," and finished her signature with long, cheerful flourishes.

Much of her trouble had arisen from the fact that she had no absorbing interest — no love, in short, for she was a woman who must love — to distract her from the grievous recollection of Emily Dickinson. Now at last a new interest came. During this winter of 1892–93 Kate Anthon "adopted" another child, Florie's twelve-year-old nephew, who now entered school at Harrow. In time Kate herself became almost an old Harrovian, and she wept with the greyheaded "old boys" when they sang "Forty years on."

On Sundays and half-holidays Florie or her sister, Lady Bertram, or their brother, came from London to Harrow to see their young nephew and to visit Kate and the family of Kate's friend Helen. Surrounded by these many warm friends, the aging woman entered on a long period of relative content. Every Sunday for many school years she busied herself joyfully with tea preparations for her young protégé, who was soon quite at ease in her small, sunny lodgings near his school. During vacation he took her with him to the large estate of which he was the sole and frail proprietor, and his widowed mother (Florie's sister) sent flowers to Kate in grateful remembrance of the tenderness shown to the little boy. When school days were over, he continued to write and to visit Kate. She was expecting him in Grasmere during the summer of 1914, but he was prevented from coming. Two months after the war broke out he was wounded and a prisoner in Germany. Although they wrote to each other, she never saw him again.

The Christmas season of 1892 brought a temporary renewal of Kate's depression. She could not wish anyone a *"Merrie* Christmas,"* she said, and on December 19 she wrote: "This is the anniversary of dear Father's death. Oh! Lila, was he not the dearest, most lovable of men? Sometimes it seems as if I *must* see him." Easter, 1893, was another depressing season, made still sadder by the death of her sister-in-law, Joanna Anthon. In July she talked of going to Harrowgate for her health, adding that it was "not far from Haworth, the home of Charlotte Brontë and her sisters." Harrowgate did not please her, however, and after a very short stay she went to the Lake District.

On the afternoon of July 22 she reached Grasmere, and even before seeking lodgings, visited Wordsworth's old home. On the register of Dove Cottage she entered in the old vigorous handwriting: "July 22d, 1893. Mrs. J. H. Anthon, New York." It was characteristic of the enthusiasm with which she pursued her literary pilgrimages. Although she sometimes complained of fatigue (and with reason), she was evidently in fair health, for she explored the countryside with a thoroughness that would have wearied a younger person. She was completely enchanted. Except for a season in Germany with Helen and her sisters and another in New York at the wedding of Edith Scott, she was to spend every succeeding summer of her life in Grasmere. In 1908 she began to live there the year round.

To Sue Dickinson Kate wrote jokingly of an old woman who had once come to a region she liked so well that she had decided to make it her "native place." Kate understood perfectly how the old woman felt.

Grasmere Lake is small, much smaller than Lake Otsego, and the surrounding mountains are softer, greener, taller. Yet in a sense Kate Scott had come home.

XV

There is one last picture of Kate Anthon. She is sitting in the garden of her friend Frank Bramley, who, she says, is not only a member of the Royal Academy but also, and better still, a charming man. She likes to visit his house and watch him paint. Now he is taking her picture, and she shakes her umbrella at him. Not easily pleased with a photograph, she has been known to tear up snapshots of herself.

The painter's wife, hovering smilingly behind Kate's chair, is dressed lightly for summer weather. From Kate's own clothes it would not be possible to guess the season. This lover of the South and of sunlight is strongly defended against a northern summer. As usual, she is dressed in complete black — trim black coat, long black kid gloves, and small black cap like a crown on her white hair. She looks regal, or rather as elderly queens might wish to look, for few of them are as handsome as Kate or as exquisite. There is no better word for the quality of this late Victorian than the Victorian word "elegance."

She spends her summers with a landlady, Miss Kirkby, in a small, two-story house of white Westmoreland stone. It is set close to the cobbled street, and from the windows of her downstairs parlor, over the window boxes of bright red geranium and blue lobelia, she has a near view of anyone passing. Many do not pass but pause and turn in, for already she has a number of friends in Grasmere; and the old Swan coaching inn, nearby, and the newer Prince of Wales, down at the other end of town on the lake, shelter many a London friend who has made the long journey to see her.

From her bedroom windows upstairs, she looks out at Helm Crag rearing its two thousand feet into the clear air. And she writes constantly of her joy in the mountains, and in the roses which clamber to the rooftree of the house, and in the scent of new-mown hay. This enthusiasm for the smell of fresh hay is another of the many enthusiasms once shared with Emily Dickinson. In every letter from Grasmere to Sue Dickinson Kate speaks of the haying. But the hay — or something like it — gives her many an unpleasant hour.

"Mrs. Anthon," says her doctor gravely, "you have a very sound constitution, but your mucous membrane isn't worth a snap."

On July 29, 1902, Sue Dickinson and her daughter Martha sail from New York for Cherbourg. They urge Kate to join them in Switzerland, and she declines. But the following year, in London, the two old friends meet once more. Sue's European stay closes with the marriage of her thirty-seven-year-old daughter to a "Captain Bianchi (Russian artillery officer) on the 19th July [1903] at the Church of the Russian Embassy in Dresden. The Captain fortunately is ordered to America (Boston) for a service of several years." So Kate writes to her sister-in-law, Lila. During the next three years she inquires punctually about "the dear Captain." Then she stops. Apparently the truth of Martha's unlucky marriage to Alexander Bianchi has at last reached her.

In the summer of 1904 Sue writes to Kate about a disturbing incident. Kate's niece, Lily Bartlett, on the strength of a childhood acquaintance with Sue, has paid an uninvited call in

Amherst and rehearsed her grievances against Kate's branch of
the family. Apparently Sue has listened attentively, if not
eagerly, until she has got the whole of the story and discovered
it to be nothing more than stale quarrels between Scotts and
Bartletts over family bequests and a disputed burial plot (Kate's
family were clearly in the right). Sue declares that she still
trembles at the recollection of Lily's visit. It is a trivial incident — of no significance except as evidence of Sue's tactlessness
in repeating a story that can only give pain. But Kate's love for
Sue is undiminished.

In 1905 Sue is once more in Europe, accompanied by her
daughter Martha (the "dear Captain" is not in the party). She
spends some autumn weeks in Paris, and Kate imagines wistfully that they are together, and that they "stray into the
Madeleine and listen to the transcendent music." With the
coming of winter Sue moves to a villa in Nice. More strongly
and urgently Kate recalls "brilliant skies and tropical warmth."
She is sorely tempted to rush for the train that Martha has
recommended, but decides to fight her battle with the fogs and
the bitter east winds. She has, in fact, no money for travel.
Although she never mentions the matter to Sue, she is still sending a large part of her income to her sister-in-law.

Sue Dickinson mentions Samuel Bowles.

"That dear, gracious, genial, charming man," Kate responds
obligingly. Then Sue dispatches an old note from Bowles,
which carries Kate back "to those happy, happy days." But
Kate has nothing more to say about Bowles. Obviously she
does not remember him very well, and it is not safe to dwell
upon those happy days.

When Sue warns her "not to let sweet, dull women drown
and smother" her, Kate is flattered and amused. "Some women
are intensely charming," she recalls, but on the whole she
agrees with Sue as to the superior conversation of men. They
improve every tea party. Unfortunately in England "the women

are painfully in excess." The men go to India or enter the army, and Kate misses them dreadfully.

A Mrs. Browning of Cooperstown comes to Europe and swoops down upon Kate. Parenthetically, it is surprising how much of Cooperstown does come to Kate and how nearly she is at home abroad. But no other visitor reacts quite like Mrs. Browning. Back in Cooperstown, she reports indignantly that "Kate Anthon is living in poverty and dying of loneliness." Quite properly the family ignore this. Kate has chosen her life, and her wants have declined with her income. But when she suffers a slight stroke of paralysis, there is a strong pull across the Atlantic. Young Edith, now married and the mother of several children, leaves her family and hurries to England. By the time Edith arrives Kate is recovering but is overjoyed to see her niece. This is the fourth time, she tells Sue, that Edith has come to her. Kate talks incessantly and happily. She is reluctant to surrender even a week of Edith's time to other friends in England. It has been many years since she has known the relief of talking freely and at her ease with a member of her own family. But Edith has duties and must go.

Since 1908 Kate has been living the year round in Grasmere. At last she is able to get together all her boxes, books, pictures, the marble clock whose welfare has agitated her through many years, her wedding silver, linens, ornamental tables, and a host of knicknacks. Now she can make a home for herself. Characteristically it is a peripatetic home. Because her landlady, Miss Kirkby, will keep a lodger only in summer, and because Kate will not give up Miss Kirkby, there are picturesque spring and fall migrations. Miss Kirkby's brother is the only person entrusted with the precious box of silver. But linens, tea tables, books, and other objects go by common carrier, with Kate following at her leisure. Does she mind? Probably not. Although she prefers Miss Kirkby to Mrs. Irving, that would not be her chief reason for returning summer after summer to the little house called "Whitebridge." The spring move to Miss Kirkby's is the equivalent of her old summer wanderings.

During her many seasons in Grasmere Kate has come to know the region almost as thoroughly as any Lake poet. Until recently she has been a stout walker and has made pilgrimages to every spot mentioned by Wordsworth or Southey or Coleridge, and she knows the history of all their work. Literary associations plus majestic mountains plus "the best bread and butter" she has ever eaten make the Lake District an enchanted region for her. But Grasmere is changing. There are too many people now, crowds of people in summer, and too many tea parties and too little reverence for the things Kate loves. She misses her old quiet summers and has come to prefer the winters. She misses the dash of the old stagecoach.

"A few horrid motor cars are tearing about Grasmere," Kate writes to her sister-in-law. She thinks them a blot on the landscape. She hates them. They are noisy and dirty, and they have a vile smell. She likes the old days and the old ways. But here comes her afternoon tea, and she wonders if there was anything so good as afternoon tea a hundred years ago. After all, "it is a sweet, calm evening, and I will sally forth and watch the men so busy getting in the last loads of fragrant hay." Then a young friend comes in an automobile, and with some trepidation Kate begins the first of a series of stately drives.

Sometimes a plaintive note creeps into her letters. She would like to have a daughter like Sue's Martha. She is too old to live alone. And sometimes, when Lila or Edith has been delayed in answering her letters, she writes with pleading anguish. But she is never really lonely. When she is not reading (her eyes are good to the end) or playing a game of patience or, with her bright smile and brighter eyes, commanding Mary Kirkby to drop housework and amuse her, she is engaged with friends. They are almost too much for her at times, and she wearies of tea parties and constant visiting; for the people in the big houses around Grasmere have taken her up. Every Sunday an officer of the Cunard Company sends her the homely treat of a dish of hominy. The Bramleys, the vicar's family, the proprietors of Butterlip How and of Huntingstile and of many another house, all are her friends.

"Mrs. Anthon [her landlady will remember proudly] was accepted by the gentry." How Kate herself would smile! But though she deprecates the notion, she has had, all her life, the sure, unconscious conviction that she *is* gentry. The respect with which she treats other people, especially those who serve her, is a result of this conviction. So are the neatness and good taste of her dress and of all the objects with which she has surrounded herself. If she has presents to give, they must be small, because of her shrinking income, but always the best of their kind. She sends to a very special shop in London for the expensive lace handkerchiefs and the elbow-length gloves that she gives to her favorites on their wedding day. For she still has favorites and is still attracted to youth and beauty.

The latest in the long series is a young girl named Ursula. The girl spends her summers with her father and sisters (the mother is dead) in a large house above Grasmere, and sometimes — to Kate's joy — they reopen the house at Christmas time. Between the girl in her twenties and the woman in her early eighties there springs up a strong, deep friendship. What they talk about no one knows, but on Kate's side it must be the same blend of humor and boundless enthusiasm and joy in life that once enchanted Florie. Ursula gives her elderly friend an anthology of poems entitled *In Friendship's Garden*. It contains Emily Dickinson's ringing affirmation, "Alter? When the hills do." But if Kate realizes that the poem was written to her, she gives no sign.

Every summer afternoon Ursula comes to take tea in the front parlor of the little white stone house. And then one day she fails to come. Miss Kirkby has laid the table, and the water is boiling. Again and again Kate goes to the window, listens intently for a well-known step, and still there is no Ursula. An

hour or so later comes a message. The girl is dead. She died
very suddenly, without warning, upon the hour that Kate was
expecting her.

("Mrs. Anthon looked very grave that day," her landlady
will recall.)

Kate says nothing. In silence she watches Miss Kirkby re-
move the tea things and put the table away. In silence she gazes
out the window, over the boxes of bright red geranium and
blue lobelia, up the towering bulk of Helm Crag. Nor is it
wise or kind to speak to her now. But it is possible to guess
what she is thinking. She is asking herself, in agony, if she will
be fated to outlive every human being whom she has loved.

They are nearly all dead or dying. Campbell Turner, Emily
Dickinson, John Anthon, parents, brother, sister — dead long
ago. The Dering sisters and Gertrude Vanderbilt — gone in
the early years of the present century. Now Sue Dickinson
begins to fail, and Kate's love, intensified by anxiety, pours out
in a flood which, if it cannot keep Sue alive, at least softens her
dying. Frank Bramley dies prematurely. Her old friend Helen
dies also, and no one dares tell Kate.

It is true that Lila Scott and Edith are living, but they are
far away and busy with their own affairs. Florie still lives, in
London, and still writes letters beginning "Dearest Friend"
and ending "Ever your loving Florie," but she does not come
to Grasmere.

"Dear Sue," Kate writes to her old friend, not long before
Sue's death, "I am more and more impressed with the excessive
brevity of everything. Surely there must be another and a
higher life. No matter what degree of brilliant genius, or
fame, or culture is attained here, all, all soon fades away. This
must be the beginning — so unfinished, so immature, so suddenly quenched in darkness. Another life we must have to
perfect and finish so many unfulfilled hopes and aspirations —
so many bitter disappointments."

This is not faith but doubt. Every assertion is qualified by

a "surely" or a "must be" or a "must have." But of course
Kate, like Emily Dickinson, has read those somber Victorian
writers for whom the loss of one kind of faith meant almost
the loss of all faith. She has come to the crucial point of doubt
on which Emily tortured herself.

2

Death is the large theme of some of Emily Dickinson's best
poems and of some of her worst. It was also a theme which she
introduced into her early acquaintance with Kate. In the summer of 1860 she wrote to Kate:

> *There is a subject, dear, on which we never touch.*
> *Ignorance of its pageantries does not deter me. I too went*
> *out to meet the dust early in the morning. I too in daisy*
> *mounds possess hid treasure, therefore I guard you more.*

The subject once introduced, apparently they did discuss it,
and Kate's faith proved stronger and serener than Emily's.
In the poem beginning "I cannot live with you," Emily wrote:

> For you served Heaven, you know,
> Or sought to . . .

In another poem ("You taught me waiting with myself") she
was more explicit: "The Heaven *you* know to understand."
    Very probably Kate did speak words of comfort and did
draw a conventional picture of the next world. Except for the
one passage quoted above from her letter to Sue, she always
wrote with calm assurance of immortality. Of course she may
have found it easier to suggest her doubts to Sue than to such
correspondents as Mrs. Scott, Lila Scott (the sister of a clergyman), or young Edith. With Sue, as Kate once wrote, she could

"plunge into the very abyss of things . . . say anything, everything, sure of divine sympathy." And to young Sue the young Emily could safely write that "sermons on unbelief" were very attractive to her. But Kate was certainly firmer in her faith than Emily. She did not mark the skeptical passages that she found in her books, and of all the Victorian writers she clung most fervently to Cardinal Newman.

The only certainty about Emily Dickinson was that she was never sure of anything. Although her technique matured, her ideas did not change. The doubt was with her all her life. In July, 1874, a few weeks after her father's death, she wrote to Higginson:

> *When a few years old, I was taken to a funeral which I now know was of peculiar distress, and the clergyman asked, "Is the arm of the Lord shortened, that it cannot save?"*
>
> *He italicized the "cannot." I mistook the accent for a doubt of Immortality, and not daring to ask, it besets me still, though we know that the mind of the heart must live if its clerical part do not. Would you explain it to me? I was told you were once a clergyman.*

Although Emily treated her childhood as an elastic quantity, she was probably — as this passage suggests — still a child at the time. She was not aware that her reaction is a commonplace of childhood. For a child's introduction to death makes a sharper impression than his elder's vague description of another world. Also his first vigorous taming for society coincides with his first understanding of death, and the one may suggest the other, the taming itself being a little death. Under two such tensions even a six-year-old may decide that life is a cheat. But as he submits to the molding of society and adopts the general beliefs, he loses the sharpness of his impressions. He is able to repress the idea of death except at crucial periods. Emily was never able to repress it. Apparently she retained the intensity of a child's perceptions.

The beginning of adolescence would have been another disturbing period. By the standards of her repressive age Emily was somewhat tomboyish, and she must have suffered more than commonly under the restrictions and taboos that now hemmed her in. This disturbance may account for the occasional melancholy of letters written in her early teens. Probably it also explains the following curious passage of a letter of 1862 to Higginson:

> When much in the woods, as a little girl, I was told that the snake would bite me, that I might pick a poisonous flower, or goblins kidnap me . . .

In her late teens she was subjected to the religiosity of the Mt. Holyoke academy, and the idea of death returned in force. She took her doubts and fears to a new friend, Ben Newton. But his early death precipitated new anxieties. In a letter to his pastor she probed uneasily into the circumstances of his death, as if she hoped to gather from the serenity of his passing the assurance that there is another life. Years later she was to be much disturbed by the fact that her friend Samuel Bowles refused to die peacefully.

In the late fall of 1850, three years before Newton's death, Emily suffered what she described as her first bereavement — the death of her ex-principal Leonard Humphrey. He died suddenly and he was young. These two circumstances were enough to shock Emily. In a letter of January 2, 1851, to Abiah Root, she imaginatively experienced her own death, not that of Leonard Humphrey. He meant little to her except as notice of the possibility of early and sudden death. Although he had certainly been a pleasant acquaintance, Emily could shudder upon hearing of the death of a stranger.

In her anxiety she wanted to gather all her friends around

her for warmth and protection. But toward the end of this letter to Abiah she threw off her depression and wrote boldly:

The shore is safer, Abiah, but I love to buffet the sea —
I can count the bitter wrecks here in these pleasant waters,
and hear the murmuring winds, but oh, I love the danger!

The sea meant a great many things to Emily — all the mysteries of love, life, death, immortality — and it could mean all of them simultaneously. Probably she herself did not always know what she intended. Through most of this letter to Abiah, however, she was struggling with the harsh idea of death. When she ended upon a note of defiance, it was as if she had determined not to let the idea of death conquer her. She would not strait-jacket her mind with the compromises of orthodox religion, but would continue her own search for meaning. The letter was written at the high-tide of her attachment to Susan Gilbert — one of the two periods in which she dealt most strongly and joyously with life.

But in the fall of 1851, when Sue went to Baltimore and was negligent, the idea of death visited Emily frequently. In 1852 Sue ended their romantic friendship by engaging herself to Austin Dickinson; a few months later Ben Newton died, and Emily withered. Long afterwards, in March, 1859, she encountered Kate Scott; and the triumphant tone returned to her letters. She was once more able to cope vigorously with life. Death diminished to a muttering on a far horizon, overridden by the tumult of love. Then Kate terminated their friendship in April, 1861 — by an odd coincidence, the month in which the Civil War began — and the idea of death broke crashingly upon Emily, never to leave her again. By her own reckoning, she died in that month, and she described her continued existence as a death in life.

Emily wrote many "death-in-life" poems. Of these, a very early manuscript, probably written about 1861, begins, "It did

not surprise me." The gist of this poem is that a loved woman
has abandoned Emily for another person, and in Emily's heart
there is a "coffin." A poem of about the mid-sixties, beginning
"Ourselves were wed one summer, dear," appears to describe
their mutual renunciation as death for both. The poem beginning "Like eyes that looked on wastes," again describes their
mutual renunciation as a death.

> To die without the dying
> And live without the life —

wrote Emily, was the "hardest miracle" that ever confronted
faith. "Somehow myself survived the night," she wrote elsewhere, but added that she was "dated with the Dead."

"I breathed enough to learn the trick," begins one poem.
Emily has mastered the trick so well that a spectator would suppose her still alive. "A great hope fell, you heard no noise,"
another poem begins. Emily is now in her coffin, waiting until
the "sovereign Carpenter" nails it down permanently. In a
poem beginning "This chasm, sweet, upon my life," she tells
her beloved that she is lying in the tomb. In another poem,
"So give me back to death," she explains that she feared death
only because it would deprive her of her beloved. Now life
itself deprives her, and "in my own grave I breathe."

Two poems, "It was a grave, yet bore no stone" and "The
color of the grave is green," appear deceptively general in
meaning. Actually they describe the grave in Emily's mind. A
more explicit poem begins "The grave my little cottage is." In
this strange little house Emily tidies her parlor and lays "the
marble tea," while she waits for real death and reunion with
her friend. A poem beginning "Because I could not stop for
Death" tells how Death comes in his carriage and takes Emily to
a little house swelling out of the ground. Then centuries pass,
each of them shorter than the day she first guessed that she was
headed toward eternity. The "centuries" may well stand for

years of her life as set off against one black day of April, 1861.

In still another poem, "Bereaved of all I went abroad," Emily writes that she is equally bereaved on a "new peninsula." The grave has preceded her. She tries to lose herself in crowds, to find oblivion in "cups of artificial drowse" (perhaps an allusion to very real sleeping draughts), but she cannot forget the "spade" that has dug her grave. Apparently the "new peninsula" is not a new friend but an attempt to forget Kate, the original peninsula. The "spade" is the jilting Emily received. More specifically, it may be the letter with which Kate broke off their friendship. In other poems it is an arrow, a bomb, a stone, a whip, or something else that suggests deliberate cruelty and violence. A poem beginning "Rehearsal to ourselves" calls it a "dirk." The dirk reminds Emily that she "died." Nevertheless, she not only cherishes it but even takes a perverse pleasure in reviewing the incidents of her ill-fated friendship.

There are many of these "death-in-life" poems (it is Emily's repetitiousness, in fact, that permits interpretation of her poems), but only one more need be mentioned — the often-quoted "My life closed twice before its close." If this poem was written after April 1, 1882, it might reflect Emily's grief over the death of Wadsworth. At no earlier period would she have had any sense of loss in connection with him, for she did not *lose* him: he remained her kind, faithful friend to his death. But the poem may well have been written years before. Of the two events referred to, one was undoubtedly the loss of Kate Scott. The other may never be identified.

In a fairly large group of poems Emily anticipated her real death. They are marred by a profound self-pity — a distinct air of "You'll be sorry when I'm dead" — and do not deserve any particular attention. In some she figures as a dying animal; in others she divides herself in two, and a first-person self lavishes pity on a dying third-person self.

A more puzzling group describe — or anticipate — the death

of the beloved. One of these ("It came at last, but prompter death") is known to have been written in the seventies. When all the poems are finally dated, it will appear that many, perhaps all, of this group were written long before Wadsworth's death, which occurred very late in Emily's life, in April, 1882. Yet if Wadsworth had been Emily's lover instead of her "ghostly father," it would have been like her to brood over his coming death. As a matter of fact, Wadsworth's death took Emily by surprise, much as Newton's had done years before. She had not had her eye on him.

In an earlier chapter it was suggested that the "Dollie" poems were written to Susan Gilbert. In two of these poems Emily died — once in self-pity ("Dying, dying in the night!") and a second time ("I often passed the village") in an effort to find a means of permanently holding Sue: they would be united in death. Emily did much the same thing in a letter of spring, 1852, to Sue in Baltimore: she imagined that they were buried "neath one willow tree."

To note the unchanging character of Emily's ideas is not to suggest that she was unusual. The ideas of youth, and especially of childhood, set like concrete; the child is always father of the man. But it is necessary to show how Emily behaved in her youth in order to show that she was behaving in the same manner at a later period. Her attitude toward Sue would be a model of her attitude toward Kate.

Two instances have already been pointed out. In her 1860 letter to Kate, as in earlier letters to Sue and Abiah, she stressed the fear of death as a reason for deeper love. Her anxiety was great; she wanted reassurance. In her letter of March, 1860, to Mrs. Holland, written shortly after Kate left Amherst, she *anticipated* Kate's death. She could see no other way of bringing about their permanent union.

In a manuscript of the early sixties, "Here, where the daisies fit my head," Emily describes herself as dead. She finds death gentle and is willing to trust her "flower" to him. Those who love her will be kind to Kate and will bury them together. In death, as in life, they will form a "single bloom." In a manuscript of the mid-sixties, already cited ("Ourselves were wed one summer, dear"), the two women are said to die.

Some puzzling verses open with the following stanza:

> I know that he exists
> Somewhere in silence.
> He has hid his rare life
> From our gross eyes.

But this is only a joke, Emily continues hopefully, "a fond ambush." In a short while her friend will leap from ambush, and bliss will be improved by surprise. But suppose one of them should die during this wilful separation? Would not the joke have gone too far?

It should be remembered that Emily freely translated the feminine into the masculine, and that she often referred to herself in the first-person plural. As for the rest, Kate did vanish into silence. By her own evidence, by the evidence of Emily's poems, she ceased writing to Emily. And even if Emily had dared question Sue, her estranged sister-in-law, there were long intervals when Sue herself did not hear from Kate. Finally, two poems using feminine pronouns ("The Stars are old, that stood for me" and "Frigid and sweet her parting face") describe the other woman as alienated and at a distance.

In a long poem beginning "Promise this, when you be dying," Emily entreats her friend to summon her in the last moments of life (there is no indication of the other person's sex). It would be natural, of course, for Emily to suppose that the absent person was more vulnerable than herself. But she may have had reasons for anxiety. Although Kate lived to a great old age, she did not look robust, and her family history of

tuberculosis would have been alarming. Also, apparently at
some time in early middle age, she underwent a serious operation for the removal of a cancerous breast.

From fearing her friend's death, Emily found it only a step
to imagining it. In a measure, the step was precautionary.
Emily tested her courage. The poem "If he were living — dare
I ask?" refers unmistakably to a person with whom Emily had
been out of touch for years. It suggests also the way in which
she might have tried, without betraying her acute interest, to
extract information from Sue about Kate. Emily "hinted
changes," talked cautiously of the passing of years, spoke of
persons connected with the one person of importance. At last
— and here she described her fears, not real events — she dared
the crucial name. "He" was dead.

Clearly the person meant by this poem could not have been
Wadsworth, who wrote regularly to Emily until he died. Nor
could she have inquired about him from Sue or her sister or
any other person she was at all likely to meet in her secluded
existence. Emily alone knew him. But how easily, and with
what apparent casualness, she could have brought Sue's conversation around to Sue's intimate friend Kate! No matter that
Kate herself did not die. Emily feared, hoped for, vindictively
desired her death, and that was enough.

There are other poems describing the death of the beloved.
Among the ironies is the fact that Kate long outlived her timid
friend, read some of the poems, and marked at least one poem
which appeared to anticipate her own death.

Many "death" poems are comparatively impersonal. They
are written from the standpoint of a spectator stopping, in bewilderment and anguish, on this side of the grave. Sometimes,
but not very seriously, Emily tries to imagine the other world.
"I went to heaven," she writes. It was a small and picturesque
town. Or she writes ("I never saw a moor") that she is as certain of heaven as of the heather and the ocean, which also she

has never seen. One poem begins, "Of death I try to think," and it describes death under the figure of a stream which a child leaps to secure a flower.

More significant are the poems in which Emily pits her reason — and not her faith — against the riddle of death. It is interesting that virtually all of them were rejected by Emily's first two editors, Mrs. Todd and Mrs. Bianchi. Like the poems addressed to a woman, accusing the beloved of cruelty, complaining of being "forgot," or describing the love affair in too intimate detail, they were reserved for *Bolts of Melody,* the revealing collection edited by Mrs. Todd's daughter, Millicent Bingham.

In a poem beginning "That it will never come again," Emily writes that there is no pleasure in "believing what we don't believe." If immortality exists at all, it is apparently so meager and deprived a state that the thought of it merely increases the appetite for life. "Their height in heaven comforts not," she writes elsewhere. The next world is a "house of supposition," a "glittering frontier" skirting "acres of perhaps." To her it looks "insecure." Hers is a "timid life of evidence," which pleads that it does not know.

"This me that walks and works must die," she writes. Perhaps there will be a future life, perhaps not; she is unable to find any certain evidence. In " 'Good night,' because we must!" she begs God, with surprising archness, to answer her serious question. Of the dead she writes ("These tested our horizon") that the hope of seeing them again is "a dice — a doubt." In a poem beginning "Which is best?" she speaks of the promised heaven "with that old codicil of doubt." It is, of course, a lawyer's daughter who demands evidence. Elsewhere she writes, "Those, dying then, knew where they went." Musing on the firm, if mistaken, trust of her fathers, she is inclined to think that fool's light would be better than no light at all.

There is no reason to believe that her faith grew stronger toward the end of her life. She remained the same turbulent, despairing, desperately hoping, passionate woman. Sometimes she wrote with a firmness that she did not feel. After the death of George Eliot, whose agnosticism evidently disturbed Emily, she wrote to her Norcross cousins: "The gift of belief which her greatness denied her, I trust she receives in the childhood of the kingdom of Heaven." But two and a half years later, in June, 1883, she wrote with deep seriousness to C. H. Clark: "Are you certain there is another life? When overwhelmed to know, I fear that few are sure." In April, 1884, about the time her health began to fail, she sent one of her doubting poems to Clark, asking if the same thoughts ever disturbed him. And in a poem of her very latest handwriting, "Some wretched creature, Savior, take," she begged that some one else be taken and that she be allowed one more hour of life.

It was not a question of doubting God. No one can doubt God, whatever he calls Him. The question was immortality. Would Emily Dickinson continue beyond the grave? More specifically, would she continue as a self-conscious being, a creature of flesh, a recognizable person with the ability to recognize, touch, love her friends? For absorption into a misty, spiritual All did not attract Emily in the least.

Sometimes, but rarely, she thought of immortality almost in the sense of Spinoza. Immortality is in this life, in the consciousness of filling a particular, an inalienable, place, and of participating imaginatively in all life past or to come. It is also in a sense of well-being, of sensuous expansiveness, of harmony with the world that is. But she was not satisfied. If the grave was the end of consciousness, then life was a cheat.

Since her question is unanswerable — and all questioning is childish that attempts to penetrate death — there is more interest in the question that her persistence raises. Why was she obsessed with death?

One answer is obvious. She lived in an age of declining faith. She mentioned Darwin, quoted from Tennyson's *In Memoriam*, and undoubtedly read Matthew Arnold. And were not Arnold's ears filled with the "melancholy, long, withdrawing roar" of the tide of faith? But the answer does not satisfy. In the work of Tennyson, Arnold, and other Victorians there is no such concentration upon the moment of death as in the poetry of Emily Dickinson.

Another explanation has been suggested. It is simply that Emily retained the tremendous impressibility of childhood. She did not harden into an adult. Death was more real to her — and consequently more terrible — than it ever was to Tennyson or Arnold or any other Victorian.

"I never hear that one is dead," begins a significant poem. The bell tolled for Emily when any one died. "Tilling" the "abyss" of death, her mind

> Had madness, had it once or twice,
> The yawning consciousness.

"Beliefs are bandaged," the poem continues. That is, the idea of death is so terrible that the ordinary mind defends against it. Emily knew no one so bold that he would dare look "that awful stranger, consciousness," in the face. It is not too much to say that she looked at it more squarely than any other poet, and she — "had madness, had it once or twice."

Both explanations are true — both account, in part, for her obsession with death and immortality — but a third is still more important. In a copy of Lamb's essay entitled "New Year's Eve," Kate Scott once marked these lines: "Whatsoever thwarts, or puts me out of my way, brings death into my mind." As woman and poet Emily Dickinson was almost completely frustrated. She wrote poetry which she could not publish. She loved where she dared not love. Again and again she insisted that she had given up life on this earth and had staked all her hopes on a life to come. The unused life in her avenged itself by confronting her with the image of death.

A lesser tragedy was the coming of old age. Although Emily

had little to say about it, she liked the idea no better than any one else. She was disturbed by the signs of old age in her friends. But in a rather vindictive poem ("Mine enemy is growing old") she rejoiced over the aging of some once-loved friend. Another poem begins, "That odd old man is dead a year." Does anyone miss him? Is it possible that anyone can love him, that he has, perhaps, a wife, hardened into old age like himself, who waits for "his wrinkled coming home"?

> Oh, life, begun in fluent blood
> And consummated dull!

It was a consummation that Emily never knew. She died at the age of fifty-five, on a May evening of 1886, attended and mourned by Austin, Lavinia, Sue, and a few friends. On the day of her burial Higginson observed with surprise that she "looked 30, not a gray hair or wrinkle, and perfect peace on the beautiful brow." It was the only peace she ever knew. And from the grave to which the small coffin was borne on a bright, flower-laden May afternoon, she continues to fling her challenging and unanswerable questions. For those who have truly felt her poems she is an inquiet sleeper.

3

It is 1910, and Emily has been dead for twenty-four years. But Kate Anthon knows what it is to grow old. From her window she looks out at a young laborer sweeping the road, and she writes with envious sadness, "He is infinitely superior to me." The old hearty appetite is gone. She cannot eat this and must be careful about that, and often it is simpler and more truthful to tell her landlady that she wants nothing at all. Her fingers stiffen; she apologizes for her crabbed, difficult handwriting. "I walk out a little on pleasant days" — the slow, cautious walk of

a very old woman — "but soon tire." The ardent traveler is
confined to one small village and at last to one small room. To
those rude enough to ask her age she turns a deaf ear. If they
persist, she remembers an old gatekeeper who was asked how
much he earned. "Why, it's like this," he answered musingly
(and Kate quotes him with malicious glee). "Some people forget to ask — and some I don't tell."

"As we grow older," she writes to Sue, shortly before her
eightieth birthday, "how much less we demand of everybody
and everything! And how much more indulgent and charitable
towards the world. A very little contents me now." This is the
period of her last great attachment — to young Ursula — and
the "little" might describe the afternoon teas on which her days
now turn.

But in one respect she is never contented. To the end of her
life she searches for more vitality in the people she meets, and
she sighs, half-humorously, over the general absence of life and
charm. With laughing approval she quotes Sue's words, "Most
people are so dun-coloured." In Kate's opinion, most people
are first-class bores. She wonders how she can bear her present
lot after knowing such women as Sue and her own "brilliant
sister Maggie." And she marks these telltale lines in one of the
letters of Charles Lamb: "I know I am too dissatisfied with the
beings around me, but I cannot help occasionally exclaiming,
'Wo is me, that I am constrained to dwell with Meshech, and
to have my habitation among the tents of Kedar.'"

Kate has not forgotten Florie, although Florie has apparently
— but only apparently — forgotten her. At some time during
these Grasmere years Kate marks a long passage in De Quincey's
Literary Reminiscences. It is a recollection and a defense of
her own passionate attachment: "But the years came . . . years
through which I was careless of all but those who lived within
my inner circle, within 'my heart of hearts'; years — ah! heavenly
years! — through which I lived, beloved, *with* thee, *to* thee, *for*
thee, *by* thee! Ah, happy, happy years! in which I was a mere

football of reproach, but in which every wind and sounding hurricane of wrath or contempt flew by like chasing enemies past some defying gate of adamant, and left me too blessed in thy smiles — angel of life! — to heed the curses or the mocking which sometimes I heard raving outside of our impregnable Eden."

Emily Dickinson, whose experience was limited by her fifty-five years, believed that the old cannot love. Surely she was mistaken. There is no diminishing of the habitual emotionalism in Kate's letters to Sue. In every line there are traces of the passionate schoolgirl who once kissed a young stranger's cheek, because she "could not help it." And Kate weeps for those happy days and quotes Tennyson: "Oh death in life, the days that are no more." Or Shelley: "On life's last steps I climb." Or she alludes unmistakably to the period of her love for Emily, and the tears blind her eyes. But in the midst of her most passionate outbreak she stops, leaves her writing desk, and returns only after a long interval, with the admission that she interrupted herself from a dread of "wearying" Sue.

Poor Sue! It is not her fault that she cannot satisfy that unappeasable desire. Doubtless she does her best. There must be something in her to incite such lines as these: "Dear, dear Sue, will I ever see you again! Worlds would I give to kiss you! — I want to see you so intensely I could cry. — Write when you can to your ever longing, ever loving Katie A. — Oh, I wish I knew all about you this minute. I fear you are not well. Do write soon — very soon. — If I could only sit by your side in the Library, with you and dear Martha and the blazing logs. I could cry to think the ocean lies between us! — When shall we ever meet! It gives me a sort of delirious joy to think of it! It is too much happiness for this world! — Good bye, my dear, dear friend. I have thought of you *so often — so often*. Ever and ever your old loving Katie 'Jane.'"

Or she thinks of the dreadful possibility that they might have failed to meet: "I cannot conceive of my life without a Sue Gilbert Dickinson! After all I believe in some way we should have met. The magnet never fails to attract. Our paths would have crossed. Kindred spirits *must* come together. Oh! the joy of being with you, to plunge into the very abyss of things, to be natural, unconventional, earnest, impassioned, to say anything, everything, sure of divine sympathy! Oh! my nature has suffered in this cold, reserved England!"

It was letters like these that Emily Dickinson once received. It was to letters like these that she responded: "O our condor Kate, come from your crags again! Oh dew upon the bloom fall yet again a summer's night."

To Lila Synnott Scott, her sister-in-law, Kate writes with a more tempered emotionalism but with a love founded on years of intimacy and of shared anguish. If she hastily describes Sue as her "dearest friend in America," she returns to specify, with a caret pointing above the line, "not relative." And a strong sisterly affection marks every letter. "Oh! to see you and kiss you! Write soon to your loving and devoted Sister Katie." She buys a pot of tulips and dedicates them to Lila. Upon the coming of her afternoon tea she imagines that Lila comes with it. In sympathy she follows Lila's steps through the garden of the old brown house (now Lila's) where Kate herself was born and knew much happiness and much sorrow. And across the blue wastes of the Atlantic she cries: "Goodbye, dearest of Lilas, I kiss you a hundred times."

In late December, 1914, she writes to Lila that she can no longer stir from the house. She "can only sit by the fire and live in the *Past*." Significantly, she has just received from Martha Bianchi, and has acknowledged in a long letter filled with wistful, reminiscent tenderness, a new volume of poems by Emily Dickinson entitled *The Single Hound*. She has reason to think of the past.

And it is a rich past. There is young Campbell Turner, dying of tuberculosis and promising God that, if he lives, he will become a minister. There is Emily Dickinson, stirred to poetry by a chance encounter. And John Anthon, classical scholar, lawyer, politician, struck down in his ripening age. And young Florie, that "passionate love adventure." And Gertrude and Helen and Ursula. Emily liked to imagine that she would meet Kate some day in heaven. She would not have found Kate alone.

It would be wrong, however, to suppose that Emily loved the more deeply, simply because she shut herself up for twenty-five years and lived with memories. Having spent her entire capital on one venture, and suffered bankruptcy, she dared not try again. For some obscure reason (temperament, childhood wounds, unsympathetic parents, or perhaps the exacting labor of creation), she did not prosper in the daily acts of living. In the absence of love she speculated constantly about its meaning.

Now psychologist and layman have tried alike, but no one has ever given a satisfactory definition of love — because it is a complex emotion, not all parts of which the definer is able or willing to recognize. There is love of beauty and God and country, love of parents and children, romantic love between two persons (by convention, of the opposite sex), mature love and immature love, love of the one and love of the many, and, finally, a very mystic and indescribable love of the All. This last seems to be nothing more than a desire to love — that is, love without apparent object. Like "love of the many" or "love of humanity," it is vague and diffuse and noble, with the nobleness of ideas that have been emptied of reality.

> . . . there's love and love [wrote Elizabeth Browning,
>   whom Kate and Emily revered]: the love of all
> (To risk in turn a woman's paradox)
> Is but a small thing to the love of one.
> You bid a hungry child be satisfied
> With a heritage of many corn-fields: nay,
> He says he's hungry, — he would rather have
> That little barley-cake you keep from him
> While reckoning up his harvests.

Without ever theorizing about the love of humanity, Kate Anthon loved many human beings. She would have been puzzled to know how one could love without loving individuals, not all of whom, as she well knew, were equally worthy. Nor would she have been long seduced by Platonism, which treats the love of the individual as a ladder to be discarded on the toilsome ascent towards love of the ideal. She would have remained in touch with earth. But would she have been equally sure in dealing with that part of love which involves sensuous pleasure? Her position was difficult.

Somewhat daringly (for a Victorian) Elizabeth Browning wrote

> Of sexual passion, which devours the flesh
> In a sacrament of souls.

But her sexual passion was legalized by marriage and consecrated by general approval (with the odd exception of Elizabeth's father, who apparently had no good opinion of any form of sexual passion). And at this point the ground would give way beneath the feet of Elizabeth's two ardent disciples.

It was unfortunate that Emily Dickinson loved a woman. She was tortured by that agent of social disapproval which she called her conscience. And as a woman in an age when few women had economic independence, she had actually no freedom of choice. Nevertheless, between love of one's own sex and love of the other, there are no real differences except those enforced by social disapproval. All other distinctions are the rationalizing of prejudices, both ignorant and learned. The ability to love one person truly is the ability to love all. That Emily attached herself to Kate was a healthier, more hopeful act than her twenty-five years of tortured isolation. Once in her life she tested reality, and she could never be entirely fooled again.

Between the experience of love and the imagination of love, however, there is a very real difference, and scholars would seem to be, of all people, least capable of recognizing it. The various biographies of Emily Dickinson are examples of scholarly myopia. On the other hand, a French critic deceived himself with the notion that Emily Brontë's works reveal a thorough acquaintance with love. There is nothing in her poems or in *Wuthering Heights* beyond the imagination of a gifted and passionate woman. But there is much in Emily Dickinson's poetry that gives proof of a real though limited experience.

The poems written during the eighteen months or so of her attachment to Kate are speakingly tender, sometimes playful, often exultant, and always directed to a very real person who is answering her love. Some of them openly address a woman; others, such as the poem beginning "I'll clutch and clutch," use imagery of a delicacy appropriate only with another woman. The person she loves is described as young, a playmate, a child sharing with Emily the childhood of love.

Still more revealing are the poems which describe her suffering after she is repudiated. She starves, suffocates, dies of thirst, freezes with cold. She arraigns her beloved for treason, cruelty, faithlessness (some of these poems are addressed to a woman, and all describe the same experience). Her tone is frantic, and her mental agony is almost unbearable. She fears that she is mad.

> To break so vast a heart
> Required a blow as vast . . .

It is nonsensical to suppose that this "vast heart" was broken by the removal of a fatherly clergyman from Philadelphia to Sacramento.

The reader of the early biographies of Emily Dickinson was compelled to forget that she was a real woman; that she loved

and hated and suffered — at something more than the common
rate, to be sure, but still in the common fashion. She was not
suffering from a delusion but from a very real and cruel rejection. This was no little white nun, no puritan ascetic, no
gentle, maidenly recluse. Her life was turmoil; her personal
symbol was the volcano. She was compounded of earthly passions, some of which, she well knew, would be stigmatized as
perverse; and for all sentimentalists she wrote bitingly:

> Such dimity convictions,
> A horror so refined
> Of freckled human nature,
> Of Deity ashamed.

Kate was the cause of Emily's anguish in 1861. But it may be
argued that her influence was transient. Although Emily wrote
that she loved once and only once, she also wrote, "We out-
grow love like other things." Did she not forget Kate and form
a passionate attachment to Charles Wadsworth? Was he not the
subject of her later poems? Undoubtedly there was a deep attachment to Wadsworth, a dependence of some kind or other,
but it may be questioned that Emily ever wrote a single poem
to Wadsworth. Good friends rarely excite much poetry. But
Emily continued to write about Katie after Wadsworth was
dead. The poem with which this book began is in Emily's
latest handwriting:

> I shall not murmur if at last
> The ones I loved below
> Permission have to understand
> For what I shunned them so —
>
> Divulging it would rest my heart
> But it would ravage theirs —
> Why, Katie, treason has a voice,
> But mine dispels in tears.

During the last years of her life, in a poem addressed to Kate by name, Emily explains that her entire life has been shaped by Kate's love and treason. It is incredible but it is true.

4 🖋

The time is August, 1914. In her eighty-three years Kate has lived through many wars and has hated them all, but she is caught up in the excitement, just as she was caught up during that first spring of the Civil War, when she broke with Emily and broke Emily's heart. Agitatedly she explains to a doubting Lila what "we" in England are fighting for. She is all English now, no trace of a transatlantic accent, except in the frequently expressed hope that America will be spared. War is dreadful; she cannot reconcile it with Christianity, and the word "civilization" seems to mock at her. When, on a bright, warm Sunday, she ventures to St. Oswald's (Wordsworth's fine old stone church, towards the repairing of which Kate generously contributes), she prays long for a murderous earth, ignorant of that "sole law" of love which Shelley and Kate believe "should govern the moral world."

Florie's nephew, the former Harrow schoolboy whom Kate loves — who was to have come to her in August — is lost in the first bloody battles of autumn. Distressful letters pass between Kate and his mother and sisters. With relief they learn that he is wounded and a prisoner in Germany. Soon Kate is writing to him at his prison address. Now Grasmere begins to lose its young men, and Kate grieves for them and for their parents. She would grieve for the Germans, too, if they were at all real to her; she never speaks of them with hatred. For her, the enemy is a vague, overshadowing evil symbolized by the Kaiser.

All her thoughts are absorbed by the war. In a way the excitement revives her. For the first time in years she speaks of making one more trip to her homeland — when the war is over and the terror of submarines has ended. One of her letters to Edith has gone down with a sinking ship; Kate herself could have gone down as easily. With stiffened fingers she knits socks and mends clothing for refugees, who are pouring into Grasmere now. She admits that she writes too much about the war to Lila, who is only mildly interested, and she resolves to speak of pleasanter subjects. But she cannot long forget it. More than ever the daily newspaper is a necessity to her. She reads all the war news, searching for favorable signs. President Wilson's notes to the belligerents seem to her very sound, very strong. She hopes they will keep America at peace. And by the grace of two weeks she escapes the sad knowledge that her native country is going to war.

On March 17, 1917, shortly after Kate's eighty-sixth birthday, the passionate heart stops beating. She dies of no particular disease except that she has lived long enough. Toward the last she is attended by her doctor, nurse, landlady, a few friends. There is no one else to come, but many will grieve.

And on those dying lips, "what name was best?" It is Emily's old question. And does Kate know

> How conscious consciousness could grow,
> Till love that was, and love too blest to be,
> Meet — and the junction be Eternity?

The question is unanswerable now. They are both dead at last, and more than an ocean rolls between them.

NOTES

CHAPTER I

The numbers below refer to the pages and lines.

3:1. Beginning on page 409, all poems by Emily Dickinson referred to in this book are indexed by their first lines, followed by the title of the book or periodical (and the page number) in which the poem can be found.

5:13. Martha Dickinson Bianchi, *The Life and Letters of Emily Dickinson* (Boston: Houghton Mifflin Company, 1924), p. 67.

5:21. Genevieve Taggard, *The Life and Mind of Emily Dickinson* (New York: Alfred A. Knopf, 1930), pp. 372–75. Miss Taggard quotes a description of Emily Dickinson by Mrs. Thomas L. Eliot (*Sunday Oregonian*, Portland, Oregon, March 19, 1899). On a visit to Amherst in 1867 Mrs. Eliot's mother was invited to the Dickinson house and seated in a room adjoining Emily's. Their conversation was carried on through an open door, and they did not see each other's face.

7:17. Louise Pound, in an article on Helen Hunt Jackson in the *Dictionary of American Biography*, mentions a tradition among the Hunt family that Major Hunt disliked Emily Dickinson. There is no convincing evidence that Emily ever saw Edward B. Hunt more than once — and then at a crowded reception in her father's house. The impression that she made on him, though disagreeable, must have been strong.

12:6. Millicent Todd Bingham, *Ancestors' Brocades* (New York: Harper & Brothers, 1945), p. 66. Mrs. Bingham quotes a letter from Austin Dickinson to T. W. Higginson, dated October 10, 1890, expressing his doubt as to the wisdom of publishing the poems. Afterwards he apparently changed his mind and became as anxious as Lavinia to get their sister's work into print.

12:17 ff. In this paragraph I have tried to indicate the gradual evolution of Lavinia's understanding, as shown by her behavior. Even an ignorant woman would come to feel that the poems were odd, embarrassing, and impossible to explain to outsiders. Mrs. Bingham (*op. cit.*, p. 146, note 9) quotes Lavinia's reply to a friend who asked her if she had not made a thorough study of Emily's poems: "Certainly not. I never looked at Emily's poems except those she showed me." Mrs. Todd recalled that she read the poems aloud to Lavinia and asked for explanations (Mrs. Bingham, *op. cit.*, pp. 21–22). She was exasperated by Lavinia's vagueness, but her own behavior would indicate that she had some knowledge of the meaning of the poems.

13:1.   Mrs. Bingham, *op. cit.*, pp. 254–55.

14:2.   Genevieve Taggard, *op. cit.*, pp. 336–37.   Miss Taggard's correspondent X has been identified as Mary Lee Hall by Mrs. Bingham, *op. cit.*, p. 371.

15:5 ff.   This account of Sue Dickinson's attitude toward editing the poems is drawn from Mrs. Bingham's *Ancestors' Brocades, passim.*

18:7.   Bianchi, *op. cit.*, p. 76.

25:35.   Bianchi, Introduction, *Further Poems of Emily Dickinson* (Boston: Little, Brown & Company, 1929), p. v.

26:13 ff.   This account of Mrs. Todd's editorship of the poems and the lawsuit with Lavinia is drawn from Mrs. Bingham's *Ancestors' Brocades, passim.*

29:32.   George F. Whicher, "Some Uncollected Poems by Emily Dickinson," *American Literature*, vol. XX (Jan., 1949), No. 4, pp. 436–40. Mr. Whicher suggests that Emily's niece, Martha Dickinson, supplied these several little poems.   After 1891, however, Martha Dickinson and her mother, Sue Dickinson, very pointedly dissociated themselves from Emily's poetry.   Not until Sue's death, May 12, 1913, did Martha Dickinson (now Mrs. Bianchi) appear to be released from some promise to her mother.   On the other hand, during the winter of 1897–98, Lavinia Dickinson was much occupied with the idea of publishing Emily's poems.   It is highly probable that she engaged Mary Lee Hall or some other friend to copy the poems which appeared in various magazines at this time.

CHAPTER II

34:10.   The most significant references to the West are found in the following poems: "When I hoped, I recollect," "I could suffice for Him, I knew," and "The Stars are old, that stood for me."

37:25.   Bianchi, *Life and Letters*, p. 76.

38:1.   James Fenimore Cooper, *Correspondence*, edited by his grandson, James Fenimore Cooper (New Haven: Yale University Press, 1922), II, 737.   Cooper did not mention Kate Scott, whose face was altogether familiar to him, but undoubtedly she introduced her foster cousin to him. There is considerable manuscript evidence of the close friendship between Scotts and Coopers.

38:19. Cooper, *op. cit.*, II, 722. Mr. Battin, mentioned by Susan Cooper, was rector of Christ Church, Cooperstown.

42:14. Bianchi, *op. cit.*, p. 76. Mrs. Bianchi spoke of "a touch of Irish blood." There was more than a touch. She also gave the erroneous impression that Kate Anthon came from Europe to visit Emily and Sue Dickinson. She came from New York. After April, 1878, she did make her permanent home abroad, but there is no record that she ever saw Emily Dickinson again.

46:27. Bagg, *Memorial History of Utica, New York*, pp. 464–65. I have seen only typewritten copies of these two pages sent to me by Miss Alice C. Dodge, Librarian, Utica Public Library. The records of Utica Female Academy were unfortunately destroyed by fire.

48:19. Bianchi, *Emily Dickinson Face to Face* (Boston: Little, Brown & Company, 1932), p. 160.

54:33. *Ibid.*, p. 141.

CHAPTER III

79:7. Mr. Whicher (*op. cit.*, p. 315) suggested that Park's sermon which impressed Emily so strongly "was almost certainly" the well-known "Judas" sermon. It is to be found in Park's *Memorial Collection of Sermons* (1902), p. 45.

84:15. Whicher, *op. cit.*, pp. 84–94; also, "Emily Dickinson's Earliest Friend," *American Literature*, VI (March, 1934), 5. In a letter supposedly written "on a snowy Sunday morning in 1848" to Susan Gilbert, Emily refers to "a beautiful new friend." Mr. Whicher assumes that this new friend was Newton. But the letter to Susan Gilbert apparently should be dated early 1852, two years after Newton left Amherst. Emily's "beautiful new friend" was probably Henry Root. Emily Dickinson had several men friends, whose significance may easily be exaggerated. I have suggested that Ben Newton was important to her chiefly because he died early. The fact of death struck deep in a sensitive imagination. The poems attributed by Mr. Whicher to Newton's influence were almost certainly written to another person, with the possible exception of a poem beginning "A book I have a friend gave." This poem has also a literary origin in Elizabeth Browning's *Aurora Leigh*, VII, 1042 ff.

CHAPTER IV

86:10. Bianchi, *Life and Letters*, p. 103.

87:4. In the introduction to his *Selected Poems of Emily Dickinson* (1924), Conrad Aiken reported a curious remark by Mrs. Bianchi. Her aunt Emily had been repressed, she said, but she herself was exhausted.

87:23. Bianchi, *Emily Dickinson Face to Face*, p. 176. In her earlier biographical sketch Mrs. Bianchi described Emily's first letters to Susan Gilbert as "too sacred for revealing" (*Life and Letters*, p. 44), and she published only some scattered excerpts. In *Emily Dickinson Face to Face* Mrs. Bianchi revealed sixteen of the "too sacred letters" but misdated most of them and omitted many paragraphs. I have been informed that letters and passages still to be published express much stronger feeling.

89:15. "And if such ardent attachments as Margaret Fuller inspired among her own sex were habitually expressed by Sappho's maiden lovers, in the language of Lesbos instead of Boston, we can easily conceive of sentimental ardors which Attic comedians would find ludicrous and Scotch advocates nothing less than a scandal." Higginson, "Sappho," *Atlantic Monthly* (July, 1871), p. 88. The whole article is a curious piece of special pleading. Emily Dickinson undoubtedly read it, as she read all of Higginson's work, and became acquainted with the fragments of Sapphic verse.

90:21. Bianchi, *Life and Letters*, p. 16.

90:24. Bianchi, *Emily Dickinson Face to Face*, p. 175.

90:28. Bianchi, *Life and Letters*, p. 31.

92:10. *Ibid.*, p. 20.

96:28. Mrs. Bianchi (*Life and Letters*, p. 43) assigns this letter to December, 1850. It was probably written three or four months later.

97:31. *Ibid.*, p. 98.

98:5 ff. Bianchi, *Emily Dickinson Face to Face*, pp. 243, 237, 214.

99 ff. The letters of Emily Dickinson to Susan Gilbert appear on pages 177–223 of *Emily Dickinson Face to Face*.

102:25. Whicher (*op. cit.*, p. 44) quotes part of this letter from Emily Dickinson to Jane Humphrey.

106:27 ff. Bingham, *op. cit.*, pp. 321–22. Mrs. Todd's understanding of the situation was also the result of a gradual evolution. She may never have been entirely certain, for it was not a matter which she could discuss intimately with either Lavinia or Austin Dickinson. On November 30, 1890, she recorded in her journal a good deal of bewilderment about Lavinia's curious attitude toward Sue Dickinson. Lavinia plainly hated her sister-in-law, yet "she seems at times to be *curiously in fear of her*, and she used to wish not to offend her." (Bingham, *op. cit.*, p. 405. The italics are mine.) But as Lavinia reluctantly admitted that certain poems were connected with Kate Anthon, and particularly after Kate's copies of Emily's letters were received, so astute a woman as Mrs. Todd would surely begin to understand. In a bibliographical note to the third series of *Poems*, I have pointed to evidence that Mrs. Todd's understanding was much clearer in 1896. Nevertheless, she chose to discount much of Kate's influence and to stress the "normal blossoming" of Emily's nature. And she repeatedly denied Emily's own repeated account of a heartbreak — of an almost unbearable emotional wound. But Lavinia's stories of Mr. Dickinson's cruelties and oppressions were more readily believed. Apparently these stories served both women as an excuse for Emily's aberrant conduct.

CHAPTER V

115:30. For information regarding weather conditions during March, 1859, I am indebted to Mr. Charles R. Green, Librarian, Jones Library, Amherst, Massachusetts.

CHAPTER VI

160:7. Introduction, *Further Poems of Emily Dickinson*, p. xviii.

CHAPTER VII

171:23. Sue Dickinson, however, retained some kind of connection with Mrs. Vanderbilt for a few years. At some undetermined period, apparently not long after the Civil War, she visited Mrs. Vanderbilt in Flatbush and became acquainted with the family of Kate's sister, Margaret Scott Bartlett.

176:25. Bianchi, *Life and Letters*, p. 74.

176:31. The truth of Emily Dickinson's pleasant but slight acquaintance with Helen Hunt Jackson is to be found in Mrs. Bingham's *Ancestors' Brocades* and Ruth Odell's *Helen Hunt Jackson* (New York: Appleton-Century Company, 1939).

182:19. The poem "Your riches taught me poverty" was sent to Sue Dickinson with this note: "Dear Sue, You see I remember. Emily." (Bianchi, *Emily Dickinson Face to Face*, p. 228). Mr. Whicher (*op. cit.*, p. 92) assumes that Emily wished to remind Sue of Ben Newton. There is no evidence, however, that Sue ever knew Ben Newton or would have had any interest in him. On the other hand, Sue was almost uncomfortably aware of the tragic entanglement between Emily and Kate. The note may have been Emily's way of telling Sue, "I have not forgotten her."

190:25. The calendar leaves inserted between the pages of Kate's Longfellow do not have a year date. However, the weekdays, which *are* given, are correct for 1861. The little volumes of poetry were a recent gift, which Kate undoubtedly reread during the winter of 1860–61. Furthermore, her books were to be in storage for nearly thirty years, a fact which increases the probability that these leaves were taken from an 1861 calendar.

CHAPTER VIII

198:32. Genevieve Taggard (*op. cit.*, p. 217) quoted Mary Bowles as saying: "Poor Emily! She is her own worst enemy."

209:8. Bianchi, *Life and Letters*, p. 67.

CHAPTER IX

211:18. Bianchi, *Life and Letters*, p. 67.

217:12. Higginson's own account is worth quoting. Regarding intimate friends, he wrote: "My child, I have never had *but* one; all others have been only acquaintances, though I have always had a profusion of those. But I never loved but one male friend with passion — and for him my love had no bounds — all that my natural fastidiousness and cautious reserve kept from others I poured on him; to say that I would have died for him was nothing. I lived for him. . . ." Mary Thacher Higginson, *Thomas Wentworth Higginson* (New York, 1914), p. 125.

219:25. Margery McKay, "'Amazing Sense' — The Application of a New Method to the Poetry of Emily Dickinson" (Swarthmore College Honors Thesis), p. 4. Miss McKay noted "surprising parallels" in the lives of Sir Thomas Browne and Emily Dickinson. Apparently she was not aware of the most surprising.

221:30. Bianchi, *Emily Dickinson Face to Face*, p. 263.

227:12. Anna Seward (1747–1809) deserves more than passing notice. In physical appearance, temperament, and personal history, she bore an uncanny resemblance to Emily Dickinson. Like Emily, she had auburn hair and eyes that could be described as auburn. In her youth she gave up a lukewarm engagement and remained at home to care for her mother and her father, who was the prebendary of Lichfield and Salisbury. The real passion of her life was for a child, Honoria Sneyd, who was brought up in the Seward family like a younger daughter. When Honoria outgrew her adolescent responsiveness, spurned her friend, and married, Anna was heartbroken. Jealousy of the girl's husband led Anna to believe that he neglected his wife, and she held him responsible for Honoria's early death. For the rest of her own life she mourned her lost friend.

Like Emily Dickinson, Anna Seward addressed a letter to an interesting stranger, Walter Scott. As she had some literary reputation and Scott was almost unknown, he was flattered by her notice and answered with enthusiasm. In her next letter Anna gave him more of her personal history than he had bargained for. She also enclosed an elegy to the lost Honoria and told Scott to regard his correspondent as among the dead. Scott thankfully dropped the correspondence, only to discover that Anna did not intend to be taken literally. For some years they continued to write, without meeting, Scott somewhat impatiently, Anna overflowingly. When he at last went to see her, he was more deeply impressed than he had expected to be.

The larger part of Anna Seward's work remained in manuscript during her lifetime. After her death Scott assumed without enthusiasm the task of literary executor which she had bequeathed him. In an apologetic preface he doubted the wisdom of publishing, but, to his surprise, the poems were well received and went through several editions. They were still in vogue toward the middle of the nineteenth century. Anna Seward was a friend and admirer of the famous "Llangollen ladies," who interested Kate Anthon.

CHAPTER X

239:8. Bianchi, *Emily Dickinson Face to Face*, p. 231.

258:22. Henry W. Wells, *Introduction to Emily Dickinson* (Chicago: Packard and Company, 1947), pp. 169–70.

Chapter X and succeeding chapters are largely drawn from the letters and manuscript diaries of Kate Scott Anthon. Many descriptions merely paraphrase her own account. Irrelevant words and sentences have been omitted without notice. Some parts of Chapter XV I owe to personal interviews with Mrs. Anthon's surviving English friends.

⚘ INDEX TO FIRST LINES ⚘
OF POEMS BY EMILY DICKINSON

This appendix lists alphabetically the first lines of all poems by Emily Dickinson quoted, analyzed, or referred to in this book. The list could have been much enlarged if I had had space to treat all poems clearly related to the friendship between Emily Dickinson and Kate Anthon. I have consulted many editions and different versions of the poems. For convenience, however, I refer the reader to the most accessible collections, unless there is some special reason for mentioning other sources. The following abbreviations have been adopted:

Poems — *Poems*, 1937.

BM — *Bolts of Melody*, 1945.

NEQ — "Poems of Emily Dickinson: Hitherto Published Only in Part," by Millicent Todd Bingham, *New England Quarterly*, XX, No. 1 (March, 1947), pp. 3–50.

Numbers following the parentheses refer to the pages of this book:

⫷⫸ BIBLIOGRAPHICAL NOTE ⫷⫸

For this study of Emily Dickinson and her friend Kate Scott Anthon, I have depended almost entirely on the poems and letters of Emily Dickinson, the manuscript diaries, letters, and family papers of Mrs. Anthon, various biographical sketches by Martha Dickinson Bianchi, and the writings and personal communications of Millicent Todd Bingham. I have also read the several full-length biographies of Emily Dickinson and many critical articles, but have found them, in the main, confusing rather than helpful. Following is a list of the chief published sources which I have consulted:

Poems by Emily Dickinson. Edited by two of her friends, Mabel Loomis Todd and Thomas Wentworth Higginson. Boston: Roberts Brothers, 1890.

I have relied upon a copy of the second edition, owned and marked by Kate Scott Anthon.

Poems by Emily Dickinson: Second Series. Edited by . . . T. W. Higginson and Mabel Loomis Todd. Boston: Roberts Brothers, 1891.

Letters of Emily Dickinson. Edited by Mabel Loomis Todd. Boston: Roberts Brothers, 1894. 2 volumes.

Poems by Emily Dickinson: Third Series. Edited by Mabel Loomis Todd. Boston: Roberts Brothers, 1896.

This volume is notable for an apparent increase in Mrs. Todd's understanding of the part played by Kate Scott Anthon. On page viii of the Preface Mrs. Todd speaks of poems which "had an obvious personal origin; for example, the verses 'I had a Guinea golden,' which seem to have been sent to some friend travelling in Europe, as a dainty reminder of letter-writing delinquencies. The surroundings in which any of Emily Dickinson's verses are known to have been written usually serve to explain them clearly. . . ." On page 33, with reference to the same poem, Mrs. Todd writes: "This poem may have had, like many others, a personal origin." On page 67 appears the poem beginning "Is bliss, then, such abyss," deprived of its last three lines, which refer to a woman. On page 73 appears "Proud of my broken heart since thou didst break it," curtailed of a very strong and obviously personal second stanza.

The Single Hound: Poems of a Lifetime. . . . With an introduction by her niece Martha Dickinson Bianchi. Boston: Little, Brown & Company, 1914.

In her introduction Mrs. Bianchi states that her mother, during the last year of her life, thought of destroying the poems and letters of Emily Dickinson. Mrs. Bianchi makes a slight and ambiguous reference to Emily's love affair and names as Emily's close friends Dr. and Mrs. J. G. Holland, Samuel Bowles, and Kate Anthon. I have consulted the copy given by Mrs. Bianchi to Mrs. Anthon.

The Life and Letters of Emily Dickinson. By her niece Martha Dickinson Bianchi. Boston: Houghton Mifflin Company, 1924.

The second part of this volume is a reprint, with many changes and omissions, of the letters of Emily Dickinson published by Mrs. Todd in 1894. The first part is a biographical sketch, notable for its many inaccuracies and its incredible account of Emily's relations with an unnamed married man of Philadelphia. There is also a grossly exaggerated and misleading account of Emily's friendship with Helen Hunt Jackson. There are three references, of varying length and importance, to Kate Anthon and her rôle in Emily's life.

Further Poems of Emily Dickinson. . . . Edited by her niece Martha Dickinson Bianchi and Alfred Leete Hampson. Boston: Little, Brown and Company, 1929.

The title of this collection is followed by a misleading "Withheld from publication by her sister Lavinia." The introduction does not name any friend of Emily's but does give a subdued and different account of the alleged love affair with a young, handsome, married clergyman.

Emily Dickinson: The Human Background of Her Poetry. By Josephine Pollitt. New York: Harper and Brothers, 1930.

This first full-length biography of Emily Dickinson names Charles Wadsworth as the clergyman hinted at by Mrs. Bianchi but minimizes his importance. Building upon Mrs. Bianchi's inflated account of the friendship between Emily Dickinson and Helen Hunt Jackson and upon Emily's statement to Higginson that she had met Edward B. Hunt and found him interesting, Miss Pollitt assumes that Major Hunt was the mysterious lover and that the two women quarreled over him. This hypothesis has been completely overthrown by the publication of new facts.

The Life and Mind of Emily Dickinson. By Genevieve Taggard. New York: Alfred A. Knopf, 1930.

This biography is an account of Emily's supposed attachment to George Gould. The evidence is Lavinia's statements to various close friends and a joking valentine from Emily to Gould, published in the Amherst College *Indicator* for February, 1850, and discovered by Miss Taggard. The rest is conjectural. Miss Taggard relies heavily on Mrs. Bianchi's account of Helen Hunt Jackson and paints a Freudian picture of Emily's relations with her father. The critical comment is valuable, as are many scattered insights into Emily's personality.

Emily Dickinson, Friend and Neighbor. By MacGregor Jenkins. Boston: Little, Brown & Company, 1930.

This slight sketch contains a few notes from Emily Dickinson but consists largely of the author's childhood recollections, apparently supplemented by the writings or communications of Mrs. Bianchi. Mr. Jenkins moved away from Amherst at the age of seven.

Letters of Emily Dickinson. Edited by Mabel Loomis Todd. New and enlarged edition. New York: Harper and Brothers, 1931.

This is the edition which I have principally consulted.

Emily Dickinson Face to Face. Unpublished Letters with Notes and Reminiscences. By her niece Martha Dickinson Bianchi. Boston: Houghton Mifflin Company, 1932.

Except for scattered excerpts in the *Life and Letters* and in an article published in the *Atlantic Monthly* (CXV, 1915, pp. 34–42), this book is the only present source of letters and notes from Emily Dickinson to Susan Gilbert Dickinson. It is also important for the increased notice given to Kate Scott Anthon. The account of Emily's alleged love affair with Charles Wadsworth (unnamed) is still further muted.

This Was a Poet: A Critical Biography of Emily Dickinson. By George Frisbie Whicher. New York: Charles Scribner's Sons, 1938.

This biography contains valuable critical comment and much background material on nineteenth-century New England. It demolishes several legends, introduces (and perhaps overstresses) Ben Newton as an influence upon Emily Dickinson, and is, in the main, sober and carefully documented.

For the alleged love affair with Wadsworth, Mr. Whicher leans upon the testimony of Mrs. Bianchi, particularly with regard to Emily's supposed intimacy with Helen Hunt Jackson. He is convinced that Mrs. Jackson made "palpable use of her friend's story" in a novel, *Mercy Philbrick's Choice*, and a short story, "Esther Wynn's Love-Letters." Ruth Odell, the biographer of Helen Hunt Jackson, has analyzed these two pieces of fiction and demonstrated that they have no connection with Emily Dickinson. On the other hand, Mr. Whicher demolishes Mrs. Bianchi's picture of Wadsworth as an impetuous lover and concludes that the minister could have had no more than a friendly interest in Emily. The erotic interest is all on Emily's side and is the product of an unstable mind.

Ancestors' Brocades: The Literary Debut of Emily Dickinson. By Millicent Todd Bingham. New York: Harper & Brothers, 1945.

Except for Emily Dickinson's own letters and poems, this book is the most important source of information about the poet. Although it deals almost entirely with the difficulties and triumphs of the posthumous publication of Emily's work, its account of the curiously strained relations among the various Dickinsons casts a very revealing light upon Emily Dickinson herself. Mrs. Bingham and her mother, Mrs. Todd (as quoted by Mrs. Bingham), emphatically deny the stories linking Emily with one man or another. Undoubtedly they speak with authority. Indeed Mrs. Bingham is so anxious to correct false impressions of the poet that she thins the love element almost to nebulosity — a mistake corrected by her next significant contribution to the understanding of Emily Dickinson.

Bolts of Melody: New Poems of Emily Dickinson. Edited by Mabel Loomis Todd and Millicent Todd Bingham. New York: Harper & Brothers, 1945.

This last important addition to the canon of Emily Dickinson is also the most autobiographical. If any poems were "withheld from publication," they are the poems in this volume. Many of them express strong emotion toward a woman, describe the love affair in too realistic detail, or bitterly arraign another person for cruelty and treason. Mrs. Bingham's introduction is very illuminating, particularly those parts referring to sections of the book entitled "That Campaign Inscrutable," "The Mob within the Heart," and "The Infinite Aurora."

"Poems of Emily Dickinson: Hitherto Published Only in Part." By Millicent Todd Bingham. *New England Quarterly*, vol. XX, no. 1 (March, 1947), pp. 3–50.

This article contains important restorations of stanzas omitted by Mrs. Todd and Mrs. Bianchi from poems of Emily Dickinson published by them. I am indebted to Mrs. Bingham for my copy of the article.

Introduction to Emily Dickinson. By Henry W. Wells. Chicago: Hendricks House, 1947.

Mr. Wells' first chapter contains a very brief summary of Emily Dickinson's life and a somewhat longer summary of the editing of her work. The book is critical and does not present any new biographical material.

Dickinson Family

Edward Dickinson (January 1, 1803–June 16, 1874) married May 7, 1828, Emily Norcross (July 3, 1804–November 14, 1882). Their children were:

William Austin (April 16, 1829–August 16, 1895), who married July 1, 1856, Susan Huntington Gilbert (December 19, 1830–May 12, 1913). Their children were:

Edward (June 19, 1861–May 3, 1898). Unmarried.

Martha Gilbert (November 30, 1866–December 21, 1943), who married July 19, 1903, Alexander E. Bianchi. No children.

Thomas Gilbert (August 1, 1875–October 5, 1883).

Emily Elizabeth (December 10, 1830–May 15, 1886). Unmarried.

Lavinia Norcross (February 28, 1833–August 31, 1899). Unmarried.

Scott Family

Henry Scott (February 14, 1792–December 19, 1873) married November 14, 1827, Catherine Mary Strong (January 14, 1800–February 20, 1843). Married January 15, 1845, his deceased wife's sister, Margaret Elizabeth Strong (July 15, 1809–August 26, 1885). By his first wife he had children:

Catherine (Kate, Katie) Mary (March 12, 1831–March 17, 1917), who married October 29, 1855, Campbell Ladd Turner (March 13, 1831–May 26, 1857), and afterwards married August 30, 1866, John Hone Anthon (October 25, 1832–October 29, 1874). No children by either marriage.

Margaret Strong (February 25, 1834–July 27, 1876), who married June 1, 1859, Dr. Homer L. Bartlett. Their children were:

Henry, "Harry" (b. April 11, 1860).

James Leland (b. June 16, 1861).

Eliza Lefferts, "Lily" (b. April 11, 1863).

Margaret Strong (June 11, 1865–January, 1875).

Frederic Wheelock (b. January 9, 1870).

Henry Augustus (March 5, 1836–June 6, 1886), who married October 15, 1868, Eliza Synnott, "Lila." Their children were:

Edith (b. December 9, 1869).
Henry (b. 1870).
Frederic (b. 1872).
Other children who died in infancy.

CHRONOLOGICAL TABLE
OF EVENTS

1829, April 16. William Austin Dickinson. Born in Amherst.

1830, December 10. Emily Elizabeth Dickinson. Born in Amherst.
December 19. Susan Huntington Gilbert. Born in Deerfield, Massachusetts.

1831, March 12. Catherine Mary Scott. Born in Cooperstown, New York.

1833, February 28. Lavinia Norcross Dickinson. Born in Amherst.

1834, February 25. Margaret Strong Scott. Born in Cooperstown, New York.

1836, March 5. Henry Augustus Scott. Born in Cooperstown, New York.

1840. The Dickinsons move from their house into one half of a two-family house.

1843, February 20. Mrs. Henry Scott dies.

1845, January 15. Henry Scott marries Margaret Elizabeth Strong.

1846, August 25. Emily begins a four weeks' visit to Boston.

1847–1848. Emily is a student at Mt. Holyoke Seminary.

1848. Emily makes new friends, Emily Fowler and Ben Newton.

1848–1849? Kate Scott and Susan Gilbert attend Utica Female Academy.

1848, late December? Ben Newton moves to Worcester.

1850, Valentine Week. Emily sends joking valentines to George Gould and Bowdoin.
Spring. Emily becomes acquainted with Susan Gilbert.
July 14. Mary Gilbert, an older sister of Sue, dies.
Summer? Apparently to console Sue, Emily writes her first known serious poem, "I have a bird in Spring."
Autumn. Austin goes to Sunderland to teach.

1850, November. Emily's friend Leonard Humphrey dies suddenly.

1851–August, 1852. Austin teaches school in Boston.

1851, late March. Emily and Sue attend a "sugaring-off" and read *Ellen Middleton* together.
September. Emily and her sister Lavinia visit in Boston.
Autumn–July, 1852. Sue teaches school in Baltimore.

1851–1852. Emily's friendship with Abby Wood becomes strained.

1852. Emily's valentine jingle to William Howland is published in the *Springfield Republican*.

June. Mr. Dickinson attends the Whig Convention in Baltimore.

1852–1853? Austin and Sue are secretly engaged.

1853, early spring. Sue visits friends in Manchester.

March 24. Ben Newton dies.

May 9. Amherst celebrates the opening of the railroad.

Summer. Emily refuses an invitation from Abiah Root.

Autumn. Emily and her sister visit the J. G. Hollands in Spring-field.

Thanksgiving. Austin and Sue announce their engagement.

December 16. Emily Fowler marries Gordon L. Ford and leaves Amherst.

1853–1855. Mr. Dickinson is a Whig Representative in Congress.

1854, January 13. Emily writes to Ben Newton's pastor.

March. In a letter to Sue, Emily speaks of "sweet Kate Scott" as a person she has never seen.

Spring. Emily and Lavinia spend six weeks with their father in Washington and Philadelphia. Emily (but not Lavinia) meets the Reverend Charles Wadsworth.

Austin graduates from law school and is admitted to the bar.

1855. The Dickinsons move back to their old house.

October 29. Kate Scott marries Campbell Ladd Turner.

1856, June. Sue visits Kate in Cooperstown.

July 1. Sue and Austin are married in Geneva, New York.

1857, May 26. Kate's husband dies in the Tremont House, Boston.

Autumn. Emily wins a prize for her bread in the Cattle Show.

1858, autumn. Emily is named a judge of the bread division at the Cattle Show.

1859, March 7. Kate, in Boston, buys a set of De Quincey.

March 10? Kate visits Sue in Amherst for the first time. Lavinia goes to Boston on a visit.

March 19? Emily shows Kate her poetry.

Late March. Emily writes an ardent first letter to Kate.

June 1. Margaret Scott, Kate's sister, marries Dr. Homer L. Bartlett of Flatbush, New York.

August. Kate apparently pays a second visit to Amherst.

August 11. Samuel Bowles meets Emily (and perhaps Kate) for the first time.

1860? Wadsworth comes from Northampton to see Emily.

1860, late February or early March. Lavinia goes to Boston. Kate makes third visit to Amherst. The "crucial night."

Late March. Emily writes a mysterious, excited letter to her friend Mrs. Holland.

April 11. Margaret Bartlett's first child, Kate's beloved Harry, is born.

1860, April 17. Emily's aunt, Mrs. Loring Norcross, dies.

June? Emily writes a letter begging Kate to visit her.

July? Kate apparently returns to Amherst, her fourth visit, and tries to break off her friendship with Emily.

July 29. Kate, in Flatbush, receives some advice from Mrs. Vanderbilt.

December. Emily begins to worry about Kate's silence.

1861, January 1? Emily writes Kate a reproachful letter.

March 19. Kate, apparently much worried, puts a curious note in her copy of Longfellow.

April. The Civil War begins. Kate breaks off with Emily.

May. Emily's cousins, Louisa and Fanny Norcross, visit and comfort her.

May 18. Kate puts another odd note in her Longfellow.

June 19. Sue and Austin's first child, Edward (Ned), is born.

July. Samuel Bowles sees Emily and writes a curious letter.

September. Emily fears that she is losing her mind.

October 22. Kate puts a third revealing note in her Longfellow.

October 31. Kate makes her fifth visit to Amherst, with Mrs. Vanderbilt. Emily is jealous and deeply hurt.

Late fall. Bowles calls, and Emily refuses to see him. Bowles sends over a book for Sue and "Mrs. Kate" to read.

1861–1862, winter. Emily fears that she will die.

1862, March 1. The *Springfield Republican* publishes Emily's poem "Safe in their alabaster chambers."

March. Bowles calls again, and again Emily refuses to see him.

April. Bowles sails for Europe aboard the *China*.

April 15. Emily writes to T. W. Higginson for criticism of her poetry.

May. Charles Wadsworth moves to California.

1863. In letters to the Norcross cousins Emily refers guardedly to her misery.

1864, March 12. The Sweetser cousins publish Emily's poem "Some keep the Sabbath going to church" in *The Round Table*.

March 20. Gertrude Vanderbilt is seriously wounded.

April. Emily is in Boston for treatment of her eyes.

Late spring (June?). Kate becomes engaged to John Anthon.

October 5. Kate sails with the Edward Clarks in the *Persia* for a winter in Paris and Rome.

1865. Emily goes to Boston for further treatment of her eyes.

May 1. Kate returns to New York aboard the *Scotia*.

1866, February 14. Sue Dickinson publishes Emily's poem "A narrow fellow in the grass" in the *Springfield Republican*.

August 30. Kate marries John Anthon.

November 30. Sue and Austin's second child, Martha, is born.

1866–1872. Kate moves in New York society and finds it boring. Emily, increasingly secluded and unapproachable, lives in her poetry.

1868, October 15. Kate's brother Henry Scott, marries her young friend Eliza (Lila) Synnott and settles in New York.

1869. Wadsworth returns to Philadelphia.

1870, August 16–17. Higginson pays his first visit to Emily.

1871. John Anthon suffers an accident.

1872, October 17. Kate sails for Europe in the *Russia* with two invalids, her husband and her brother Henry.

1872–1873. Henry Scott recovers and goes home. The Anthons try one doctor after another — in London, Mentone, Rome, Florence, Munich.

1873, May 12. In Vevey, Switzerland, Kate learns that her husband is doomed.

October 27. The Anthons sail for home in the *Wyoming*.

December 3. Higginson visits Emily again in Amherst.

December 19. Kate's father dies.

1874, June 16. Emily's father dies in the Tremont House, Boston.

Spring. Kate takes her dying husband to Cooperstown.

October 29. John Anthon dies.

1875, January. Kate's ten-year-old niece Maggie Bartlett dies. Kate's sister Margaret is ill with tuberculosis.

June. Mrs. Dickinson is paralyzed. Emily becomes her nurse.

August 1. Sue and Austin's third child, Thomas Gilbert Dickinson, is born.

November 10. Kate and Margaret sail in the *Scythia* for a winter in Mentone.

1876, May 27. Kate and Margaret return to America in the *Scythia*.

July 27. Margaret Scott Bartlett dies.

Helen Hunt Jackson calls on Emily.

Autumn. Austin Dickinson is seriously ill. Sue and Emily are estranged.

Mid-70's. Emily writes to Charles Wadsworth under cover of her friends, Dr. and Mrs. J. G. Holland.

1877? Kate returns to Amherst, her sixth visit, and tries to renew her friendship with Emily. (The most probable date is about April 19 or November 10.)

1878, January 16. Samuel Bowles dies.

April 10. Kate sails in the *Bothnia* to live abroad.

Autumn. Helen Hunt Jackson and her husband call on Emily.

November. Mrs. Jackson publishes Emily's poem "Success is counted sweetest" in *A Masque of Poets*.

1879, June 6. In a Swiss resort Kate meets Florence Eliot and Florie's elderly mother. The three travel together in Switzerland, Italy, and southern France.

1880, August? Charles Wadsworth calls on Emily.

September 5. Florie and Mrs. Eliot return to England.

October 3. Distracted and ill, Kate goes to England.

October 28. Florie and Kate arrive in Florence.

1881, January 21. Mrs. Eliot sends for Florie, who refuses to come.

April 28. Florie and Kate leave Florence.

April 29. Florie goes to England, Kate to Lausanne.

August 17. Kate is at Château d'Oex with her nephew Harry Bartlett. She makes a new friend, young Helen.

December 9. Kate is in Clevedon, near Bristol, with Florie and Mrs. Eliot.

1882, April 1. Charles Wadsworth dies.

November 14. Emily's mother dies.

1882–1883. Kate and Florie spend six months at Tunbridge Wells.

1883, July 10. Kate and Florie are in the Scottish Highlands.

October 5. Young Thomas Gilbert Dickinson dies.

1883, November. Kate goes to Lausanne. Florie remains in London to study music. Kate's brother suffers a mental breakdown. Mrs. Scott, her stepmother, is threatened with blindness.

1884, January. Mrs. Scott sends for Kate.

Early February. Mrs. Scott sends a cable, apparently countermanding her letter.

February 14. Kate suddenly leaves Lausanne and goes to England.

March 1. She takes her farewell of Florie and sails in the *Gallia* for America.

Late May. Kate's brother is brought to Cooperstown.

Late spring. Emily suffers the first attack of her fatal illness.

1885? Emily writes a letter to Kate and composes some forgiving poems.

1885, February. Kate buys Buxton's two-volume edition of Shelley.

August 3. Florie is engaged and her fiancé writes to Kate.

August 26. Kate's stepmother, Margaret Elizabeth Strong Scott, dies.

Late fall and winter. Alfred Corning Clark and his wife take care of Kate.

1886, April 17. Kate sails in the *Elbe* for England and Florie.

May 15. Emily Dickinson dies.

June 6. Henry Augustus Scott dies.

Summer and early fall. Kate is in Scotland with Florie and Mrs. Eliot.

October. Kate's niece, Edith Scott, goes to England in the *Celtic*.

1886–1887. Sue Dickinson agrees to edit Emily's poems, then refuses.

1887. Florie marries and goes to the Isle of Wight on her wedding trip.

March. Kate and Edith go to Tunbridge Wells and then to the Isle of Wight.

Early summer? Florie tries to do district visiting. Kate intervenes.

August. Florie and her husband join Kate and Edith at a resort on the North Sea.

Late October. Edith returns to America.

1888–1889. Edith pays a winter visit to England.

1890, Summer. Edith comes to England and tours Wales with Kate.

October 1. Edith sails for America, and Kate settles at Clifton, near Bristol.

November 12. *Poems by Emily Dickinson*, First Series, appears. Sue and Lavinia are estranged.

1891, January 2. The London *Daily News* reviews the *Poems* harshly.

March 7. Andrew Lang writes an unfavorable review for *The Illustrated London News*.

March 26. Kate decides to visit America.

May 10. Kate postpones her sailing and goes to Ventnor.

May 13. Her sister-in-law Lila and her invalid nephew Fred arrive at Ventnor.

June 24. Kate sails in the *Havel*.

July 1. Lila and Fred follow in the *Trave*.

Summer. Kate visits in New York, Cooperstown, and Utica. She asks Albert Matthews to get her Emily's *Poems*.

1891, September 20. Kate arrives in Amherst.

October 6. She returns to England in the *Havel*.

October 30. Lavinia writes to Kate, begging for copies of Emily's letters and poems.

November 9. *Poems by Emily Dickinson*, Second Series, appears.

November 23. In a letter to Edith Kate acknowledges a clipping about Emily Dickinson sent by Mrs. Clark. Someone (Fanny Dering?) sends Higginson's *Atlantic Monthly* article about Emily, and Kate marks it.

Mid-December. Sue Dickinson writes Kate a disturbing letter.

1891–1892. Kate endures a winter of anguish.

1892, February. Kate again marks Higginson's article.

February 13. She prepares to answer Sue's December letter and sends Lila an account of her Amherst visit and of the quarrel between Sue and Lavinia.

April 5. Kate goes to Clevedon for relief.

May 15. She hears that Campbell Turner's mother is dying.

July 26. Kate flees to Harrow to be near Florie and Helen.

Winter. She "adopts" a Harrow schoolboy, Florie's nephew and becomes more cheerful.

1893, Summer. Kate tours the English Lake District.

July 22. She pays her first visit to Grasmere.

1894, November 21. *Letters of Emily Dickinson* appears. Among the letters are three taken from Kate's copies.

1895, August 16. Austin Dickinson dies.

Kate pays her last visit to America to attend the wedding of her niece, Edith Scott to Henry Johnston.

1896, September 1. *Poems by Emily Dickinson*, Third Series.

November 16. Lavinia Dickinson files suit against Mabel Loomis Todd and David P. Todd.

1898, March 1–April 16. Lavinia's suit is decided in her favor.

May 3. Edward (Ned) Dickinson dies.

1897–1898, winter and spring. Some poems of Emily's appear in various magazines, probably furnished by Lavinia.

1898–1899, winter. Lavinia employs Mary Lee Hall to edit a new volume of poems.

1899, August 23.   Lavinia Dickinson dies.

1902, July 29.   Sue Dickinson and her daughter Martha sail for Europe.

1903, July 19.   Martha Dickinson marries Alexander E. Bianchi.
Summer.   Sue and Kate meet in London.

1905. Sue makes another trip to Europe.

1908. Kate begins to live the year round in Grasmere.
November.   Kate has a slight stroke, and Edith hurries to England.

1913, May 12.   Sue Dickinson dies.

1914, October.   Martha Dickinson Bianchi publishes *The Single Hound*
and sends Kate a copy.

1917, March 17.   Kate Scott Anthon dies in Grasmere.

1924. Mrs. Bianchi publishes *The Life and Letters of Emily Dickinson*.

1929. Mrs. Bianchi publishes *Further Poems of Emily Dickinson*.

1930. The Centenary edition of Emily's collected poetry appears.
Genevieve Taggard's *The Life and Mind of Emily Dickinson* and
Josephine Pollitt's *Emily Dickinson: The Human Background of
Her Poetry* offer interpretations of Emily's life.

1931. Mrs. Todd republishes the *Letters of Emily Dickinson*.

1932, October 14.   Mrs. Todd dies.

1935. *Unpublished Poems of Emily Dickinson*, edited by Mrs. Bianchi, is
published.

1937. A new collected edition of Emily's poems appears.

1938. G. F. Whicher's critical biography, *This Was a Poet*, is published.

1943, December 21.   Martha Dickinson Bianchi dies.

1945. Two important new books are published: *Bolts of Melody: New
Poems of Emily Dickinson*, edited by Mabel Loomis Todd and
Millicent Todd Bingham, and *Ancestors' Brocades* by Millicent
Todd Bingham.

1947, March.   Stanzas of Emily's poems omitted by Mrs. Todd and
Mrs. Bianchi are restored by Mrs. Bingham in an article entitled
"Poems of Emily Dickinson: Hitherto Published Only in
Part," *New England Quarterly*, XX, No. 1 (March, 1947), 3–50.

1950, May. Mrs. Bianchi's heir, Alfred Leete Hampson, sells the manuscripts of Emily Dickinson to Gilbert H. Montague, who gives
them to the Harvard University Library.

INDEX